J

The American-Scandinavian Review

VOLUME VI   JANUARY-FEBRUARY, 1918   NUMBER 1

Published Bi-Monthly by THE AMERICAN-SCANDINAVIAN FOUNDATION, 25 West 45th Street, New York

Yearly Subscription, $1.50.   (One dollar to Associates of the Foundation.)   Single Copies, 25 cents

Entered as second-class matter, January 4, 1913, at the post-office at New York, N. Y., under the act of March 3, 1879
Copyright, 1916, The American-Scandinavian Foundation

HENRY GODDARD LEACH, *Editor*   HANNA ASTRUP LARSEN, *Literary Editor*

Advisors

New York, HAMILTON HOLT   Copenhagen, HARALD NIELSEN
Stockholm, CARL LAURIN   Christiania, CHRISTIAN COLLIN

CONTENTS

FOUNDED BY NIELS POULSON, IN 1911

ESTABLISHED 1746

ROYAL COPENHAGEN PORCELAIN
≋ *and* DANISH ARTS, *Inc.* ≋

563 FIFTH AVENUE, Near 46 th St.. NEW YORK

ROYAL COPENHAGEN PORCELAIN is the most beautiful art Pottery in the world—both in design and decoration. It is the work of the great Danish artists, designers, and craftsmen, and strikes a new note in applied art. The figurines of animal life are interesting studies of nature, and are in all cases taken from original models by noted sculptors. The splendid coloring exhausts the range of the palette, and its rich charm will add immeasurably to the effect of your table or room. TEA SETS, DINNER SERVICES, Breakfast Sets, either individual or family, Centerpieces, Vases, Plaques, and Flower Holders at reasonable prices. Beautifully illustrated booklet sent on request.

"Peasant Girls in Sunday Costume"
Modeled by Bultox, S. C., $55.00

A NATIONAL HIGHWAY!!

Links the
GREAT NORTHWEST
and the
ATLANTIC SEABOARD

The trunk line of the Erie Railroad is between Chicago—where one can connect from terminals of western lines—and New York—where trans-Atlantic steamship connections are made. Other important cities served are:

Akron	Jamestown	Elmira
Pittsburgh	(Chautauqua Lake)	Binghamton
Youngstown	Bradford	Cleveland
Oil City	Buffalo	Cincinnati
Meadville	Rochester	and many
Cambridge Springs	Corning	more

Courteous employees, excellent dining-car service, modern sleeping-cars, reasonable fares and the Erie motto, "Safety always," insure a pleasant trip.

Interview your local ticket agent, or address

ERIE RAILROAD COMPANY

R. H. WALLACE
General Passenger Agent
NEW YORK

SELMA LAGERLÖF

The Swedes in America should give their friends here these books as gifts for Christmas and for other occasions.

Start now to collect the beautiful new Northland Edition of this Swedish writer whose fame has spanned the world.

THE NORTHLAND EDITION

Nine volumes, for the first time in a uniform limp leather binding, of these great short stories and novels. Each volume, Net $1.75. Nine Volumes, boxed, Net $15.75. Any bookstore will be glad to show you this edition.

Translated by Velma Swanston Howard.
JERUSALEM.
THE EMPEROR OF PORTUGALLIA.
THE GIRL FROM THE MARSH CROFT.
THE WONDERFUL ADVENTURES OF NILS.
THE FURTHER ADVENTURES OF NILS.

Translated by Pauline Bancroft Flach.
THE STORY OF GÖSTA BERLING.
THE MIRACLES OF ANTICHRIST.
INVISIBLE LINKS.
Translated by Jessie Brochner.
FROM A SWEDISH HOMESTEAD.

Published by DOUBLEDAY, PAGE & CO., Garden City, New York, who will be glad to send free to any admirer of Miss Lagerlöf an attractive 81-page booklet about her life and work.

Reading THE NATION every week

Places you in sympathetic relation with the things that make life richest—yet that are often swept aside in the rush of every day—Art, Literature, Music, Drama.

Saves you the bother of hunting among thousands of events for just those that are interesting and valuable for you to know.

Although it is accurate and discerning in its examination of a subject, yet the editorial perspective of THE NATION is broader than that of any other periodical in the world.

For Fifty Years America's Foremost Critical Review.

10c a copy

$ 4.00 a year

THE NATION

20 Vesey Street, New York City

Clip this coupon and send with $1.00 for an experimental subscription of four months.

CHRISTMAS GIFT LIST OF THE FOUNDATION

Ten per cent. discount to all "Associates"

"Scandinavian Classics"

Vol. (VII) Marie Grubbe

A Lady of the Seventeenth Century

By J. P. Jacobsen

Translated by Hanna Astrup Larsen

Jacobsen's famous novel is at last presented for the first time in English.

The *Nation*, in its issue for June 7, regretted that the Foundation had not yet included in its series of SCANDINAVIAN CLASSICS " such significant time-tested works, for example, as . . . J. P. Jacobsen's *Niels Lyhne* and *Fru Marie Grubbe*." At that time *Marie Grubbe* was already in type.

The translator is well known to *Review* readers as Literary Editor and contributor to other magazines.

(VIII) Arnljot Gelline

A Verse Romance

By Björnstjerne Björnson

Translated by William Morton Payne

As editor of the *Dial* (Chicago) and essayist, Mr. Payne has proved his fine sympathy for Northern literature.

Of Björnson's *Arnljot Gelline* H. H. Boyesen says: "Never has he found a more daring and tremendous expression for the spirit of old Norse paganism than in this powerful but somewhat chaotic poem. Never has any one gazed more deeply into the ferocious heart of the primitive, predatory man, whose free, wild soul has not yet been tamed by social obligations and the scourge of the law."

(IX) Anthology of Swedish Lyrics

From 1750 to 1915

Collected and translated by Charles Wharton Stork.

This is a careful and representative selection from the great Swedish lyrists, Bellman, Wennerberg, Rydberg, Runeberg, Snoilsky, Karlfeldt, Heidenstam, Fröding and many others., Dr. Stork appeared as a translator last year with a volume of Fröding "like a fresh wind out of the Northland" (*Pittsburgh Post*) where " the thirsty may drink liquid lines to his heart's content." (*World*, N, Y.)   Price $1.50 each.

"Scandinavian Monographs"

Volume III

The King's Mirror

Translated from the Old Norwegian of the 13th Century

By

Laurence Marcellus Larson

Professor of History in the University of Illinois

This is the first English translation of the book of instruction used at the court of Hakon the Old. It will be welcomed by Norwegian scholars everywhere: for the *Speculum Regale* is the chief Norwegian prose monument from the period when the sagas were written down in Iceland. Professor Larson furnishes also a long and valuable introduction. He is widely known as author of *Canute the Great* and a history of England.

Price, $3.00

THE AMERICAN-SCANDINAVIAN FOUNDATION

25 West Forty-fifth Street, New York

CONTRIBUTORS TO THE YULE NUMBER

FRIDTJOF NANSEN, Norwegian Minister on Special Mission to the United States, is best known in this country as an explorer. At the age of twenty-seven he made his famous expedition across Greenland on skis. In the years 1893 to 1896 he established a new record to the North Pole. Retiring to the professorship of zoölogy in Christiania, he came before the world as political spokesman for Norway in 1905. After the separation, he represented Norway as the first minister to the Court of St. James's. He is at present professor of oceanography in Christiania. Among his numerous books are *Farthest North* and *In Northern Mists*.

IVAR KIRKEGAARD is a Danish-American poet and editor. As an officer in the Danish army, he was stationed near the Slesvig border, where he had an opportunity of going over the old battle grounds and interviewing people who still remember the fight of 1864.

K. KARSTENSEN, the Danish poet, has found a sympathetic interpreter in Miss Jane Campbell of Philadelphia.

J. C. LINDBERG is connected with the State Normal School in Spearfish, South Dakota. He has translated Oehlenschläger's *Hakon Jarl* for the University Studies of the University of Nebraska.

EDWIN BJÖRKMAN needs no introduction to readers of the REVIEW. As a former scholar of the Foundation and the translator of Strindberg's *Master Olof* in the SCANDINAVIAN CLASSICS, he has been closely associated with the work of the Foundation. Mr. Björkman has recently returned from Sweden, where he studied the political situation.

AMELIA VON ENDE is a native of Poland, but came to this country at an early age. She is a musician and was for some time a teacher and head of a girls' school, in which she tried to realize some of the ideas of Ellen Key. In recent years she has been a critic and reviewer of art, music, and literature for the *Nation*, the *Dial*, and other publications, and has lectured on contemporary foreign art and literature.

FANNY ALVING won the 1917 prize offered by the woman's magazine *Idun* in Stockholm with the charming story *The Three Cottages*, the first part of which appears in this issue. It will be remembered that Selma Lagerlöf's career as a writer began with the award of a prize from *Idun*.

FRIDTJOF NANSEN

THE
AMERICAN-SCANDINAVIAN
REVIEW
298883

| VOLUME VI | JANUARY-FEBRUARY · 1918 | NUMBER 1 |

The Mission of the Small States

By FRIDTJOF NANSEN

An Authorized Interview

WE are a small nation, we Norwegians, yet we are a nation with a right to exist and to determine our own fate. We have chosen to remain neutral and do our best to keep out of this war, believing that thus we may serve humanity. It is true, our neutrality has been grievously violated. I am sure I am not over-stating the case when I say that one-third of our merchant marine has been destroyed; that is, more than one million tons of Norwegian ships have been sunk, and over seven hundred of our brave sailors have been killed. If the destruction is to go on at the same rate, Norwegians will no longer be a seafaring nation—we who had once the third merchant fleet of the world, inferior only to the fleets of England and the United States. We are not wanting in resentment, and we do not forget the claims of honor, but it is possible for a false ideal of honor to insinuate itself, and surely a people whose sons face death again and again, as our sailors do, without even the privilege of defending themselves, need not fear the stain of cowardice upon its honor. Let me remind you that American neutrality, too, was violated with the sinking of the *Lusitania*, and you did not go to war; you stayed your hand, because you are a peace-loving people. We have protested against the outrages on our ships, but we do not feel that our honor demands we should declare war on the guilty power and thus invite annihilation. We should be only an atom whirled into chaos.

I have been asked why the five small neutrals do not enter the war; their quota of perhaps a million and a half of soldiers would be enough, some people think, to turn the scales in favor of the Allies. Yet the most elementary knowledge of military tactics should convince anyone that five small scattered units do not make an army. A large, concentrated force could crush them one by one. How, for instance, could our men be brought into the field? Denmark would be conquered before we could come to her assistance, and Sweden's long coastline would lie open to the attacks of the German fleet now idle in the Baltic. The situation in Scandinavia is so complicated that no human being can foretell what would happen if any one of the three countries should be dragged into the war, but our most likely fate would be to become another Roumania. No, I fail to see that even a temporary military advantage would be gained by our taking active part on the side of the Allies.

The great duty and mission of the small states now is to keep the peace so far as it lies with them. A time will come when they will be required to tie again all the fine threads of intellectual and commercial intercourse that have been broken so ruthlessly. Even after the Franco-Prussian War, in 1870, German and French scholars, working in the same field, refused to co-operate or even to know anything about one another's progress, while Belgians who read German were looked upon with disfavor in France. Yet the hatreds engendered by that war were as nothing in intensity and duration compared with what this war will surely bring in its wake.

It is the task of the neutrals to keep unbroken the chain of human development. At present every available brain in the belligerent countries is pressed into service to invent means of destruction or means to avoid destruction. Even here in the United States a vast amount of energy has already been deflected into the channels of war work and will be so more and more. I cannot conceive that this great nation, having put its hand to the plough, will turn back before universal peace is attained, but I believe that only a few among you know the magnitude of that which lies before you. The longer you carry on the war the more your normal life will be disturbed, and even after the war we must be prepared to see all the present belligerents busied, for many years to come, in repairing what has been laid waste. But human development cannot be thus suddenly stopped like a clock without incalculable damage, and, therefore, civilization itself demands that some should remain outside the conflict that is now drawing almost the whole world into its vortex.

The fact that we Scandinavian nations are small does not prevent us from fulfilling this mission. England was not much larger than Norway to-day, certainly not larger than Sweden, when she produced Shakespeare, and the world owes a debt of gratitude to Holland, the Greek cities, and the Italian republics. Indeed, small states have, in some respects, an advantage over the larger. Their culture is more homogeneous. An idea can more quickly penetrate to all the people within their borders and set its stamp upon them. They become a more closely-knit organism, almost a single personality, and thus their influence is more direct and intensive. France is perhaps the only large country that has a well-defined individuality in this sense. Germany made her finest contributions to civilization when she was yet split up into small, weak members.

Large states are the victims of their size. Rome fell because her strength was drained by her colonies. All her talent was absorbed by the work of defending and administering her distant possessions, and as a result she made no contribution of great and permanent value except in the domain of jurisprudence. In the arts she excelled only in architecture, which requires some of the same constructive qualities of mind as those of statesmanship (the arch was a Roman invention), but in the imaginative arts she brought forth only a pale imitation of the glory that was Greece.

Russia is a modern example of the evils of unwieldy size. While traveling through Siberia I had an opportunity to observe conditions at first hand. Not a road can be built nor a school-house erected in Siberian country districts without orders from Petrograd. Even a very efficient government could not possibly administer a vast region from such a distance—least of all with the miserable means of communication that exist there. As a consequence, Siberia is still dark with ignorance and all her splendid resources undeveloped. If we then turn to the small states, we find Denmark with its perfect organization, and Norway with a popular education on as high a level as any in the world.

The future may show a return to a condition of more and smaller states, and we may live to see the map dissolving again into the component parts that have been artificially welded together. When the doctrine that might is right perishes from the earth, as assuredly it must some time perish, there will be no need of large states. The present war is being waged for the most elementary principles of justice that ought to be self-evident and will some time be accepted as a matter of course. Though I am not optimistic enough to believe that the present war will be the last—for I am afraid that the fires of hatred kindled by it will smoulder and break out again—yet I have faith in a time when all war will be at an end. It may be a commonplace, still it is pertinent to remember that private combat as a means of enforcing right and vindicating honor has gone by the board. National combat will go, too. Humanity will find out other means of settling difficulties than by slaughtering half the human race and plunging country after country into bottomless misery.

At present all large states are imperialistic, not necessarily in the sense of wanting territorial expansion, but in the sense of putting their ultimate reliance in force. Small states, in the nature of things, can not be imperialistic in this sense, and therefore they have a peculiar mission to seek out and find the new paths that humanity must tread in order to abolish war altogether.

Something new will rise out of this war. A new sense of human brotherhood will be born of its hatreds. Already there is a growing body of internationalists in every country, and they are not so small a minority as might appear on the surface. But they must not fall into the mistake of trying to wipe out all national peculiarities and substituting a new international culture. Even if it could be done, such a culture would be barren. We still need patriotism, not to breed enmities as in the past, but to stimulate each nation to its highest possibilities. Each has something special to give, and I, for one, mourn when I see a nation disappear from the face of the earth.

All culture is first national and grows and expands as various races meet and fructify one another. There has never been any great civilization built without outside influence, unless it should be, possibly, that of the Incas of Peru, though we know too little about them to say positively that they were not stimulated by some outside current. We do know that Chinese civilization stagnated when the caravans ceased to bring their quickening influence from the West. England, France, and Germany have given one another much. Germany has, perhaps, given least, because she was for two hundred years too utterly exhausted by the Thirty Years' War to originate much, except, perhaps, in the domain of music, but she has assimilated and organized. German scientists have developed the ideas of Darwin and Pasteur. Kant, who is accepted as the quintessence of Germanism, built on British thought; and Goethe, their great poet, was deeply influenced by England. On the other hand, Germans claim Shakespeare as an essentially Teutonic spirit and are fond of saying that they understand him better than his own countrymen do.

This mutual fructifying cannot take place without national individuality, and I can not look forward with any enthusiasm to a time when the world may become one great community with but one language. I am afraid it would be a drab-colored world. I can hardly imagine French literature written in German or Shakespeare in French, and Heine cannot be conceived as anything but a German.

We three Scandinavian peoples, alike and yet diversified, have made our contribution to the world's sum of achievement. I trust I may say, without being boastful, that it has not been inconsiderable. We each have our capacities and ideals that the world would be poorer for losing. We know full well that the road to the stars is difficult and steep, over mountains and valleys. We are now in the deepest valley we ever crossed; there seems almost no road to the heights again, nothing but darkness wherever we look, and the dawn seems far away. May the new morning come and come soon, and, above all, may we never forget that the stars are always shining in the blue above the clouds.

We look to this great nation of the future, the nation of free men and women; men of thought, men of action, lead the way.

SCANDINAVIAN COMMISSIONERS TO THE UNITED STATES
(And Two Hosts)

From left to right: N. W. Böeg, Commercial Advisor to the Danish Legation; J. E. Böggild, Commercial Advisor to the Danish Legation; H. G. Leach, Secretary of the American-Scandinavian Foundation; Dr. Fridtjof Nansen, Norwegian Minister on Special Mission; H. P. Prior, President of the American Society of Denmark, on Special Mission to the United States; W. H. Schofield, President of the American-Scandinavian Foundation; Johan Baumann, Delegate of the Norwegian Government; Dr. Hjalmar Lundbohm, Delegate of the Swedish Government; Axel Robert Nordvall, Delegate of the Swedish Government. The photograph was taken November 4 at the home of Mr. J. G. Bergquist on Long Island.

A Memorable Dinner

A really memorable evening in international friendship was the dinner given by Professor W. H. Schofield, as President of the American-Scandinavian Foundation, at the Harvard Club in New York, November 2, in honor of the Scandinavian Commissioners to the United States. Among Mr. Schofield's guests were trustees and representatives of the American-Scandinavian Foundation, as well as other prominent Americans from varied walks of life. Dr. Frederick Lynch, former president of the Foundation, thus commented upon the dinner in his weekly letter to *The Christian Work:* "The dinner was a private dinner, so I am not at liberty to report the remarks made by the eminent guests and by the president. But I am sure I am violating no confidence in saying a word or two about one of the most interesting evenings I ever spent. After Professor Schofield had told us, in most delightful manner, of the hospitality shown him by the kings and peoples of the Scandinavian governments, and had told in a few words the origin of the Foundation, and what it was attempting, he called upon Professor Nansen. It was my first sight of the great explorer and scientist. He is a tall, straight, handsome man. His face might be that of a poet instead of that of explorer and scientist. Indeed, he is a poet of some note. He is now a professor in the University of Christiania, and everybody agreed that the Norwegian government made a happy choice in sending him as head of the special mission to the United States. He speaks excellent English—what visitor from abroad does not? And he won the hearts of everybody present by his story of the courage of the Norwegian sailors in this great war. It was interesting to see Nansen and Peary sitting side by side. Each of them, when they came to speak, paid high tribute to the courage and skill of the other. Dr. Lundbohm and Mr. Nordvall, the Swedish delegates, are also very interesting men. Dr. Lundbohm is one of the most famous geologists of Europe. In his remarks he said one thing that Americans might well hope is true. He said that Americans should think in big terms, having so vast a country. He illustrated it by referring to geology. In Sweden he said there was only a narrow land, running north and south, and geologically one thought in terms of that circumscribed area. In America there were vast expanses in either direction, and geologically one thought through every age in the earth's history. So, he said, Americans ought to think big thoughts, hold great ideals, take broad, generous outlooks upon all problems. He also felt that our freedom from traditions was in our favor. The past was Europe's; the future would be ours."

Founder's Memory-Beaker

Speech by the President of the Foundation at the dinner given by him in honor of the Scandinavian Commissioners to the United States, at the Harvard Club, New York, on November second.

IN olden times, gentlemen, in Denmark, as in all the North, it was the custom at the *arv-öl*, the inheritance banquet, of a chieftain or the head of a household, to pass around a so-called "memory-beaker" among those present, the heir having drunk from this beaker and consecrated himself to the service of the clan or family.

Now this Foundation owes its existence to the munificence of a high-minded Dane, who amassed a goodly fortune by industry in this country, and with fine public spirit put it at the service of his old and new countrymen, that it might work for the common profit on both sides of the Atlantic and redound to the advantage of many generations to come. I refer to Niels Poulson. If it were not for him, we should not be gathered together to-night to do what we can to fortify the friendly feeling that exists between Scandinavia and the United States and, in general, to carry on the beneficent work in which this institution is engaged. We, the Trustees of the American-Scandinavian Foundation, are Poulson's heirs, and our whole thought is, and shall ever be, to fulfil our Founder's wishes with regard to his bequest, and to safeguard it for the benefit of mankind. No one of us receives a cent for his labors. On the contrary, we are all put to much personal expense of time and money to meet the obligations we have assumed. But we do all we do gladly; for we believe in the undertaking Poulson's generosity made, possible, and we feel that if we generously give of our energy to make his gift fruitful we shall encourage other benefactors to make a like disposition of their wealth. To-night, then, in public before you, we would do what we have often done in private, pledge

"FOUNDER'S MEMORY-BEAKER"
PRESENTED TO THE AMERICAN-SCANDINAVIAN FOUNDATION BY WILLIAM HENRY SCHOFIELD, SECOND PRESIDENT, 1917

our best efforts so to conserve Poulson's gift that it may bring forth good fruits of general well-being, to his rejoicing were he here, and to that of all other large-spirited men.

If it is right that we should drink to Poulson's memory to-night, it is right that we should do it as fittingly as possible, and according to the custom of his native land. So I have brought with me this silver cup, which I propose to offer to the Foundation as a permanent memory-beaker in which, on important occasions like this, to honor Poulson. It is, I think, as handsome an object of its kind as now exists. I secured it several years ago in Norway, and have cherished it since then as a delight to my eye. But the time has come, I feel, when it can be put to larger service. It is almost exactly two hundred years old. Until it came into my possession it had not, I was told, been out of the family of Böresen for whom, in 1720, it was wrought as a work of art. My hope is that after another two hundred years it will still be in the hands of *our* family, the self-perpetuating family of Trustees of this Foundation, and that Board after Board of them will drink from it to their Founder, and to his ideals of American-Scandinavian co-operation for the advancement of knowledge and for ever-increasing sympathy in the bonds of peace.

This beaker, gentlemen, is now filled, not with old Danish mead, for that is not obtainable; not even with famous Carlsberg ale—though I personally should have liked in that way to recall the memory of the great Jacobsen, who, in a way that Poulson remembered, gave a large fortune to promote learning and science, literature and art—not even with pure American beer, such as could be produced by the distinguished Danish chemist, Dr. Max Henius, here present, likewise a zealous public servant in this his adopted land. No, gentlemen, not with these, for they cannot to-night be had, but with the sweet wine of that land where our beloved soldier boys are risking their lives for freedom—the wine of fair France.

Officially, as President of the Foundation, I shall, with your permission, drink first. Then I shall offer the beaker to the chief Commissioner from Denmark among our guests. After him, let all drink to Poulson's memory as the cup passes, bearing in mind also the success of this Foundation, and the success of the cause of liberty overseas.

The Fall of Dannevirke and Dybböl

By IVAR KIRKEGAARD

THIS IS THE FIRST OF TWO ARTICLES
ON THE DANES IN SLESVIG

THE preliminary battle against Prussianism was fought by the Danes at Dybböl in 1864. From the high roads of Holstein the Austro-Prussian army, under the command of Field Marshall von Wrangel, invaded the ancient Danish soil of South Jutland, called Schleswig by its conquerors, overwhelming and crushing all resistance by a series of successive well-prepared and well-directed assaults. In the course of seven months, the eagles from the Hohenzollern and Hapsburg crags successfully broke the wings of the embattled Danish falcon, who fought his battle alone—with all the world looking on, in pity, it is true, but also in silence.

We know the result: Danish Slesvig, as also Holstein, soon became part and parcel of Prussia, and their conquest was made the corner-stone in the building of the German Empire. Prussia forced the extension of its boundary, not to the national and natural line, where the German tongue ceases to be spoken, but far beyond, over Danish hills and homes, fields and farms, to Ribe on the North Sea, and to the foot of the Skamlingsbanke on the Little Belt. Now the Dybböl hills guard a German naval station in the harbor of Sönderborg, and in their home nest, in the fortified harbor of conquered Kiel, the U-boat adders coil, ready for their spring on the merchantman, through the canal and the North Sea, protected and sustained by the forts and mine channels of Heligoland.

The pretext for the invasion and subsequent occupation of Holstein and Slesvig was, in brief, the Austro-Prussian claim that Denmark had no legal title to the two duchies and that the Teutonic allies consequently would hold them until the Duke of Augustenborg's title to them could be settled; but having won the title from Denmark by force of arms, Berlin solemnly proclaimed to the courts of the world that the Duke had no claim to the duchies whatsoever, but that, on the contrary, the Danish title, which Prussia now held and intended to keep, was legally perfect in every way. So it happened that the capacious German waste-basket, which now also contains the Belgian scrap of paper from 1914, had its bottom lined with a package of Prussian sworn statements marked "*Schleswig, 1864.*"

This perfidy is now common knowledge, but it took some time before the liberal nations of Europe saw clearly that the insurgency of Holstein and South-Schleswig against Denmark, the young German Federation at its Frankfurt headquarters, as well the ambitions of Austria, were all but pawns in the great game of the Brandenburgers;

that the maze of conflicting war issues involved and the labyrinths of ambiguous legalities and misleading proclamations, prepared and strewn broadcast by the Chancellor and his servitors, were but a cunning ruse to cover his arrogant plan of creating a new empire by means of Prussian cannon and bayonets.

Another factor in the motive for the attack was the wish to crush Denmark's newly-found liberty, guaranteed by the free Constitution granted on June 5, 1848, when Frederik the Seventh abdicated his autocratic power in favor of a popular government. In fact, the issue of to-day, so well clarified and defined by our President, was also that of 1864: autocracy against democracy.

The ambush on French liberty by the houses of Hapsburg, Hohenzollern, Bourbon, Romanoff, and Hannover, had been frustrated by the genius of a Napoleon, but the great issue was only postponed, and autocracy also found its genius, its tower of strength, its very apotheosis of masterful, ruthless statecraft, in von Bismarck. He saw his choice: either the imperial sceptre, held by divine right and the grace of God, or the people's will freely expressed, and Bismarck soon made his decision in favor of a sceptre and sword. Hence the forcible suppression and the weakening of a little neighboring state, which had dared to discard an autocracy for a democracy, was necessary to him. Denmark had prospered by her peaceful revolution and, furthermore, had allowed her dangerous ideals of government by the people to strike root in Germanized—but as yet far from Prussianized—Holstein. Dybböl fell, and democratic Denmark was bled white. France shortly after found her Sedan and witnessed the crowning of a German Emperor in the Versailles of its exiled Bourbons. Now, on the fifty-year anniversary of the fall of Slesvig, Prussia's first and nearest prey, we see the assault on parliamentary England and republican France through Belgium.

Slesvig was, however, not relinquished by outraged Denmark without a stiff fight, and the resistance offered during the seven cruel months of war is a heroic example of a nation's supreme sacrifice and soldierly courage in the face of certain disaster. Denmark met the invaders at the forts of Dannevirke, originally built by King Götrik (died 810), strengthened by Queen Thyra, the great grandmother of England's conqueror, King Canute the Great, and garrisoned by the great Valdemars against the Vends, in the latter part of the twelfth century. Here, at this southern outpost of Denmark, between the rivers Sli and Trene, where his forefathers had fought back the hordes of Hun and Vend and Saxon, had stopped Attila's ravaging hosts, defeated the Vendic forefathers of the Prussian, and silenced the cymbals of victorious Charlemagne, here, on February 2, the Danish soldier of 1864 first measured swords with the Austro-Prussian invader.

The Austro-Prussians had 60,000 men, and before the war was over their armies numbered 90,000 well-trained soldiers, equipped with the very latest in cannon and firearms, while Denmark could muster but 35,000 men, many of them without uniforms and equipment of any sort during the first weeks of the war. Yet this attack resulted in a defeat of the men of the spiked helmets, who were beaten back at the Mysunde line by two impetuous Själland regiments. This first assault, however, proved also to be the last. The Danish staff, headed by General de Meza, gave orders to evacuate the entire Dannevirke line of fortifications three days later and to retire to the fortified positions of Dybböl and Fredericia, seeing in an immediate retreat the only means of saving the small army from sudden and certain annihilation.

Public opinion in Denmark, as also the military chroniclers of England, at first condemned de Meza's strategic move as an almost traitorous blunder. Later they understood that the cool strategist and keen fighter, famed from hard-won battles in the three years' war in the forties, had made his decision wisely, and that the Dannevirke position was untenable with an army composed of less than 70,000 men. Its center was fourteen miles in length, its left wing twenty-four miles, while the whole extent of the line from the stronghold to Frederikstadt was about twenty-five miles long.

The engineers of the line had, in fact, based their defensive calculations upon the assistance of an auxiliary army to be sent by Sweden-Norway, the friendly brotherhood of the North. In the mind of the Danish people, as in the great hearts of Norway's and Sweden's academic youth, in the songs of Björnson and Ibsen, ancient Dannevirke was the fortress of Scandinavia, where the Dane in bygone centuries had defended not only his own heritage but the entire North. Here the new-born Scandinavianism of unity and brotherly love was to receive its baptism of fire.

But this army never came; neither did the expected assistance from England and France, who then feared one another; nor from the Russia of the Romanoffs, always unreliable in friendship and pledge. Bismarck magnanimously proposed to divide isolated Denmark with Sweden; and, although his offer was rejected with contempt, his masterful intrigues in Stockholm and St. Petersburg stayed Sweden's hands. Not all of the Swedish officers, however, could be held back by government policies. They volunteered in great numbers, obtained forthwith commands at Dybböl and, as usual, distinguished themselves as the most dauntless fighters Europe has ever seen. Many Norwegians also laid down their lives for their Danish brothers.

It was not officers that Denmark needed, however, but brigades; and yet de Meza's pathetically thin lines of troops undoubtedly

From a Painting by O. Bache

GENERAL MAX MÜLLER AT SANKELMARK

would have fought their foes stubbornly here, as later at Dybböl, if
a severe frost had not converted their natural defenses of moats and
swamps into an easy passageway for the attackers.

With but one-third of the troops necessary to defend his extended
front, his lines open to attack and vulnerable on every point, de Meza
saw that the stand at Dannevirke would quickly lead to the out-
flanking and surrounding of his army. The retreat was conducted

with great efficiency and stanchly defended. Hardly a cannon was lost, though the progress of the army, over icy roads and exposed to the sleet and biting winds of early February, made the five days' march a veritable nightmare of hardships. Horses with broken legs and screaming in agony littered the roads. They were mercifully shot, and the artillerists put the harness on their own shoulders. When the pursuing enemy was first sighted, two regiments of the rearguard, 1st Copenhagen and 11th Vendsyssel, were ordered to detain him. Although they had but two cannon, they gave battle to the Austrian pursuers with sixteen and, in addition, not less than three squadrons of hussars. They met the shock of cavalry with the bayonet, advanced on the enemy twice and successfully held him back. This happened at Sankelmark near Flensborg. Both the colonels, three lieutenant-colonels, sixteen captains, and all the officers of one of the companies fell, but the retreat was covered, and the Danish soldier had again proven his courage.

The Danes reached Dybböl Hill in comparative safety a few days later, and they soon had their garrisons and reserves established on the Isle of Alsen, in and near the city of Sönderborg. About 12,000 men were stationed there to hold the Dybböl chain of ten forts, which were drawn across the mainland peninsula from the Bay of Vemmingbund to a narrow part of the Als Sund and extended about a mile and a half. . This narrow hilly passage to the bridges of Sönderborg on sea-girded Alsen, became a Thermopylae, unsung, perhaps, but as well defended as the Spartan pass. The odds were tremendous. In all the so-called forts, which were built in 1852 and were insufficient as a shelter for troops and almost worthless as a means of shelter, its handful of defenders had but two twelve-pounders, dating from 1756 and 1767 respectively, and rifled in Copenhagen. The rest were inefficient smooth-bore guns, while the Prussians, from the very beginning of the siege, mounted a battery of modern rifled cannon on the hills of Broager south of Vemmingbund and brought into play the largest cannon then invented, some of which were brought up from the strongest fortifications of Prussia. The Danes, who had not dreamed of cannon ranging over a mile, soon found that the Broager batteries could effectively enfilade their whole line of defense, and the vedettes, thrown out in front of the forts, quickly realized that their firearms were still more out of date. They used muzzle-loaded muskets against the Prussian *Zündnadel*, which easily fired five shots to their one, and when using the ramrod, they exposed their upstanding bodies to all the five shots of the crouching foe.

Of what use was their eager bravery! They demanded constantly to be led face to face with the enemy, so that they could use their bayonets as their fathers had done with such glorious results in the forties, but discovered all too soon that such small victories as were won in close battle cost them more than half their numbers even before the hand-to-hand fighting had commenced. The forts became slaughter-houses during the three months of carnage. The English author, Auberon Herbert, who witnessed the Dybböl battle, thus vividly describes the horrors so manfully faced: "From the 2d of April up to the 18th, a cannonade was directed against this army, exceeding at times in violence the bombardment of Sebastopol. This little army had to be exposed without shelter to shells often falling at a rate of thirty and upwards in a minute. Here for two weeks this has been borne by a handful of men who, throughout that period of suffering, when death was sown around them alike in every quarter—in the ruined forts, under the broken parapet, on their line of march, in their sleeping quarters, wherever they set their foot, whether they rose up or laid them down—have stood with a full understanding of the sheer hopelessness of their position and with despair staring them sullenly in the face."

Previous to the final storming of the Dybböl forts, on April 18th, the Prussians had made three parallels of elaborate trenches, digging their protected zigzag ditches to the very base of the forts. The last Danish gun had been silenced and the forts were razed. Fortified by liberal doses of "Branntwein" the Prussians went into the slaughter. They bore the Danish defenders down and pressed them back to the bridges by sheer weight of numbers; but of such desperate nature was the resistance offered that in two forts they were forced to shoot defenders who ran to the powder magazines with burning fuses intent upon the blowing up of the invaders—and incidentally of themselves. At a third fort, the Prussian flag had just then been victoriously raised on its pole in a picket fence of gleaming steel, when a Danish corporal suddenly smashed his way back to the invader's flag, tore it down and broke the pole. He was promptly spitted on Prussian bayonets. These examples of the determination of the outnumbered and overmatched troops will suffice. The Danish general fell; so did his chief-of-staff, his colonels, and captains. In fact, the greater number of the officers leading the defenders on the last day of Dybböl died on the hill—among them most of the Swedish volunteers.

Such, then, was the heroic defense of Danish Slesvig on the Dybböl-Banke in 1864. The victorious Prussian cannonade sounded the death knell of Danish hopes, and the Government at Copenhagen, appalled by the slaughter at Dybböl, ordered the abandonment of the still stronger Fredericia lines. The roads to North Jutland were open, and the invaders swept forward to the Limfjord country. Alsen fell on June 29—and at the peace of Vienna, October 30, Denmark gave up her title to the duchies.

The battle of Dybböl cost Denmark 8,000 men.

In the cemetery of Sönderborg can be found a monument in an enclosure guarding the graves of a few of the Swedes and Norwegians who gave their lives for Denmark. The touching Danish verse inscribed upon it loses in translation, but these last lines will express its silent appeal:

> *Brothers beloved*
> *In anguish and sorrow we buried you*
> *here and in our hearts.*

From the lofty parapet of the embattled Dybböl windmill the visitor can, on a summer day, count grave after grave in the barley and clover fields on the Hill where the weary soldiers found lasting rest—little green enclosures with flower-covered mounds, hedged by wild roses. On the Slesvig battle-days, Danish women in conquered Sönderborg place their wreaths of flowers on the graves of the silenced host.

Their flowers are red and white—the colors of Denmark.

The Danish Tongue in Slesvig

Danish Poem by KARSTENSEN.   English Verse by JANE CAMPBELL.

> *Long, long enough have I been peasant maiden*
> *At my wheel spinning in lowest place of all,*
> *Gnawing at bones, while vaunting German damsel*
> *Sat in my high seat of honor in the hall.*
> *But gladly now I'll take my own seat;*
> *Foremost too I'll go in the dance, as is meet.*
>
> *Well I recall how, in the days so olden,*
> *Silk-clad I roamed in my mother's garden wide,*
> *In my hair pearls and ornaments all golden,*
> *Knights, noble, stately, gathered at my side.*
> *Queen was I then, crown upon my head,*
> *And with King Valdemar, the dance, too, I led.*
>
> *But bitter days came when, with Hendrik the Black Count,*
> *My husband captive from me had gone,*
> *While over broken wall, Vendish hordes stealing,*
> *Stealthily moving, came on, ever on.*
> *Then was I cast in thrall's quarters base,*
> *And German damsel danced in the Danish woman's place.*

No more the Court was I allowed to enter.
  Scarce could I rest, e'en in the peasant's cot.
Under foot trodden, cast aside with roughness,
  Bitterly groaning at the hardships of my lot.
But peasant now it was befriended me,
Many long nights through, weeping with me silently.

But times are changing, thank God, they're changing.
  Again in high places dare I to stand,
Though German damsel's fan may hap oft to strike me,
  For away goes she not, but struts about the land.
But strut as she may, boldly I say,
From the dance German damsel will be soon danced away.

A New Year's Carol

J. C. LINDBERG

I walked along a dreary road,
  And Sorrow walked beside me.
A little bird came warbling by;
  In song he seemed to chide me:
    We, we, we,
    We are free,
    We warble in glee,
For upward soar our longings—don't you see?

I paused; I could not comprehend
  The joys that stirred within me,
While constantly this messenger
  In singing sought to win me:
    We, we, we,
    We are free,
    We warble in glee,
For upward soar our longings—come with me.

And then I saw how petty were
  The ills that had annoyed me,
And I resolved I too would sing
  The song that overjoyed me:
    We, we, we,
    We are free,
    We warble in glee,
For upward soar our longings—come with me.

OLD LADY ON A SOFA

AUTUMN IN MEDELPAD

FROM A PAINTING BY CARL JOHANSSON

BLUE FLOWERS
From a Painting by Lauritz Ring

COMRADES

FROM A PAINTING
BY ERIK WERENSKIOLD

The New Swedish Cabinet

By Edwin Björkman

TO every genuine believer in modern democracy, and to every one anxious for the preservation of the good relationship between this country and Sweden, the news about the formation of the Edén-Hellner-Branting coalition ministry must have come with a great sense of relief. What was wrong before was not that Sweden had a Conservative government, but that its government was in the hands of a minority group against which an overwhelmimg majority of the nation had repeatedly declared itself. Furthermore, this state of affairs had continued so long, and the opposition had become so embittered, that those most familiar with the temper of the Swedish people—that "slow people full of fire"—had begun to think some kind of serious upheaval almost inevitable. And, lastly, the foreign policy of the ruling minority was so one-sided in its orientation that it had already put Sweden in a false position toward some of her best friends among other nations.

Viewed from within, the inauguration of the new Government means a return to self-government in the accepted modern sense. It means also that the menace of starvation, which has been hanging like a black cloud over the people, can be met by reasonable measures that need not involve the country in other risks of an equally serious nature. Viewed from without, the advent of the new ministry means a restoration of faith and good will in quarters where Sweden undoubtedly had come to be regarded with a distrust bordering on resentment. It means that the private sympathies or opinions of petty officials will no longer be permitted to obscure and thwart and misrepresent the will of the people. It means that democracy here will be able to treat directly, and without danger of misunderstanding, with democracy over there.

This is the third time since the abolishment of the Four Estates, in 1865, that Sweden has a cabinet containing no official representatives of the Conservative party. It is the second time the country has a government that must be classed as radical. It is the first time in Swedish history that members of the Socialist party have entered the ministry. In this connection, it may be well to remember that Hjalmar Branting, as the first Socialist member of the Riksdag, was elected for the first time in 1897, and that then he was elected by Liberal votes on the Liberal ticket.

The new cabinet contains six Liberals under the leadership of Professor Nils Edén, now prime minister; four Socialists under the leadership of Hjalmar Branting, now minister of finance, and one independent, Dr. Johannes Hellner, minister of foreign affairs.

Edén is professor of history at the University of Uppsala—an absolutely clean man, with a mind of rare clarity and penetration; a firm believer in the right of the people to rule itself, but one who, nevertheless, will not let himself be swayed unresistingly by any sudden gust of public opinion. His very balance and fearlessness have stood in his way at times. When Karl Staaff died, in 1915, Edén would undoubedly have succeeded him at once in the full leadership of the Liberal party but for his own divergence of opinion from the bulk of the party membership on the question of military preparedness. On that question his position was almost identical with that of the Conservative party, and in consequence thereof he had to encounter a great deal of distrust from the more radical elements within the Liberal party. Both he and they have learned much from the great war, and to-day Professor Edén has the full confidence of every faction within his own party, while also enjoying the respect of both Conservatives and Socialists to an unusual degree.

There are many who think Hjalmar Branting the strongest man in Sweden to-day. He is certainly one of the best hated and best loved men in the country. Even his worst enemies have to admit his ability and his honesty. He is probably the only living Swedish politician whose name is known, and well known, all the world over. In spite of his leadership of a party often classed as revolutionary, he is cautious and practical, free from all dogmatic devotion to any form of theory, and thoroughly versed in every detail of public business. As the principal leader of the opposition, he has been fearless in his criticism, but also courteous and reasonable. It is significant that he has been entrusted with the ministry of finance. In recent years, the air has been full of sensational rumors about the management of the National Bank of Sweden, a government institution with a monopoly on the issuing of bank notes. These rumors will now undoubtedly be settled—either by reform or by refutation.

Hellner, the new foreign minister, has long held a prominent position within the Department of Justice, has twice served on the International Court at the Hague, and has once before belonged to the cabinet. Lately he has been one of the leaders in the Swedish lumber industry. In November, a year ago, he was sent to London as one of the four official delegates entrusted with the task of negotiating a complete commercial settlement between Great Britain and his own country. While belonging to no party, he has the confidence of all the political groups with the possible exception of the seceding Socialist extremists, and he is regarded with no less respect and confidence in Washington and London than in Stockholm.

The reputation for ability held by these three leaders is to a large extent shared by the other members of the ministry, including the two ministers without portfolio, one of whom, Professor Östen Undén, is the youngest man who ever held a cabinet position in Sweden. Eliel Löfgren, Liberal minister of justice, is a brilliant lawyer and equally brilliant writer on political subjects. He has, during the entire period of the war, represented Swedish ship owners in England, where he is widely known and liked. E. A. Nilson, Liberal minister of war, is a business man from Örebro and one of the party's principal experts on public finances. As a member of the auditing committee of the Riksdag, he has rendered conspicuous service. Axel Schotte, Liberal minister of civil affairs (as he was in the Staaff cabinet of 1911-14), is governor of one of the northern provinces and a man of great organizing capacity. Alfred Petersson of Påboda, Liberal, is a small landowner who now holds the agricultural portfolio for the fourth time, having graduated from Conservatism, through moderate Liberalism, to a position on the extreme left of his party. He has been Professor Edén's rival for Liberal leadership and has been mentioned as a possible prime minister.

Baron Erik Palmstierna, Socialist minister of the navy, came into the public eye for the first time when, as a dashing young naval officer, he dared to throw himself actively into the revivalist movement that swept Sweden during the first decade of this century. Verner Rydén, Socialist minister of ecclesiastical affairs (and, therefore, head of the educational system of the country), is a public school teacher and probably the most widely hated man within the cabinet. Strong-willed and strong-viewed, he frequently moves on the verge of arrogance, and his opponents have learned to fear his sharp tongue, but for all that he is one of the shrewdest men within the party and well versed in public affairs. Östen Undén, Socialist minister without portfolio, is a brilliant young jurist and won a professorship at Uppsala last spring in the face of bitter Conservative opposition. This opposition was largely based on his biting criticism of Germany's attitude toward international right and law during the war. Edward Petrén, Liberal, has long been a permanent official within the Department of Justice and has once before served as minister without portfolio.

What is known about the men in the new cabinet indicates that, one and all, they will place the welfare of their own country above everything else, and also that they will regard a policy of genuine neutrality as essential to the present and future safety of Sweden. Apart from this basic sentiment, they are all known as having strong leanings toward the side of the Entente Allies. Neither threats nor bribes can move them into an unwarranted break with Germany, but, on the other hand, they will be sure at once to put an end to all future attempts at turning Sweden into a catspaw for Germany or placing the interests of their own people behind those of the domineering neighbor to the south.

Charles Haag

By AMELIA VON ENDE

THE FIFTH IN A SERIES OF ESSAYS ON
SCANDINAVIAN ARTISTS IN AMERICA

THERE is much in the setting an artist affects for himself and his work that reveals his character and his calibre. The amateur's studio in Greenwich Village, fitted out in the firm conviction that the atmosphere of that art center alone will be a source of inspiration; the studio apartment of the struggling artist, with its pretense at elegance in the workshop where he receives potential patrons, and the ill-hidden poverty of the living-room in which the family is confined; these are some of the conventions to which the average artist living in New York becomes a slave. Rare exceptions are the men who scorn the fads and fetishes of their fellow-artists and dare to live their own lives, ungoverned by the social and esthetic canons of others.

Such an exception is Charles Haag. He needs no artistic setting to proclaim him an artist. He does not require the society of his fellow-artists to stimulate his creative gift. The lingo of the studios, their gossip, their customs, are distasteful to him. He will not be confined within their cliques, nor conform to their conventions. He is first of all human, broadly, inclusively human. That was the impression I received when I first met him some ten or twelve years ago. He had just exhibited his *Mother* at the National Arts Club in New York and was acclaimed by a few and discussed by all. He moved about among the men and women in evening full dress with an ingenuous, kindly sympathy beaming from his florid countenance. Yet one instinctively felt that he was a stranger in that fashion show.

That was the time when he was giving expression to his social conscience in groups like the *Immigrants* and the *Strikers*. In that monument to the mother of Gustave Stickley he had symbolized motherhood. He had created the image of a mother, of everybody's mother; for the predominant sentiment in Haag, the man and the artist, is his consciousness of universal brotherhood. Out of that consciousness grows his sympathetic treatment of certain types of the people. The struggle of the newcomer for a living and the tragedy of labor, over-burdened and underpaid, he senses as though they were his own. There is no trace in him of that professional snobbery which places an artist upon a pedestal, far above his fellow-beings. Artist or artisan alike are of the people, and Charles Haag never for a moment forgets the bond of human fel-

THE IMMIGRANTS

Labor Union

lowship that binds him to the lowest as to the most exalted of the race. Were he to be asked about his political and social creed, it could be expressed in the three words that greet one from every roadside in France: Liberté, Egalité, Fraternité. Nor does he merely cherish this ideal of the great humanitarian dreamers of the world: he lives it.

The second time I met Charles Haag was in the West, where he had gone to execute some commissions and had settled in a quaint old log house on the wooded shores of Lake Michigan. The figure of a working man resting upon a rock, at the entrance to the Henry Demarest Lloyd estate in Winnetka, is one of the works of that period. . It epitomizes the problem of poverty and toil, the weary pilgrimage of ill-paid labor. He came near winning the prize in the contest for the Altgeld memorial, but the committee decided otherwise. So the country is deprived of the opportunity to see a statue of one of its most humane governors modelled by one of its most human artists. Nevertheless the West seems to suit Haag; he feels more at home there than in the East. The people are less sophisticated, less given to accepting as infallible the standards of an academic art or a fashion of the day. Their minds are more open to the appreciation of beauty, whether it bears the stamp of official approval or not. He has exhibited in the Art Institutes of Chicago, Milwaukee, Minneapolis, and St. Paul, and has been warmly praised by the critics. He has won the friendship of many of Chicago's most intellectual and most cultured men and women, and the experience has broadened and deepened his reading of life and his art.

When I saw Charles Haag again, it was at his home in Silvermine, near Norwalk, this summer. A simple farmhouse, one hundred and sixty years old, on the road from Winnepauk to New Canaan, it has a garden sloping down to the river and acres of meadow and woodland. A peaceful quiet spot it is for a peaceable quiet worker. From its Puritan plainness outside and inside, people with conventional ideas about art and artists would never suspect that one of the most striking personalities in the art world of this country lives there. A fireplace in the dining-room closed in with masonry by its former owners is adorned with figures of Haag's quaint fancy. Above, two green dragons stretch forth their heads, carrying lanterns in their mouths. Below, the head of an old man, a genial Santa Claus, bobs forth, guardian of the whilom hearth, smiling a hearty greeting at the visitor. A vase of clay, a carved candlestick, home-woven rugs and table-runners embroidered in original designs—the work of his artist-wife, Sophia—chests, tables, chairs of charmingly simple lines, a few heirlooms of foreign stamp, make up the furnishings of the house. But from cellar to attic it seems to extend a warm welcome. Haag has not spoiled its old-fashioned physiognomy by modernizing touches. Nor has he attempted to improve upon the surroundings by landscape garden-ing. A few flowers, an arbor of grapes, shrubbery, fruit-trees, and a well-kept vegetable garden at some distance from the house com-plete the impression of a simple, but comfortable, home.

The studio, in the former barn, is of the same unstudied sim-plicity. A few hangings where they serve a purpose and a few flowers relieve the severity of the workshop, but there is an atmos-phere of dignity about it, the dignity of earnest and sincere work. There are a few specimens of Haag's earlier production. A pow-erful allegorical composition, the *Wheel of Progress*, the figures of children, men, and women forming the spokes, the spirit of Time turning it slowly and deliberately, with eyes looking out pensively into the dim future, is the most ambitious. Vigorous of conception and strongly modelled is the figure called *Effort*, in which every muscle is tense with the will to achieve an end. The bronze called *D'accord* shows a man and a woman harnessed to a plough and trudging along under the yoke, earnestly and willingly, each determined to co-operate with the other in the fulfillment of their duty. A female figure tenderly wrapping the folds of her mantle about a cat, with another cat following it, would make an appropriate memorial for the Society for the Prevention of Cruelty to Animals. There are several fountains; one set up in Youngstown, Pennsylvania, shows water-sprites drinking on one side of a spring, on the other side a buffalo. Unique in design is a triangular fountain with figures clinging to a rock under the three arches meeting above, suggesting the force imprisoned within.

A surprise was in store for me when Haag showed me his recent works. Living close to nature, in communion with the forest, his imagination alive with the nature-myths of Scandinavian lore, he has begun to carve in wood the epic of the forest. He has taken pieces of oak, walnut, chestnut, bay, and pine and has made them into figures that symbolize the spirit and suggest the story of the trees. Only a man loving the woods as he does could conceive and successfully realize such a plan. To him, wood is not merely wood; it is part of the tree, part of the forest, of living, growing, ever-creating nature. Charles Haag sees the hidden relation between all living things and associates the life of man with the life of the tree. He conjures the very spirit of the living tree out of a piece of dead wood. It is amazing how plastic wood becomes in the hands of this artist. He has released from their sleep the forest sprites of ancient lore, has visualized and embodied them in their own ele-ment. From the trunk out of which they rise to the deepset eyes which see without pupil and seem to hold in their depths something of the mystery of the forest, these creatures of his fancy are superbly alive. Conceived in reverence of nature, in love of the open, they reflect the wholesome attitude of Charles Haag towards life. There is pathos and humor and an indefinable subtle charm about them which sets them apart from anything modern sculpture has achieved.

Haag's woodland sprites are neither nymphs nor dryads. They are not ideal human forms. They show no attempt at "anatomy," at careful observation of the canons of the sculptor's art. They seem to have simply grown—risen out of the wood. There is Father Oak, broad of base, the powerful trunk crowned with a head of Olympian dignity, a symbol of virile strength, holding in his hand the acorn, the seed of the future. There is the Walnut, a sturdy fighter, hard and tough of fibre, defiant of pose; and there is the Chestnut, bare of limbs, with but a few leaves clinging to a droop-

Bronze in the Metropolitan Museum *Charles Haag, Sculptor*

D'ACCORD

ing hand, a pathetic embodiment of the tragic fate that threatens his race in this country. The young Pine is a figure of a young girl, exquisitely graceful of form and chaste in conception. The moss-grown trunk is an old man whose hair and beard cover his body. A short stubby block of wood with a gargoyle face is the wood-knot. Another grotesque figure, the head bending around its axis, suggests the hollow tree. More purely allegorical are the *Forest-Singer*, the figure of a tall man, an exalted expression about his open lips; the *Secret of Nature*, a woman with a finger on her lips, and the *Sanctity of Nature*, a female figure with clasped hands and the stamp of solemn religious fervor upon her brow. Thus do pathos and humor alternate in the work of Haag and prove the essentially human quality of his art, and this is the source of its compelling power.

A series of figures representing the people of the woods and suggesting our own country's early history illustrate this quality even more forcibly. They are pioneers blazing a trail, sturdy forms of men and women clearing the forest and making the wilderness blossom and bear fruit. They are rolling logs; they shoulder the axe; they trudge along sickle in hand; or, like the old man of the forest, they stop in their pilgrimage, to rest on a heavy staff and look about. Path-finders, strugglers, builders of a new world, they are the salt of the earth. Real, without being repulsively realistic, they are the work of a man who faces the facts of

A VIKING IN THE WOODS. WOOD CARVING BY CHARLES HAAG.

life without blinking, who has pondered much over the past of our country and is following with his eyes the vision of a dim future. No native artist has grasped more deeply the spirit of Lincoln than has Charles Haag, a Swede by birth and an American by adoption. Even now, as I close the eyes to my immediate surroundings, I imagine myself in that studio and see from the corner by the door the good plain face of old Abe, beardless, yet unmistakable, rising out of a log and flanked by a rail, looking out upon a world which has sadly changed since his time. And from the opposite wall smiles down upon me the relief-portrait of another representative American: Walt Whitman. To have singled out those two men as special objects of his hero-worship is significant. It gives us the measure of the man and artist, Charles Haag.

There are moments when his democratic conscience is troubled by the knowledge that all is not as it should be. Then the spirit of the critic and the reformer in him awakens and incarnates its protest against the *status quo* in a composition of powerful satire. There is a cast in his studio which at first glance I took for a caricature on cubism, but as I looked at it longer, an impression which had long lain dormant in my memory suddenly detached itself and stood out clear and well-defined. During trips to and from Staten Island, in the hours when the skyscrapers of lower Manhattan are lit up, I had always been fascinated by the top of the Singer tower. I fancied that an Oriental idol was squatting there, heavy with trappings of gold and jewels, an image of Mammon ruling the destiny of the human ants squirming in the streets below. Haag's cast is that idol: straight, rigid, and hard in outline; one questions whether it harbors a soul. It squats in its material security, immovable, immutable, a weird uncanny adaptation of the skyscraper to human proportions. Of a milder sarcasm is a group of figures in wood. An old countrywoman, one hand in the thick folds of her skirt, as if feeling for her pocket-book, looks down kindly from a square pedestal upon a group of four men: a pleading lawyer, a scheming financier, a popular politician, and a society dude. The allegory is obvious: the four figures tell the economic story of a country whose backbone is the rural population.

The art critic will be puzzled by the versatility of Haag's work, and will attempt to enroll him in this or that school or group. But Charles Haag defies such an attempt. No academy, museum, gallery, or studio has given him his astonishing knowledge of all the arts that are founded upon the plastic sense. Like the artists of the Renaissance, he can wield many tools. There is no doubt in my mind that his familiarity with the ways and the work of the people have helped him to acquire that craftsmanship. Some of his admirers comment upon his spirituality. It is his love of nature, his reverence for creation that have given him this rare quality. Love of nature and of our fellow-beings keep the soul sweet, the mind open and the heart young. If it is the privilege of great artists never to grow up, Charles Haag, the sage, the poet, and master craftsman, is one of our greatest artists, for he is a child at heart.

The Three Cottages

By FANNY ALVING

Translated from the Swedish for the REVIEW

PART 1

IT WAS a wonderfully serene spot; so at least thought ꞁthe little lady from Stockholm. She had been sitting still a long time, leaning back and looking about her. To the left was the manor-house, and to the right stretched a long lane of gigantic elms. It ended somewhere far down in the valley, but seen from the garden chair it appeared endless; for in the far distance the crowns of the trees melted into a dark green maze that extended over half the horizon.

Not a sound was heard in the yard except the rustling of the newspaper as the pages were turned, and that was not often; for the master of the house, the brother-in-law of the little lady, read it with old-fashioned thoroughness. Here everything was done thoroughly. It seemed as though Time had chosen this remote spot to stand still and catch his breath.

The little lady's eye dwelt on one object after the other. Over all there was a sleepy calm. Not a living creature was to be seen in the valley, and the valley itself looked as though it had just been unpacked from a toy-box, the stillness was so wooden and the colors so fresh and bright. The fields made neat little squares prettily painted in light green and gray. To the left of the lane stretched a bit of straight and empty road, and to the right lay three small cottages on a green patch in the sunlight. It seemed as though she might have lifted them by the chimneys, had she wished it.

"Who lives in those cottages?" she asked.

"Crofters on the manor."

"It must be delightful to live down there."

"I dare say. But I doubt if they have any sense of it."

"Why not?"

"I don't believe people of that kind care about such things."

"What makes you think they don't?"

"That is my experience. I have been watching them for many long years, and they seem to me absolutely stolid."

The little lady sat still for a few moments looking down at the cottages. "I wonder," she said slowly. "Why should they be differently made from us?"

"I don't know, but they are different, that is certain."

"That sounds snobbish to me. If some one else said it, I should be angry."

He folded the paper slowly and precisely, yawning as he did so.

"As you please, but the fact is that the people here are awful dullards, and so are people of that class everywhere. Their emotions are quite satisfied by a dram and a pancake."

"Shame on you! You are very cynical."

"No, I am not, but you, like all ladies of culture, have what is known as imagination. When you look at that red cottage you fancy yourself within it, peeping out through the window, and getting a great many esthetic impressions. But at present it is not you who are sitting in there; it is an old woman, who doubtless wipes her nose on her petticoat, and whose son is the gawkiest individual I have ever seen. He always stands gaping and never says a word. I have often wondered what he is staring at."

He smiled at the recollection.

The little lady smiled too. "Perhaps he sees things that you cannot see."

"Not he," came the answer decisively.

"What does he do? I mean, what is his trade?"

"He is a carpenter."

"And how is his work? Good or bad?"

"Not bad. Pretty good, in fact. But to plane off a board requires no great intelligence."

"And who lives in the other cottages?"

"In the cottage to the left there is an old couple. The overseer claims that they fight. I don't know anything about it, but he has probably not invented the tale. And farthest to the right lives an old woman."

"Do you know them?"

"Know them? I have spoken with them once in a while. The boy comes up here to do carpenter work when it's needed."

"And that is all you know about them?"

"Yes, and all I care to know."

"My dear boy, I think it's you who are the dullard," said the little lady categorically.

"What do you mean?" He looked a trifle surprised.

"The plain truth, Ernst, is that you sit here with a row of mysterious cottages before you, and you don't know a thing about the people who live in them. And yet there's nothing so amusing as folks in cottages."

"Amusing?"

"Yes, amusing. I hope you don't imagine that people like you and me are amusing?"

"You are not tiresome," he said humorously.

"Oh, yes, I am dreadfully tiresome—dismally tiresome, and you are not a bit better."

"One can't accuse you of flattering," he said smiling.

"No, but how could we be amusing?   All educated people are so awfully like one another."

"Are they?"

"Disgustingly like one another.   Have you never noticed how education clips people's claws, so you can't tell whether they belong to an ape or a cat?   They have just the same curve and just the same length, every last one of them."

He looked at her.   "So that's your philosophy!"

"Yes."

"Do you mean that it would be better if all civilization were wiped out, and everybody lived according to instinct?"

"I didn't say that, but I do say that uneducated people are interesting, because they have not smoothed themselves down till they have lost all individuality."

"Because they never reflect over themselves."

"No, they are as God made them, and it would be jolly to see what God really did create."

"Then you must be what they call spiritual."

"Perhaps," she said a little pertly, "but that may wear off in time."

"Let us hope so, and in order to get over it more quickly, I think you should go down and visit the cottages."   He nodded toward the valley.   "If you can squeeze any originality out of the people down there, you must put it in a bottle and cork it tightly.   Then you can take it out and ponder over it in the long evenings."

"I will, and when you get tired of Mr. Ernst Löfmark, I'll let you peep into my bottle."

"And see an old couple fighting, a woman with a lout of a boy with eyes like saucers, and yet another old woman thrown in?"   He gave a teasing little laugh.   "But with these expectations I'll take a nap.   Good-by, so long."   He nodded and sauntered slowly across the clean-swept yard into the house.

The little lady sat still for a while in the garden chair.   Over the valley rested the sun-baked air, warm and motionless, heavy as with invisible weights.   Suddenly she felt as though the three cottages lay behind a thin curtain, which she could see through but could not lift.

The green spot, which from the manor had seemed no larger than the palm of a hand, was not so tiny when seen near by.   It consisted of three pastures.   Nor were the colors so brilliant when one walked over it; in fact it was rather a lonely stretch with grass bitten short by the sheep and strewed with an amazing number of rocks.   The little lady could not rid herself of a feeling of disappointment; for there was not the slightest trace of any home comfort about the place.

It looked lonely, poverty-stricken, and almost repelling. It might have been a playground for giant children who had amused themselves by throwing rocks here at the beginning of time. But the playground was deserted; time had crumbled the rocks, and now human beings had vainly tried to make themselves at home there. Two paths started to cross the short grass, but they had not been able to carry out their purpose. They struggled along in unsteady bends, made anxious leaps over dried up bits of swamp, and sometimes hid under the grass for long stretches. Here and there, clumps of dwarfed trees crouched low and timid, peeping after them.

The three cottages stood on top of a little hill, and the paths evidently led up to them, for they both seemed to stop at a gate in the fence at the foot of the slope. The gate was green with moss and was fastened on one side with a leather strap. The little lady took it off, and the gate fell askew at once as though from old habit. At the same time, it emitted a strange moaning sound almost like the cry of an animal, but this was probably due to the fact that it had but one hinge.

She left it open, for she meant to go back soon, and there was something about the sound that she did not care to hear again.

The first cottage was right within the gate. She did not go up to the door at once, but stopped under an old crabbed pear-tree near a hawthorn thicket. She heard voices on the other side of the bushes. One, shrill and strangely cynical, was evidently an old woman's voice.

"You will have to wait," she said sharply.

"But when I am so thirsty?"

"You will have to wait, that's all."

"You gorilla!" said the other voice. It was the feeble voice of an old man and sounded as though the speaker were grinding the words out between his teeth.

"Gorilla, did you say?   I'll pay you back for that!"

There was no reply.

"Gorilla, you said?   You old wretch who can't stand on your own feet.   You won't get a drop."

"But when I'm almost dying from thirst!"   Again it was the man's voice that spoke, but in a different tone. It sounded like a child's fretful persistence.

"So much the better, then maybe we'll get rid of you."

The woman was evidently busy chopping wood; for her words came in jerks, and the sentences were punctuated by the blows of an axe.

A strange feeling came over the little lady under the pear-tree. She was not afraid, but she would have liked to turn back. She knew nothing about the people behind the thicket, but the two voices seemed like living creatures, clear and distinct, and vibrant with hate. They were like two serpents hissing at each other in there.

She took a few steps forward with a curious sense of passing into an unreal world. She told herself that she was silly and overwrought, but the air lay heavy over the path, and the old pear-tree was crabbed and bent, while all traces of humanity seemed to belong to bygone ages. Behind the copse was a gray wall, on which a wagon wheel was hanging from a nail. The wheel was red with rust and the wall gray with lichens. A luxuriant dark green growth of brier rose covered a tumble down stone fence. Over all there was a peculiar odor of decay.

A few steps more brought her within view of the garden. It was an overgrown plot with a round flower-bed in the middle. The border was edged with stones, and everything seemed drearily gray and poor.

Not far from the pear-tree, by the thicket, sat an old man in a wheel-chair, and a few steps from him stood an old woman gathering fagots in her apron. She had a round, ruddy face and a pair of black eyes. For a moment they met the eyes of the little lady; then she bent down again.

The path leading to the other cottages went straight past their entry. The house was gray with age. In the window was a geranium, and near it sat a yellow brindled cat, so still that it might have been made of china.

The little lady walked quickly past the entry. She did not know why she was suddenly frightened. There was no reason for it. Perhaps it was only the clicking of her heels on the flat stones that sounded with such startling distinctness, almost like the report of a gun, through the uncanny stillness of the small yard. She could feel four eyes in the back of her neck.

The little lady sat on a sofa of pine. It was without ornament but skillfully painted to resemble oak. Before her, by the wall, stood a bed, also without ornament, but skillfully painted to resemble walnut. Above the bed hung a calendar in a carved frame which was only stained. It was not an ordinary frame but a little work of art, and she looked at it in surprise.

"Who made that frame?" she asked.

"Anton made it," said the old woman at the hearth.

"Really?" said the lady. It was the fifth time she had been told that it was Anton. "He must be a jack-of-all-trades," she said, and she meant it.

"Yes, he's handy at most anything," answered the old woman.

The lady looked at her as she cleared the coffee. She was a tall woman with handsome features, but appeared older than her age, because her teeth were gone. She moved a little awkwardly, and was a trifle too tall for the fireplace, which was of the old-fashioned kind with a brick hearthstone and a low hood. It certainly was a squat and inconvenient old fireplace. There could be no doubt of that.

"But why hasn't Anton, who is so clever, rebuilt the old fireplace?"

The old woman smiled a little with her toothless mouth. She had a pair of beautiful brown eyes which met those of the little lady.

"Yes, it's a little inconvenient, but we think it's so pretty," she said.

"Yes, it is pretty," admitted the lady.

"You see, we're rather inclined to like what is old, both Anton and I. Some folks don't feel that way, and new things are finer, of course, and yet——"

"I am glad to hear it. I, too, like old things."

The brown eyes brightened. "I don't know just how to say it, but when I stand by the old fireplace cooking, I think of all the others who have stood there before me, and somehow I like it. I don't know if you understand just what I mean?"

"Yes, I think I do."

"If we rebuilt the fireplace I don't believe it would ever be the same——"

"No, it certainly wouldn't."

"And so with the whole cottage. It is small and poor, and of course it's inconvenient, but sometimes I feel as if all that is old— all that's gone—is sitting round about me and looking at me from the corners. And I like that. I don't think I could ever have the heart to rebuild the cottage. Besides I think it might seem strange to the house-goblin. But now I suppose you are laughing at me."

No," said the little lady softly. Why should I laugh at you?"

The brown eyes looked at her. The little lady thought they were the most faithful eyes she had ever seen. They made her think of the eyes of a horse and seemed to have the same far-away look.

"I like you very much. I can't remember that I have ever before chatted this way with anyone. There's no one here that I can talk to about these things."

"But Anton?"

"Well, yes, but you see we always think the same, so there isn't much to talk about. We feel in the air what the other one is thinking, and so it gets to be very quiet."

"Does Anton believe in the goblin?" asked the little lady, after a pause.

"Believe in it? No, not exactly, but you see when one is born so far up in the country, there are so many things that are queer. I don't think Anton could go to bed contented, if he thought he hadn't treated the goblin right—if there is a goblin."

"What could he have done?"

The old woman did not answer at once.   She stood looking out through the low window and seemed lost in thought.

"Oh! anything that wasn't right.   If he had been unkind to me or to any creature on the place—or if he hadn't done his best in everything."

"Do you believe the goblin cares about that?"

"I don't know."   She took her eyes from the window and began to arrange the coffee cups.   But I suppose you know that the idea with the goblin is that everything in the place is to be good and made better.   And he thrives only in respectable places.   Anyone who isn't hard working and kind can never get the goblin to thrive.   Never in the world."

The little lady looked at her without speaking.

"If you are to be perfectly frank, you believe in the goblin?" she asked presently.   "You believe that he really exists?"

The other woman met her eyes.

"That he exists?   That, of course, I don't know.   But when one is alone in an old cottage like this—and besides I may tell you that in the cottage next to ours, there has never been any real comfort."   She made a movement with her head in the direction of the window.   "The one you passed."

"Is that so?"   For a moment she saw again the yard and the wheel-chair.

"It seems as if there can never be any real happiness there.   He was terribly cruel to her for many long years before he had to take to the wheel-chair.   Perhaps you saw an old man in a wheel-chair?"

"Yes."

"He often struck her, and he beat the children till they were half dead.   None of them ever visit their home, and I know they don't intend to come for his funeral; for they have often said they wouldn't.   The doctor said he hadn't a long time left to live, and she told him so."

"Why did she do that?"

"Because he is afraid to die.   Do you know, I think it's awful."

"Yes," answered the little lady softly.

The brown eyes gazed at her with a pensive expression, as if they were pondering something.   "You musn't think that I want to talk ill of them, but I think of them sometimes.   It isn't natural—is it? —that a man should beat his wife and children, just because he is stronger than they?"

"No, but I suppose he has a quick temper."

"Yes, but *she* never had a temper before he got to be helpless in the chair.   Yet she's good to everybody else."

"Is she hard on him?"

"Dreadfully. But tell me, ma'am, you who understand such

things, is it natural that one who has always been kind should become spiteful toward a poor lame man in a wheel-chair?"

"I don't know. But there are people who need to be punished."

"Yes, but a poor lame man who has to die soon? Will you think I am foolish if I tell you what I think?"

"What is it?"

"That neither of them can help it. Sometimes I think there are powers round about us that no one can resist. And we musn't wake them; for then they'll just make sport of us, and we are no longer masters of ourselves."

"You mean the goblin?" the lady asked hesitatingly.

"Well, no, but one thing and another. We surely oughtn't to deny that anything can exist. I believe we should just simply do our best all the time; for after all that's the only thing that help us."

"Yes," answered the little lady.

"And isn't it foolish to laugh at something you know nothing about?"

"Yes, indeed."

The lady sat silent for a while.

"I should think it must be lonely here," she said at last.

"That is what people say when they come here, but it doesn't seem that way to us. We think we have more things here than we can really keep track of."

"What kind of things?" said the little lady, in some surprise.

The old woman looked embarassed. "Well, it may seem stupid to a fine lady like you, and it may be silly to speak of it, but we're just alike, Anton and I. We find such company in everything around us. When Anton was small, we had names for all the trees here, and, do you know, ma'am, we use them still, and sometimes when new ones grow up we christen them by some name. But now I suppose you think I'm quite crazy, ma'am."

"No, indeed I don't."

The brown eyes gazed at her. A serene light glowed in their depths. "I hardly understand how it is, but I've never longed for people. It seems to me that we have enough with all the other things round about us, and if you only keep your eyes open there is so much going on here in the wilderness. There are so many animals, and they have so many doings. And sometimes there's a wind, and sometimes the rain comes, and you know it can rain and blow in such an endless number of ways. Do you know, it seems that everything has its own way of living, no matter how dead it looks. Are you fond of walking in the forest, ma'am?"

"Yes, indeed."

"As for me, I'd rather walk in the woods than go to church. Do you think I'm talking in an unchristian way?"

"No, I think it is beautiful."

"Sometimes I wonder if it's right to think like that."

"What wrong could there be in it?"

"I don't know, but sometimes I have a feeling that it is, and I don't want to do anything unchristian; for I am no heathen."

"No, certainly you are not," said the little lady.

"But now you must have a cup of coffee, ma'am," and she made a motion toward the cups on the table.

"Thank you, that will taste good."

The coffee was not very good compared to that which was probably being served in the garden of the manor-house, but the little lady drank two cups.

"I should like to have seen Anton," she said.

"Yes, I wish he were here, but he's at the overseer's, building a stable. You see, he's a carpenter."

The lady sat looking about her, and her eyes unconsciously rested on the frame around the calendar. "But isn't it tiresome work for a lad who can make frames like that?"

"Tiresome? He gets two and a half kronor a day, and we can live on half of it. He never drinks, you see, ma'am, but he likes to amuse himself with such little things instead, and I think that's fine."

"Of course it's fine. Has he never thought of doing only that kind of work?"

The old woman smiled a little with her toothless mouth. "That kind of work? People don't pay anything for such things, do they?"

"You think not?"

The brown eyes twinkled. "Then we'd get rich in a year, for Anton can carve out a thing like that in an evening. He has only to bring in a branch from the hawthorn bush and put it on the table and sit and look at it—"

"And you think that is nothing?"

"It's nothing for Anton. He can cut out almost anything, if he only sits and looks at it a while. But I think it's pretty and nice to have. If you care for that frame as a little remembrance, ma'am, I'll take it down."

A blush spread slowly over the little lady's face.

"Thank you! But isn't it almost too much to accept?"

"Then I can tell Anton that he has made something that a fine lady from the manor-house cared to carry with her." She stepped up on the edge of the bed and took down the calendar.

The lady stood looking at the frame she held in her hand. She looked at it a long time. "I will tell Anton that myself," she said.

(To be continued)

Editorial

WAR AND GOOD-WILL The REVIEW in this, its fifth YULE NUMBER, can no longer wish its readers peace on earth. A year ago we still belonged to the blessed community of Four Neutrals. This Christmas most of our readers are belligerents; after nearly three years of waiting, America has been forced to enter the war in defense of world democracy. Our young soldiers are crossing the seas with much the same spirit of high idealism as that which actuated Christian knights of the middle ages who consecrated themselves to the defense of the distant Holy Sepulchre against the infidel. The task we have set for ourselves is no less difficult than that of the crusaders and demands the uttermost sacrifice of our lives and resources.

War on earth, but still good-will to men. In spite of our own anxieties, Americans can pause to offer a message of good-will to the three neutral nations of Northern Europe. Misunderstandings there have been, during the year, between them and us, blindness due to ignorance. Happily the horizon of our relations daily grows clearer. We realize that no one of the Scandinavian countries can enter the war at this time without becoming more of a liability than an asset to the Allies. Of the moral sympathy of the great mass of all the Northern peoples with the cause of democracy, we are assured. The visiting Scandinavian Commissioners have realized the essential friendliness of the American people. It seemed necessary for us to place a temporary absolute embargo against the nations bordering on Germany, as a preliminary to a world-wide economic adjustment. Yet we have no desire to drive them against their will into economic dependence upon Germany. Their governments, we understand, have now submitted to Washington full statistics of their commerce and consumption. We believe that it will not be long before trade is resumed, on the restricted basis made imperative by the war, and hope that on Christmas Day complete good-will and understanding will be in the ascendant between the United States, Sweden, Denmark, and Norway.

THE NORWEGIAN NATION ROUSED All the brutalities hitherto perpetrated by Germany upon peaceful Norwegians on the high seas pale before the account of the attack on a fleet of merchant vessels under British convoy on October 17. Four Norwegian, two Swedish, two Danish, two English ships, and one Belgian were destroyed by Germans raiders, which had followed the convoy through the night and opened fire at daybreak. Three men asleep in the forecastle of the *Silja* perished at the very first shot. Not only were the crews given no opportunity to save themselves, but it was evident to the men that the Germans were shooting to kill quite as much as to sink the vessels. Twelve men in one life-boat were killed by a single shell. Nine men had their boat splintered under them and managed to board their sinking ship, where they signalled for mercy, only to be answered by a shower of shells. Two women were shot as they struggled in the water. The tales brought in by the survivors, who made their way back to Bergen after unspeakable suffering, have shaken the Norwegian nation to its depths.

We sympathize with Norwegians who feel maddened by the sense of impotence, as their Government protests and protests again and yet again without avail. It is inevitable that the bitter futility of words should drive them almost to despair. Yet these notes have not been in vain. They have clarified the situation, and they will go down into history among the most terrible indictments of the German people. The last note of the Norwegian Government was framed in no uncertain terms. We welcome likewise every individual action, such as that of Roald Amundsen, who has returned all his German decorations, and we hope the rumor is true that Norwegian longshoremen have refused to load or unload German vessels.

DENMARK'S
MODEST
DEMANDS
With negotiations for American supplies pending, the Danes have bent their energies to utilizing their own resources and making every pound of food yield its utmost amount of nourishment. They have applied to the task the same scientific skill that built up their industrialized agriculture —now unhappily ruined. We lament the slaughtering of Denmark's fine herds and the passing of Danish butter and bacon from the markets of the world, but the picture has a brighter side. Through this finely-balanced food production and organization, the Danes have been saved from the starvation that seems imminent among some of their neighbors. The grain situation has been worked out on the principle: food for human beings first, then for animals. The hogs were the first to be sacrificed, since it was found they consume a disproportionate amount of grain compared to the number of calories they yield for human consumption. The cows were saved as long as possible, in order not to cut off the milk supply, but in time most of them have to go. The empty breweries, idle since the injunction against using grain for beer was issued, have been made into vast storehouses for salt and dried meat. If sufficient artificial fertilizers can be imported, the yield of grain will be greatly increased next year, and in the meantime a consistent rationing of bread is stretching the present supply as far as possible.

The Danes will not starve. Nor will they freeze, though they have to practice strict self-denial in the use of heat, light, and even city water. The men made idle by the curtailment of street car and railroad service have been mobilized as wood-choppers and peat-cutters. Many brain-workers, too, have tried their muscles on the unwonted toil. Wood is used to replace coal in private houses, and even that is used sparingly; for instance, a family living in an apartment of six rooms can only heat three. The coal is saved for manufacturing, and with 100,000 tons coming every month from England and the same amount from Germany, making in all two-thirds of the normal consumption, it would be possible to keep most of the manufacturing plants going, if raw materials could be obtained. This is Denmark's greatest need at present. About one-third of the population is dependent upon manufacturing, and the menace of unemployment in the winter is very grave. The Danes need from us copper for electric wires, lubricating oils, lead and iron for ammunition for their own neutrality guard, steel plates for their ships, fats for margarine, and Argentine hides for their leather industries.

It is to our advantage to grant these modest wants of Denmark, so far as we have the power. The Merchants' Guild of Copenhagen furnishes an absolute guarantee that no goods manufactured from our raw materials shall be sold to our enemies. Of the total amount passing through the hands of the Guild during the war years, only two-tenths of one per cent. have gone astray, and England has officially recognized the fact that the Danish merchants can handle the whole export situation better than the British Government itself. We can safely trust their vigilance. We must not allow the superb Danish shipyards to lie idle at a time when the Allies are in such dire need of tonnage, nor the Danish skilled workmen to tramp the streets when the whole human race needs to conserve every pound of its labor supply.

FRIENDLY AID CAMPAIGN The editors of the REVIEW are grateful to all Associates for their prompt and generous response in the "Friendly Aid Campaign." On December 1, 945 of the 4,000 required new Associates had been subscribed. Thank you!

TRUE SONS OF ICELAND A large number of Canadians of Icelandic origin are serving in the armies of our Allies. They were among the first to respond, and Icelandic names were found on the first list of Canadian dead and wounded. Many prominent men have testified to their splendid loyalty, among them the Lieutenant-Governor of Manitoba, Sir James A. Aikins, who estimates that, out of an Icelandic population of twenty thousand in the province, one thousand men are at the front. One entire regiment, the 223d, is made up chiefly of Icelanders and officered by them.

Current Events

Denmark

❡ The new tax law, passed by the Rigsdag after considerable opposition from Conservatives, will increase the revenue of the state by nearly a hundred million kroner. Its most drastic clause is the additional tax on wines and beer and on tobacco in all forms. The retail price of all alcoholic drinks will be at least doubled, while cigars and cigarettes will be such luxuries that the workers in tobacco factories have protested violently against the measure as endangering their means of livelihood. The law provides, furthermore, for a special income tax, distinct from those already levied by the state and municipality, to apply to all who own property valued at 15,000 kroner or more or who enjoy an annual income of 6,000 kroner or more. It will be graded at from .90 to 14.50 per cent. ❡ A loan of 60,000,000 kroner has been taken up by the Government and was fully subscribed almost as soon as announced. ❡ These extraordinary measures have been necessitated by the extra expenses due to the war, the "neutrality guard," the counting of cattle, the rationing system, the buying and storing of food and fuel, and the extra pay for Government employees to meet the increased cost of living. Moreover, it is expected that there will be a great falling off in the customary revenues; the tax on excess profits due to the war is likely to dwindle to almost nothing, and the customs receipts have fallen off with the decreased importation. ❡ Some thousands of the men mobilized as a "neutrality guard" have been allowed to return to their homes, largely in order to save the heavy expense of keeping so large a force under arms. ❡ The employees of the Government, numbering fifty thousand, have formed an organization to insist on a permanent and thorough revision of the pay-roll, a measure which they claim was imperative even before war prices set in. Many bitter words were spoken at the organizing meeting, where, for instance, one prison inspector declared that the prisoners had better food than he and his colleagues could afford to buy. Many professional men took part in the meeting, including school principals, civil engineers, and officials in the police, railway, and customs departments. ❡ The permanent Arbitration Court recently declared against the Waiters' Union in a suit brought against five leading restaurants which had engaged women as waiters. The court held that, as the restaurants were paying the women the same wages as men, the hiring of women could not be considered a breach of contract. The men's union was sentenced to pay the costs. ❡ Six young fishermen, of from seventeen to twenty-one years of age, were instantly killed by the explosion of a huge mine that had drifted ashore near Thyborön.

Sweden

⁋ A meeting to consider ways and means of economic co-operation after the war was arranged by the chambers of commerce and business organizations of the three Scandinavian countries, and was held in the Riksdag building in Stockholm, September 14 and 15. The chairman of the meeting was Mr. K. A. Wallenberg, the banker. Several members of the Government were present. Professor Bredo Morgenstierne of Christiania spoke of the need for a careful preliminary study of the whole situation, and ended with an urgent appeal to the three brother nations to stand by one another, even at the cost of sacrificing some of their individual interests. The chief topics of consideration were questions touching the customs, shipping, and the right to utilize natural resources such as mines and waterfalls. ⁋ Representatives of manufacturing interests and technical experts met in Stockholm, September 19, to discuss the means of devising substitutes for the various things now unobtainable. Chief among these are mineral oils for fuel and for machinery, and experiments have been made, though not with perfect success, for utilizing wood tar oils for both purposes. Motors have been reconstructed to allow the use of tar oil, and many parts of machinery hitherto imported are now made in Sweden. No substitutes have been found for fats and for the raw materials of the textile industries. ⁋ Electricity has long been in use for household and agricultural purposes in Norrland, Dalecarlia, Vestergötland, and other districts where great electric plants are located. An effort is now being made to extend the use through all the country districts, and especially intensive work is being done in Uppland. ⁋ The importation of coal from Germany has decreased from 2,859,750 tons for the first six months in 1916 to 634,138 for the first six months in 1917. The need of the Swedish manufacturers is so great that they have been anxious to pay almost any amount for fuel, and the German Government has taken advantage of this fact to increase the price by 25 kronor per ton in violation of all contracts. ⁋ Since Sweden now has a complete embargo on meat, it was necessary to obtain a special license to export cattle that had to be sacrificed on account of the dearth of fodder in the fall. Permission was given at the beginning of September to export 5,000 animals to Norway and Finland, and at the beginning of October to export 6,000 animals to Germany. The latter roused some criticism in Liberal newspapers as likely to interfere with the American negotiations. ⁋ Two monuments have been raised by the inhabitants of Bohus Län in southwestern Sweden over the graves of German and British victims of the North Sea battle whose bodies drifted ashore and were buried there. ⁋ About fifty Swedish concerns took part in the great annual market of Nisjnij Novgorod in Russia.

Norway

❡ A standardized coarse bread, made by mixing rye with wheat, is sold at a moderate price in Norway with the aid of a state subsidy. Until recently this bread was sold in unlimited quantities, but, beginning November 1, the Government has introduced the rationing system which has long been in use in Sweden. The object is to make people eat freely of potatoes, which are fairly plentiful. Experiments are also made with preparing potatoes in huge drying machines for mixing in the bread and with substituting barley and oats for wheat flour. ❡ The movement to make Norway self-supporting in the matter of food has resulted in increasing the tilled area of the country by twelve per cent. in 1917. The two preceding years show an increase of about four and a half per cent. each. The park surrounding the summer palace of the King and Queen at Bygdö was pressed into service for raising potatoes and was said to promise a harvest of a thousand barrels. ❡ A Norwegian concern, called the Borregaard Company, has acquired the property of the Kellner Partington Paper Pulp Company, valued at a hundred million kroner. It includes the Sarpsfos waterfall and a large part of the ground on which Sarpsborg is built, besides extensive forests in Norway and Sweden, and a plant in Salzburg, Austria. The annual product of the company has been 150,000 tons of wood pulp. The acquisition is considered the greatest step that has yet been taken to make Norwegian industry independent of foreign capital. ❡ After the Luxburg revelations, *Morgenbladet* in Christiania published, a—confessedly incomplete—list of Norwegian vessels that had disappeared leaving no trace. The list included fourteen ships the fate of whose crews the Norwegian Government had not been able to ascertain even by inquiry of the British Admiralty. A few days later, the paper published another list of thirteen vessels known to have been sunk in routes to and from South American ports covered by the telegraph system centering in Argentina. This takes into account only those lost since the unrestricted U-boat warfare went into effect. ❡ The United States Government has issued a license for the exportation of the provisions required by Roald Amundsen for his coming expedition, and he intends to start for the northern coast of Siberia in his new boat *Maud* in June, 1918. Amundsen has a state subsidy for the expedition of 200,000 kroner, and an additional donation of 50,000 kroner from Mr. A. F. Klaveness, the ship-owner, has just been announced. The explorer has himself staked his entire fortune on the trip. ❡ The municipality of Christiania has a "fuel central" operating with a budget of 24,000,000 kroner. An enormous supply of wood has been laid in for the winter, and ration cards are issued to the people.

Books

ARNLJOT GELLINE, a Verse Romance. By Björnstjerne Björnson. Translated
from the Norwegian with an Introduction and Notes by William Morton
Payne. SCANDINAVIAN CLASSICS, Volume VIII. New York: The American-
Scandinavian Foundation, 1917. Price $1.50.

In the lyric-epic poem *Arnljot Gelline*, we have Björnson in his first, purely
Norse, period. The hero is an outlaw who joins the forces of King Olaf Trygvason and falls with him in the Battle of Stiklestad for the cause of Christ against
the older gods. The story is told in a series of vivid episodes, each with a mood
and metre of its own. To a reader unable to appreciate the stern reserve power
of Norse poetry, such a piece will seem bare in subject and abstruse in style, but
to him who catches the tone it will be rich in inspiration. The alternations of
gloom and radiant vision are like the changing lights of a broken storm on the
North Sea.

Dr. Payne has followed the original in rhythm and rhyme, with the result that
he conveys to the reader much of its atmosphere. He is most happy where the
verse is freest and least rhyme is required. Here his phrasing has great directness and dignity, together with a sweep that carries one along breathlessly. In
the more set passages, the inversions of the English are at times disturbing.
Fortunately the great moments come where the translator is most completely
submerged in the scenes and emotions of the poem. A compact introduction
and notes with full quotations from the *Heimskringla* and Björnson's other
sources make the volume attractive alike to the general reader and the scholar.

C. W. STORK.

ANTHOLOGY OF SWEDISH LYRICS FROM 1750 TO 1915. Translated in the original
meters by Charles Wharton Stork. SCANDINAVIAN CLASSICS, Volume IX.
New York: The American-Scandinavian Foundation. 1917. Price $1.50.

This splendid volume of SCANDINAVIAN CLASSICS, representing the product
of forty-five modern poets, is the first comprehensive collection of Swedish lyrics
in English. Some of these have appeared before in American periodicals, and
the poet-translator became well known to English-reading students of Swedish
literature last year through his *Selected Poems of Gustav Fröding*.

Dr. Stork has wisely followed his customary method of giving us, first of all,
good English poetry. But he has also followed the original with sensible faithfulness and has realized fully his double difficulty and responsibility as a translator and, in a sense, as a pioneer anthologist. The most striking characteristic
of this collection is the translator's sympathy for Swedish poetry in general, and
his scrupulous efforts to reproduce the spirit of the original. In this he has been
surprisingly successful, even in the rendering of Bellman, whose unique improvi-
sations can seldom be appreciated apart from the music. Dr. Stork's enthusiasm
for Runeberg is well founded, and even admirers of the Swedish will find it decid-
edly worth while to read aloud the translation of *Sven Duva*, the hero of which,
a simple-minded Finnish Horatius, has no parallel in modern literature.

The value of this anthology is enhanced by the addition of all the editorial
accessories that are necessary in a work of this kind, such as indexes, brief biographical notes, and an historical sketch of Swedish poetry. It will be heartily
welcomed by all lovers of good verse, and the translator should feel encouraged
to add another volume, of a more historical character perhaps, including some
Swedish folk songs and such names as Charlotta Nordenflycht, Julia Nyberg,
Vitalis, Hedborn, Karl August Nicander, and Wilhelm von Braun.

ADOLPH BURNETT BENSON.

Brief Notes

The index of the AMERICAN-SCANDINAVIAN REVIEW, Volume V, will be ready December 15, and may be had free by application to this office. Those who desire may send in the six numbers for 1917 with $1 and have them bound attractively in cloth with gold lettering and the seal of the Foundation stamped in gold on the side. The volume will be returned postpaid.

Madame Signe Lund has won the $500 prize awarded by the National Arts Club for the best musical setting for the prize poem "The Road to France," by Daniel M. Henderson. Madame Lund comes of the distinguished Norwegian family of artists of that name. She is an American citizen and has two sons in our army, one in France already.

An interesting excursion was made by the Ygdrasil Literary Society of Madison, Wisconsin, on July 29, to the little town of Muskego. The first Norwegian newspaper of America appeared there just seventy years ago, and three years earlier the first Norwegian church was built there. The most eminent son of Muskego, Colonel Hans Heg of the Fifteenth Wisconsin, was commemorated in an eloquent speech by Professor Julius E. Olson.

The REVIEW joins with the many friends all over the country who congratulate Mr. Henry Hertz upon his seventieth birthday. Mr. Hertz has at all times been active in public service for his adopted country and particularly for the Danes in the United States. He is a member of the Foundation Advisory Committee of Chicago.

The Series of *Scandinavian Classics*, and Hustvedt's "Ballad Criticism" and Hovgaard's "Voyages of the Norsemen," in the *Scandinavian Monographs*, were printed for the American-Scandinavian Foundation by this Press.

Dear Reader:

¶ This is a time for service.

¶ If you believe in the REVIEW, in the cause for which it stands and for which it gives its best efforts, you will help the REVIEW. If you believe in it fully you will take pride in this service.

¶ One of the ways in which you can help lies in buying goods from our advertisers. Not to buy them just for this purpose, but when with little extra trouble you can as well buy an article from a REVIEW advertiser as from another, do so.

¶ You will be helping all along the line. Our advertisers expect results. They are entitled to them. If results fail to come, advertisers drop out. But when results come as they should advertisers stay in, and we are able to get more advertisers. This adds to our income and helps us to make a better magazine for you to read. It lessens the drain on the funds of the Foundation, so that these can be put to other patriotic purposes.

May we count upon your help?

Yours faithfully,

THE ADVERTISING MANAGER

"one of the few"

"Your organization represents one of the few real groups of craftsmen in the printing field,"

says an eminent authority on the typographic arts, in writing to us recently. . . It is our aim to merit this commendation. . . . . The measure of our success is reflected in the quality of our work, as exemplified in *The American-Scandinavian Review*. . . . We solicit inquiries from the readers of this magazine.

REDFIELD-KENDRICK ODELL CO.

INCORPORATED

Printers . Engravers . Map Makers

311-319 WEST 43d STREET
NEW YORK CITY

"SWEDEN"

A MAGAZINE OF SWEDISH ART AND LITERATURE

WITH TWELVE ART SUPPLEMENTS IN COLORS
Reproductions of Paintings of Most Famous Swedish Artists

CONTENTS

NOT FEEDING GERMANY by HANNA ASTRUP LARSEN. An article of great importance, an interesting version of facts.
THE LYRIC POETRY OF SWEDEN by DR. CLEMENT BURBANK SHAW with translations into English of twenty-five Swedish songs. Never published before in this couutry.
SWEDEN AS A TOURIST COUNTRY. Compiled by R. J. COLLIN. Richly illustrated.
MAMSELL FREDRIKA by SELMA LAGERLÖF, translated from Swedish by Pauline Bancroft Flach.
SWEDISH FOLK DANCES by NILS BERGQUIST.
FRITHIOFS SAGA, translated by DR. CLEMENT BURBANK SHAW. Two cantos are given.
YOUTH, WOMEN, AND ANTIMILITARISM by ELLEN KEY, translated from the Swedish by ARTHUR G. CHATER·
THE WORK OF THE AMERICAN-SCANDINAVIAN FOUNDATION by DR. HENRY GODDARD LEACH.
IN THE DAYS OF '49, translated from an old letter describing the trip to America fifty-three years ago.

Fox Hunter.—Oil Painting by BRUNO LILJEFORS.
Famous the world over for his Animal Paintings

Seven of the twelve art supplements are reproductions in colors of famous Swedish artists. Anders Zorn, Bruno Liljefors, H. R. H. Prince Eugen, Carl Larsson, Karl Wilhelmson, Carl Nordstrom, and N. Kreuger are represented.

Sweden with its wonderful nature and remarkable literature and art is little known throughout America. All research has been directed elsewhere, and Sweden has remained the obscure giant of the north. This magazine will give the American an opportunity to know a little more about Sweden.

It is excellent as a Christmas present.
Price $1.50

Fill in This Blank.   ORDER IMMEDIATELY

Waldemar J. Adams & Co.
    573 Lexington Avenue, New York, N. Y.

Kindly send......copy "Sweden"

Name..
Address...
City and State ....

After Bathing.—Oil Painting by ANDERS ZORN.

WALDEMAR J. ADAMS & CO.
573 Lexington Avenue,
and 516 Third Avenue, New York

SELECT CHEERFUL CHRISTMAS REMEMBRANCES FROM

1000 Unique, Thoughtful and Distinctive **Gifts** Described and illustrated in our great 1917 Gift Book—a collection of practical suggestions which carry a message of thoughtful giving, of dainty simplicity and of beauty with usefulness. Published by **Pohlson**

Increase the joy and add to the good cheer of this Christmas by giving things that are "different." We originate, and specialize in, thoughtful, personal and friendly little gifts—charming, out-of-the-ordinary things that cause pleasant thrills on Christmas day.

Discriminating Specialty Shops and Gift Departments everywhere are now showing our new ideas for the holidays. Just look for the Pohlson things.

Tasteful cards, rhymes of cheerful sentiment and a "doing up" that lends the final touch, all combine to make each gift complete and personal.

If you wish to shop by mail, we shall be delighted to meet your requirements. Our new 72-page illustrated catalogue will be sent free with any of the gifts shown above, or on receipt of 6c. in stamps.

1851

1803

997

1009

1838

1839

995

995—**Shopping List** of leather and convenient to the shopper - - $0.60

1838—**Data Booklet** of green leather. For pocket of shopping bag - - - - - - - - .50

997—**Tight Wad Bill Fold** of tooled leather - - - - - - - - .50

1009—**Pair of Candlesticks** with Bayberry candles - - - - - 1.00

1838—**Yarn Holder** for crocheting. Painted wood - - - - - - 1.25

1803—**Uncle Sam Savings Bank** - .50

1851—**Marjorie Knitting Needle Protectors** - - - - - - - .50

1839—**Bob and Betty Book Ends,** painted - - - - - - - - 1.25

ASK YOUR DEALER OR WRITE US

1038

POHLSON GIFT SHOPS, Pacific Bank Building, PAWTUCKET, RHODE ISLAND

TRADE NOTES
*News and Comment on Exports and Trade
Conditions Between America and the Scan-
dinavian Countries*

SWEDISH MATCH COMBINE
It is reported from Stockholm that all leading Swedish match factories have been merged into a new corporation, divided into 400,000 shares at 200 crowns each. This concern will be the largest of its kind in the world, with an annual output of 5,000,000,000 boxes.

SCANDINAVIAN STEAMERS RESUME SAILINGS
After an interval of some months, the Scandinavian-American Line has resumed its sailings, with the departure of *Hellig Olav* from New York, November 20. The Norwegian steamer *Bergensfjord* arrived, bringing 1207 passengers, said to be the largest number ever carried by the Norwegian-American line on a single voyage; she returned with passengers November 20.

SCANDINAVIAN COMMERCIAL CONGRESS
Great developments are anticipated from the meeting of the Scandinavian Commercial Congress, held recently at Stockholm. The president of the Congress was Mr. Wallenberg, the former minister for foreign affairs. "After War" trade was discussed by such velin, respectively, of Sweden, Norway, and Denmark. experts as Messrs. Heckscherer, Morgenstjerne, and Scho-

HALVOR JACOBSEN IN FULL CHARGE.
Halvor Jacobsen, New York representative of the Scandinavian-American Line, has taken over the firm of A. E. Johnson & Co., which for many years has been the general agent for the passenger department of the Steamship Company in this country. The line has agencies in all the leading cities.

AMERICAN-SCANDINAVIAN TRADE

The New York *Commercial* has published a series of five articles dealing with the future trade development between the United States and Norway, Sweden, and Denmark. It is shown that Russia will be a big field for business, utilizing Scandinavia as a clearing-house for goods and traffic.

NORWAY DENIES NICKEL RUMOR

It is authoritatively denied that Norway is to resume shipments of nickel to Germany. The story gained currency that the Christiania nickel factory would start operations in January. As the metal is principally used in the manufacture of torpedoes it would appear that the Norwegians would be the last people to furnish munition to a country that persists in sinking its merchantmen.

AMERICAN TRACTORS POPULAR

American tractors attained great popularity in Norway, and as soon as embargo restrictions are raised a big field is opened up in that country for such motors as are especially suited for road and farm purposes.

CEMENT INDUSTRY AFFECTED

The coal shortage has greatly affected the Danish cement industry. The amount of coal annually needed for the purpose of manufacturing cement is 200,000 tons.

DANISH GOVERNMENT TO AID

The Danish Government has arranged with butter producers for 1,600,000 pounds of butter to be disposed of weekly at two crowns a pound. The Government will pay the difference between this figure and the market price, which is 20 to 25 per cent. higher.

J. M.

FINANCIAL NOTES

*Notes About Issues in the Financial World
Most Interesting to Readers of the Review*

AIDED THE LIBERTY LOAN

According to U. S. Treasury statements the sections where Scandinavian-Americans reside in greatest numbers were foremost in exceeding their second Liberty Loan quotas. Many well-known people of Scandinavian descent were on the local committees boosting the Government bond issue.

SWEDISH JOINT STOCK COMPANIES INCREASE

New companies numbering over 1500 with a paid-in capital of $80,000,000 were formed in Sweden during the past two years. Total bank deposits in private institutions at the close of 1916 amounted to $700,-000,000.

DENMARK INCREASES TRAFFIC RATE

The Minister of Traffic proposes to increase the rates on certain classes of goods with a view of producing an additional revenue of 12,000,000 crowns.

STATE BANK OF CHICAGO

It is doubtful if any banking institution has larger deposits from Americans of Scandinavian descent than the State Bank of Chicago. Founded in 1879 under the name of Haugan & Lindgren, the bank in 1905 increased its dividend rate from 6% to 8%, in 1907 to 10%, in 1908 to 12%, in 1915 to 16%. Oscar H. Haugan, one of the directors, is a trustee of the American-Scandinavian Foundation. He is manager of the Real Estate Loan Department.

Scandinavian Trust Company
56 Broadway, New York

Paid-in Capital and Surplus, $2,500,000

THIS company has been established to meet the large and growing business and financial relations between the United States and the Scandinavian countries, and for the purpose of providing facilities for general and domestic banking.

A. V. OSTROM, President

B. E. SMYTHE, Vice-President   T. BARTH, Vice-President

MAURICE F. BAYARD, Treasurer   D. CARDOZO, Asst.-Secretary

BOARD OF DIRECTORS

JOHS. ANDERSEN.................................J. Andersen & Company
KNUT BACHKE...........................Andresens Bank, Christiania
CHARLES E. BEDFORD..................Vice-President, Vacuum Oil Company
JAMES F. BELL......................Vice-President, Washburn-Crosby Company
JOHN E. BERWIND.............Vice-President, Berwind-White Coal Mining Co.
R. R. BROWN...................First Vice-President, American Surety Company
WILLIAM R. COE...............................Chairman, Johnson & Higgins
GERHARD M. DAHL.....................Vice-President, Chase National Bank
S. E. DAHL.......................Centralbanken for Norge, Christiania
W. EDWARD FOSTER.............Treasurer, American Sugar Refining Company
SAMUEL L. FULLER...........................Kissel, Kinnicutt & Company
EDWARD F. GEER...Shipowner
CHARLES S. HAIGHT.......................Haight, Sanford & Smith
G. KAMSTRUP HEGGE...................Den Norske Creditbank, Christiania
EDWIN O. HOLTER..Attorney
FREDERICK W. HVOSLEF.....................Bennett, Hvoslef & Company
N. BRUCE MacKELVIE.........................Hayden, Stone & Company
ALEXANDER V. OSTROM..President
BIRGER OSLAND..............General Western Agent, Norwegian-America Line
E. A. CAPPELEN SMITH...............................Guggenheim Brothers

Den Danske Landmandsbank Hypothek-og Vekselbank

Paid up Capital	:	80 Million Kroner
Reserve Fund	:	16 Million Kroner

(about $25,600,000)

COPENHAGEN
(DENMARK)

PROVINCIAL [BRANCHES:

Aalborg	Elsinore	Nykjöbing F.
Bandholm	Holbäk	Nykjöbing S.
Bramminge	Kallundborg	Nysted
Esbjerg	Kolding	Rödby
Eskildstrup	Maribo	Saxkjöbing
Fejö	Nakskov	Sönderho
Fredericia	Nordby	Vejle

(*Telegraphic Address:* LANDMANDSBANK)

THE BAND TRANSACTS EVERY KIND OF LEGITIMATE BANKING BUSINESS:

Opening of Current Accounts.

Acceptance of Deposits for fixed periods or subject to notice.

Safekeeping and Administration of Securities.

> (These can also be made for Joint Accounts, *i. e.*, in the names of two or more persons, each with equal right to dispose of the funds.)

Purchase and Sale of Danish Bonds and Shares.

Purchase and Sale of Banknotes, Cheques, etc.

Collection and Discounting of Bills.

Issue of Circular Letters of Credit, Cheques, etc.

Telegraphic Transfers to all parts of the world.

CENTRALBANKEN FOR NORGE

Amalgamated with the Christiania Banking Houses

THO. JOH. HEFTYE & SÖN   and   SEV. CHR. ANDERSEN
(Established 1769)   (Established 1845)

Capital:

Covered by stocks and bonds easy of realization deposited in the State Bank of Norway	Kr. 7.500.000
Paid-up in cash............................	" 12.500.000
Reserve fund............................	" 7.450.000
	Kr. 27.450.000
Deposits and current accounts............	Kr. 167.413.444

Prompt collection of Norwegian inheritances at moderate charges.
Special attention given to Collections.
Accounts of Banks, Merchants, and individuals solicited.
Deposits received at highest rate of interest.

Oversea and Letter of Credit business.   *Remittances to all parts of Scandinavia*

CHRISTIANIA - - - NORWAY

EMPIRE TRUST COMPANY

120 Broadway   NEW YORK   580 Fifth Avenue

London Office, 41 Threadneedle Street

Resources, February 28, 1917, Over $46,000,000

The Fifth Avenue Office of this Company, corner 47th Street, is accessibly situated for anyone desiring the services of an Uptown Banking Institution.

Careful and courteous attention given to any business entrusted to it.

Interest may be arranged upon accounts subject to check.

Certificates of Deposit, maturing at a date to suit the needs of the depositor, issued at favorable rates of interest.

EMPIRE SAFE DEPOSIT COMPANY

Safe Deposit Vaults

FINANCIAL NOTES Continued

THE TRADE ACCEPTANCE ISSUE

An address delivered by Lewis E. Pierson, chairman of the board of the Irving National Bank, dealing with trade acceptances, is of particular significance during the war. Mr. Pierson spoke before the War Convention of American Business of the Chamber of Commerce of the United States held at Atlantic City. He showed that the true relationship between business and banking is much closer than generally is realized. The bank has issued the address in pamphlet form.

BIG BANKING SUCCESS

As evidence of the need for closer financial co-operation between this country and the Northern nations of Europe, the Scandinavian Trust Company of New York is rapidly forging to the front as a considerable factor in international finance. It has recently been admitted as a member of the Federal Reserve Bank of New York.

CHRISTIANIA BANK DEPOSITS INCREASE

During the first half of 1917, the ten largest banks of Christiania received deposits aggregating $157,000,000, or 43 per cent. more than in the corresponding period last year.

GUARANTEES

Swedish bankers are reported to have taken the initiative in the forming of a national league which shall have for its purpose guaranteeing to the American Government that there shall be no resale of goods purchased for home consumption.   J. M.

Norwegian America Line

Modern Twin Screw Steamers
16,000 tons displacement, 530 feet long, 16½ knots speed

Route

Steamers take the shortest route (North of Scotland), direct to B e r g e n, f r o m whence railroad and steamship connections may be made to all points in Scandinavia, Finland, R u s s i a and other parts of the Continent. Bergen - Kristiania Scenic Railway may be used without extra charge.

All passengers must secure passports or consular certificates

Travellers

can arrange for all details of travel in Norway, Sweden, Denmark and other parts of the Continent during the voyage, as representatives from Bennett's Tourist Office are stationed on board our ships for the purpose of furnishing information in regard to train connections, securing sleeping car and hotel accommodations, arranging itineraries, etc.

No Contraband or Ammunition Supplies Carried

Accommodations: The steamers are new, modern and efficiently equipped for the utmost safety and comfort of passengers. First-class staterooms are situated amidships on the Promenade and Shelter Deck. Cabins De Luxe on upper promenade.

For further particulars apply to

NORWEGIAN AMERICA LINE PASSENGER AGENCY, Inc.

8 and 10 Bridge St., New York   General Passenger Agents for United States and Canada

HOBE & CO.	BIRGER OSLAND & CO.	REIDAR GJÖLME
General Northwestern Passenger Agents	General Western Passenger Agents	General Pacific Coast Agent
123 South Third Street, Minneapolis, Minn.	115 So. Dearborn St., Chicago, Ill.	115 Cherry St., Seattle, Wash.

NORWAY MEXICO GULF LINE AND SWEDISH AMERICA MEXICO LINE

Regular service between GÖTEBORG, CHRISTIANIA and STAVAN-GER and NEWPORT NEWS, VA., HAVANA, CUBA, GALVESTON, TEX., and NEW ORLEANS, LA.

Passengers Carried   Wireless Apparatus

AGENTS

FEARNLEY & EGER, Christiania   SANDSTRÖM STRANNE & CO., Ltd., Goteborg

FURNESS WITHY & CO., Ltd., New York, N. Y. and Newport News, Va.

32 BROADWAY

JAS. P. ROBERTSON	FOWLER & McVITIE	LYKES BROS.	GEO. PLANT
111 West Jackson Boulevard Chicago, Ill.	Galveston, Tex.	Havana, Cuba	1119 Whitney Central Bldg. New Orleans, La.

The Travel Number *of*
THE AMERICAN-SCANDINAVIAN REVIEW

will be ready on February 15. It will be an American Travel Number, and will contain an article by CHRISTIAN LEDEN on his explorations in the Hudson Bay region, with many pictures, an account of a trip on foot through the White Mountains, a story of a tour through Whittier Land, a picture in colors of the most northerly church in the world, painted by BAYARD TAYLOR, and other unusual features.

Single Copies, Only Twenty-five Cents.

A. E. JOHNSON & CO., INC., 1 BROADWAY, NEW YORK
GENERAL OFFICES: Passenger Department

117 N. Dearborn Street, Chicago, Ill.
236 Nicollet Ave., Minneapolis, Minn.
702 Second Ave., Seattle, Wash.

1 BROADWAY, NEW YORK

544 Market St., San Francisco, Cal.
248 Washington St., Boston, Mass.
24 Tronto St., Tronto, Ont., Can.

SWEDISH AMERICAN LINE

(SVENSKA AMERIKA LINIEN)

Direct Passenger Service between **New York and Gothenburg, Sweden.**
Short Route to **Sweden, Norway, Denmark, Finland, Russia** and other
parts of the European Continent

Twin-Screw S.S. "STOCKHOLM"
Length 565 Feet.   22,070 Tons Displacement
Largest Steamer in Service between America and Scandinavia

Twin-Screw S.S. "Stockholm"

is provided with all modern safety appliances,
and every care is taken to give the passengers
a safe and comfortable journey.

*Unsurpassed passenger appointments in
First, Second and Third Classes.*

RATES
[To Scandinavian Points:

First Class . . . . $150.00 and up
Second Class 105.00
Third Class 62.00

*Reserve Berths Now and Secure Tickets Through
Nearest Local Agent or*

NIELSEN & LUNDBECK, General Passenger
Agents, 24 State Street, New York.
MARTIN MAURD, General Western Agent, 183
N. Dearborn Street, Chicago.
NILS NILSON, General Northwestern Agent, 127
S. Third St., Minneapolis.
BRATTSTROM & CO., General No. Pacific Agents,
117 Cherry St., Seattle, Wash.
A. HALLONQUIST, General Agent, 396 Logan Ave.,
Winnipeg, Man., Can.

The Splendid S.S. "Stockholm" is in regular service between New York and Gothenburg.
Apply to nearest agency for sailing dates.

The American-Scandinavian Review

VOLUME VI   MARCH-APRIL, 1918   NUMBER 2

Published Bi-Monthly by THE AMERICAN-SCANDINAVIAN FOUNDATION, 25 West 45th Street, New York

Yearly Subscription, $1.50.   (One dollar to Associates of the Foundation.)   Single Copies, 25 cents

Entered as second-class matter, January 4, 1913, at the post-office at New York, N. Y., under the act of March 3, 1879
Copyright, 1916, The American-Scandinavian Foundation

HENRY GODDARD LEACH, *Editor*   HANNA ASTRUP LARSEN, *Literary Editor*

Advisors

New York, HAMILTON HOLT   Copenhagen, HARALD NIELSEN
Stockholm, CARL LAURIN   Christiania, CHRISTIAN COLLIN

CONTENTS

FOUNDED BY NIELS POULSON, IN 1911

ANNOUNCEMENT

THE ROYAL COPENHAGEN POR-CELAIN AND DANISH ARTS announce that they have discontinued their old Showrooms at 256 Fifth Avenue, near Twenty-eighth Street, and have assembled the products of the Royal Copenhagen factories in their establishment at

563 FIFTH AVENUE

(Near Forty-sixth Street)

You are cordially invited to call

D. B. UPDIKE
The Merrymount Press
232 SUMMER STREET
BOSTON

· · ·

PRINTERS OF FINE BOOKS FOR
BOOK CLUBS, INSTITUTIONS, AND
PRIVATE PERSONS
&c. &c. &c.

The Series of *Scandinavian Classics*, and Hust-vedt's "Ballad Criticism" and Hovgaard's "Voyages of the Norsemen," in the *Scandinavian Monographs*, were printed for the American-Scandinavian Foundation by this Press.

Scandinavian Monographs

VOLUME III
The King's Mirror
*Translated from the Old Norwegian of the 13th Century
With an Introduction and Notes*

By LAURENCE MARCELLUS LARSON
Professor of History in the University of Illinois

THIS is the first English translation of the book of instruction used at the court of Hákon the Old. It will be welcomed by Norwegian scholars everywhere: for the *Speculum Regale* is the chief Norwegian prose monument from the period when the sagas were written down in Iceland. Professor Larson furnishes a long and valuable introduction. He is widely known as the author of *Canute the Great* and a history of England. Price $3.00.

This volume is a companion piece to the superb viking facsimile text edition of the manuscript *Speculum Regale* edited by Professor George T. Flom, and published by the University of Illinois. Price $15.00.

The above two volumes will be sold together to Libraries and Associates of the Foundation for $16.00, express free.

American-Scandinavian Foundation
25 West 45th Street, New York

UNDERWOOD

FIRST GRAND PRIZE—SUPREME HONOR
Panama-Pacific International Exposition, 1915

"The Machine You Will Eventually Buy"

UNDERWOOD BUILDING   NEW YORK CITY

THE SCANDINAVIAN CLASSICS

Ten per cent. discount to all Associates

Two volumes are sent annually free to Sustaining Associates

"The series is, in its dignified simplicity, a beautiful testimony to a literary solicitude which we hitherto have not been accustomed to associate with modern American culture. . . . This undertaking, which is not in the least forced, but just well done."
—August Brunius in *Svenska Dagbladet*.

If you want to show your American friends the high level of Northern culture, you can do no better than to present them with a set of the SCANDINAVIAN CLASSICS.   These books are carefully translated by competent writers.   They are printed from hand-set type and handsomely bound in a uniform red cloth edition with gold lettering.   No pains have been spared to make them worthy of the great literary works they contain.   If you do not wish to order the whole set, you will find each volume complete in itself.

The following nine volumes are now ready:

Comedies by Holberg
Three most characteristic plays by "The Molière of the North," the first great modern in Scandinavian literature.

Poems by Tegnér
"Frithiof's Saga" and other poems by the lyrist who revealed the beauty of Swedish literature to Longfellow.

Poems and Songs by Björnstjerne Björnson
A catechism of Norwegian patriotic ideals.

Master Olof
Strindberg's historical - religious drama, whose hero has been called "as uncompromising at moments as Ibsen's Brand, but more living than he."

The Prose Edda of Snorri Sturluson
Mythical tales of the North written by a master of Old Norse Prose.

Björnstjerne Björnson

Modern Icelandic Plays
"Eyvind of the Hills" and "The Hraun Farm" by Jóhann Sigurjónsson, the young dramatist of Iceland.

Marie Grubbe.   A Lady of the Seventeenth Century
The first of J. P. Jacobsen's two great psychological novels.

Arnljot Gelline
In this verse romance Björnson has found the most "daring and tremendous expression for the spirit of Old Norse paganism."

Anthology of Swedish Lyrics
A wonderful array of lyric achievement is revealed in this volume of Swedish verse, from 1750 to 1915, collected and translated by Charles Wharton Stork.

In course of preparation are translations of Heidenstam's *Karolinerna*, Selma Lagerlöf's *Gösta Berling*, and Jonas Lie's *Familien paa Gilje*.

Price, $1.50 each

The Foundation publishes also another series of books: "Scandinavian Monographs"

THE AMERICAN-SCANDINAVIAN FOUNDATION
25 West Forty-fifth Street, New York

CONTRIBUTORS TO THE MARCH-APRIL NUMBER

CHRISTIAN LEDEN is a native of Norway. He gained his first experience of Arctic explorations in 1909 as a member of the expedition sent out by the Danish Government to West and North Greenland. Afterwards he visited East Greenland with the support of King Haakon. In 1911 he made a short trip through northern Canada as a preliminary to the three years' journey described in this number of the REVIEW. Mr. Leden is now in New York. His article in the *Outlook* on "Mobilizing the Arctic" recently attracted attention.

ALLEN H. BENT is the author of a *Bibliography of the White Mountains* and a frequent contributor to the *Appalachia*, the journal published by the Appalachian Mountain Club. He is chairman of the publishing committee of the club and was formerly its secretary.

The editors of the REVIEW take particular pleasure in being able to give their readers again a sonnet by MAURICE FRANCIS EGAN, the American friend of Denmark, now visiting his native country.

CARL JOHANNES SÖDERGREN is professor of New Testament exegesis at the Augustana Seminary in Rock Island. He is himself a graduate of that institution and has served the Augustana Synod as pastor, teacher, and editor.

HENRIK IBSEN's poem on "The Death of Abraham Lincoln," presented here in an English version by Professor Schofield, is in many ways so pertinent to the present situation that it has particular interest to-day.

KARL GUSTAF DERNBY is Swedish fellow of the American-Scandinavian Foundation for 1917-1918 and is now engaged in chemical research work at the Rockefeller Institute in New York.

LILLA FRICH, of Minneapolis, is at present serving as supervisor of food education and demonstration with the New York State Food Commission for New York City.

MARGARET OF CONNAUGHT, SWEDEN'S ENGLISH CROWN PRINCESS, WHOSE DISTRIBUTION OF CANDLES TO THE POOR OF STOCKHOLM EARNED HER THE NAME OF "LUCIA," THE FAIR YOUNG SAINT WITH A CROWN OF BURNING CANDLES ON HER HEAD

THE
AMERICAN-SCANDINAVIAN
REVIEW

VOLUME VI   MARCH-APRIL · 1918   NUMBER 2

A Chapter from My Eskimo Travels

By CHRISTIAN LEDEN

Photographs by the Author

ON July 17, 1913, which chanced to be my thirty-first birthday, I embarked in the sealing vessel *Nascopie* at Montreal to begin what was to prove a long and arduous journey. The Norwegian consul for Canada and many other friends had risen in the misty dawn to wish me godspeed, and as the boat passed out of sight of their waving handkerchiefs I felt that it might be my last glimpse of friends for an indefinite time. I was setting out to make ethnographic studies among the Eskimo tribes living to the west and northwest of Hudson Bay. The desire to learn something about these unknown tribes had been growing in me ever since my first exploring trip in Greenland four years earlier, and I had, as early as 1911, been so fortunate as to secure the aid of their Majesties King Haakon and Queen Maud as well as of the University Museum at Christiania and several private persons in Norway. I was going alone; for I dared not take a white companion into a country so full of perils and empty of comforts, and moreover one has a better opportunity of learning to know the daily lives, beliefs, and emotions of primitive folk when living as one of them. I had arranged to have the *Nascopie* take me down the Gulf of St. Lawrence, around the peninsula of Labrador, and across Hudson Bay to its western coast, where I was to be left alone with the Eskimos.

After four days of rainy and foggy weather, a magnificent view of the Labrador mountains and icebergs burst through the clouds. As we glided slowly along, the gray sail of a Newfoundland fishing-smack or a schooner would now and then streak the blue of the sky, but such signs of human presence grew rarer and rarer, and finally the last sail sank beneath the southern horizon. We had passed

The "Nascopie" Among the Icebergs

beyond the pale of civiliza-tion, and nothing but the roar of calving icebergs and the shriek of sea-gulls broke the silent desolation.

The waters of Hudson Strait and Hudson Bay were alive with seals and walruses, sunning themselves on the ice-floes; the latter are queer-looking animals with their stiff moustaches and long tusks. The walrus hunter needs steady nerves and a sure hand, for the wounded animal always turns on its assailant, and its ugly tusks are most unpleasant to face. Nevertheless, the Eskimos are untiring in their pursuit of it; for not only is the meat excellent for food, but they have an old religious belief that the spirit world sends them game, and if they fail to kill it, the unseen powers will be angry and refuse to give them any more.

At the mouth of the Churchill River I left the *Nascopie*, and my real explorations began. The river mouth forms an ideal natural harbor, where a dozen ships could safely anchor, and beyond the coastline stretches a long row of spruce. There is an appealing home-likeness about this bountiful growth to the Arctic traveller, who is accustomed to barren tracts and ice-fields. Only a few miles north of Churchill the tree-growth ends, and the last spruce tree is the sign post at which the Eskimo turns back to his Barrenground. The beginning of tree-growth, which to other men seems essential to life, is to the Eskimo the end of the world.

I found both Eskimos and Indians camping in the neighborhood of Churchill for the sum-mer. These two races have the most decided antipathy for each other, and while they may no longer fight out their prejudices by force of arms, they have their camps at least four miles apart and see as little of each other as possible.

The Northernmost Spruce Tree, the Sign Post at Which the Eskimo Turns Back to His Barrenground

The Indians call the Eskimos "the wild creatures who eat raw meat," and the Eskimos, in their turn, refer to the Indians as "Etkailik" or "the dirty people." Besides these two tribes, a census of Churchill would include a Scotch fur-trader, three or four white men of the Royal Northwest Mounted Police, and a missionary.

CHURCHILL, THE OUTPOST OF CIVILIZATION

I had arranged with the Hudson Bay Company for a small wooden schooner to take me northward from Churchill about the middle of August. While waiting for it to arrive, I began the work of collecting ethnographical specimens and data. Meanwhile I established myself in my Arctic tent, and found that this portable home, which had been constructed in accordance with my explicit directions, was a success. It was shaped like a bag, with a waterproof floor and an outer covering that made it practically two tents. In the space between the outer and inner wall, the cold was tempered, and there I stored my instruments and provisions. This double device proved very satisfactory; it kept out the mosquitoes in summer and the drifting, penetrating snow-dust in the fall; it proved equal to the most violent gale, and by means of it I accomplished the miracle of miracles in Eskimo land of keeping my bedding dry during a snowstorm.

My tent had to serve as photographic studio as well, and to make this possible I had it dyed to produce the necessary light for developing plates and films. The outside canvas was yellow and the inside green; with the window of the inner tent shut, I had my dark room and a substitute for the photographers' red lamp.

As I did not care to depend entirely on game, I had brought a goodly supply of provisions, the chief item in which was pemmican. This is the most concentrated food an Arctic explorer can carry, and, when prepared after a scientific recipe, contains all the necessary food elements. My Norwegian pemmican, made at Thorne's factory, consisted of the best kind of dried powdered beef, fat, fruit, and vegetables. After eating a quarter of a pound of this, a man has had practically as much nourishment as if he had partaken of an elaborate course dinner, and his appetite is as well satisfied. It can be eaten from the can just as it is or powdered and made into a filling for a sandwich—a hasty meal that does not bring indigestion—but if there is time and a fire, it is better to heat it, either thinned with water for soup, or as a meat dish. Pemmican is used in the Norwegian army and has great possibilities as a food for large forces in the field. A man can carry a month's rations in his knapsack, and with a cup of coffee or tea it makes a meal fit for a king. So far, however, it is only the Norwegians who have been able to manufacture it in a really satisfactory way.

Besides the indispensable pemmican, I got from the Army ,and Navy Store in London dried powdered milk and eggs, some dried fruit and vegetables from northern latitudes, coffee, tea, salt and pepper, and some especially prepared biscuits of oats and wheat mixed. For cooking I had a Swedish *primus* stove and a supply of coal oil. My whole outfit weighed scarcely two tons.

After waiting four weeks for the promised schooner, I began to fear the approach of winter and decided to start out in a little open boat for a tribe living around an inlet about three hundred miles north of Churchill. I hoped to reach them before the bay should freeze. It was hard to assemble a crew, however, for the Eskimos did not relish the thought of a boat trip along the dangerous western coast. At last I succeeded in persuading a half dozen of them to accompany me, but the terrific September gales made it impossible to leave for another two weeks, and it was the end of the month before the sea grew calm enough to start. We made a queer-looking party—I with my outfit and provisions, the Eskimos with their skin tents, seal oil, wives, children, and dogs—all setting sail in an open boat for the unknown north.

Christian Leden

My chief pastime during the long October evenings on this hazardous and comfortless journey was to watch the northern lights that set the sky aflame every evening. There was a curious blending of colors with a predominance of orange, green, violet, and yellow. Before a storm, these lights seemed strangely affected, suggesting wild ghosts in a midnight dance. The Eskimos said the souls of the dead were dancing. They have a great reverence for what they see in the sky. They did not approve of the observation instruments I directed toward the firmament, and declared that if I did not stop "shooting the sun" with my sextant we were sure to have bad weather.

. These Eskimos differed from those I met farther north in being very poor sailors. Whenever there was a storm, they wanted to pull in among the breakers and rocks near the shore instead of keeping to the open sea. Their *angakok* or heathen priest, who was chief of my night crew, would often keep me awake with his yelling and singing, as he implored the spirit world for good weather and a lucky voyage.

After a fortnight of slow and rough sailing, with hungry dogs, seasick women, and squalling children all making their presence felt in the little open craft, our trip came to a disastrous end. A fearful northeast snowstorm came upon us just as we were in a dangerous place. We could see nothing and do nothing against the terrible gale, which lasted for four days. On the second night, the boat was forced by the raging waters over the reefs, and was at last thrown up by the breakers on the shore several feet above the usual high-water mark. Fortunately no lives were lost, but much of the outfit was either damaged or washed overboard, and the boat itself was full of holes in the sides and bottom.

My Eskimo followers and I were now in a pitiful state, alone on a deserted, barren coast, terribly far from any other human beings, absolutely isolated until the ice should form on the big rivers. Wet, frozen, hungry, and sleepless, we were still forced to battle against the fierce snowstorm. We managed to wade out to the boat through the breakers, and, after several trips, succeeded in bringing to land what was left of my supplies. Fortunately my scientific instruments were for the most part uninjured, and my guns and ammunition, which had been sealed in air-tight and waterproof cases, were still in good condition. If these had been spoiled, I should indeed have fared badly, for most of my pemmican and other concentrated food had been lost, and I realized that I should have to depend on hunting to give me sufficient food during the rest of my long journey in No-Man's-Land.

My double tent was saved, but for some time after the wreck I lived with the Eskimos, who had managed, in spite of the terrible weather, to save and put up some of their deer-skin tents. Their camping-place, for some queer reason of their own, was three miles from the wreck. Later I succeeded in transporting my own tent there and putting it up. My clothing caused me the most acute suffering. I had lost all except the garments I had on, and these were not of fur seal, but of common seal, which is adapted only for summer use in the north. As soon as winter weather sets in, the seal-skin collects frost on the inside, and, besides, my garments had been wet in the wreck, and I had no fire for drying them. I could not take

OUR LAST CAMP BEFORE OUR BOAT WAS WRECKED

them off at night, but crawled into my sleeping-bag, dressed as I was, and thawed them out. The result was that I was wet all night and frozen all day.

These miseries lasted for six weeks, until the snow grew hard enough to build houses from, and the rivers froze so that I could go with a dog team back to Churchill and get fur for winter clothing. To be sure, we were killing plenty of deer, but by this time they had their winter coat of long-haired skin, which the Eskimos think it a sin to cut or make into garments. The summer skins we had with us had all been lost in the wreck, and so I had no alternative but to make the long journey back to the Indians and get furs from them.

My daily journal, which I kept with some difficulty and not regularly, will give an idea of the life we lived for the first few weeks after we were wrecked.

Sunday, October 12, 1913. What a terrible life we lead! Not a bit of sleep last night! The Eskimo tent where I had my night quarters was blown down during the night, and it was not possible to do anything about it. I had to get up and shake the snow from my bedding every now and then to escape being choked. A half yard of snow within the tent, and my clothing and sleeping-bag are frozen together. I am homeless in the worst of snow-storms.

Wednesday, October 15, 1913. The snow-storm has turned into a regular blizzard and is raging worse than ever. I can not get outside. To live in tents now becomes more impossible every day, but the snow is not yet hard enough to enable us to build snow-houses. Our dogs lie outside, shrieking with cold and hunger like a human being in pain. They try to break into our tents and eat the little food left inside. If only the weather would give us a chance to get out and hunt reindeer! We need meat badly both for men and dogs.

October 26, 1913. The maximum temperature is −17 degrees Centigrade, and the minimum −23 degrees. Although this is not very cold, it is enough for this time of year. However, everything might be all right if a terrible blizzard had not come up again. Very little food is left in the camp, and by to-night I shall have no fuel. My coal oil, of which I managed to bring a little to my tent from the wreck the other day, is so far gone that I have only sufficient to cook a cup of tea. Nobody knows what a cup of tea means to you under such circumstances, unless he has learned through similar experiences.

October 27, 1913. The blizzard is raging like doomsday, and it is impossible to get outside. My double tent is quite snowed down. It is very nearly dark inside even at noon. I have a piece of ice beside me, from which I chip off small pieces with which to quench my thirst. The space between my inside and outside tent is filled with snow.

The Eskimo "Crazy Illatnak" with the Indian Half-breed and His Wife

I have made my will to-day, as I do not believe that I shall get away alive from this place if the blizzard lasts many days longer. It is impossible to keep the blood circulating in such weather in a little tent where one has no place to move and is without any heating apparatus or anything hot to eat. I am a prisoner in my tent without fuel or food. My clothing is frozen on my body. I will go into my sleeping-bag and try to thaw out my frozen rags.

It was November before I could start out for Churchill with the dog team. My companions were a half-crazy inland Eskimo named Illatnak, a lad who answered to the name of Attornok, and a half-breed Indian and his wife, whose lives I had saved when they were wrecked not far from our camp. We saw great herds of reindeer on the way, and once we had a more unwelcome visit from a pack of Barrenground wolves, who sometimes follow the reindeer.

When I had reached Churchill and fitted myself out with good winter clothing of deer-skins, I made up my mind to continue my travelling with the Eskimos, in spite of all obstacles, until I had secured the ethnographical information and collections I wanted. It took me about three years to finish my work, during which time I investigated seven Eskimo tribes. I had many a struggle before I reached civilization, but the Eskimo says that a man never talks much about difficulties and dangers—they are for him to overcome, and if he can not master them he is no real man. Even now, as I sit here, in this restless city, and look back upon my experiences, I feel the call of the wilderness. My thoughts and longings return to the ice-fields of the north, where my friends the Eskimos still live the same vigorous and happy life, free from all the petty troubles and worries of civilized life.

On the Trail in the White Mountains

By ALLEN H. BENT

NO SCANDINAVIAN needs to be told the value of mountains as playgrounds or as training grounds. Pleasure, health, and freedom are always to be found on the heights, and together these things mean happiness. First to be climbed in the United States—two hundred and seventy-five years ago, for climbing began early here—the easiest to be reached to-day from the large cities of the northeastern part of the country, and with the largest mileage of trails, are the White Mountains, a region, roughly speaking, forty miles square in northern New Hampshire.

In recent years, the Federal Government has taken part of the group as a Forest Reserve, which means that within its boundaries live timber can not be cut nor camp-fires lighted, except by special permit. The Government is making trails, and there are many small local clubs, composed mainly of summer residents, that are interested in trail work, nor should the work done by the Dartmouth (College) Outing Club be forgotten.

Longer in the field than any of these, however, is the Appalachian Mountain Club of Boston, organized more than forty years ago and with a membership at present of over two thousand. The Club came into being for the purpose of making the mountains of New

England more accessible, and to-day it has nearly two hundred and fifty miles of trails, three stone huts in charge of caretakers during the summer months, and ten open log shelters. The new guide book of the Club covers the ground thoroughly; with a copy of this and the maps that accompany it, and, with a compass in his pocket, the tramper cannot go far astray, provided he does not attempt too much and uses caution in fog and storms; for in the usual climbing months, July, August, and September, there are once in a while long and severe storms and also dense fogs. If you have ever faced a gale of a mile a minute, with driving snow or ice particles, you will not care to repeat the experience. Only two or three years ago, a September storm held a little group of shivering people snow-bound in one of the A. M. C. huts for four days, with the wind blowing a hundred miles an hour. The same storm blew the Chocorua Peak House entirely to pieces and did thousands of dollars' worth of damage to trails. In 1900, two strong men lost their lives on the way up Mount Washington in a similar storm in July. At other times of the year, even greater caution is necessary. Fortunately such storms are rare, but when they come, do not hesitate, but get down into the timber quickly.

While the mountains are interesting at any time of the year, and many prefer the winter months, when ski and snow-shoes can be used, a majority find it pleasanter and more convenient to go in summer or early autumn. The beginning of summer, with its long days and delicate colorings, is theoretically the best time, but it has one drawback, the presence in the woods of vast armed bands of mosquitoes, black flies, and midges, and these things have to be considered by anyone who values his peace of mind or his reputation; for the amount of suffering they cause and the profanity they encourage are in an inverse

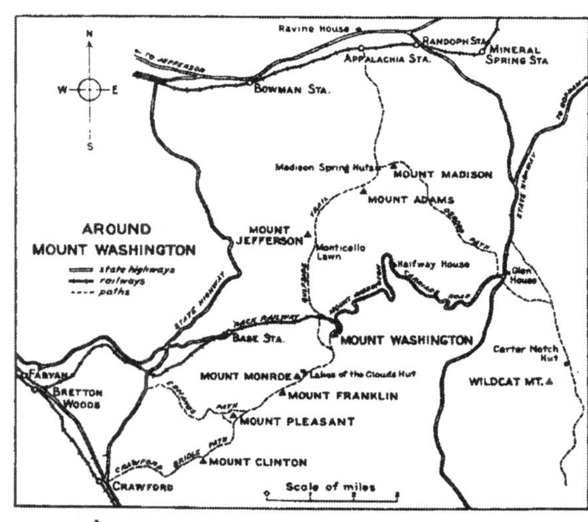

ratio to their size. I have no positive information about the imps that drove Peer Gynt out of Dovrefjeld, but somehow I have a feeling that they were the European relatives of the black flies and midges of the American mountains.

In some respects, the last half of September, and frequently the first part of October, proves the best time of year for tramping in New England. The air is cool, and the coloring is beautiful beyond all superlatives, while the first snow on the mountain tops adds to the contrasts. Some years, however, there are long storms at that season. Twice I have not been able to see a mountain for four days, but it is no use trying to foretell the weather—not in New England, and a part of its charm, after all, is its variety.

The advice usually given, "Don't tramp in the woods or climb mountains without a companion," is sound, but if you must go with only your camera or your thoughts for company—and I confess I like to stand alone on the heights—be sure at least to tell where and how you expect to go.

The novice will do well to take counsel of his friends who have gone on the trail before. The experienced climber knows that stout clothing must be worn, that strong and comfortable shoes and a sweater or something of the kind to put on at the end of the climb are absolute necessities; nor does he need to be told that, while lungs and muscles can be easily trained, a strong heart is necessary to begin with. Nor should the mental equipment be overlooked.

Now Mr. Hiker, Mrs. Hiker, or Miss Hiker, let us be off. The two best centers for intensive climbing are Randolph, at the northern base of the Presidential or Great Range, and the Glen House, seven or eight miles away, at the eastern base of Mount Washington. Let us begin with the latter. The Glen House is about 1,600 feet above the sea, and Mount Washington, the highest point in New England, 6,293 feet, so that 4,700 feet is as much climbing as can be done on one mountain, but that can be made as hard or as easy as you like. We will ignore the cog-wheel railroad on the other side of the mountain and begin with the easiest

"WE WILL IGNORE THE COG-WHEEL RAILROAD"

route, the carriage road, eight miles in length. The upper part of this is above the trees and has fine outlooks; it is worth going over at least once, but it can be saved for the down trip some time. Of trails to the summit, the one by Huntington Ravine is difficult and even dangerous; it ought not to be attempted by the inexperienced. From the east side, the most popular trail is by way of Tuckerman Ravine, which has snow until the end of July. This is the shortest and one of the most satisfying. While the ascent from the road, starting about three miles south of the Glen House, has been made in less than two hours, it is wise to allow twice that time.

Nearly a mile farther south on the same road, another interesting path makes its start, the Glen Boulder Trail, so called from a big stone poised on the

"Tuckerman Ravine, Which Has Snow Until the End of July"

mountain side. Passing this landmark, we go on by way of Boott Spur, which can also be reached by a branch from the Tuckerman Ravine trail. From the Glen House yet another trail starts through the Great Gulf, which, like the so-called ravines bearing the names of the botanist Tuckerman and the geologist Huntington, is really a cirque, carved by an old residual glacier into the side of the mountain. The early explorers, before the days of trails, ascended from the east, and the first trail, made more than a hundred years ago, started from that side.

Beginning in 1819, when Abel Crawford and his son, Ethan Allen Crawford, began their path from what is now the Crawford House, the west side became the popular approach, and remained so for many years. This is now the region of the railroad and the big hotels. From Bretton Woods, the Mount Pleasant path joins the Crawford path above the tree line, and three years ago a new trail through the Ammonoosuc Ravine was added to the west-side trails. It is possible also to start farther south by the old Davis path, reopened in 1910. From the railroad at Bemis station, eight miles below the Crawford House, and a thousand feet above the sea, it is fifteen miles to the summit.   This route is the longest of all, and requires two days; for an early start is hardly possible.   For a dozen miles or so it is a wilderness trail, but there are several peaks just off the path that should be ascended.   It joins the Glen Boulder-Boott Spur path and then crosses over to the Crawford path.   The summer after it was opened, the present Councillor of Improvements of the A. M. C. and I spent two days on the trail without meeting a soul, though it was in the height of the climbing season.   We went by easy stages, for it was warm, we had heavy packs, and the berries required some attention. Blueberries and raspberries are pretty sure to stop the hiker, but they should be regarded as a special favor of Providence and should not be counted on.   The same year in early June, when I was helping to trim the trail, we had snow squalls and frost feathers at the same time as the wild flowers bloomed all around us.   They are not to be seen in such profusion at other times of the year, though the Greenland sandwort and other Arctic plants bloom a little later.   There is another kind of Arctic inhabitant that the hiker should be on the lookout for, a little butterfly whose nearest relatives are in distant Labrador.   He was stranded here in the ice age.

From the north, Mount Washington is reached by the Randolph path, a little over ten miles from Randolph station; so it will be seen that the tramper has the choice of at least ten routes up the highest of the mountains, every one interesting, and several with variations and cut-offs. From Randolph there are three or four ways of reaching the A. M. C. huts at Madison Spring, the hardest way, through King Ravine, being the most interesting.   In the wildest part of the ravine there is a choice of going under or over the tremendous boulders—subway or elevated. At the huts, food and lodging for a limited number may be obtained during the months of July, August, and September. At Madison Spring the first of the Club huts was built in 1888. A second was added in 1911, for it is a popular location.   They are at an altitude of 4,800 feet, in

"A Choice of Going Under or Over the Tremendous Boulders—Subway or Elevated"

a col between Mount Madison, 5,380 feet, and Mount Adams, 5,805 feet, the latter being the next to the highest and one of the most interesting of the White Mountains. For those who wish to spend some time on the very summit of Mount Washington, there are hotel facilities.

"Near the Lakes of the Clouds, at an Altitude of About 5,000 Feet, Is the Second of the Club Huts"

On the other side of Mount Washington, near the Lakes of the Clouds, at an altitude of about 5,000 feet, is the second of the Club huts, a day's tramp from Madison Spring. The third of the Club huts is in Carter Notch, 3,450 feet above sea level, reached by a good trail four miles long, starting back of the Glen House. This is a day's tramp from either of the other huts or from Randolph, so that a four days' tramping trip, going light, is possible.

There are, of course, other good climbing centres, the Crawford House and the Profile House, for people who do not have to count the cost, and Waterville, Jackson, and North Woodstock for those with more moderate purses. On the outskirts are Intervale, Bartlett, Whitefield, Twin Mountain, Shelburne, Gorham, and Jefferson on the railroad, and Benton, Easton, Whiteface, Wonalancet, and

"On the Very Summit of Mount Washington"

"At the Huts Food and Lodging May Be Obtained"

North Chatham in secluded side chapels.   The large summer colonies
at Bethlehem, Sugar Hill, and North Conway are made up of people
who enjoy the mountains from the verandas, or who have motor
cars to take them to the beginning of the trails.   In the lake country to
the south are many low mountains with beautiful outlooks, while to the
north and northeast is a region of wooded heights only now being
partly opened up.   In this latter region, near the Border Mountains,
is said to be the finest of all the notches.   A rough trail was opened
to it, the Mahoosuc Notch, last summer, and some day a camp will
be built there, and a trail cut to Grafton Notch, just over the state boundary in Maine.

The most independent mortal on earth is the man with knapsack and blankets on his back. Properly trained and equipped, he can stay out one night or for weeks. For such the open front log and bark shelters of the Appalachian Mountain Club

"The Open Front Log and Bark Shelters of the Appalachian Mountain Club"

were built. They accommodate from six to ten people, though frequently more squeeze in, and they are free to any one who wishes to use them, but the Club expects that they will be left clean, and that great caution will be observed with firewood and fires.

Of course, there are trials on the trail. I have suffered from heat when climbing in February, cut trails during snow-storms in September, had to change all my plans because of a fog that shut out all of the world beyond a radius of twenty feet, lost my glasses fighting off "yellow jackets," and had the broadest of views ruined by the smallest of insects. Heat and wet have a way of upsetting our plans, not to say our dispositions. There are days when pack and feet both seem made of lead, and evenings when camp-fires refuse to burn, and black flies torture you, but if you have had such experiences on the trail, look backward and see if the pleasures do not outweigh the trials. The winding trail, the brook beside it, the balsam-laden air, the sunshine and shadow, the wonderful clouds, the rugged cliffs and peaks looming ahead, the sunset coloring, the light of the camp-fire, the peace of it all, are not these the things that live in the memory? If you have not yet had such experiences, the pleasures and trials are all before you.

A Picture

By Maurice Francis Egan

Small, lemon-tinted blossoms dot the shore
Where rocks are touched by ripples; butterflies
Made by the sun in silver shine and rise
Upon the Sound in rays that westward pour.
Gulls glide and float and in the soft air soar,
Creatures of grace; they watch with eager eyes
The crystal depths—a sudden dart! There dies
An argent fish—the gull sails as before:

A splash of foam, and swift a young athlete,
All ivory and rose, dives to the cool
And brilliant waves; another dauntless springs
And yet another, swimmers strong and fleet,
To whom the sea belongs by Viking rule—
And, over all, a Danish skylark sings:

Helsingör, Morning, June 16, 1917.

The Three Cottages

By FANNY ALVING

Translated from the Swedish for the REVIEW

PART II

IT was no secret to the little lady that she was inclined to be romantic, but when she caught sight of the third cottage, she opened her eyes wide. Did it really look like that, or was it all a creation of her fancy? It seemed as though all the saga books in the world had suddenly spread out their pages before her.

Yet all she could see was one window that peeped at her from between two cherry-trees. It was fairly large and had small square panes. She had seen similar windows before, but none just like that. It seemed to look at her both wisely and cautiously. The gray branch of an apple-tree crossed it diagonally. Above the cherry-tree she saw the top of the chimney. A little potato patch lay between her and the knoll. The vines grew high and luxuriant, and she had to hunt for the path. It crept under the potato vines along the edge of the ditch, and when it reached the foot of the knoll it hid under the grass. If one did not know it was there, one could hardly find it.

A little gray half-timbered cottage stood under a clump of fruit trees, looking as if it were asleep. It was a long time since it had noticed that anything happened to it. It had not felt it when the paint fell off and the moss crept over it. The trees had grown strong and wound their arms about it, protecting it from the severest storms. The fire ladder had tired of standing at attention and had sunk down on the moss, where it seemed to lie sleeping across what had perhaps, once upon a time, been a yard. The little lady had to step over it to reach the entry. It was a low gray entry with a low gray door, and in the door stood a key as large as if it belonged to a church. She knocked a few times, but no one answered. She knocked once more, then turned the key and stepped in.

She stood for at least a minute peering in without seeing anything, but then her look encountered a pair of small dark eyes.

"Good day," she said, nodding.

"Why, bless me!" said a voice which expressed the most unfeigned surprise, and an old woman rose from a chair by the window.

The little lady had never seen such an old woman. It seemed as though a very old pig had dressed itself in a red-checked kerchief and an old jacket and a gray woollen dress. Unconsciously she glanced down the sleeves. No, it was not a pair of cloven hoofs that stuck out, but a pair of human hands, small hands, wrinkled and gray, human hands that had worked and toiled till they lost their shape.

—

The old woman did not boast much of a chin, but she had a nose that resembled a snout and a skin that might have adorned an old leather cannon. It was yellow-brown and rough, and around the eyes it had amused itself by blowing up a number of little pouches. But in the midst of all this shone a pair of human eyes, a pair of small dark human eyes, there was no doubt of that.

"To think that I should get such fine company!"

The little lady smiled pleasantly. "I thought it would be nice to step in as I passed." She took one of the tiny hands that were extended to her. It was a very cold little hand.

"That's very kind of you."

The room was quite dark. It had two windows, but a heavy curtain hung before one, and the apple-tree shaded the other. The little lady felt herself almost like a vision, as she stood there in her white dress, which seemed actually to give out light. Perhaps the old woman felt it too.

"It's real grand for any one like me to get such fine company." Her voice sounded a little shy.

"Then perhaps you don't get company very often?"

"No, but please sit down. You're not afraid to sit down, are you?"

"Why should I be afraid?" The little lady sat down on a blackish chair near the hearth. The old woman remained standing in the middle of the floor.

"Why, I suppose there's nothing here to sit on that's like what you're used to."

The lady looked around a little. "I think it's very pleasant here," she said.

"But I suppose you think it's frightfully old-fashioned?"

"That isn't any fault is it? Don't you, too, think the old things are cozy?"

The small eyes met hers for a moment. "Oh, yes, I do, but I'm so old myself."

"How old are you?"

"Well I'm so old I really ought to be dead. I'm eighty-eight years old, I am."

The lady looked at her. "I should never have guessed it."

A slight tremor passed over the old face. "Shouldn't you? Bless me, you say it just like Anton." She nodded toward the window. "He's my neighbor, he and his mother. He's a good boy."

"So Anton is good, is he?"

"Yes, I should say he's good. He and his mother are kind folks. He splits wood for me, and before he splits it he hauls it home from the woods, for I can't stand to do as much as I used to."

"No, that's not to be wondered at."

The old woman had returned to her chair, which stood in front of a queer old table.   The lady had never seen anything like that table; it looked as though some one had once upon a time laid a plank over a carpenter's bench and called it a table.   The plank had never known paint.   It was partly hidden under an old newspaper, beside which lay a pair of spectacles and a bit of hard, dry rye bread.

"No, it isn't any wonder, but, do you know, sometimes I feel it even now.   You see, I've always been used to working—and to go here and help an old woman for nothing isn't a man's job, is it?"

"But haven't you any children that could help you?"

The old woman did not answer at once.   For a moment she gazed out into space, but suddenly she roused herself.   "No, I haven't. It would have been nice if I had."

The lady looked down at her hands.   On the left there was a narrow brass ring.   "But you have been married?"

"Yes, I was married for four years, but then he died.   It's sixty-one years ago come Michaelmas.'

"And have you lived here alone ever since?"   There was a trace of astonishment in the little lady's voice, which she could not conceal.

"Yes, I have lived here.   You see, ma'am, I was born in this house.   Haven't you noticed that it's kind of a peculiar cottage?"

The little lady looked about her.   It was a peculiar cottage, there was no doubt of that.   She had never been in a room with walls of blackened logs with moss growing in the cracks.   She had never sat by a fireplace made of stone slabs and earth, but surely that was not what the old woman meant.

"Perhaps you haven't noticed how high it is under the roof?"

It was a roof of sooty beams, and some one had pasted under it a scalloped border cut from newspapers.

"It's a lovely roof," she said.

The old woman nodded.   "It is that," she said.   "This house was built for soldiers.   My father was a soldier, and at that time the soldiers wore a high cockade on their caps; so it wouldn't do to build a low roof.   Not for them."   The old cracked voice had a note of dignity.

"You mean they couldn't have walked upright?"

The old woman nodded.   She really looked like an aged pig confirming something with a nod.

"Just so.   But my father could walk in this cottage as straight as a candle, and he wasn't a small man either.   When I was a little girl I thought it was such fun to look up at the cockade on his cap; it seemed so high up.   But now there's nothing but the roof left."

"That was a long time ago."

"Yes, it's a long time ago.   Sometimes I think it's a very long time. There were two soldiers living here then, for we have another room across the hall." She nodded toward the door. "And now there's only me left."

"And the others?"

"They're gone." The room was quite still for a few moments. "I can tell you that when a body gets to be eighty-eight years old she's seen right many pass away."

"Yes."

"And sometimes I get to wondering why I'm not taken."

The lady did not answer, and the reason was that she could not speak. She felt a strange impulse to weep. The room was small and dark, the floor old and black, the hearth low and gray. On the hearth lay a few sticks of fallen branches, decaying in the centre. The bit of rye bread by the newspaper on the table looked as if that, too, might have had a tale to tell.

"I suppose it gets pretty dark here in the winter?" she asked at last.

"Yes, it does that, but Anton is so kind, he splits wood."

"But even so?"

"And then, of course, I can go to bed."

"And there is kerosene." The lady spoke cheerfully. She felt an irresistible desire to say something cheerful.

The little narrow eyes peeped up at her for an instant. "Yes, in the store."

"And perhaps Anton helps you to get a few things home once in a while?"

There was no immediate answer. "Yes, he does that when there is anything to bring."

There was something in the voice that told more than many volumes.

"I suppose you have some little aid in your old age?" she said, still cheerfully.

"Oh, yes, I've had poor relief ever since I got so poorly I couldn't work. That's nine years ago now."

"And how much does that amount to in this parish?"

"It's ten pounds of bacon, twenty-five of rye, and twelve of wheat, and six kronor besides."

"For how long a time?"

"Why, for a year, of course." The old woman's voice sounded a bit astonished.

The lady was silent for a moment. "But that can't last you a whole year?"

The tiny dark eyes looked at her. "No, it doesn't last the whole year, of course it doesn't."

"And when that is gone, how do you manage?"

"Well, then—of course it's a little hard, but it's a shame to complain. God has always given me good health, and that's a blessing, isn't it?"

"Yes, indeed, but you can't live on that."

"No, that you can't, but still it would be worse if a body were sick."

"But how do you manage when there is an end of the poor relief?"

"Why, I try to make the gifts of God go as far as possible."

"But after that?"

"I always get a loaf when they bake at the neighbors. I get that regular, and they lend me the paper."

The lady sat searching for words. "You have some very pretty furniture," she said at last. It was the third time she spoke in that cheerful voice. She had suddenly noticed something that roused her curiosity. In an obscure corner of the fireplace stood an old iron pot on three legs, but it showed no trace of having been used for cooking. Everything looked strangely empty. Through the door of the old oven she could plainly see that no baking had been done in it for a long time. From the fireplace her eyes wandered to the bed. It was an old-fashioned bed made fast to the wall and with a striped cotton curtain which concealed almost the whole bed and extended beyond it. Perhaps it was just as well.

The woman sat looking at her with her small, dark eyes. "You said it so kindly," she remarked suddenly.

"What do you mean?"

" I mean that the manor folks are real kind."

The little lady sat looking at the fireplace for a while. "But suppose you should be ill?"

"If I should be ill? Why, I'll tell you. We have sort of an agreement about that, the neighbors and I. They look in——"

"Every day?"

"No, not every day. That would be too much to expect. But we have the smoke."

The lady looked at her with a puzzled expression.

"From the chimney," said the woman in reply to the question in the other's face. "When they see there's smoke rising in the morning, then they know I'm alive. We've agreed about that."

"And if there isn't any smoke?" asked the lady, her voice trembling a little.

"If there isn't any smoke? Why then——" The little dark eyes gazed into the fireplace, as if they saw something unusual there. "Why then," she repeated, "I want to tell you that I'm not afraid to die."

Mr. Löfmark sat at the table in the yard cleaning his gun when the little lady stepped out from the lane.

"Well," he said, smiling a little, "you look very solemn."

"That is because I feel solemn," she replied, sitting down in the garden chair.   "I have rarely felt so solemn in my whole life."

"Really?   And what have you got in your bottle?"

"I have got—but I hardly think there is room for it all in a bottle. In the first place, I have seen a vendetta, and it was no less gruesome because it was not bloody."

"Excellent!"

"And I have met a poetess who did not know she was a poetess."

"That is absolutely impossible."

"And thirdly I have found out what your lout of a carpenter sees when he stands staring."

He glanced up from the gun.   "And what is it?   I am really curious to know."

"You will soon know, and you will even see it, for I brought a specimen with me.   But the fourth thing I hardly know whether I can show you."

"Why not?"

"Because I can't describe it.   I am afraid it would sound bombastic."

"You might try."   He peered into the barrel of his gun with a half smile.   "I promise to be charitable."

"In that case, I may tell you that I have seen the most beautiful image of human dignity that it has ever been my good fortune to meet."

He glanced up from his gun and looked at her.   Her expression startled him.   "Down in those hovels?" he said, with a slight motion in the direction of the cottages.

"Yes," she said, "in those hovels."

THE END

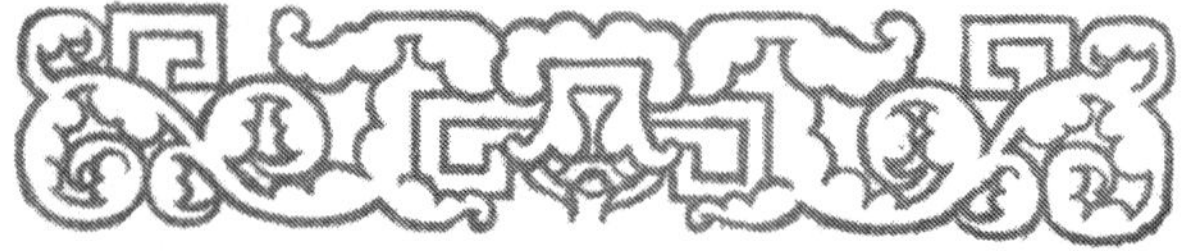

David Edström

By CARL JOHANNES SÖDERGREN

THE SIXTH IN A SERIES OF ESSAYS ON SCANDINAVIAN ARTISTS IN AMERICA

A MAGNIFICENT eagle with wings spread for flight is the first creation of David Edström's art since his return to America after many years' sojourn in Europe. In its light upward sweep, defying the hardness of the sculptor's materials, it is an emblem of the human spirit that struggles eternally toward the light, and it seems not unfitting that this buoyant symbol of victory should be placed in the community where the artist's own early fight for existence began. It is the mature work of one who has himself overcome obstacles that would have daunted all but the strongest, and who finds himself now "the friend of princes" and an artist of European fame.

Born in 1873, in the thrifty province of Småland in Sweden, Edström came to America a lad of seven with his immigrant parents. They settled in Burlington, Iowa, where David attended the public schools, until he was fourteen. Afterwards he moved to Ottumwa in the same state and there earned his living by the poorest kind of labor—selling newspapers in the street,. working in the packing-houses or as a section hand on the railroads. But the fire of the born artist burned within him and gave him no rest. He was thrown so violently between the extremes of high ambition and crushing despair that, finally, the realization of his dream became to him a matter of life and death. At the age of twenty-one, he bade his parents and friends farewell and started out to "beat" his way, after the manner of a tramp, to New York. Arrived there, he shipped as a coal-heaver on board a Danish steamer and so managed to reach Stockholm, the goal of all his longings.

Naturally, the doors of opportunity did not swing open of their own accord to the penniless tramp, whose work-hardened fingers could hardly hold the tools of his art. The powers that ruled in the Academy thought him mad, but his impassioned determination created opportunities, first to demonstrate his talent, and then to realize his consuming desire for study and self-expression. By sheer dogged persistence he gained an entrance into the Technical School and, two years later, into the Royal Academy of Fine Arts. While a student there, he sold his first sketch for fifteen hundred dollars. A serious illness, brought on by want and exposure, threatened to bring his brilliant career to an untimely end, but the favoring climes of bleak Lapland and of sunny Italy restored him to his former vigor. Moreover, the art atmosphere of Italy brought the first fruits of his genius to full and strong maturity.

These early hardships, however, were a matter of choice rather than of necessity. He preferred to starve rather than to prove false to his vision, or rather, he forgot all about life and death in the single-minded pursuit of his ideal, while he consistently refused to cater to the merely conventional, fashionable, or popular. The struggle has not been in vain. Out of this "astounding career," says Haldane Macfall, "has evolved

David Edström, Sculptor

THE OLD HUNCHBACK

David Edström, Sculptor

PORTRAIT BUST OF LUCIA HIGGINS

a personality and a vigorous soul, such as was bound to utter itself in rare fashion and compelling art." Having run the full gamut of human experience, Edström knows life writ large. He has travelled from the top to the bottom and from the bottom to the top again on the far side of the valley, and there is no shade of feeling or variety of sentiment to which he is a stranger. To overcome the obstacles that barred his way required an almost superhuman energy, and that very effort has set free the native strength of his spirit, the elemental power that makes each one of his works seem a distributing center of dynamic force.

Leading art critics of the old world and numerous writers in the art journals both of Europe and America have borne abundant testimony to his achievements. Among them, W. G. Blaikie Murdock, writing in the *American Magazine of Art*, mentions him with Carl Milles as one of the two men in Sweden whose work towers high above that of all others. Edström has exhibited successfully in London, Berlin, Amsterdam, Paris, Florence, Vienna, Munich, Gothenburg, and, most recently, in America. To his friends he seems something of an orator and a poet too, and one of the rarest treats that life has offered to the present writer is the "flow of soul" which Edström pours out in a gathering that understands and enters into rapport with his inspiration. The high order of mind and character that have emerged out of the fire like a fine Damascus blade give him the penetrating vision and impassioned ardor of the prophet. For he is a seer, simple and direct as a child, but fearless and strong as the prophet of a new dispensation.

Three years ago he returned to the country which he still considers his own, and which he loves above all others, because it gives the freest play to human endeavor. When visiting his old home in Ottumwa, he was welcomed enthusiastically with a banquet, in which citizens of all races were glad to take part. There and then, he promised to design the Soldiers Monument which the county of Wapello proposed to erect in honor of its heroes of the Civil War, and the work has now progressed so far that we can appreciate its lofty monumental character. The great eagle, measuring five feet in height and eight feet in the spread of its wings, which is to be poised on top of a high column, is completed, and the sculptor is now at work in his New York studio on the four reliefs that are to decorate the base. They constitute a human epic of war: first the parting; then the mad charge; then the soldier's death in the forest, as the battle rushes past him; and, lastly, a quiet scene which the artist calls "Reconstruction," a woman and boy ploughing in the cold light of the morning sun that rises over the prairie.

Better than an extended description, the following partial catalogue of Edström's works may serve as a cloud of witnesses to indicate the present scope

David Edström, Sculptor

SISTERS

David Edström, Sculptor

RHAPSODY

of his art and the vein of his genius: *Young Peasant Girl, Hermaphrodite, Industry, Triumph of Labor, Old Peasant, Old Italian Soldier, Caliban, Fear, Envy, Pride, Poverty, Lucifer,* the *Siren,* the *Hunchback,* the *Athlete, Two Souls, February, Ophelia,* the *Sphinx,* the *Cliff,* the *Clouds, Day and Night, Rhapsody, Fiat Lux.* In *Caliban* there is degradation, agony, and dawning hope, while *Poverty* has been described as "one cry of horror out of the depths." The wasted figure of *Ophelia* is like an incarnate sigh. Of the *Sphinx* one critic says that "it is impossible to be unmoved by the uncanny scrutiny of those eyes, as of a bird of prey ranging the world in search of quarry." The *Clouds* gives the half-veiled contour of two lovers in close embrace, moving in airy flight

David Edström, Sculptor

Old Italian Soldier

toward distant harmonious spheres. The wind, which carries them along, seems to threaten a momentary disruption, but over all there is an earnest of a glorious consummation of undying hopes. Face speaks to face in a language that is not of this earth. The whole is a surpassingly original and unique conception. *Fear* is a cringing, gibbering petrification of the subject, a figure rolling on its back, drawing up its knees, curling its toes, and literally screaming out its abject terror. A child on seeing the picture of it said: "I should hate to be alone with that thing at night." *Rhapsody* is constructed in flowing lines like the melting measure of a poem, to convey a sense of aspiration, like the soul of a flower forcing its way through the hard soil, pouring forth its fragrance as a holy sacrifice to life. A few of Edström's conceptions are forbidding in the extreme, but in the great ellipse in which this artist moves, sharp contrasts are inevitable to complete the circuit of the rounded whole, and, in the words of Rodin, the true artist finds in ugliness itself the beauty of truth.

His portrait busts all live and speak, but more than that, they think and feel, and the thoughts are always those of the heart. Every portrait seems to condense an entire biography and to give us the very essence of the personality with pitiless psychology. Among his more recent busts is that of the late Princess Patricia of Connaught. Earlier portraits are those of his Excellency Erik von Trolle, Countess Alice Trolle, Baron Beck-Friis, the Portuguese singer Senor Francisco D'Andrade, Dr. Franz Oppenheimer, and others.

Some critics believe that Edström's portrait busts represent the most successful part of his artistic accomplishment, and this is a high compliment, since nothing else makes such demands on the artist's skill. Yet such comparisons are futile; his portraits and imaginative works can not be compared, inasmuch as they belong to different categories. In the latter, too, he divines with the same subtle intuition, but there his subject is the heart of the world. He never notes the merely pretty, never embellishes nor ornaments. Overlooking useless detail, he seizes the meaning of the whole and cuts to the very center, cleaving the form and revealing the very soul. With the true eloquence of the poet and the orator he makes us forget the language to listen to the message itself. He seems to set free the spirit of the material in which he works, and Collins Baker once said of his statues and statuettes that they were "stone lit up with spirit. Extraordinarily his dead material seems to flicker up with indwelling life, looking so you would swear they had just moved, almost imperceptibly, and had again composed themselves into immobility."

David Edström, Sculptor

CALIBAN

At present Edström's thoughts are centered on monumental tasks. Of his genius in this realm the *London Times* wrote: "The most interesting of Edström's works are sketches which seem to demand an architectural setting and sometimes even to suggest it. For instance, the little sketch of the two Putti might be continued in a frieze; and as we see it, it is a mere fragment like a broken piece of music. The fine *Mother and Child* is evidently meant to be a part of some larger whole; but it and most of these sketches make us wish to see the larger whole and to discover whether Mr. Edström has an architectural sense equal to his lyric power." Surely the architectural sense of such pieces as the *Sphinx*, the *Five Continents*, and the *Cliff*, the sculpturesque grandeur in some of his portraits, and many recurring hints in all his works, speak of power to create colossal designs for great spaces. They give us promise of a monumental sculptor of the highest rank—a promise that is already redeemed in his partly completed Soldiers' Monument and is, no doubt, destined to show a yet richer fulfillment.

Portsmouth Doorways

By A RAMBLER ABOUT PORTSMOUTH

When Associates from the West or tourists from Scandinavia ask the advice of the Editors of the REVIEW about a few days' sight-seeing, we never send them to Wall Street or Niagara Falls. These things are obvious. When Americans go to Europe we seek out the old as well as the new. Our thirteen original colonies still offer much of interest to the quiet traveler. Boston should be a center for many expeditions, and nowhere can the life of the eighteenth century and early years of the Republic be studied more pleasantly than in Portsmouth, New Hampshire. For the following paragraphs we are indebted to one who knows Aldrich's "Old Town by the Sea."—*The Editors.*

BEFORE the Revolution, Portsmouth was the capital of New Hampshire. For many years New Hampshire, like Massachusetts and unlike Connecticut and Rhode Island, had a governor appointed by the Crown—a petty viceroy; and by a chance unusual, if not unique, in British colonial records, the governorship became virtually hereditary in a native family—that of Wentworth. While the Province was still under the authority of Massachusetts, John Wentworth, a Portsmouth man, was for five or six years Lieutenant-Governor of New Hampshire. After an interval, when New Hampshire was given an independent charter, his son, Benning Wentworth, was named Governor; under him, a Portsmouth man, William Pepperell, commanded the forces which captured Louisbourg from the French; Pepperell was rewarded by a baronetcy. Benning Wentworth, who had no son, was succeeded by his nephew, John Wentworth. This second John Wentworth, later a baronet, remained in office till the Revolution.

The family bore a Yorkshire name distinguished in England, and seems to have been recognized as remotely akin by Lord Rockingham and Lord Fitzwilliam. Other Portsmouth families and worthies were of more nearly gentle origin than was frequent in the Northern colonies. Champernoune, for example, who left no descendants, was

THE DOORWAY OF THE WARNER HOUSE (ABOUT 1715), THE OLDEST BRICK RESIDENCE IN PORTSMOUTH, BUILT BY CAPTAIN ARCHIBALD MACPHEADRIS. IT WAS BEGUN UNDER QUEEN ANNE AND COMPLETED UNDER GEORGE I.

Staircase in the Moffatt-Ladd House (about 1760). Now Kept Open for the Public by the Colonial Dames of New Hampshire

of the Champernounes of Dartington in Devon; the Sherburnes were allowed by the Herald's Office to bear the arms of Sherburne of Stonyhurst in Lancashire; the Penhallows sprang from Cornish gentry; and so on. In pre-Revolutionary Portsmouth, names like these generally distinguished the members of His Majesty's Council, most of whom were more or less related by marriage, if not actually by blood. George Boyd, the last councillor appointed by the Crown, was the son of a cousin of that Boyd, Earl of Kilmarnock, who was beheaded on Tower Hill for loyalty to the Stuarts in 1746; and George Boyd lies in the North Burying Ground of Portsmouth under a stone bearing the arms of Boyd of Kilmarnock. Portsmouth, in brief, though a small provincial

The Governor Benning Wentworth House Near Portsmouth (about 1750). Not Open to the Public. Though Simple in Detail, This House Is Planned for Regal Ceremony

seaport, was at one time a royal capital and a town whose aristocracy, though engaged in commerce, had more than usual claim to its innocent social pretence.

Portsmouth trade, originally in fish and timber, had long been considerable. The still abundant woods of the region had combined with the depth and the safety of its harbor to make it a center of ship-building. Ship-building requires skilful artisans. These conditions developed certain unusual features—excellent construction of houses, almost always wooden; an instinctive sense of proportion in the design of these; something like a local

The Jacob Wendell Doorway
(late eighteenth century)

The Rice Doorway (about 1800)

style of architecture; exceptional refinement of detail, particularly in mouldings and carvings; and beautifully delicate, simple furniture.

Since the Revolution, Portsmouth has had the good fortune of less prosperity than the other seaports of early New England. In consequence, despite at least two disastrous fires, one in 1806, the other in 1813, it still retains more of its eighteenth-century aspect than could otherwise have been the case. A number of houses remain, mostly in decay, which show how stately the **surroundings of the provincial** gentry were; and there is at least one street—Gates Street—where almost every house, of well-to-do though not aristocratic kind, shown on a map of 1813, and presumably then fifty or sixty years old, is standing to this day, though many are superficially altered.

Any traveler who will pass a few hours in rambling about the streets of Portsmouth will therefore find himself rewarded by many glimpses of what an American royal capital was like under George III. The things to look for are the proportions of the old houses, the delicacy of their cornices and their window mouldings, and, above all, the

Fort Constitution (New Castle). There Has Been a Fort at the Point from Early in the Seventeenth Century. The Gate Here Shown Is of about 1812

simple but admirable details of their doorways. Often, too, the roofs with their dormer windows and their massive chimneys are of unusual merit; and the so-called "hip roofs" of the houses built after 1750 mark something like a local style.

In general, of course, the interiors are not accessible to the public. The greater number of old houses are either still occupied by people of such quality as originally built them or else used as tenements, and so equally private. Fortunately there are now three houses in Portsmouth regularly open to the public during summer months. Two of these are among the finest of the eighteenth century; the third is later, giving an admirable example of what surrounded Portsmouth ship-captains from 1800 to 1850. In all are examples of Portsmouth furniture, though most of the furniture now in the two older houses is rather more elaborate than was generally made in Portsmouth.

The first, and most noted, of these three houses is on Market Street. Built about 1760 by the Moffatts, it has never had an interval of decay. During the nineteenth century, it was owned by the Ladds, who have recently put it, for a long term of years, in the hands of the Colonial Dames of New Hampshire. The Colonial Dames

An Old Pump Near the Site of the South Meeting House, Destroyed in 1910

have restored its original features, furnished it in accordance with its period, and opened it as an historical museum. It has retained its generous garden and outbuildings; its details, particularly the cornices, chimney-pieces, and staircase, are the acme of New Hampshire splendor under George III. Its great hall, probably the most dignified in New England, still retains the original pictured paper. The scale of this hall, however, renders the general plan of the house at least awkward, if not inconvenient.

And convenience was the chief feature of Portsmouth houses in general. So the second accessible house is in some respects more typically interesting. This is the Wentworth-Gardner house, on the river, at the foot of Gardner Street. It was built about 1760 for Thomas Wentworth, a brother of the last royal governor; confiscated during the Revolution; bought by the Gardners; again sold; for many years little better than a tenement; and lately restored and elaborately furnished by Mr. Wallace Nutting. The simple plan is that regular in eighteenth-century Portsmouth: a central hall, with a beautifully generous and easy staircase, on the landing of which is a large Palladian window; parlors on each side; behind one parlor the comparatively small but comfortable dining-room; behind the other, across the hall, the commodious kitchen. On the second story is an upper hall, exceptionally delicate in proportion and detail, but in general design of the orthodox Portsmouth type. At each side of the hall are two large bed-rooms. Everywhere, the detail of cornices, chimney-pieces, and so on, is admirable. And the furniture collected by Mr. Nutting makes every room in itself a museum.

The third accessible house is on Court Street. Here the chief man of letters who came from Portsmouth, Thomas Bailey Aldrich, passed his boyhood. His memories of this he has left us in his *Story of a Bad Boy*. After his death, Mrs. Aldrich restored the house to the condition in which it must have been when he lived there about the 1840's. This was not a period of the finest artistic sense anywhere; but her wonderful appreciation of atmosphere— what may not excessively be termed her supreme good taste—has made the house, in its exquisite harmony, a beautiful work of art. Were any detail of its somewhat prim and slightly heavy simplicity allowed to be modified by the more conscious refinements of later eclectic taste, there might be a false note. As it stands there is not even a false overtone or undertone.

These houses, always open to the public in summer, will give any traveler a remarkable impression of the aristocratic New Hampshire of the eighteenth century; and of the later New Hampshire to which pre-Revolutionary times had become a tradition. And the pictures of Portsmouth doorways, and the like, which accompany these words will perhaps lure to the old town visitors who might not otherwise have thought it worth their while. Should any of these have friends who have friends in Portsmouth, a word of introduction may perhaps afford them opportunity to see some of the still private interiors which remarkably preserve the atmosphere of olden times. Even without these, however, Portsmouth will reward any visitor who loves tradition, who loves the picturesque, and who wants to breathe the air of ancestral New England.

FORT-POINT LIGHT (NEW CASTLE). ON THE SITE OF ONE OF THE EARLIEST LIGHTS IN NEW ENGLAND. IT MARKS THE MOUTH OF THE PISCATAQUA

The Murder of Abraham Lincoln

By Henrik Ibsen

Translated by W. H. Schofield

They fired a shot over yon in the West,
And Europe suddenly shook.
Heigho!   How the courtiers, gaily dressed,
Showed anxiety in their look.
Alas!   Old Europe, with order and law,
With rules for each single case,
With a name unmarked by stain or flaw,
With virtuous griefs that bitterly gnaw,
Your pallor grew apace.

Unicorns, eagles, and similar beasts
In mourning-wax are pressed.
Courts abandon all thought of feasts,
And dispatches go distressed.
Cotton-magnates, sons of renown,
Hosts from the land of lies,
Stood ready to raise up peace's crown,
When a single revolver shot brought down
One man—a President dies.

And so you took fright.   You old world pact!
Why at this should you grieve so sore?
A Prussian performance, the Dybböl mean act,
Our world had witnessed before.
Oh, never does a brother his brother slay!
You recall the unlucky Pole?
Copenhagen suffering the English foray?
And the Flensborg grave? and Sonderborg's play?
So wherefore this present dole?

The ruddy plant that yonder grows
And startles you with its bloom,
Is only the graft of our Europe-rose,
Which finds in the West more room.
You planted it there, this vigorous wand,
America made no request.
You it was who, with most natural hand,
Bound the martyr's blood-red order-band
On Abraham Lincoln's breast.

With promises broken, and vows forgot,
  With treaties revealed unsound,
With sin upon sin availing naught,
  You have fertilized history's ground.
And so you expected (by what right?)
  A crop of the finest kind!
See!   Now grows your seed—a flaming sight!
You wonder! sad o'erwhelming plight!
  For grain, stilettos you find.

Where law relies on the point of a knife,
  And justice is done by the gallows,
Hope for the future has far more life
  Than here where words kill and malice.
Men's will is waking and holding court;
  Down the fabric of lies it smashes.
But worms must first eat out the skull,
And time must first the past annul,
  And reverse its capes and sashes.

A demon rules with eternal might.
  Only try to twig his proboscis!
The dust must domus aurea *bite.*
  To ruins went Nero's colossus.
But first had the vices of Romans to go
  O'er the earth from pole to pole,
Tyrants their apotheosis show,
And emperors' golden statues glow
  Like gods on the Capitol.

The whole went to pieces, circus and hall,
  Temples and columns fell low.
Arcades and arches were trampled small
  By the hoofs of the buffalo.
New buildings rose on the sites of old,
  And the air was pure for a time.
Again renewal seized a hold;
Now rises the pest from the swampy mould,
  And is wafted from clime to clime.

But if in rottenness' swamp we go,
  I cry not out against all
The poison-flowers proud that grow
  In fulness of time's great hall.

Just let the worm work.   Till it cleans the room
The structure won't fall away.
Just let the "system" sink into gloom.
The sooner will Vengeance hold its doom
On Hypocrisy's final day.

Photo by Wilse

AT THE ROYAL SAETER

THE MEETING OF THE THREE KINGS AT CHRISTIANIA, NOVEMBER 28, WAS NOTABLE CHIEFLY AS THE FIRST VISIT OF KING GUSTAF TO THE NORWEGIAN CAPITAL SINCE THE DISSOLUTION OF THE UNION. WHILE KING CHRISTIAN WAS CORDIALLY GREETED, THERE IS NO DOUBT THAT THE WARMEST, MOST EARNEST WELCOME WAS GIVEN TO THE SWEDISH KING, WHO THUS SHOWED HIS WILLINGNESS TO LET OLD WOUNDS BE HEALED, AND TO WORK WITH NORWEGIANS AND DANES FOR THE COMMON GOOD OF THE NORTH. THE PHOTOGRAPH SHOWS THE ROYAL VISITORS ON A QUIET LITTLE OUTING TO THE ROYAL SAETER NEAR CHRISTIANIA. QUEEN MAUD IS LEADING THE WAY, FOLLOWED BY CROWN PRINCE OLAF; NEXT COME KING CHRISTIAN, KING GUSTAF, AND KING HAAKON, IN THE ORDER NAMED

Editorial

"Making Sweden Safe To the foreign observer, the recent fall of
for Democracy" the Conservative ministry in Sweden appeared due to the failure of its foreign
policy. Swedes know that the change would have taken place even
had there been no Luxburg affair; for the main issue of the election
that brought a Socialist-Liberal government into power was the
demand of the people for a thorough revision of the constitution. Yet
it is true that this internal political campaign was in its essence a
fight between the spirit of two ideas, the idea of Prussian autocracy
and that of British-French democracy. It is not for nothing that
Swedish sympathies in the war are divided almost on party lines.
The ideal of the Swedish Conservatives is the efficient German
feudal government with a powerful royal ruler, a firmly intrenched
bureaucracy, and a rather insignificant popular representation. The
ideal of the Liberals is British parliamentarism with a strong parliament and cabinet.

The Swedish Riksdag is almost as old as the British Parliament.
From time immemorial there has been in Sweden a struggle between
the two powers, king and people, with sometimes one in the ascendant,
sometimes the other. The last era of despotism ended in total failure
in 1809, when King Gustaf IV Adolf was deposed, and Sweden got
the constitution which, in its main features, is still in force. By it
the king, together with his cabinet, exercises all executive power and
has full control of the army and navy in peace as well as in war; he
can propose laws, but can not levy taxes. The Riksdag has the
same power as the king of proposing laws, but has the sole right to
levy taxes. The king can choose his ministers as he likes, but they
are responsible to the Riksdag. The exact measure of this responsibility, however, is not defined in the constitution and has always been
a bone of contention between the Liberals and Conservatives.

The Liberals have insisted upon a parliamentary government
after the British pattern, by which the cabinet is chosen from the
party that has a majority in the lower house, that is, in Sweden, the
second chamber of the Riksdag. To the Conservatives "parliamentarism" has always been "un-Swedish" and fraught with every
imaginable evil. Possibly some of their animosity towards England
may be traced to this source. The doctrinaire Conservatives in
Sweden are inspired by the same peculiar views on democracy as
those launched by G. K. Chesterton. The only cabinet they approve of is one made up of Conservative or—what in fact comes to
the same thing—"non-political" officials. As for the Riksdag, and
in particular the second chamber, they would prefer to degrade it

into a mere voting machine to approve the king's propositions. They consider the Riksdag a far less important part of the government than the bureaucracy, and this bureaucracy, consisting of absolutely permanent officials, is the strong wall of Conservative power.

The constitutional reforms which the new government will try to realize include: the abolishment of all property qualifications for voters in the elections to the first chamber; suffrage for women; obligatory parliamentary government; control of the foreign policy by the Riksdag through a permanent committee. These points are common to Socialists and Liberals. Beyond this, the extreme Socialists have a much more far-reaching programme, including disarmament and the establishment of a republic, but these need not be considered here.

We may expect years of trouble and obstruction before the programme of the government can be fully carried out. Political feelings are perhaps more bitterly violent in Sweden than in any other country. We have a few "great Swedes," who are also the most pro-German element of our population, who will never consent to an amendment of the constitution, but will obstruct it by every means in their power. The radicals have a strong weapon in their control of the budget, which is settled by common voting of the two houses. As they have a majority in the Riksdag, they can refuse to vote money for the royal family or for the army and navy and so on, thus forcing any cabinet to resign. Yet this is a two-edged sword which, we may be sure, will be used sparingly. The able men who constitute the new cabinet will do all in their power to adjust differences by peaceful means. And it is a hopeful sign that the king himself has loyally accepted the will of the people and chosen a cabinet that represents the majority.

If the constitutional question can be finally settled, the Swedish people can meet the future full of confidence, and those who have predicted the ruin of trade, industry, and general prosperity will see the country flourish as well under democracy as under a bureaucratic regime.

KARL GUSTAV DERNBY.

REDS AND WHITES At this writing it is impossible to say what turn IN FINLAND events may take in Finland. Last December, with Finland's independence acknowledged by Russia, France, Germany, Austro-Hungary, Sweden, Norway, and Denmark, with the Scandinavian countries looking on in sympathy and promising whatever they could spare from their own depleted stores to relieve hunger among their Finnish neighbors, there seemed every reason to await the best. The bourgeois government under Judge P. E. Svinhufvud (who recently returned from Siberian exile) seemed about to establish stable conditions, and there was hope of a Finnish republic. Then came the revolt of the proletariat, backed by the Red Guard and with the moral support of the Bolsheviki. The Government is defended by the so-called White Guard. The struggle is aggravated by the old racial rivalry between *svekoman* and *fennoman*, most of the Swedish Finns belonging to the bourgeois party, the Finns proper to the revolutionists. The former have in their favor property, education, the traditions of self-government, and hatred against the oppressor, Russia. The latter have numbers, popular jealousy of the privileged classes, and racial prejudice against the Swedish element in the population. We can only hope that the distracted country may be able to settle its own affairs and not fall into the arms of Germany.

PONTOPPIDAN AND GJELLERUP   Mail advices from Scandinavia confirm the cabled report that the Nobel prize for literature has been divided between Henrik Pontoppidan and Karl Adolf Gjellerup. These two Danish authors have both passed their sixtieth birthday, and their appointment again raises the question of whether it is well to make the Nobel prize a "veteran medal" for men whose most productive period is over, instead of an encouragement to those who are still in the thick of the fight. Neither of the two possesses the overmastering genius that would entitle him to the prize as a matter of course, though Pontoppidan has a fine and distinctive talent, which he has developed along highly specialized lines. Vilhelm Andersen says of him that modern Denmark could be reconstructed entire from his books. Gjellerup, on the other hand, has roamed far afield for his subjects, and by his residence in Dresden has voluntarily exiled himself from his own country without gaining any commanding international position. His appointment has been received with marked coolness in Scandinavia.

These two winners of the Nobel prize have, in their youth, gone through a somewhat parallel development. Both were the sons of clergymen. Gjellerup followed the family traditions so far as to take the final examinations in theology, but almost at the same time he was swept into the modernist movement and became a disciple of Brandes, Darwin, and Spencer. It was not long, however, before he realized that he was not at home in the radical camp, and, in the eighties, he left it as abruptly as he had entered it. For a while he turned to old Norse subjects, and, besides his original works, translated the songs of the Edda. His later dramas of modern life are an attempt at reconciling his Greek love of beauty and naturalness with the altruistic principles of Christianity. Pontoppidan, in his youth, was under the influence of the Grundtvig elements, and became a teacher in a folk high school conducted by his brother, but he soon revolted against what he conceived to be the insincere lyricism in the mixture of religion and patriotism that characterized the movement. His novel, *The Promised Land*, deals satirically with the folk high schools; the unfortunate hero of *Lykkeper* is a clergyman's son, and in *The Kingdom of the Dead* he uncovers the defects of the church. Yet, with all his critical probing, Pontoppidan is inspired by a deep love of his country and his people and an earnest desire to free the best elements in them from all weaknesses and hypocrisies.

JOHN ERICSSON MONUMENT   It appears that the Congressional Committee plan to go ahead with arrangements for the construction of the John Ericsson memorial in Washington, although the Memorial Commission expressed its willingness to let the matter wait until after the close of the war. The Commission have been highly gratified by the response they received from all parts of the country. For a while it was feared that the uncertain conditions now prevalent would make it impossible to secure the $25,000 which it was planned to add to the Government's appropriation of $35,000. The actual amount subscribed, however, is nearer $30,000 than $25,000. Much of the credit for this splendid result must be accorded to the enterprise of the chairman, Mr. S. Adolf Eckberg, who personally raised one-fifth of the sum. Special thanks are due also to Dr. Hjalmar Lundbohm, who came in at the last minute and supplied the balance of $3,000 before it was known that late subscriptions would more than make up the total. Of this amount, 8000 kronor was raised by friends of the movement in Sweden, the remainder being Dr. Lundbohm's personal contribution.

THRIFT STAMPS AND PATRIOTISM   Readers of the REVIEW need not be told that the American Government has never appealed in vain to its citizens, and that when it is a question of giving financial assistance the people respond with a will. The two Liberty loans demonstrated to what an extent this question of war revenue was understood by the nation. And it is no less gratifying to see with what readiness men, women, and children throughout the United States are entering the War-Savings campaign which, in some respects touches the individual much more directly than the former loan drives. There has never been a time that so searched out the character of the country as the present war. The War-Savings Stamps now offered for sale by the Government permit each and every one to lend a hand. As a means of teaching the public to save, this War-Savings Stamp campaign has already done a vast amount of good. The REVIEW gives its whole-hearted endorsement.

A New
Donation

The American-Scandinavian Foundation announces a gift of five thousand dollars from Mr. C. Henry Smith to endow an "Illustrated History of Scandinavian Art." This is the third large donation received within the year and is, in some respects, particularly gratifying as a mark of the widening influence of the Foundation. While the original endowment was established by a Dane, Niels Poulson, the first large special gift was made by a Swede, Mr. Charles S. Peterson, who recently donated three thousand dollars to the Scandinavian Classics. The next was contributed by an American, Mrs. Henry G. Leach, who put five thousand dollars at the disposal of the Friendly Aid Campaign to make the Review self-supporting. The third comes from a Norwegian, Mr. Smith, who thus completes the circle of the four races most vitally interested in this work. Furthermore, the three donations represent the East, the Middle West, and the far West, Mrs. Leach being a resident of New York, Mr. Peterson of Chicago, and Mr. Smith of San Francisco. Though living at a distance, he has followed the development of the Foundation through the Review and has become convinced of the importance of its mission. He recently visited the headquarters of the Foundation in passing through New York on his way to Norway. Mr. Smith is a native of Christiania and came to San Francisco shortly before the great fire. Since then he has built up a very successful exporting business.

The Annual
Meeting of
The Foundation

The Trustees of the American-Scandinavian Foundation, at their annual meeting, on January 19, re-elected the following officers: for president, Professor William Henry Schofield; for vice-president, Mr. John D. Hage; for treasurer, Mr. William H. Short; for secretary, Dr. Henry Goddard Leach; for counsel, Mr. Henry E. Almberg; for auditors, Mackay, Iron & Co. The president reported that he had been appointed by Harvard University to give a series of lectures in Middle Western colleges and universities from the beginning of February to the end of May, and that he would use the opportunity to speak of the work of the Foundation.

During the year, four trustees, Mr. A. E. Johnson, Mr. C. A. Smith, Mr. Oscar H. Haugan, and Mr. E. V. Eskesen, have resigned because of inability to take active part in the work. Their resignations have been accepted by the Board with regret and with appreciation of the services they have rendered. To fill the vacancies created, the Board, at the annual meeting, elected Mr. Charles S. Peterson to succeed Mr. Johnson; Mr. John G. Bergquist to succeed Mr. Smith, and Mr. Edwin Olaf Holter to succeed Mr. Haugan. Mr. John Aspegren was also elected a trustee to fill one of the places created by the Board in authorizing an increase of its membership from fifteen to seventeen. The election of a successor to Mr. Eskesen was postponed until another meeting. Mr. Peterson is one of the Swedish members of the Advisory Committee of the Foundation in Chicago and has shown his interest in many ways, notably in his generous gift to the CLASSICS. The other new trustees are residents of New York. Mr. Bergquist by birth is a Swede, an engineer by profession; he recently became a life Associate of the Foundation. Mr. Holter, the son of Norwegian pioneers in Montana, is a lawyer and business man. He has been active in various kinds of public service, the most far-reaching of which is perhaps his work as a member of the State Prison Commission and the State Parole Board, when he helped to shape the policies that resulted in the destruction of the old Sing Sing prison. Mr. Aspegren, of the firm of Aspegren and Company, is president of the Swedish Chamber of Commerce for the United States of America. He served as president of the American-Scandinavian Society during the years 1914 and 1915 and by his financial support made possible the Concerts of Scandinavian Music in Carnegie Hall. Owing to a severe illness, Mr. Aspegren has not yet accepted his election as trustee of the Foundation.

THE   The REVIEW began its sixth year under very bright
REVIEW   auspices. The Friendly Aid Campaign started a move-
          ment of general helpfulness beyond our most optimistic
hopes. Every mail has brought us letters full of praise and good wishes; they have come from all the states and from foreign countries. In three months, 708 of our Associates ordered and paid for a full year's subscription for one or more of their friends. Hundreds of others helped to enlarge our circle by buying single copies for presentation or by giving us names of persons to whom we could write. Probably a majority of the 708 ordered more than one subscription, some two or three, some five or six, and so on all the way up to fifty. On February 15, we had received 2,768 new subscribers.

We never knew the REVIEW had so many friends. Naturally the editors are deeply moved and gratified by all signs of appreciation for work faithfully done. Far above and beyond this, however, is the knowledge that many thousands of readers are aiding us in the task to which the REVIEW is consecrated. In the midst of all the stern, grim duties that confront us as a nation, the REVIEW is helping to keep the lamp of international friendship burning, to clear away misunderstanding, and create good-will. It is striving to keep open the channels of friendliness that unite America with the Northern neutrals and the various groups of our citizens—Swedes, Danes, Norwegians, Icelanders, and colonial Americans—with one another. The task is one that calls for all the help our readers can give us.

Current Events

Denmark

⁋ The American "Christmas present," the release of several ships carrying supplies to Denmark, was received by the Danes in the same cordial spirit of friendliness in which it was offered. The coffee was especially welcome; the supply at Christmas time was at a very low ebb, and the want of the accustomed drink was one of the severest privations in this heatless, lightless, and alcoholless winter. ⁋ Professor L. V. Birk of Copenhagen last autumn visited England and was received by the minister of the blockade, Lord Robert Cecil. The minister permitted Professor Birk to publish a letter in which he explained the position of the Allies and reiterated his statement that Denmark had observed her obligations most carefully in the present war. He added the interesting words: "Our action in the matter is not dictated by a desire to injure Denmark. You referred to certain attacks on the Danes in one or two English papers. I regret those attacks. There has always been a traditional friendship between England and Denmark, and it may be that if we had stood by Denmark in 1863-1864 we should not now be faced with the devastating war originated by German militarism." ⁋ Denmark has refused the request of Iceland for a national flag. In 1915, an Icelandic flag was authorized for use in Iceland and its territorial waters, while the Danebrog remained the national emblem to be used by merchant ships in foreign waters. The present resolution, which was passed unanimously by the Althing, called for the substitution of the Icelandic for the Danish flag both at home and abroad. It was refused by the king on the ground that it would be better to treat all the differences between the colony and the mother country at a special conference instead of dealing with the disputed points one by one. ⁋ The Danish merchant marine in 1917 lost ships amounting to 128,780 tons, or more than twice as much as in 1916. The sailors killed during the year numbered 171, making Denmark's total loss 219. The toll of men and ships has been steadily rising throughout the war, and as Denmark's fleet, even before the destruction began, was inadequate to her needs, the outlook at present is very dark. ⁋ The street cars in Copenhagen and Frederiksberg will soon be run entirely with electric power from Sweden. A cable passing from Lagen in Sweden, under the Öresund, and across Elsinore has been used very successfully for some time. It is now being greatly strengthened and will no doubt help to relieve the present medieval conditions in the Danish capital. ⁋ An increased number of crimes has been one of the by-products of the war in Copenhagen, where the dimly-lit streets favor the operations of thugs and thieves.

Sweden

❧ The situation in the east is full of complications for Sweden. While the great majority of the Swedes emphatically do not want Finland back as a part of the kingdom, there is a warm sympathy between them and the Swedish population in the neighboring country. The emissaries sent out to secure the recognition of Finland as an independent state went first of all to Stockholm. King Gustaf's careful greeting to them, conditioned on the attitude of Russia, drew down on him the frankest criticism from his own subjects, while his later full and free recognition, following that of the Bolsheviki, was acclaimed with enthusiasm at home. The head of the Finnish delegation, Minister Gripenberg, declared it to be the greatest day of his life. Recently the Finnish bourgeois party, to which practically all the Swedish Finns belong, has been sending appeals for aid across the border, and there is a strong feeling among the Swedes that they ought to help their kinsmen with money, food, and ammunition; many think Sweden should even intervene to restore order by force of arms, but the government has refused to take action beyond sending a ship to bring home Swedish subjects. ❧ The Åland question is another difficulty. The island was Swedish until 1809 when it was forcibly taken away, and, in spite of forced Finnish settlement for propaganda purposes, the inhabitants are still Swedish in sentiment, and have repeatedly petitioned to be restored to Sweden. The present government of Sweden may be counted upon to resist all temptation to military adventure such as the seizing of Åland, but naturally there is a desire to get rid of the menace of Russian fortifications within fifty miles of Stockholm. The publication of certain state papers by the Bolsheviki has not contributed to lay the "Åland spectre" with which the Activists have long tried to stir up the old fear of the Muscovite. It is seen that the Russian Government tried to secure the consent of France to the annulment of the Åland treaty, by which Russia is bound not to erect permanent fortifications on the island. While there is no indication either that France agreed or that the new Russian Government would follow the same policy, the matter has left a feeling of uneasiness in Swedish minds. ❧ On the other hand, the conquest of the Baltic provinces by Germany, vastly increasing her power in the adjacent waters, forebodes a "German menace" that may soon loom even larger than the old "Russian menace." ❧ The cabled report that Branting's resignation from the ministry was due to ill health is confirmed by mail advices. His successor as minister of finance is F. W. Thorsson, a man who, originally a shoemaker, has come up from the ranks of the labor party. He has held many important local offices and has been for some years a member of the Riksdag.

Norway

❧ The negotiations long carried on in Washington by representatives of the Norwegian Government resulted in a definite offer from the United States, but unfortunately this offer was not found acceptable by the Norwegian home authorities. The American terms require Norway, in return for food amounting in 1918 to 500,000 tons, to forego all re-export to Germany and practically all export of home products except the usual percent of fish. As a matter of fact, Norway at present exports hardly anything else to Germany, and re-export has long been a punishable crime. We may infer therefore that it is not the actual curtailment of trade with Germany which moves Norway to refuse our Government's offer. The true reason is the belief that Germany would instantly seize upon such an agreement as a pretext for declaring war on Norway, destroying the Norwegian coast cities, and seizing the fleet which is now so useful to our Allies. It is probable that some compromise may be reached. ❧ Meanwhile the Norwegians are making tremendous efforts to increase their own food production. The amount of grain raised has been almost doubled; yet it is not sufficient. American motor ploughs have been imported in large numbers. Measures for enforcing the cultivation of fallow lands by law and mobilizing citizens for agricultural work are being discussed. ❧ General dissatisfaction with the delay of the Government in introducing the rationing system almost led to the fall of the Knudsen ministry. Popular clamor was appeased, however, with the resignation of the minister of provisions, Oddmund Vik. Birger Stuevold-Hansen was appointed in his place. ❧ The British Government has cancelled its agreement to purchase 85 percent of the Norwegian export of fish, and the obligation has been taken over by the Norwegian state. The transaction involves the sum of possibly a hundred million kroner a year. ❧ An important discovery has been made in the refinement of whale oil so that it can be used for the manufacture of oleomargarine. Manufacturing according to the new method has already begun, and, it is hoped, will greatly relieve the shortage of fats. ❧ Another woman has taken her place in the Norwegian Storting. She is Miss Sara Christie of Trondhjem and, like her predecessor, Miss Anna Rogstad, is a teacher by profession. ❧ The Norwegian merchant marine at the beginning of the new year consisted of 1,669 ships with a total tonnage of 1,996,214. This shows a loss for the year of 367 ships with a total tonnage of 566,181. From the beginning of the war, the vessels known to be wrecked by war measures were 702, with a total tonnage of 1,031,778, and with them 875 sailors perished. Besides, 53 other vessels have disappeared, at least two-thirds from causes due to the war, and more than 700 sailors have been lost with them.

Books

A DANISH CLASSIC

Marie Grubbe, a Lady of the Seventeenth Century. By J. P. Jacobsen. Translated from the Danish by Hanna Astrup Larsen. Scandinavian Classics, Volume VII. New York: The American-Scandinavian Foundation, 1917. Price $1.50.

(From the *Westminster Gazette* for December 15, 1917)

For one's own complacent ignorance of the great works of other nations there is only one real excuse—the keen delight with which it is at times disturbed. To be ashamed of not having sooner read the work of Jonas Lie or Alexander Kielland is a sensation altogether forgotten, obliterated, as it instantly was, by the deep satisfaction of discovery. And such satisfaction is ready for those who had never so much as heard of J. P. Jacobsen when they take up the admirable translation of *Marie Grubbe*, the earlier of the two novels on which his fame in his own country has long securely rested, prepared by the American-Scandinavian Foundation, in whose excellent series it forms the eighth.

Jens Peter Jacobsen, born in Jutland seventy years ago, died in 1885 after producing a number of poems, some short stories, translations of Darwin's two major volumes, and two novels, *Marie Grubbe* and *Niels Lyhne*. Georg Brandes thus hailed him as the re-creator of the Danish language; the man who "tuned" it, in his critic's phrase, as language requires every now and then, like any other instrument, to be tuned, so as to fit the thoughts of a new generation. No translator, however gifted, can give to a foreign reader the quality which enables him to estimate such a claim to greatness as this; but Miss Larsen's version does at least retain the extraordinary beauty, vividness, and accuracy of Jacobsen's imagery, and that high colouration that puzzled and even displeased his earlier critics.

The story of Marie Grubbe (the girl mentioned in Hans Andersen's *Goose Girl*) is based on a minute and careful study of historical documents, to which Jacobsen devoted years. He called it "Interiors of the Seventeenth Century." But, although these interiors, and some exteriors too, are given with wonderful faithfulness and a power of evocation so strong that one accepts the medium without any troublesome sense of its strangeness, the real interest of *Marie Grubbe* lies not so much in its rich and violent background as in the development of character. In Marie, however much he may have relied upon letters, documents, and records, Jacobsen has created a real woman—a woman whom we see and know, and who yet retains that element of the profoundly mysterious that belongs to the most fascinating of actual beings. We see her—we realize her rare and special beauty, with its pallor, its spiritual quality, its underlying passion and fierceness, expressed at times in the eyes, of which he gives so remarkable a description; and we accept as absolutely true to type her strange career, her child's adoration of the Danish Paladin, Ulrik Christian; her marriage to the Viceroy of Norway, Ulrik Frederik Gyldenlöve; and all her subsequent strange adventures of the heart, culminating in her final marriage to a poor ferryman. Nothing could be subtler and more searching than the analysis of her feeling for Sti Högh, her second lover; its rise, development, and death are traced with the utmost delicacy—a delicacy which gains in artistic value from Jacobsen's power to delineate with equal sureness and firmness scenes of wild and unbridled passion—such as that in which Marie tries to kill Ulrik, where she whips his mistress Karen, or where she confesses her love to the rude farm-hand, Sören. Nor is Marie the only character that lives before us; the whole population of her world is there, given often in a few simple touches of apparently external description, but always given, solid, actual. They are real, but she is supremely interesting—interesting partly because one never quite understands her, any more than she understood herself, and despite of the fact that her life, ending in failure and negation, suggests such dreary questions—questions to which Jacobsen has no answer to give.

DEN NY KURS I AMERIKAS UDENRIGSPOLITIK. By Roger Nielsen. Copenhagen: Nyt Nordisk Forlag. 1917. 173 pages.

It is, perhaps, something of a coincidence that at a moment when American readers are being presented with Professors Robinson and West's *The Foreign Policy of Woodrow Wilson*, published by the Macmillan Company, a book in Danish, written in this country by a Danish-American, but issued by Nyt Nordisk Forlag in Copenhagen, treats of the same subject for the benefit of those interested in Scandinavian affairs and familiar with the languages of the North.

As a matter of fact, *Den Ny Kurs i Amerikas Udenrigspolitik* (The New Course in American Foreign Policy) by Roger Nielsen, comes at a most opportune time to show the people of Scandinavia in just what way President Wilson handled the country's affairs during certain periods when only the most accomplished statesmanship could avoid collisions with the outside world.

Mr. Nielsen, who is associated with the well-known Danish-American newspaper, *Den Danske Pioneer*, in Omaha, Nebraska, has much to say about President Wilson and William Jennings Bryan, while the latter was Secretary of State. The Mexican crisis, in fact, occupies the major portion of the book. There is also a foreword by Mr. Bryan. On the whole, the work is a credit to the author and also to the Danish publishing house which has been the means of bringing it to the attention of the reading public in Denmark. Much good can come from an enterprise that stands for the retention of the friendship always existing between the Scandinavian countries and the United States. The American President appears in his true colors as the standard bearer of democracy against autocracy. Considering that it is a Danish-American who has become the medium through whom such presentation has been effected, there is good reason for asserting that Mr. Nielsen's book takes its rightful place among works that are of direct importance to America in this world-war. Translated into English, this book no doubt would find many interested readers. JULIUS MORITZEN.

Brief Notes

The American-Scandinavian Society at its annual meeting in New York, January 21, elected the following officers and trustees: for president, Mr. Henry E. Almberg; for vice-president, Mr. Halvor Jacobsen; for secretary, Miss Therese C. Holm; for treasurer, Mr. Edwin O. Holter; for auditors, Mr. Emil Johnson and Mr. Gerhard Hille; trustees for three years, Mr. F. C. W. Rambusch, Mrs. J. de Neergaard, Dr. H. G. Leach, Mr. John Hartell; for two years, Dr. H. V. Barclay, Mrs. Effie Danforth McAfee, Mr. A. N. Rygg; for one year, Dr. Augusta Vedin, and Mr. C. K. Johansen to succeed Dr. J. Hoving, resigned. Dr. H. G. Leach, the vice-president, presided at the meeting. It was voted to send a letter to the retiring president, Mr. Rambusch, who has gone south for his health, thanking him for his devoted service and wishing him a speedy and complete recovery. Thanks were also voted to the other retiring officers; to Dr. and Mrs. Leach, Mr. and Mrs. Rambusch, and Mr. and Mrs. Lagerlöf, who entertained the members of the Society at three Round Table evenings; and to the committee which recently arranged a very successful banquet for Dr. Fritjof Nansen.

BRIEF NOTES—Continued

Karen Borneman, Hjalmar Bergström's celebrated play which was at one time suppressed by the censor in Denmark, has been played four weeks under the title *Karen* in the Greenwich Village Theatre, one of the new small intimate theatres of New York. The performance was, on the whole, excellent, and the audience, which was distinctly of an intellectual type, was very appreciative. The translation is by Mr. Edwin Björkman.

Mr. Julius Moritzen contributed a series of five notable articles on "Scandinavian-American Trade Relations" to the *New York Commercial* in October and November. He pointed out the probability that Scandinavian ports would supersede German ports after the war as the connecting links in trade between Russia and America.

In Rochester, New York, a new organization, the American-Scandinavian Association, has been formed to bring together men and women of Scandinavian descent for social and educational purposes. The organization will disseminate information concerning American institutions and stimulate interest in the history of the Scandinavian countries and their contribution to the development of America. Mr. Andrew Gustafson is secretary.

Dr. Haakon Styri, formerly "docent" at the Technical Institute in Trondhjem, has been appointed assistant professor of metallurgy at the Carnegie Institute of Technology at Pittsburgh. Dr. Styri studied at the Carnegie Institute in 1910, before the incorporation of the Foundation, as a scholar of the American-Scandinavian *Society*.

Dr. Julius Lincoln of Jamestown, New York, has made a visit to the Western front to study the war at first hand with a view to giving lectures at Swedish Lutheran churches in this country.

A translation of Ibsen's long narrative poem "Terje Viken" has been published by H. F. Rosing of Minneapolis.

The Editors regret that, through an oversight, King Saint Olaf was referred to as Olaf Trygvason in the book page of last number.

HOUSEHOLD HINTS

POTATO RECIPES

Among the European countries that can teach us many lessons in food economy, Denmark is conspicuous. It is interesting to note that the Danish Government considered a study of food sufficiently important to establish a Laboratory of Nutrition Research in Copenhagen. Dr. M. Hindhede, author of *Protein and Nutrition* and *What to Eat and Why*, is the director. He is regarded as one of the leading nutrition experts of today. In his laboratory experiments, he is selecting the cheaper foodstuffs and combining them in such a way that they will fully meet the requirements of nutrition.

He refers to the potato as the "best article of food I know of." For ten months he had human subjects living on potatoes and margarine alone. Their strength and health during that period were not only maintained but improved. Dr. Hindhede's experiments prove to us the food value of the potato and make us appreciate it as one of nature's bread foods. In its composition we find much starch, some protein, and fat. It is also rich in mineral matter. A medium-sized potato contains the same food value as a large-sized roll and as much iron as the yolk of an egg. It may rightly be called the king of vegetables, reigning supreme in our diet. At this time it is of particular value as it furnishes one of the best of wheat substitutes. The potato is a food of which the palate does not tire and it may be used in so many different ways without monotony. Even at the present price of potatoes, a diet, such as Dr. Hindhede suggests, could be provided at a low cost when compared with other food of the same nutritive value.

CREAM OF POTATO SOUP

Boil three medium-size potatoes in boiling salted water until soft. Rub through a strainer or potato ricer. While the potatoes are cooking scald one quart of milk with one sliced onion. Remove onion and thicken the milk with two tablespoons of flour which has been mixed with two tablespoons of water until smooth. A little of the hot milk should be added to the flour and water mixture before it is added to the hot milk. Stir while adding and until milk begins to thicken. When the milk is thickened add the potato, $1\frac{1}{2}$ teaspoons salt, $\frac{1}{4}$ teaspoon celery salt, $\frac{1}{8}$ teaspoon pepper, a few grains Cayenne, and 1 teaspoon chopped parsley. Serve hot.

SAVORY POTATOES

Slice six boiled potatoes and put a layer in a well-greased saucepan. Sprinkle with salt and pepper, add a layer of finely chopped onions, finely chopped parsley, and repeat until all the potatoes are used. Cover with $\frac{1}{2}$ cup full of water and let simmer for 20 minutes. Add $\frac{1}{2}$ cup full of milk and cook fifteen minutes. Remove to a serving dish and sprinkle with $\frac{1}{2}$ cup full of grated cheese.

POTATO BREAD

To 1 cup hot mashed potato add 1 cup hot liquid which may be water or milk or half and half. Add $1\frac{1}{2}$ teaspoons salt, 1 tablespoon fat, 2 tablespoons syrup, mix, and let stand until lukewarm. Add $\frac{1}{2}$ yeast cake which has been mixed with $\frac{1}{4}$ cup lukewarm water and enough flour to make a dough stiff enough to knead. Knead mixture until smooth and elastic to the touch; put dough in a greased bowl, cover and let rise to double its bulk. Shape into two loaves, put loaves in well-greased bread pans, let rise to double their bulk and bake in a moderately hot oven about 50 minutes.

POTATO DROP COOKIES

Cream ¾ cup fat, add 1¼ cups sugar gradually and continue creaming until mixture is thoroughly creamed. Add 1½ cups hot mashed potatoes and 1¾ cups of flour which has been mixed and sifted with 2½ teaspoons baking powder, 1 teaspoon cinnamon, ½ teaspoon cloves, and ½ teaspoon nutmeg, add ½ cup chopped raisins and ¼ cup chopped citron. Mix ingredients thoroughly and drop mixture by teaspoonfuls on to a well-greased pan, and bake in a moderately hot oven from 15 to 20 minutes.

POTATO AND APPLE PUDDING

Pare 3 apples and cut in eighths, and cook with ¼ cup sugar and ¼ cup full of water until mushy. Add 2 medium-size potatoes which have been boiled and mashed. Add 1 tablespoon fat, 1 well-beaten egg, ⅛ teaspoon ginger and the grated rind of ½ lemon. Pour into a well-greased baking dish and bake in a moderately hot oven from 30 to 40 minutes. Serve with a lemon sauce.

POTATOES O'BRIEN

Arrange 6 boiled potatoes which have been cut into cubes, 2 cups white sauce, 1 green pepper, finely chopped, ¼ cup pimentos finely chopped, in layers, in a well-greased baking dish. Sprinkle top with ½ cup finely grated cheese and bake in a moderately hot oven until heated throughout and nicely browned on top.

POTATO PANCAKES

One and one-half cups of grated or mashed potatoes, ½ cup flour for raw potatoes or 1 cup flour for mashed potatoes, ¾ cup milk, 1 egg, 2 teaspoons baking powder, ¼ teaspoon salt, ⅛ teaspoon pepper, 1 teaspoon melted fat. Mix the ingredients. Shape into cakes. Sprinkle them with flour. Brown on both sides on a well-greased griddle.

POTATO BISCUITS

One cup mashed potatoes, 1½ cups flour, 3 teaspoons baking powder, ⅓ cup fat, 1 tablespoon syrup, 1 teaspoon salt. Add the flour, baking powder, and salt mixed and sifted to the mashed potatoes. Rub in the fat, add the syrup and work mixture into a dough. Roll out to ½-inch thickness. Cut into biscuits. Bake on a griddle. Brown on both sides, split, butter, and serve.

SOME NORWEGIAN RECIPES
RICE SOUP WITH MILK

Cook 1 quart milk with ¼ cup rice and a small piece of stick cinnamon in a double boiler until rice is soft. Add sugar or salt to taste and serve.

BARLEY SOUP WITH MILK

Cook 1 quart milk with ¼ cup barley in a double boiler until barley is soft. The barley should be soaked over night before cooking. Season with sugar or salt to taste, and serve.
Note.—Tapioca, sago, or oatmeal may be cooked in the same way.

FRUIT SOUP

Boil 1½ quarts water, 8 prunes, ¼ cup raisins, 1 sliced lemon and ¼ cup sago until sago is transparent. Add 1 cup fruit juice, sweeten to taste, serve hot or cold. A little stick cinnamon and a few cloves may be added to the mixture while cooking.

NORWEGIAN BREAD

To 1 cup boiled barley mush add 1 cup hot liquid, 1 tablespoon fat, 2 teaspoons salt, ¼ cup syrup and let stand until lukewarm. Mix ½ yeast cake with 2 tablespoons liquid and add to the lukewarm barley mixture. Stir in enough flour to make a dough stiff enough to knead. Knead mixture until smooth and elastic to the touch; put into a well-greased bowl, cover and let rise to double its bulk. Shape mixture into loaves and put loaves into well-greased bread pans. Let rise to double their bulk and bake in a moderately hot oven about 50 or 60 minutes.

LILLA FRICH.

EDITORIAL ANNOUNCEMENT

The editors have in preparation a **WAR SERVICE NUMBER** and a SCANDINAVIAN-AMERICAN HISTORICAL NUMBER

The forthcoming June-July issue will be as attractive as its predecessors. It is hoped that it will contain, among other features, an international article by BRANTING, and a rollicking, humorous story by ENGSTROM.

THE AMERICAN-SCANDINAVIAN REVIEW

TRADE NOTES

*News and Comment on Exports and Trade
Conditions Between America and the Scandinavian Countries*

U. S. EXPORTS BREAK RECORD
For the year 1917, the United States export trade totalled $6,226,000,000. The largest export figures of any year before the war were around $2,500,000,000.

SWEDISH FOOD CONFEREES AT LONDON
Marcus Wallenberg, brother of the former Swedish Foreign Minister, and Robert A. Nordvall, formerly at Washington representing the Swedish Government as special commissioner, are in London negotiating with American delegates regarding food shipments for Sweden.

FUEL EMBARGO WINNING OUT
While the majority of the newspapers sent up a hue and cry when Dr. Garfield issued his sudden order for the five-day industrial shutdown and "coalless" Mondays, there are indications that the measure has aided in relieving the railroad congestion, which was its main purpose.

MOTOR EXPORTS AFTER THE WAR
In the opinion of P. S. Steenstrup, of the General Motors Export Company, steps should now be taken to make secure the position of this country as the chief center for motor cars when the war ends. Last year's export of motor cars amounted to 75,000 vehicles at a value of $80,000,000.

NORWAY INCREASES MANUFACTURING

Since the war Norway has begun to make greater use of her unsurpassed water-power facilities for manufacturing purposes. The Norwegian Chamber of Commerce, of New York, is proving a strong link in bringing the two countries together in a commercial direction. Trade promises to be on a large scale following the war.

AMERICAN DYE INDUSTRY GROWS

The organization of American dye manufacturers has recently been effected as a result of chemical research work which now puts this country's products on an equal footing with the best that Germany used to produce.   J. M.

FINANCIAL

*Notes About Issues in the Financial World
Most Interesting to Readers of the Review*

A CORRECTION

The REVIEW is in receipt of a cablegram from Den Danske Landmandsbank of Copenhagen stating that their paid-up capital now amounts to 100 million kroner, and their reserve fund to 25 million. We are glad to make this announcement to correct the figures printed in the Christmas Number of the REVIEW. The Landmandsbank has branches in every part of Denmark and transacts legitimate banking business of every kind, making telegraphic transfers to all parts of the world.

HANNEVIG & CO., NEW YORK BANKERS

American financial circles are more than ordinarily interested in the establishment in New York City of a new banking institution by Christoffer Hannevig, of Norway, who has opened up handsome quarters at 139 Broadway. The name of Hannevig is famous throughout the world, and shipping enterprises will base the main financial operations of the new house. Mr. Hannevig has associated with him his brother, Finn Hannevig, John M. Grant, and A. Stolt, the latter as chief of the general banking work. The capital of this new Norwegian bank is $1,000,000. Ultimately the name of the institution will be the Marine Trust Company.

ISLAND OIL AND TRANSPORT CORPORATION

Among the most interesting transactions of recent date is the offering of $1,000,000 Island Oil and Transportation first lien collateral 7 per cent. gold notes for the purpose of providing funds for the construction of a pipe line from the Tepetate oil district to the Gulf of

Mexico, and the further development of properties controlled by the company. At the price of 99 and interest, and yielding over 7 per cent., these notes are considered by financial experts especially suited for investment purposes. The Island Oil and Transport Corporation has made some of the most surprising strikes for oil in the whole Mexican territory.

PROGRESS OF SWEDISH CHAMBER OF COMMERCE

Despite the difficulties in the way of trade with Sweden, the Swedish Chamber of Commerce of the United States made steady progress during 1917. As a matter of course, the past year proved a critical period in the Chamber's history, but 126 new members were nevertheless added to the list and the *Swedish-American Trade Journal* continues to be the most valuable auxiliary.

Scandinavian Trust Company

56 Broadway, New York

MEMBER FEDERAL RESERVE BANK OF NEW YORK

Paid-in Capital, Surplus and Profits, $2,600,000

OFFICERS

ALEXANDER V. OSTROM.........President
B. E. SMYTHE ....Vice-President
MAURICE F. BAYARD............Treasurer
D. CARDOZO ....Asst. Secretary

BOARD OF DIRECTORS

JOHS. ANDERSEN......................................J. Andersen & Company
KNUT BACHKE..............................Andresens Bank, Christiania
PHILIP G. BARTLETT............................Simpson, Thacher and Bartlett
CHARLES E. BEDFORD..................Vice-President, Vacuum Oil Company
JAMES F. BELL.....................Vice-President, Washburn-Crosby Company
JOHN E. BERWIND...................Vice-President, Berwind-White Coal Co.
R. R. BROWN ....First Vice-President, American Surety Company
WILLIAM R. COE...........................Chairman, Johnson & Higgins
GERHARD M. DAHL.....................Vice-President, Chase National Bank
S. E. DAHL.........................Centralbanken for Norge, Christiania
W. EDWARD FOSTER.............Treasurer, American Sugar Refining Company
SAMUEL L. FULLER.........................Kissel, Kinnicutt & Company
EDWARD F. GEER.......................................Shipowner
CHARLES S. HAIGHT..........................Haight, Sanford & Smith
G. KAMSTRUP HEGGE...................Den Norske Creditbank, Christiania
EDWIN O. HOLTER.......................................Attorney
FREDERICK W. HVOSLEF.....................Bennett, Hvoslef & Company
N. BRUCE MacKELVIE...........................Hayden, Stone & Company
C. M. MacNEILL ....President, Utah Copper Company
ALEXANDER R. NICOL ...Treasurer, Atlantic Gulf & West Indies Steamship Lines
ALEXANDER V. OSTROM.......................................President
BIRGER OSLAND...............General Western Agent, Norwegian-America Line
E. A. CAPPELEN SMITH..............................Guggenheim Brothers
THOMAS THACHER..........................Simpson, Thacher and Bartlett
NIEL A. WEATHERS..........................Simpson, Thacher and Bartlett

NORWEGIAN ADVISORY BOARD

KNUT BACHKE...................Andresens Bank, Christiania
CHR. BONGE ....Bergens Kreditbank, Bergen
F. BRUENECH...... Christiania Bank og Kreditkasse, Christiania
S. E. DAHL................Centralbanken for Norge, Christiania
G. K. HEGGE..............Den Norske Kreditbank, Christiania
KR. JEBSEN.....................Bergens Privatbank, Bergen
CHR. THAULOW .....Den Nordenfjeldske Kreditbank, Trondhjem

Bolsheviki Repudiating Loans

The entire world is concerned in the announcement from Petrograd that the Bolshevik Government intends to repudiate all foreign loans. Large quantities of Russian securities are now held in this country. The British Chancellor of the Exchequer, Bonar Law, however, is of the opinion that it is unlikely that Russia can entirely cancel its national debt, as it would make it impossible for the country later to secure necessary funds elsewhere.

Stock Exchange Developments

The *Financial World* figures that during the past year, in 104 common and preferred stocks and bonds, based on highest and lowest prices of the year, there was a shrinkage of $3,023,000,000 in market values. As to the change for the better, which came with the beginning of the new year, railroad stocks discounted Government control, and investors, says the *Financial World*, "are now looking toward Washington with hope and confidence."

Norwegian Pulp Company Transaction

England is more than ordinarily interested in the recent sale to Norway of the Kellner Partington Paper Pulp Company, mentioned in the last number of the Review. Lord Robert Cecil informed Parliament that the amount of money concerned in the transaction was around 100,000,000 kroner. The English interests did not part with their holdings without regret, but international conditions made it essential that the enterprise should rest exclusively in Norwegian hands.

Consolidated Stock Exchange

The speculative world has been receiving many small investors in recent years who have taken advantage of the odd-lot offerings that the Consolidated Stock Exchange has been pioneer in placing at the disposal of wage-earners. Under the presidency of J. Frank Howell, this financial institution has rapidly risen to a place of importance in the investment history of the country.

Scandinavian Exchange Rate

The *New York Evening Post*, in its special financial number issued at the close of the year, refers to the high rate for Swedish exchange as follows: "The heavy deposits in American banks to the credit of Swedish merchants may explain much of the rise in Scandinavian exchange. The depreciation of New York exchange at Stockholm to the extent of 63 per cent., not long ago, was one of the mystifying features of this financial situation, since, during the first eight months of 1917, exports from this country to Sweden were 30 per cent. greater than her exports to the United States."

World Bank for Federal System

The creation of a foreign-exchange bank in the United States as part of the existing Federal Reserve system has been proposed in a bill now being drafted by Senator Owen, of Oklahoma, chairman of the Banking and Currency Committee. Max May, vice-president of the Guaranty Trust Company, and a recognized authority on foreign exchange, is aiding Senator Owen in the draft of the measure. It is expected that many millions of dollars will be saved Americans in business by the adoption of the proposed plan.   J. M.

NORWEGIAN AMERICA LINE

Modern Twin Screw Steamers

16,000 tons displacement, 530 feet long

16½ knots speed

Accommodations:

The steamers are new, modern and efficiently equipped for the utmost safety and comfort of passengers. First-class staterooms are situated amidships on the Promenade and Shelter Deck. Cabins De Luxe on upper promenade.

For further particulars apply to

NORWEGIAN AMERICA LINE PASSENGER AGENCY, Inc.

8 and 10 Bridge St., New York   General Passenger Agents for United States and Canada

HOBE & CO.
General Northwestern Passenger Agents
123 South Third Street
Minneapolis, Minn.

BIRGER OSLAND & CO.
General Western Passenger Agents
115 South Dearborn Street
Chicago, Ill.

REIDAR GJÖLME
General Pacific Coast Agent
Arctic Bldg. Third & Cherry Streets
Seattle, Wash.

NORWAY MEXICO GULF LINE AND SWEDISH AMERICA MEXICO LINE

Regular service between GÖTEBORG, CHRISTIANIA and STAVAN-GER and NEWPORT NEWS, VA., HAVANA, CUBA, GALVESTON, TEX., and NEW ORLEANS, LA.

Passengers Carried   Wireless Apparatus

AGENTS

FEARNLEY & EGER, Christiania   SANDSTRÖM STRANNE & CO., Ltd., Goteborg

FURNESS WITHY & CO., Ltd., New York, N. Y. and Newport News, Va.

32 BROADWAY

JAS. P. ROBERTSON
111 West Jackson Boulevard
Chicago, Ill.

FOWLER & McVITIE
Galveston, Tex.

LYKES BROS.
Havana, Cuba

GEO. PLANT
1119 Whitney Central Bldg.
New Orleans, La.

Recommendation for Associate
of the
AMERICAN-SCANDINAVIAN FOUNDATION

I nominate ....

Address ....

GENERAL OFFICES: Passenger Department

117 N. Dearborn Street, Chicago, Ill.
236 Nicollet Ave., Minneapolis, Minn.
248 Washington St., Boston, Mass.

1 BROADWAY, NEW YORK

544 Market St., San Francisco, Cal.
702 Second Ave., Seattle, Wash.

SWEDISH AMERICAN LINE

(SVENSKA AMERIKA LINIEN)

Direct Passenger Service between New York and Gothenburg, Sweden

Short Route to Sweden, Norway, Denmark, Finland, Russia and other parts of the European Continent

Twin-Screw S.S. "Stockholm"

Length 565 Feet.   22,070 Tons Displacement

Largest Steamer in Service between America and Scandinavia, is provided with all modern safety appliances, and every care is taken to give the passengers a safe and comfortable journey.

Unsurpassed passenger appointments in First, Second and Third Classes.

NIELSEN & LUNDBECK, General Passenger Agents, 24 State Street, New York.

MARTIN MAURD, General Western Agent, 183 N. Dearborn Street, Chicago.

NILS NILSON, General Northwestern Agent, 127 S. Third St., Minneapolis, Minn.

BRATTSTROM & CO., General No. Pacific Agents, 117 Cherry St., Seattle, Wash.

A. HALLONQUIST, General Agent, 396 Logan Ave., Winnipeg, Man., Can.

The American-Scandinavian Review

VOLUME VI MAY-JUNE, 1918 NUMBER 3

Published Bi-Monthly by THE AMERICAN-SCANDINAVIAN FOUNDATION, 25 West 45th Street, New York

Yearly Subscription, $1.50. (One dollar to Associates of the Foundation.) Single Copies, 25 cents

Entered as second-class matter, January 4, 1913, at the post-office at New York, N. Y., under the act of March 3, 1879
Copyright, 1916, The American-Scandinavian Foundation

HENRY GODDARD LEACH, *Editor* HANNA ASTRUP LARSEN, *Literary Editor*

Advisors

New York, HAMILTON HOLT Copenhagen, HARALD NIELSEN
Stockholm, CARL LAURIN Christiania, CHRISTIAN COLLIN

CONTENTS

FOUNDED BY NIELS POULSON, IN 1911

THE HOLY CITY
JERUSALEM II

By SELMA LAGERLÖF
Translated by Velma Swanston Howard

Recent military events about Palestine add new interest to this latest book, "Jerusalem II," by the distinguished winner of the Nobel Prize. It is a continuation of her already famous epic, "Jerusalem," and yet it is complete in itself.

The religious upheaval that took the Dalecarlians to Jerusalem places them in the colony founded here by the Gordons, Americans. The highest level of this writer's genius is touched in this story of persecution and physical hardship. *Net $1.50.*

The Northland edition, leather. $1.75.

DOUBLEDAY PAGE AND COMPANY
GARDEN CITY, NEW YORK

D. B. UPDIKE
The Merrymount Press
232 SUMMER STREET
BOSTON

. . .

PRINTERS OF FINE BOOKS FOR
BOOK CLUBS, INSTITUTIONS, AND
PRIVATE PERSONS
&c. &c. &c.

The Series of *Scandinavian Classics*, and Hustvedt's "Ballad Criticism" and Hovgaard's "Voyages of the Norsemen," in the *Scandinavian Monographs*, were printed for the American-Scandinavian Foundation by this Press.

If you are looking for color—visit

THE SCANDINAVIAN
ART SHOP

728 MADISON AVENUE
Near 64th Street
NEW YORK

The Shop will move to
Bar Harbor, June 15

Orders for Carl Larsson Nurseries Executed
Painted Furniture for Country Homes
Wool-embroidered Smocks

THE SCANDINAVIAN CLASSICS

Ten per cent. discount to all Associates

Two volumes are sent annually free to Sustaining Associates

"The series is, in its dignified simplicity, a beautiful testimony to a literary solicitude which we hitherto have not been accustomed to associate with modern American culture. . . . This undertaking, which is not in the least forced, but just well done."
—August Brunius in *Svenska Dagbladet.*

If you want to show your American friends the high level of Northern culture, you can do no better than to present them with a set of the SCANDINAVIAN CLASSICS. These books are carefully translated by competent writers. They are printed from hand-set type and handsomely bound in a uniform red cloth edition with gold lettering. No pains have been spared to make them worthy of the great literary works they contain. If you do not wish to order the whole set, you will find each volume complete in itself.

The following nine volumes are now ready:

Comedies by Holberg

Three most characteristic plays by "The Molière of the North," the first great modern in Scandinavian literature.

Poems by Tegnér

"Frithiof's Saga" and other poems by the lyrist who revealed the beauty of Swedish literature to Longfellow.

Poems and Songs by Björnstjerne Björnson

A catechism of Norwegian patriotic ideals.

Master Olof

Strindberg's historical-religious drama, whose hero has been called "as uncompromising at moments as Ibsen's Brand, but more living than he."

The Prose Edda of Snorri Sturluson

Mythical tales of the North written by a master of Old Norse Prose.

J. P. JACOBSEN

Modern Icelandic Plays

"Eyvind of the Hills" and "The Hraun Farm" by Jóhann Sigurjónsson, the young dramatist of Iceland.

Marie Grubbe. A Lady of the Seventeenth Century

The first of J. P. Jacobsen's two great psychological novels.

Arnljot Gelline

In this verse romance Björnson has found the most "daring and tremendous expression for the spirit of Old Norse paganism."

Anthology of Swedish Lyrics

A wonderful array of lyric achievement is revealed in this volume of Swedish verse, from 1750 to 1915, collected and translated by Charles Wharton Stork.

In course of preparation are translations of Heidenstam's *Karolinerna*, Selma Lagerlöf's *Gösta Berling*, and Jonas Lie's *Familien paa Gilje.*

Price, $1.50 each

The Foundation publishes also another series of books: "Scandinavian Monographs"

THE AMERICAN-SCANDINAVIAN FOUNDATION
25 West Forty-fifth Street, New York

CONTRIBUTORS TO THE MAY - JUNE NUMBER

HJALMAR BRANTING has been, throughout the war, the open friend of western democracy, believing the ideals for which the Entente is fighting to be the same as his own. At the beginning of the spring drive he published in *Social-Demokraten* a fervent prayer that Prussian militarism might be again defeated as it was at the Marne. Branting was born in Stockholm in 1860, a member of the intellectual class. He entered the Social-Democratic ranks by way of journalism and, in 1908, was sent to the Riksdag on the Liberal ticket, the first Socialist to enter that body. He has made himself to a remarkable degree the personal leader of the democratic elements in Sweden.

HENRIK WERGELAND was in Norway the moving spirit of the struggle for freedom that shook Europe in the first half of the nineteenth century. He would have gone, like Byron, to fight in Greece if he had had the means, and wrote of England as the "sharp-beaked eagle rising from her foggy nest to aid the Greeks." A visit to Paris, in 1831, fired him with memories of the July revolution of the year before. Though Norway had already achieved political freedom, he set himself the task of liberating his countrymen intellectually and socially. His early death in 1845 cut short many schemes for the betterment of the common people. His occasional didactic vein appears in the verses, "Lowly Are All Thy Ways," while his pure poetic gift is shown in the scintillating fragment, "The Dream Genius Speaks." The translator, Illit Gröndahl, is a Norwegian man of letters living in London.

RAGNA BERGLIOT ESKIL is a young Western writer, an occasional contributor to the REVIEW.

ALBERT ENGSTRÖM is known as a cartoonist as well as a writer. He is the editor of the humorous paper *Strix* in Stockholm and the author of numerous volumes of stories and sketches. Charles Wharton Stork is a frequent contributor of verse translations.

ARNE GARBORG, though much younger than Björnson, Ibsen, and Lie, may be said to belong to the same literary constellation, and is the only one yet writing. He is less widely known, partly because he has chosen the *landsmaal* as a medium for many of his most characteristic works. Among these are the somber stories of religious life among the peasants and the long poem *Haugtussa*, from which we print two fragments. The translator is Miss Thora Grönvold, teacher of Norwegian and English in the high schools of Faribault, Minnesota.

OLIVER A. LINDER is himself a popular writer on Swedish life in America. A collection of short stories and poems by him was published under the title *I Västerland* as the first volume in the series of Swedish-American literature inaugurated by the Augustana Book Concern. Mr. Linder has been in newspaper work for more than thirty years and, as editor of *Svenska Amerikanaren* in Chicago, is one of the foreign-language editors who render America loyal service by interpreting her ideals to those newly arrived.

DR. MAURICE FRANCIS EGAN AND HIS GRANDSON, MASTER FRANCIS O'REILLY

Our American Minister to Denmark Contributes to the Current Number of the *Yale Review* a Sympathetic Article on Scandinavian Ideals and Problems. Writing of Denmark's Hope that England, Russia, and the Moral Force of the United States Would Prevent Her National Extinction, He Closes Thus: "These Hopes Are Gone. Denmark Fed England, She Exported Certain Products to Germany, She Had Made Herself the Foremost Scientific Agricultural Nation of the World, She Was the Freest, She Was Working Out the Ideals of Her National Life Without Desiring to Acquire Territory or to Infringe on the Rights of Others; but the Moment the United States Entered the War, She and the Other Scandinavian Nations Gave up Hope of Any Protection or Help, and They Have Now Determined to Band Together in an Industrial and Economic Union. The World Has Deserted Them, and They Have Determined to Do Their Best to Become Independent of the World."

THE
AMERICAN-SCANDINAVIAN
REVIEW

VOLUME VI   MAY-JUNE · 1918   NUMBER 3

The Forward March of Democracy

By HJALMAR BRANTING

A Speech in the Riksdag when the Conservative Ministry, by Refusing to Consider a Revision of the Constitution, Took the Step that Led to Its Fall

MR. SPEAKER, Gentlemen: The answer we have just heard confirms the rumors, that have been circulating for the last few days to the effect that the Government would refuse to grant the demand formulated in the interpellation, that it should "devote all its power and influence to creating conditions favorable to a revision of the Constitution." In my opinion, it is a matter of regret that the Government has thus missed an opportunity to do a great deed. Its refusal seems based on the mistaken supposition that a revision of the Constitution at the present juncture would tend to divide our people. I am convinced, on the contrary, that it would unite us as nothing else could. It would demonstrate that the party in our country which has often in the past resisted progress is capable of rising above old prejudices and viewing the situation with a wider outlook, an outlook worthy of the great times in which we live.

We supposed, when the interpellation was made, that the Swedish Conservatives would have been sufficiently impressed with the international movement for political equality, which is advancing the world over, to show clearly that they too had learned something from the passing events. We supposed that they would modify their former principles enough to unite with the other parties in seeking a line for the continued progress of our country on the only possible basis, that of democracy.

There is no need of expatiating on that world-wide development from which we too can learn a lesson. I need not dwell on the experiences of our great neighbor in the east, except to say that, whatever her present troubles, one fundamental fact remains: the power of the Czar, that corner-stone of reactionism in Europe, has crumbled in the dust and, in all human likelihood, will never rise again. If we turn to the south, we hear voices there too rising and demanding reforms in tones that will not be denied, and we can hardly conceive of a Germany emerging from a world war the same junker-ridden country that went into it. Similar reports come from Austria; there is discord indeed, but with it a conviction that the future belongs to democracy. As for Hungary, the people are in the midst of a struggle for universal suffrage; the powerful opposition has been broken and has been forced back from the position where it was entrenched before the war. In England, woman suffrage in particular has taken a great forward stride. . . . So we see that democracy is advancing there too.

From a painting by Richard Bergh

HJALMAR BRANTING

It may be said, perhaps, that we cannot compare ourselves with the great belligerent countries, that we small neutral nations have more than enough to cope with in providing the means of our own material subsistence, without thinking of constitutional reforms, now while the world is on fire. But even if we admit that, what are the facts? In the midst of the world war, Denmark has taken whatever steps remained for the complete democratization of a constitution that was democratic even before. There too, the problem of woman suffrage has been solved; there too, the equality of citizens in the elections for both chambers, which we here are putting forward as an uncompromising demand, has been safeguarded. Norway must be counted out, but for the excellent reason that reforms have progressed so far in Norway that there is no immediate reason for direct continuation. In another neutral country, however, in Holland, which in many ways has come in closer touch with us during the war, a truly universal suffrage has been adopted under a system more liberal than that formulated in this country by any party except the Socialists, keeping the franchise entirely distinct from any question of taxes paid or anything of that nature. The movement has been carried through by all parties in full accord and with the support of the Conservatives, who have known how to yield to the imperative demands of the situation.

In view of these facts, it is not too much to say that, in the midst of convulsions more violent than Europe has known for centuries, the nations—and not only the nations but the conservative parties— have felt and sensed that, in order to live and to attain that very unity which our prime minister has pointed to as necessary in these trying times, the antiquated privileges of the ruling classes must be swept away. Such unity can be reached on democratic ground and there alone. This has been realized everywhere, and it is a pity that the Swedish Conservative party, unlike conservative parties in other countries, should put itself on record as not having known the time of its visitation.

Clearly, the present great upheavals have their effect even on the countries not directly involved in them. Issues are raised and become vital in a way that would not have happened but for the tremendous events round about us. We are fully aware that these issues must be met by each country in accordance with its own particular needs and the division of power between its classes. There can be no question of our adopting Russian methods or Russian measures, as we have sometimes been accused of wanting to do. These may be justified and explained by the conditions that gave rise to them, but are not to be followed blindly. We have no intention of patterning ourselves after others, and yet I believe the brief survey I have just made of the forward march of democracy everywhere will bring home forcibly the similarity of conditions in all capitalistic countries. Democracy is coming and can not be downed. It can no more be downed in our country than in others. I am constrained to say it: there is something small in a policy that refuses to recognize and admit this fact. Such a policy sees in the development of a democratic age nothing but the fact that on these points party programmes differ, and one might risk getting "no" for an answer here and there, if one were to venture a bold stroke. This is not the attitude we looked for. We hoped that the mere influence of the times would bring thinking men, even those of a different political complexion from ours, to another viewpoint.

The Government, however, chooses to point to the great tasks for which, as the prime minister again explains, it was formed, namely to uphold an inviolable loyalty to all sides, and to relieve, as far as possible, the daily increasing difficulties that harass our national housekeeping. These are great tasks indeed, and no one can for a moment accuse our party of failing to appreciate their importance or of undervaluing what is really being accomplished in their solution. So long as the loyal co-operation with the Riksdag, which the Government initiated, continues in the same spirit, without concealment of any important measures whatsoever, so long we shall continue to respond with that appreciation for which the prime minister has just expressed a certain amount of gratitude.

But suppose we return to the question which was the subject of the interpellation. What has the Government done about that? Happily the answer is not a mere no. In the first place, it recognizes, in the most unequivocal terms, the paramount importance of these problems. Furthermore, it admits that a constitutional reform is now knocking at our doors and refers the matter to the verdict of the people in the elections.

Herein lie two concessions: firstly, that the question has been put and can not be shoved aside; secondly, that it must be answered by the people. I hope that the verdict of the people will be respected more than it has been on many former occasions; for therein lies the new spirit. Yet there are drawbacks even in this appeal to the elections. The electorate, which is to pronounce the verdict, is decimated by those very restrictions on the franchise which we want to remove, and against which the mass of the people are now aroused. Women are still excluded, and many members of the poorer classes still fall before the numerous limiting clauses that make our so-called universal suffrage unworthy of the name as commonly understood in other parts of the world. Nevertheless, we have ourselves, we willingly admit it, pointed to the decision of the polls. In the closing words of the interpellation, we expressed the hope that the Government would pledge itself to co-operate in a democratic revision of the Constitution in accordance with the will of the people as indicated in the coming elections. There is a connection here, and I will by no means underestimate the importance of the fact that the views of the Government and our views to a certain extent coincide.

All emphasis is now laid on the elections. We hoped that the Government would act sooner, but the Government refers us to the elections. Very well. Then let us meet at the polls, each party with its own banner, its own watchword, its own record. I understand from the answer of the Government that these elections in the autumn of 1917 will be of the utmost significance. The nation will be the judge, and the Government must at least assume the responsibility of seeing to it, as far as possible, that its judgment is respected. The determination of the Government to put the issue to a test can hardly mean anything less than willingness to abide by the decision of the elections in full and complete loyalty.

That is the least; that is the minimum of co-operation. History will hardly call this refusal to take up a task statesmanlike. Yet it is something not to work against progress; it is something not to plant oneself rigidly and obstinately and uncomprehendingly in the way of that which is inevitable. It means at least a pledge not to obstruct the efforts which the rest of us are making to rally the Swedish people around a real solution of the problems that confront us. In that spirit I, for one, would fain read the answer of the Government. The Swedish people will be heard. May it speak so plainly that no misunderstanding and no misconstruction shall be possible for any one, whoever he be, after the people shall have spoken.

Lowly Are All Thy Ways

By Henrik Wergeland

Translated from the Norwegian by Illit Gröndahl

"Lowly are all thy ways and plain!
This gives the proud and purblind pain;
Their life is hidden from them.
Traceless its days do disappear;
Like Jordan to the silent mere,
They toward the grave are flowing,
Nor deed nor honor knowing.

But came to Jordan's silent shore
The World's Redeemer not of yore?
—To Nile or Euphrat' never:
Well then! Let Jesus betake him
To thy life-river's shaded brim—
How well, though softly gliding,
His image there abiding!

Each morning call him! Without fame
Day dawneth not in such a name:
Therein begin thy labor.
'T will have, though without pomp it be,
Greatness enough for Him who'll see
Of things their core and meaning,
Not how they may be gleaming."

Jens Jensen: Landscape Architect

By RAGNA BERGLIOT ESKIL

"IT has the feeling and the spirit of the prairie!" Thus exclaimed a city-weary old prairie pioneer as he gazed at the slow, wandering lagoon in Humboldt Park, with its marshy shores and lily beds, its irregular, ragged banks—rock-jutted here and there—

JENS JENSEN

and its suggestion of the free, languid strength of the prairies he had known in his youth. And so, indeed, Jens Jensen, the designer of "Prairie River," had meant him to feel, as he had meant him to rejoice when he could see again (edging a Chicago boulevard) in a long, uneven, tree-and bush-lined grass lane, the prairie road he had swung along in the young pioneer days.

Jens Jensen, perhaps the leading landscape architect of his sort in the world, is a philosopher and a poet of outdoor planning, besides being an artist in this field. He believes passionately in the right of all people to have a part in nature. His creed is that, in these days of crowded civilization, it is absolutely essential for each individual to be able to get away from his fellows to some free spot of nature where he can get the peace and solitude that will give him soul quietude and soul growth.

There is little formality about Jens Jensen's landscapes. His free and sunny spirit will not be stifled by the established forms of garden conventionality. The only place where he suggests the mathematical symmetry of the continental ideas is in an occasional flower garden, but even then there is a grace and hominess about the scene rarely found in formal garden architecture. Mr. Jensen believes that the feeling of the controlled nature spot should reflect the scenery of the surrounding wild landscape—not copy it, but interpret it. For instance, in a prairie section the spirit of the rolling, flat land should be emphasized; in a mountainous region the spirit of the mountains; in a ridge district the beauty of overlying strata of rock, while a park along the shore of the sea or a large lake should call attention to the majesty and bigness of the water. Every line which he draws on his canvas of living things suggests this. He does not build a lagoon beside an ocean, nor does he simulate mountains in a flat area, nor disregard the rocks in the ridge section of the Blue Mountains. Like the portrait painter, who is able to reflect the soul of his sitter, he catches the soul of the landscape—a living thing to him—and then lets it emanate from his frame of grass and trees and flowers.

Every detail of his gardening carries out this unconventional and true idea. He uses not ornamental, clipped shrubbery, but native trees and hazel-nut brush, wild gooseberries, raspberries, blackberries, grapevines, and whatever else in tree and shrub is at home in that region. The shores of his artificial lakes are not "parky," but, like the "Prairie River," are muddy and marshy and weedy, except where the children are to wade. His walks are not of cement, but of indigenous materials, small pebbles, blocks of stone, or mulled tamarack and cedar bark; sometimes they are just plain "cow-paths" or "deer-trails," and perhaps there is a bit of "corduroy" along some wider road. Rustic bridges of young maple poles cross little streams that trickle and fall in true woodland fashion, and everywhere are easy seats where one may sit until the peace of the scene has encompassed one's soul. Or, if one would be sociable, there are picnic grounds

Jens Jensen, Architect

PRAIRIE RIVER IN HUMBOLDT PARK

and golf links and tennis courts and council fires and concert places and open-air theatres—and, by the way, in these open-air theatres Mr. Jensen believes America's contribution to the world stage will be developed. Even the conservatory in Garfield Park, although it is the largest in the world, has not the stiffness and touch-me-not air usual in greenhouses. The spirit of the tropics is portrayed in this landscape gardening under glass, and one is constantly charmed with the little poetic nooks of seeming fairy arrangement that are revealed at every turn.

This holding to the true, which Jens Jensen shows in his portrayal of nature, he also shows in his dealing with men. "The only really honest big man there's been in Chicago's public service," some one has said of him—which statement, let us hope for Chicago's sake, is an exaggeration. "The graft-fighting Dane," as he has been called, hates dishonesty, and especially the dishonesty that expends itself to the public detriment. With the money and the patronage that have passed through his hands, first as superintendent of Humboldt Park, then as superintendent of Garfield Park, and then as superintendent and architect of the West Parks system, Mr. Jensen, if he had been corruptible, could easily have become an immensely wealthy man. But his undeviating principle, "Never accept any money for influence," and his determination that, as far as he could bring it about, the people were going to get every cent's value out of their park appropriations, drew him into hard conflicts with the grafters who were mulcting the West Park funds, and made his name a headline feature, time after time, in the Chicago papers for some ten or eleven trying years.

His first graft fight was twenty years ago, as superintendent of Humboldt Park, with an interest-protected sidewalk contractor who

Jens Jensen, Architect

A Tangle of Grasses

was attempting to provide cheaper material and work than the specifications called for, and his second was with a combination of coal grafters who were delivering short weights of coal to the heating and power plant of this park, while they charged the city for full-weight loads. This latter, especially, proved a pretty stiff graft to expose, for the influences back of it were some of the most powerful in Chicago, but Mr. Jensen finally managed it, at the personal cost, however, of being ousted from his position. A reform park board that soon came in, though, demanded his reinstatement, and he was made superintendent and landscape artist for the whole extensive West Parks system. But the personnel of this board changed shortly, and the graft machine back of the new members was so strongly entrenched that it even dared try to remove the trained employees of the West Parks and fill their places with its political henchmen. Mr. Jensen, of course, was immediately up in arms against this new move, and after a bitter struggle the merit rule was absolutely established, and the park employees who started in with Mr. Jensen are still there. After that fight—about eight years ago—Mr. Jensen gave up the superintendency and opened a private office, though, fortunately for Chicago, he still retains the position of consulting architect for the West Parks system.

Since leaving the superintendency, Mr. Jensen, besides laying out public parks in smaller cities—Racine, Wisconsin, for instance—designing numerous private estates and university grounds throughout the country, training park superintendents and landscape designers in his own offices, and lecturing before colleges and clubs and associations interested in the out-of-doors, finds a great deal of time to champion the movement for more state and national parks. Especially has he been interested in the park reservations in the Great Lakes commercial region, for his slogan is: "A free spot of nature within the reach of every person." He it was who, some eighteen or nineteen years ago, started the agitation to save the famous sand dunes along the Indiana coast for a national park, so that Chicago and the steel cities could have this near wild spot, and it has been his eager desire to see a school of landscape architecture established on a part of the dunes; for he believes that this unique meeting-place of the plant life of the north and the south, the east and the west, would make an ideal location for a landscape school. Yet his energies have not been confined only to his home territory. Through talks and illustrated lectures he has given of his vigor and his enthusiasm to every public park project in the country, and only last spring he signally aided, by his candid report, the battle which the New York club-women were waging to save Riverside Park from the encroachment of the New York Central interests. Wherever the people's outdoor recreation spots are in danger, Mr. Jensen's militancy for the right may be counted upon.

Mr. Jensen has been in this country only thirty-six years. He was born of Danish parents in Dybböl, Slesvig, close beside the sea, on an estate that had been handed down from father to son for almost four hundred years; and he received his first training in an agricultural school in Jutland, later finishing in the famous *Landbrugskole* near Copenhagen. It need hardly be said that this country—especially Chicago, which scarcely knew then what landscape gardening meant—did not, when he first came, give his unique ideas a very warm welcome. He learned what it meant to go hungry, but he persisted in believing that the work he had set out to do would find a place. He made his entry into the Chicago park system by taking a job as a common laborer, and now he is hailed by both American and European critics as a really great creative landscape architect.

But more than his wonderful gardens, his contribution to this country has been revealing the individual, personal beauty of America to herself, and inspiring in thousands of people a hitherto unrealized appreciation and understanding of nature.

The Dream Genius Speaks

By HENRIK WERGELAND

Translated from the Norwegian by ILLIT GRÖNDAHL

A diamond is my imagination,
Cut thousand-edged; my reason ever
Peers through it as through a kaleidoscope—
Or 'tis a Chinese game which in a thousand
Fresh forms my reason puts—Halloo!
I split asunder easily, arising
A hissing rocket, coming down as ten.
Same time I play upon a sleepy sexton:
Who hears bell-ringing—and upon a grocer:
Forthwith he bacon smells—a maid: she laughs,
Her pillow kissing—then I touch a king:
He struts and feels majestic, seeing that
With phosphorus I paint him, rex, rex, rex!

Isaacson's Death

By ALBERT ENGSTRÖM

Translated from the Swedish by CHARLES WHARTON STORK

IT looked as if old Isaacson would have a hard time to die. The pastor had been with him twice, with an interval of fourteen days, but after each call he brightened up, and lay there giving orders about the care of his garden and observing everything as if nothing was the matter. He began to be actually troublesome.

Like most mariners, Isaacson had been sailing a number of years before he returned to cultivate his native soil, and he did it then like a good fellow. So gradually he developed until he was now the owner of a full half-allotment of land, and of the best boats and fisheries on the island, and had risen to the second rank in the tax assessor's list. But what availed him worldly honor and elevation now that he was to die?

He lay on his bed and groaned and thought over this fact. He thought over other facts too. . He had been a great sinner and a great rascal, both with liquor and with women, white women and black women and yellow women. But when one is away for months at a time from wife and children, and comes into the heat around the line, one can not steer a straight course. God, who permits whatever takes place, had surely also permitted his sinful desires and acts. Though the priest said that it was the evil one who brought all this about! But God at any rate permitted that the evil one should play the mischief with mankind.—All of this kept going around in Isaacson's head. He groaned and wailed, because his sickness was on him again. There was something that pushed from beneath his stomach up against his breast and squeezed his heart, and he thought, as he had thought now for many weeks with each attack: This is surely death that's coming. This time it oppressed him worse than ordinarily, and he rang the cow-bell which had been laid on a chair by the bed.

His wife came in. She was a person of sixty years, sunburnt and wrinkled, sinewy with fishing-work, knotty and bent.

"I think I'm going to have more pain, Johanna! You'd best send after the pastor."

"You're foolish with your pastor. Is he to keep going back and forward like a ninny every time there's something stuck in your gizzard? You'll never die, never. Shall I give you a glass of wine?"

"Yes, give it to me; perhaps then the pain in my breast will ease a little—Thanks, Johanna—Oi! oi! oi!—Aye, but there's something there that ought to be eased—hoho!—hm-hm!—It's hard to die. Ah! I've been a great sinner."

Johanna's face grew dark.   "Oh yes, I heard enough of that when you were confessing.   You were a villain, that you were; were false to me with each and every, though you gave me your promise in church.   But now you have your punishment."

"Did you come and listen when I talked with pastor?   Dev— but it's all the same—Oi! oi! oi!—Give me a glass now!—Thanks, Johanna, you're always kind—oi!—oi!—now death 's a-coming!"

Isaacson's eyes seemed to stare through the roof and the air out into somewhere where his wife could not see.   She became frightened.

"Isaacson dear, don't die, don't die!"

"Give me a glass, that eases me a great deal!—Thanks, Johanna dear.   But now go and tell the children and grandmother to come in, for this time it's serious.   I know it—don't cry, Johanna, it's no use now!"

With apron over her eyes, his wife went out into the kitchen, where the rest of the family were eating their midday meal.   With trembling hand Isaacson put a glass of port wine to his lips.   It was remarkable how much good it did him.   He remembered a certain drinking-orgy in Hamburg—a tavern where the whole crew of the brig *Leontine* drank strong-beer and schnapps.   There was a fight, and Isaacson broke off a coat-hanger and banged the Germans over the head till the police came.   Then he sneaked up a stairway to a girl, who helped him out through a window, and he ran down a dark alley to the harbor and hid in a barge.

Everything stood out clearly in his memory;   all too clearly, he thought, for these were but sinful recollections—he had done nothing good in his life.   Nothing?   Yes, he had tended his garden, and it surely says in the Bible that man shall cultivate and tend his land. That at least he would be able to say when shortly he should stand before the Throne.

But now the kitchen door opened, and grandmother came in first. Grandmother was an old woman of eighty-eight years, little and brown, and twisted, like a pine-tree by the coast.   After grandmother came Alida, the youngest daughter, a round-cheeked girl of twenty; the son Victor, flaxen fair, with down around his lips; and David the man-servant—all with solemnity impressed on their countenances in the form of wrinkled eyebrows.   But Alida sobbed quietly.

Old Isaacson, pale yellow in complexion, lay there on the bed and picked at the coverlet.   The wine had gone to his head, for our Lord is merciful even to those about to die; and he smiled.   He had thought to make a big scene, that was the one thing that supported him now, because his testament was clear and final.   He had made arrangements about his establishment, with the very beginning of his sickness.

"I know I'm beginning to suffer and that it's as good to arrange things first as last. Give me another glass, Johanna!—Thanks, Johanna; it's clean wonderful how it eases my chest. Now there must be a funeral of course. There's two hundred rix-dollars laid aside for it. Heeheehee!—funeral of an old sailor. But there shan't be any funeral with weeping and gnashing of teeth, but with gladness and rejoicing—heeheehee! There shall be clapping of hands and violins, and trilleryfillery-rumtumtollery, for here rests old Isaacson six feet under the earth—fallery—with a fine cross and a verse o' the Psalms and a fir-twig crown on his gallant breast. For pastor said to me according to Holy Writ that no sorrow shall be hereafter, nor either weeping or wailing any more, for behold! the former life has passed away. And afterwards ye shall make a little peep-hole in the grave, so I can get air and look at the stars, for after the Judgment a sailor must take his observations, when he has no soundings. Won't you take a glass of wine too, Johanna? What the devil are you standing and glowering at me for? Don't you see that I'm sick, plague take you? Don't you understand that I'm holding on and keeping up, you snivelers? I remember when old Storm sailed right up to the shore with his sloop and jumped down onto the beach and said to the owners: 'Here's your damned boat!' I was only a younker then, but devil take me if I didn't understand him. For now I lay to on the shore of Eternity and say: 'Here's your boat! Battered it is, and the rudder's away, and the keel's gone; the heart in my carcass has no captain left, 'tis foul and cracked and sinful; but the flag's flying, anyhow.' What does the Lord say then? Why, our Lord takes me under the arms and says: 'Thanks, old Isaacson, that you came to land right here by me!' And then there come angels with whisky and brandy—and beer—and wings like new-washed sails, and then they carry me to—to—Table Bay and Zanzibar and Singapore—and—and—then come—sharks—and yellow devils—and wine—and—"

Isaacson had fallen asleep.

Grandmother's eyes stood out, because she hadn't heard so much sinfulness in a long time. Johanna's look was unfathomable, but the hired man said: "Devil's in me if the master doesn't get well!"

The day after, Isaacson sat up in bed, weak and sallow, and wanted meat soup. A week later he got on his cloak and examined the farmyard. After a month he was Isaacson again.

People said that Isaacson would never die. But he died. Next time I shall describe his funeral, pretty much as I was told about it.

Drawing by Helen Peale Jacobs

Current Illustrations

THE POSSIBILITIES OF THE 'CELLO AS A SOLO INSTRUMENT ARE REVEALED BY HERMAN SANDBY, WHO RECENTLY DELIGHTED A NEW YORK AUDIENCE WITH A RECITAL INCLUDING WORKS OF SIBELIUS AND ARRANGEMENTS OF SCANDINAVIAN FOLK SONGS. IN KANSAS CITY SANDBY PLAYED THE SOLO PARTS IN THE PERFORMANCE OF HIS OWN WORKS BY THE KANSAS SYMPHONY ORCHESTRA, CONDUCTED BY ANOTHER DANISH ARTIST, CARL BUSCH.

WHEN ELSA UELAND TOOK THE PRESIDENCY OF CARSON COLLEGE FOR ORPHAN GIRLS IN PHILADELPHIA, SHE DECLARED HER PURPOSE OF GIVING HER PUPILS "THE JOY OF LIFE AND THE JOY OF WORK." OUR YOUNGEST COLLEGE PRESIDENT IS A MINNEAPOLIS GIRL OF NORWEGIAN STOCK, THE GRANDDAUGHTER OF THE FAMOUS PEASANT-POLITICIAN, JOHAN GABRIEL UELAND

Courtesy of "Every Week"

Courtesy of Architecture

Poster by Jonas Lie

THE ACCIDENT OF WAR BRINGS TWO GREAT NORWEGIAN EXPLORERS HERE AT THE SAME TIME: NANSEN, PERHAPS THE GREATEST LIVING EXPONENT OF NEUTRAL RIGHTS AND DUTIES; AMUNDSEN, A CITIZEN OF THE WORLD, PROTESTING AGAINST GERMANY'S OUTRAGES ON THE SEA. AS THE GUEST OF OUR GOVERNMENT, HE LECTURED THROUGHOUT THE COUNTRY. THREE THOUSAND PEOPLE HEARD HIM AT THE MEETING IN THE CENTURY THEATER, NEW YORK, ARRANGED UNDER THE CHAIRMANSHIP OF MR. EDWIN OLAF HOLTER

A Class at Gustavus Adolphus, the First American College to Introduce the Ling System, Now Used in the American Navy, and the Instructor of the Class, William Söderlund

Mr. Söderlund's Corps of Boy Scouts in the City of St. Peter Serves as a Practice School for the Gymnastics Class in the Normal Department at Gustavus Adolphus

Two Fragments from Haugtussa

By ARNE GARBORG

Translated from the Norwegian by THORA GRÖNVOLD

I

INTRODUCTION

To you, you hills and marshes pale
At dawn of day,
You mountains strong, where great birds sail,
I sing my lay.

To you, you heather, brown and sere,
Where dreams abound,
I sing, when eve and dawn appear,
Of life unfound.

I know you well, you Troll-home grey;
At somber night,
I dream in fear, then must alway
Watch for your flight.

I know you well, your wild unrest,
Relentless sea;
You oft strike terror in my breast
And misery.

I know the struggle vain and grim
'Gainst Berg-troll's gloom.
God save us all from shattered limb
And pitfall's doom!

I know you well, I know your dread,
Who conquered stand:
I see your strife, the path you tread
Through Shadow-land.

I, too, have fought that struggle black
For many years,
With spirit strong, but breaking back
And heart-wounds fierce.

You hover near, you needs must stay,
Poor broken soul.
You tear my flesh to break away
And reach your goal.

I know full well the struggle vain
'Gainst torrent's will;

The boat o'erturned, a minor strain—
Then all is still.

A lark sings out from greening tree
A conqueror's song.
The wind sweeps from a dark-blue sea
Full fresh and strong.

And e'en though with us sorrows stay,
And weakling Fear,
We must believe the lark's sweet lay:
That Spring is here!

II

AT SET OF SUN

From out the sea appears a fairy-land
  With hills and trees.
'Tis pictured clear against a heavenly strand
  In night-blue peace.

Oft have I seen it veiled in golden foam
  O'er yon grey beach.
It is the shrine of peace, celestial home,
  We strain to reach.

The shimmering mountain-peaks are held in charm
  Of captive sleep,
Till, kindled by the sunset's fiery arm,
  To flames they leap.

When day sinks down in molten golden fire
  In marshy dales,
There springs to life a land of light and lyre
  And fairy-tales.

The evening landscape evanescent shines
  In magic old.
Like silver glows the air; then amber wines;
  Then rose; then gold.

But soon the splendor pales; the fairy-land
  With hills and trees
Again stands clear against the heavenly strand,
  In night-blue peace.

As wearily the path of life I tread,
  I fain would run
To reach that land which ever on has sped
  At set of sun.

Writers of Swedish Life in America

By Oliver A. Linder

THAT the Swede in this country becomes too quickly American-
ized is an assertion commonly made, though perhaps not war-
ranted by an earnest and intelligent survey of the facts. It is
claimed that he is prone to discard all the manners and customs that
were his by virtue of heritage and upbringing, but even though we
assume this to be true, I am not sure that it can be called a fault; it is
at most a virtuous resolution carried out too literally. For if the Swede
comes to this country with the conscious purpose of carving out his
future here, of building himself a home, and making America his own
country and that of his children, the all-important problem of "making good" demands that the change should be effected in him as soon
as possible. Yet the question has another side, which I would ask
you to consider.

The Swede in America, though he is not so clannish as some other
racial groups, has strong social instincts that lead him to seek out his
countrymen. He will walk many miles to hear the old Swedish melodies
fiddled or sung, and will announce his approval by a deafening clapping with his monstrous hands. Swedish singing societies are found in
almost any city with enough Swedish inhabitants to form a quartette,
and the typical Swede will insist on celebrating Midsummer with a
dance around the May-pole. In these short hours he will lay aside
all that smacks of the new and enjoy the old to his heart's content.
While in this mood, he is little else than a Swede, and if any one
should fling an insult at the beautiful blue and yellow flag that flut-
ters merrily in the summer breeze above his head, he would fight for
its honor as lustily as he would huzza for Uncle Sam's red, white, and
blue that floats at its side. He is also inclined to eat *lutfisk* and
risgryngröt on Christmas Eve and to attend *julotta* in the morning, as
he did at home. These customs cling to him a long time, often for
life.

Yet all the time he is steadily Americanizing himself, even to the
extent of preferring to speak his broken English instead of his mother
tongue. Not that he is ashamed of his own language, but rather he is
eager, in his awkward way, to learn the new, which he feels is the key
to success. He does not attempt to found a new Sweden on American
soil. He came here because America was different from his native
land, and he is sometimes so conscious of this difference that he fails
to give due recognition to what he left behind. He determines to
like this country, and he does like it. He makes the wise decision
of adapting himself to the bride with whom he expects to spend a
lifetime, even though he may be compelled to disregard some of the

nice things his old mother would have liked in him, and herein he is
in perfect accord with the teachings of the Good Old Book itself.

Now and then we do find small communities where the Swedish
element dominates, and here we may instantly recognize a spirit
distinct from the American spirit, though by no means hostile to it.
For a while, the whole community has a Swedish color and character,
but this is likely to pass when the second generation becomes dominant. The Swede does not cling so tenaciously to the customs and
modes of his old country as do many other immigrants. In consequence, there is but little of what might be called Swedish-American
folk-life, and herein lies the explanation of the fact, so often brought
forward, that stories dealing with the life of Swedes in America lack
background. There is no atmosphere of environment to make the
figures stand out.

If I have succeeded in setting forth effects in their relation to
causes, I may perhaps be pardoned for this otherwise inexcusably
long introduction, in which I have tried to make plain that the Swede
in America does not yield the same rich store of material for the
novelist as does the immigrant of almost any other nationality.

He has, however, been made the theme for fictional treatment
by a number of writers. Greatest in volume, but least in value and
significance, is that produced in Sweden by persons who have lived
in this country for longer or shorter periods, sometimes for years,
sometimes only for months. On coming back to the old country,
they find only too ready a market for stories "knocking" America,
and so they fall easy victims to the temptation of writing their own
experiences and observations on this side of the big water. As a
rule, they have done this with no understanding of that which they
were not interested in, and with little sympathy for that which they
did not understand.

Thus Henning Berger has devoted his undeniable talents to creating in the mind of his readers an impression of America as a place
full of snares and pitfalls in which the Swede will, sooner or later, be
lost. On reading his stories of Chicago—where all his American characters live and move—one might believe that the Swedes in that city
were a conglomeration of cheap adventurers, half-starved frequenters
of low Bohemia, and sheepish fatalists—failures in every respect.
During the half dozen years he lived here, Berger saw no other phase
of their lives than the sorry plight of a few men and women whose
souls were dead, either from exposure or voluntary self-destruction.
He has no desire to tell the truth, nor does he know the truth.

Hilma Angered-Strandberg is another talented writer of fiction
who has drawn on the experiences and observations of a few years
in America for stories pretending to be descriptive of life among the
Swedes. Like Berger, she has rather a narrow horizon, which tends

to a short perspective and limited types. *På prärien* ("On the Prairie"), her earliest American story, caused a sensation and not a little scandal, when first published, because of its pretended description of life at one of the Swedish-American colleges. Several well-known and highly respected persons yet living were grossly caricatured in her book and ridiculed for their American ways. The story was, at most, founded on second-hand gossip. Neither in *På prärien* nor in any of her later works does this author even attempt to portray the Swedish-American in the making. That which is common does not interest her; that which does not sicken through utter wretchedness, or compel momentary attention by gaudy emptiness, seems to her dull and draws from her contempt and derision rather than an even superficial pity.

A few others, such as J. L. Stockenstrand, Ernst Lindblom, Ernst Berg, and Alfred Kämpe, have made attempts at picturing life among the Swedes in America, but they do not get much beyond the outlines, and moreover they have sometimes eked out their limited material by drawing on their imagination, which provides a poor substitute.

Now, any one who is to give a true and intimate picture of the soul of a nation or of any stratum in a nation must be one with what he describes to the extent that he feels, or at least possesses memories of having felt, the same glorious joy of victory, the same despairing sadness over the grave of dead hopes, the same momentary weakness or daring defiance; he must have fallen before the same temptations and bravely crawled back into line again in the same way as the men and women he portrays. He must have been a part of what he depicts, must not only have observed it, but felt it.

There are perhaps only two or three writers that stand out distinctly as giving a searching and intimately true picture of Swedish life in America. They are Gustaf N. Malm, Johan Person, and Anna Olsson. Person has been more prolific than the other two and has undoubtedly a firmer grip on his material, but in spite of that, I am inclined to place Malm at the head, on account of his deeper understanding and wider sympathy. When his *Charli Johnson* came out, in 1909, he was quite unknown even to those who keep abreast of productions in this field. There were evident crudities in the book; the picture was often crowded with unessential details, and the tendency to sermonize made itself too strongly felt. Yet the reader willingly overlooked these common faults of the beginner for the refreshing directness, the keen obervation and pleasant good humor, and the ardent, at times exalted, enthusiasm for the true and noble, and the hatred of everything bad and small and mean that breathed from his pages.

The conviction was borne in on us, as we smiled and wept and cursed with his heroes and heroines, that this was real life. It is true that here and there some purist would sneer at the broken Swedish Malm put in the mouth of his characters, but this dialect was neither manufactured, nor was it used for the purpose of ridiculing, as other authors have done. It was simply the mixture of Swedish and English which is as natural to the farmer of Nebraska or Kansas as his blue overalls. Without it, the picture would have been incomplete.

In the years since the appearance of *Charli Johnson*, Malm has written a number of short stories and has developed, in this field, a great strength of expression as well as delicacy of feeling. He knows the Swedes of the prairie states in the Middle West through and through. An instance of this type was the Christmas story *Peace and Good Will* which appeared in the Yule Number of the AMERICAN-SCANDINAVIAN REVIEW, in 1915, having been awarded the first prize in a contest arranged by the magazine.

In temperament there is every possible difference between Malm and Johan Person. Person deals preferably with the Swedes of the cities, while Malm devotes himself to those who live in the country. *I Svensk-Amerika*, a collection of short stories, published in 1900, contains much of the best of Person's work. He pays more attention than in his later stories to the environment in its influence upon the phenomena of change in his countrymen. He was then yet too close to his own experience not to look on their struggles with sympathy, and, side by side with his wholesome humor, there ran a vein of true pathos.

The years have brought a decided change in his point of view. There has crept into his style a satirical note, which sometimes borders on contempt and aversion. He has not much love for the men and women of whom he writes; he waxes sarcastic over their failures, caricatures their weaknesses, and heaps high-brow ridicule on their childish pride in what is sometimes very small achievement. His sympathies have dwindled, and in their place has come a supercilious attitude. Meanwhile he has perfected his technique; he sees clearly even to the smallest detail, and his style has gained distinction. His collection of essays, *Svensk-Amerikanska Studier*, published in 1912, gives an excellent bird's-eye view of the Swede in America, and will probably have lasting value as the best serious book of its kind.

Wilhelm Berger has written half a dozen or more volumes of short stories and, recently, a collection of articles called *Svensk-Amerikanska Meditationer*. He writes along the same general lines as Person, covering some phases of his subject more thoroughly, but neglecting others. His field of observation is more narrow, but within it he seems to have come in closer contact. His short stories, however, lack atmosphere; what happens in them could have happened anywhere. There is a little more satisfaction to be gained from C. W.

Andeer's *Augustana-folk*.   These stories are told without much pretension to art, but they bring into clear view the life in Swedish Lutheran parishes throughout the farming districts of the northwestern states.

A sharply defined individuality meets us in the short stories of Anna Olsson.   They have keen observation, kindly feeling, a style with an intuitive sureness in essentials, and a rich, bubbling humor. If there is hidden a sting, you prefer to laugh it off.   This author has for some reason, which no one is inclined to accept, confined herself to an illogically narrow field—the immigrants from a single province, Värmland—and, in spite of their good qualities, her stories tend to produce a feeling of monotony.

Quite recently, however, a book came from her pen in which she breaks away from these self-imposed limitations.   *En prärieunges funderinger* describes the musings of a curious, wide-eyed child, as she toddles among the farmer-folk of the little Kansas town where her father was a pastor.   In a few passages here and there the writer succeeds in creating impressions of scenes and conditions with picturesque vividness, although this, of course, is not her predominant aim.

Ernst Skarstedt is not a writer of fiction, but has, in his way, contributed largely to our knowledge of life among the Swedes in America.   Besides his series of books dealing with the biographical history of his countrymen on the Pacific slope, he has written *Vagabond och redaktör*, in which he details his own experiences as a newcomer and in many years of roving.   He is a keen observer, but a poor psychologist, and it is a good thing, therefore, that he generally leaves the interpretation to the reader.   The last-named book, where it is not controversial, is a rich source of intimate details revealing Swedish life in America.

There is then, quantitatively, but little written of Swedish life in America for reasons that I have tried to make clear in the beginning of this article.   If I am right, it serves also to explain why no American author has gone to the Swedish-Americans for material, the only exception, so far as I am informed, being Willa Sibert Cather.   In *O Pioneers*, as well as *The Song of the Lark*, the chief characters are Swedish immigrants and their sons and daughters, who are pictured with truth to life and without any attempt at overdrawing.

The Chicago Norwegian Club

ON July 4, 1917, the Chicago Norwegian Club celebrated Independence Day by opening its distinctive new club-house on North Kedzie Boulevard, with a performance of Hostrup's old comedy,"Gjenboerne." Thus fittingly did it initiate its enlarged opportunity to take a leading part in the cultural and social life of the

Norwegians in Chicago. In late September, it entertained the important Congress of American and Canadian Engineers and Architects of Norwegian birth or descent, which convened in Chicago at the club's invitation. Its future plans contemplate the holding of art exhibitions by Norwegian artists, concerts, plays, lectures, and the entertainment of prominent visiting Scandinavians.

The new club-house is rarely beautiful and individual among Scandinavian clubs in this country, with its reminiscent note of Norse patterns. The architects, Joachim C. Giaver and Frederick P. Dinkelberg, have succeeded in carrying out, in brick construction, the Norwegianized château style; and the interior decorations, too, are of characteristically Norse flavor. The auditorium on the first floor, with its white raftered ceiling, reminds one of the halls in Norway, and the oak beams and consoles in dragon design of the roomy club-room on the second floor, the huge "peis," planned by Christian Boggers, and the unique iron chandeliers and the wall lights, the work of Emil Björn, suggest an older period. A little nucleus of paintings by Norwegian artists already adorn the walls. The whole atmosphere of the club is of cheeriness and Northland hospitable comfort, and a fine sense of good taste in the ornamentation and conduct.

The present Chicago Norwegian Club dates back only from 1911, when it was formed by the union of the venerable Norwegian Quartette Club and the old Norwegian Club. Its membership now is about two hundred and eighty.

Editorial

Loyal Swedes It is an absurd injustice based on individual exceptions to judge Americans of Swedish descent apathetic toward the war. The first death in Pershing's Expedition was that of a Swedish-American. The descendants of the soldiers who heard the call of freedom in the seventeenth century and followed the leadership of Gustaf Adolf across the battlefields of Germany will be found, in whatever land they live in, the most eager defenders of constitutional democracy. Almost overnight there has grown up a spontaneously organized council of Swedish-American defence called "The John Ericsson League of Patriotic Service." Judge Harry Olson of Chicago is president of the League. Its headquarters are likewise in Chicago, in Room 1347, Conway Building, at the corner of La Salle and Washington Streets, with Mr. Werner Melinder as managing secretary. Collector of Customs Harry A. Lund is president of the Minnesota District Council, and Professor Alfred J. Pearson of the State Council of Iowa. Strong district and local committees are being formed at various points from New York to San Francisco. The League will work through other agencies and promote and coördinate the numerous patriotic activities among Swedes throughout the country. The formation of the League is due to the vision and energetic initiative over a period of many weeks of its general secretary, Mr. Edwin Björkman, the author, director of the Scandinavian Bureau of the National Committee on Public Information. It may be regretted that the name of John Ericsson has again been multiplied by this organization. There are other Swedish-American names that conjure up democratic images: John Morton, for example, who cast the deciding vote for the Declaration of Independence; John Hanson, first President of Congress and the United States after the adoption of the Articles of Federation. But in times of national emergency, Ericsson stands forth as the man who offered Lincoln not only his Swedish inventive genius, but his life if need be, in the cause of freedom.

The "Sons" to the Rescue Knute Nelson raised a quick stir of applause at the mass meeting in New York, on March 16, when he spoke of the Scandinavians flocking to our colors. In introducing Captain Roald Amundsen, the venerable senator said: "Wait till the casualty lists come in, and you will see the Johnsons, the Knudsens, the Larsens, the Nelsons, and the Amundsens taking their place with the rest." Scandinavians are loyal beyond question, and they will soon be tied even more closely to their adopted country by the common bond of sacrifices made and trials faced.

Norway's At this writing, the trade agreement between our
Plight government and that of Norway is not ratified, as
exception has been taken to certain clauses in the
proposed compromise. The delay is most unfortunate for Norway.
It ought to be clearly understood that the agreement, even if ratified,
in no way guarantees that Norway will receive anything whatsoever.
It means simply that the blockade is lifted to the extent of permitting
the Norwegians to buy food wherever they can and bring it home as
best they can. But every week that passes sees a tightening of the
world's markets. Australia and Argentina are under Allied control;
our own crops are needed for ourselves and our Allies, and it is understood that no American wheat can be spared for the Northern neutrals. Meanwhile the Norwegians are living on the scantiest possible
rations of bread that is said to "look like sand and taste worse,"
with the prospect that even this will be at an end before summer is
over. Our government has shown its good-will by releasing a certain
amount of petroleum, drugs, and coffee for shipment to Norway, but
the main issue of staple food remains unsettled.

An especially unfortunate feature of the embargo is the hindrance
it places in the way of the Norwegians helping themselves. In order
to carry out their plans for increasing their tilled acreage, they need
motor machinery to take the place of the work-horses killed for lack
of fodder, benzine to run the machines, and phosphates and potash
to be used with their own Norway saltpeter for fertilizing. One hundred and fifty motor plows purchased by their government and
urgently wanted in the spring plowing are being held here, while
shipments of seed and fertilizers are, of course, also delayed. We
hope some means will soon be found to aid this friendly neutral—a
neutral which, in the words of one prominent Norwegian, is "more
anti-German than America itself."

Class War Since our last issue appeared, that which we feared for
in Finland Finland has happened; to the horrors of civil war has
been added the even more sinister menace of German
occupation. It is difficult to apportion the blame. The situation
in Finland presents some of the same irreconcilable elements as that
in Ireland. Only so long as they were united by fear of Russia, could
the Svekomans and the Fennomans act together; that fear removed,
they fell apart. It is fair to remember that Finland's small Swedish
population has been, not only the bearer of culture, but also the
political backbone of the country, and that it deserves the chief credit
for having preserved the forms of self-government, so that Finland
stood ready to take her place among the constitutional democracies
of the world. Judge Svinhufvud was named as the president of the
new Finnish republic, and we have no conclusive evidence that the

White government was thinking of calling in a German prince; in fact, the rumor has been denied in the strongest terms. When the Red revolution broke out, and unspeakable atrocities were perpetrated by the Russian soldiers and Finnish "Hooligans," the Whites looked to Sweden for aid, but the Swedish government, very properly, refused, on the grounds that such a step would involve not only Sweden, but Norway and Denmark, in the world war. The Whites then turned to Germany. It appears that at any rate the first troops sent from Germany were not regulars, but members of the old Finnish battalion with some German volunteers.

The Reds, on their side, claim that they represent the real Finnish people and dispute the legality of the election by which the Whites secured a majority. They protest against being identified with the "Hooligans" who have joined them and retort on the Whites by accusing them too of committing cruel acts. They assert that their opponents have sold themselves to Germany, and that the small upper class does not really desire an independent Finland, since it would be hopelessly outvoted and therefore would much prefer to be under Germany or Sweden.

The Reds have been recruited largely from the laboring men of the cities. The Whites include the property-owning classes, the intellectuals—among them the poet Bertel Gripenberg and the artist Gallén-Kallela—many Socialists, and a large part of the peasantry. In Norway and Sweden, the Syndicalists and Left Socialists, who are under the influence of Bolshevik ideas, have expressed their sympathy with the Reds, while moderate Socialists like Branting have repudiated them.

THE BALTIC   The bear's paw, which has been the terror of Sweden for centuries, is withdrawn, and in its place has come the mailed fist. Every schoolboy in Sweden knows that the Baltic provinces, now taken by Germany, contain cities associated with the proudest victories in Swedish history. When the Baltic was a Swedish lake, the land on which Petrograd now stands belonged to Sweden; Finland and Åland remained Swedish till 1809. The Russian colossus, increasing at the rate of 140 square kilometers a day for four hundred years, has pushed Sweden back so far that no further encroachment is possible without touching land that has been Swedish since prehistoric times. But the face of the Baltic is suddenly changed. The Russian colossus has fallen to pieces, and with it the last shred of an excuse for pro-Germanism has vanished. The German clutch on the Baltic provinces, on Finland, and Åland is a new menace more grim than the old. It should drive Sweden to a closer alliance with the Western powers and particularly with Denmark and Norway.

CONSERVING HISTORICAL MATERIAL A remarkable old journal, written by Ole Nattestad, the first Norwegian settler in Wisconsin, and printed in Norway in 1839, has recently been presented to the State Historical Society in Wisconsin. This is said to be the only copy of the book extant; its loss would have been irretrievable. The case suggests the need of a nation-wide organized effort to collect and preserve the hundreds of other documents, printed or in manuscript, that bear on the history of Scandinavians in America. Not only is there danger that much invaluable material shall be lost, but the investigator at present is baffled and discouraged by the difficulty of using materials scattered all over the country and often imperfectly catalogued.

Fortunately this important work has been taken in hand by an organization which is, in every way, equipped to carry it out successfully, namely the Minnesota Historical Society. A splendid fireproof building has just been erected in St. Paul by the State, for the purpose of the Society. The superintendent, Dr. Justus Solon Buck, has announced that the organization will specialize in building up a library of Scandinavian-American material. As a nucleus it has acquired, through the coöperation of the University of Minnesota, an extensive private collection of pamphlets, books, newspapers, and periodicals, formerly the property of Mr. O. N. Nelson. This has been arranged and catalogued and will be put in charge of a trained librarian familiar with the languages and history of Scandinavia. The Society ought to have the coöperation of all who possess or know of any old documents that will add to our knowledge of Scandinavian history in America.

NONSENSE The ignorance of Americans in regard to the Northern countries is greatly exaggerated by Scandinavian visitors to our shores. We hear from them the story of the American debutante who had a Great Dane dog but did not realize that Hamlet was a Dane, and the anecdote about the clerk in the State Department who addressed a packet to "Christiania, Sweden." Do these stock examples indicate more than that the layer of geographical knowledge is thin the world over, and that one searching for it must go a little deeper than ballroom belles and office boys? One who scans our newspapers during the war receives daily conviction from the mass of short cablegrams and long Sunday stories that Scandinavia is very much upon our political map. Among the college, literary, artistic, scientific, and tourist professions you will often discover really subtle valuations of the intellectual offerings which are the chief contribution of the Northern countries. At this writing, the weekly magazines are spread before us. In one of them, *The Nation,* a journal of only a few pages, we see at least three pertinent passages. The first is an editorial about Sweden's lost Baltic provinces.   The second is an appreciative note about a recent book by Professor Christopher Nyrop of the University of Copenhagen entitled *Is War Civilization?* The third is a long review of Ibsen's *The Wild Duck* on the New York stage.

HOLBERG THE
ENGLISH MIND
The Norwegian Holberg scholar, Viljam Olsvig, spent several weeks this spring as a tourist in America.   The sum impression to be derived from Mr. Olsvig's life researches in Holbergiana is that Holberg was in spirit an Englishman.   That the influences of his student residence at Oxford are not more obvious in his works may be explained by the argument that this world genius was not the imitator but the peer of the Englishmen with whom his creative mind associated.   His fresh, forward-looking English ideals wrestled with the gloomy tradition-worship of German thought.   He opened up the windows of Denmark and Norway and gave their sombre schoolrooms a Western exposure.   Is not Holberg, like Shakespeare, as much an historical epoch as an author—the purest spiritual force in the North in the eighteenth century?   He who has been named "The Molière of Denmark" may some day be rechristened *The Englishman of Scandinavia.*

THE REVIEW
The Friendly Aid Campaign officially closed on March 30.   It is hoped that the late returns now rapidly coming in will round out the full number of 4,000 new associate subscribers and enable us to report complete success in our next number.

The editors have in preparation numerous articles of vital interest, among them: a constructive essay pointing out the possibilities for American trade with the North after the war; a presentation of both sides in the Finnish struggle; an analysis of the Young Socialists in Scandinavia and their part in a world-wide movement; an interpretation of Holberg as an intellectual link between Scandinavia and England in his time.   A South Jutland Number is being prepared by authorities in Europe.   The National Service Number will be what its name implies—a record of service, primarily of that rendered America by citizens of Scandinavian blood.

A later issue will contain an account of the very successful lectures and other work of the president of the Foundation, Professor Schofield, in the "Scandinavian states" of the Middle West, where he is spending the spring months.   Local societies of the Associates of the Foundation have been formed in Galesburg and Rockford, Illinois, and in Beloit, Wisconsin.   A strong Wisconsin Council of the Foundation is to be organized at Madison.

Current Events

Norway

¶ The split in the Socialist party is deepening under the influence of the proletarian upheaval in Russia and Finland. It is estimated that about one-half of organized labor belongs to the radical wing which is led by Martin Tranmael and has for its organ *Klassekampen* ("Class War"), edited by Eugene Olaussen. Its programme calls for the confiscation of all food, the cessation of military drill, the closing of all industries not manufacturing the necessities of life, and the regulation of export and production by means of labor councils to be appointed by the various unions. ¶ *Socialdemokraten* warns its followers, the regular Socialists, against this form of labor dictatorship. Since no regulation or confiscation can create food out of nothing, it would only lead to the discredit of the Socialist party and very likely to its defeat at the polls in the autumn elections. ¶ Living conditions in Norway furnish a sinister background for the prophets of revolution. Expenses have risen on an average 110 per cent. since 1914. The reduced rations in force since the end of March allow each person 150 grams or about a pound and a half per day of breadstuffs, including flour, cereals, rice, beans, and peas. Some addition is made for those who do manual labor. It should be remembered that, even in normal times when meat is obtainable, Scandinavians are not meat-eaters, and that fresh vegetables are also scarce in northern latitudes. The workingmen, in particular, depend upon bread and butter with tea and coffee for at least two of their three meals. Now coffee is doled out in rations giving about one cup per day, while tea is almost unknown. For butter there is oleomargarine made of fish or whale oil. White bread is obtainable only upon the prescription of a physician. ¶ The Christiania Steel Works have secured government support for the establishment of a rolling-mill for the manufacture of steel plates to be used in ship-building and other industries. At the beginning of the new year, 125 ships were being constructed in Norwegian shipyards, and 98 others were contracted for. Most of these, however, were of wood, and averaged only about 240 tons. The construction of larger steel ships will be begun as soon as plates can be procured from Sweden or by home manufacture. ¶ The nickel works at Ringerike have been obliged to close for lack of fuel and will probably not be reopened during the war. The much larger nickel refining plant at Christiansand has not yet been put in operation since it was partly destroyed by fire. The manufacturers expect a government embargo on nickel. ¶ The rebuilding of the burned district in Bergen is proceeding very slowly.

Denmark

¶ Denmark's new liberal constitution goes into effect with the general elections which have been announced for April and May. The Radical Zahle ministry has been in power since June, 1913, a longer time than any other Danish government except the notorious Estrup cabinet, which held office for nineteen years during the reign of Christian IX. In order to avoid a change of policy during the war, and yet insure a representation of all parties, three ministers without portfolio were appointed in August, 1916. They were Christensen, Liberal; Rottböl, Conservative; and Stauning, Socialist. The resignation of the two first-named means that the truce is ended, and the parties are ready for a trial of strength at the polls. ¶ The cessation of imports of raw materials from America and England has resulted in the closing of many factories. Efforts are made to relieve the sufferings of the unemployed by direct pecuniary help from the state and commune, amounting sometimes to as much as three-fourths of the usual wages. Large agricultural and building enterprises have been started both by the government and through private initiative in order to provide as many as possible with work. Several of the leading banks have together guaranteed the sum of 30,000,000 kroner as a loan to the communes for this purpose. In spite of all efforts, there were in January 40,000 persons out of work, 18,000 of these in Copenhagen. ¶ The situation has been used by the Syndicalists as an occasion for demonstrations against the government, the property-holding classes, and the "bourgeois" element of the Socialist party, which they accuse of being in league with the oppressors. A demonstration on January 29 was comparatively peaceful, though large numbers of unemployed took part. A more serious riot followed on February 11, when the mob broke into the stock exchange building, attacking the members, and smashing furniture and windows. The rioters were driven away after a pitched battle with the police. Among those arrested was Chr. Christensen, the editor of the Syndicalist organ, *Solidaritet*. The riots were the worst Copenhagen has experienced in the memory of men now living. In many of the cities of the provinces similar demonstrations took place. ¶ The cheap, well-cooked dinners of the communal kitchen in Copenhagen have proved so popular that the kitchen is being enlarged to serve 24,000 portions daily. ¶ The city of Copenhagen has spent over 25,000,-000 kroner for special poor relief in 1917. ¶ The East-Asiatic Company earned the gratitude of people in Denmark by sending the Diesel motor ship *Fionia* to Copenhagen with a load of delicacies from the Orient, including tea, sago, and rice, which were sold at prices barely covering the expense of transportation. It was meant for a Christmas ship, but was delayed till January.

Sweden

❧ Early in February a small squadron under Commodore Åkerhjelm was sent to Mäntyluoto in Finland and returned crowded with refugees. Danes and Norwegians, as well as Swedes, were transported free of charge by the Swedish government. Naturally, the tales of horror they told increased the excitement in Stockholm, where many of the victims were well known. Even so pronounced a pacifist as Ellen Key was among those who petitioned the Swedish government for intervention. The extreme or Left Socialists, on the other hand, looked on the struggle as a part of the world-wide proletarian revolt against the oppressors' class and threatened a general strike if the government departed from its policy of "hands off" in Finland. In reply to their interpellation in the Riksdag, Prime Minister Edén stated that the government would refrain from armed intervention, and would continue to prohibit the exportation of or transit trade in arms across the border as well as the formation of auxiliary troops on Swedish soil. It would not, however, place obstacles in the way of individuals who wished to join the White Guard. ❧ A deputation from Åland, consisting of five members, headed by the mayor of Mariehamn, the only city in the archipelago, waited on King Gustaf, on February 2, with a monster petition signed by 7,000 people, begging to be taken back into the kingdom of Sweden. The king made a cautious reply to the effect that he hoped the matter could be amicably settled with a free Finland. ❧ The inhabitants of Åland had suffered so much from the cruelties perpetrated by the two thousand Russian soldiers, who were running wild over the islands, that the Swedish government finally decided to send a small police force to defend the helpless people. The expedition was authorized by the Riksdag against fifteen votes, representing, no doubt, the Left Socialist group, and the time limit of the occupation was set as March, 1919. In spite of the effective policing by Swedish troops, the Germans have now seized the islands without heeding the protests from Stockholm. The matter has caused both anger and apprehension in Sweden. Branting, according to an interview in the Paris *Temps*, warns his countrymen that Germany may possibly intend to offer them the islands on conditions that it would be dangerous to accept. He adds that Sweden will never consent to an alliance with the group of Baltic states under German influence. ❧ The speech from the throne at the opening of the Riksdag was remarkable chiefly for its frank acceptance of the coming revision of the constitution. The king spoke of the present times of stress as an incentive to "strengthen our people through extended political rights and through far-sighted social reforms." He mentioned woman suffrage and equality in the communal franchise as measures that would come up for consideration.

Brief Notes

Some recent addresses by the Secretary of the American-Scandinavian Foundation: February 25, Loyalty Meeting of Swedish-Americans at Hartford, Conn.; "Sweden and the War from the Point of View of Democracy." February 26, American Geographical Society, New York: "The Voyages of the Vikings." March 10, Jamestown, N. Y.: "Sweden and the War from the Point of View of Democracy." March 11, Kane, Pa.: the same. March 17, Intercollegiate Cosmopolitan Club, Columbia University: the same. April 1, Scandinavian Society of Philadelphia: "Scandinavia's Sons in the United States." April 11, Ethical Culture School, New York: "Vikings Past and Present." April 20, Swedish Colonial Society, Philadelphia: "The Voyages of the Vikings."

The Fiftieth Anniversary of the American Scandinavian Society of Philadelphia was celebrated on April 1 by an evening of speeches, banquet, and music. Loving cups, flags, and other souvenirs were presented by the various Scandinavian beneficial societies of Philadelphia which have sprung in the course of the years from the parent organization. The first president in 1868 was C. G. Grönbeck. The president for 1918 is William Jörgensen. William Weber was chairman of the anniversary committee. The hall was decorated with great American flags from the Navy Yard at Philadelphia. The banquet closed with a beautiful tableau representing Columbia rising from a group of Denmark, Sweden, and Norway in national costumes.

Edwin Björkman contributes an article in the February *Scribner's* on "Sweden's Position in the War." He emphasizes the anti-autocratic sympathies of the great unprivileged mass of Swedish people. Mr. Björkman has recently returned from Sweden, where he has been during a great part of the war. Two other articles by the same author appear in *The World's Work* for February and *Everybody's* for April. Mrs. Björkman contributes an article about Sweden in the *Delineator* for March.

The January number of the *Atlantic Monthly* has a lucid article by Christian L. Lange, General Secretary of the Interparliamentary Union, on "Scandinavian Cross-Currents." Mr. Lange groups his statements under the heads: Anti-German Denmark, Pro-Ally Norway, Anti-Russian Sweden, and Scandinavian Co-operation.

The friends of the Foundation are now found in Asia, Africa, and Australia, besides Europe and America. From Melbourne we have recently received a number of reprints of articles on the Normans by a Norwegian, Mr. Henry Norman, who writes to convince the British of the great part which the Norwegians have played in their history.

The tenth volume of *Islandica* (1917) contains two Latin texts edited like its predecessors by Dr. Haldór Hermansson.

The Wild Duck was presented by Arthur Hopkins as the first in a series of Ibsen performances with Madame Alla Nazimova in the principal feminine roles. It was the first English performance of the play in New York and drew large audiences to the Plymouth Theatre during March and the first week of April. The acting throughout was of high artistic excellence. The revelation of Ibsen's powers as a comedian was perhaps its most striking feature.

Dr. Max Henius lectured under the auspices of the Danish Women's Civic League in New York on March 14. His subject, "Denmark, Past and Present," was treated in a delightfully original manner, and his illustrations were likewise a departure from the stereotyped views.

Weekly courses in modern Icelandic and Danish are being offered at Columbia University by Miss Holmfridur Arnadottir, who recently came to this country from Iceland to study our educational system.

The following books have been received: *The Utopian Way,* by John Veiby; *Walking Trips in Norway,* by N. Tjernagel; *Paa Kongevei* and *Flytfugl,* by Sigurd Folkestad; *Dikter,* by Axel Fredenholm, and *Krigs-og Fredsproblemer,* by Arnold Raestad. Among pamphlets received are: *The International Bearings of War,* by G. Th. Mejdell, and *The Beginnings of the Norwegian Press in America,* by Albert Olaus Barton, published by the State Historical Society of Wisconsin.

TRADE NOTES
News and Comment on Exports and Trade Conditions Between America and the Scandinavian Countries

NORWEGIAN SHIP ARRIVALS

According to the annual report of Consul General Ravn, Norwegian ships to the number of 2,799 and registering 4,027,066 tons entered ports within the New York consular district during 1917. Of the 781 steamships that arrived in the port of New York, ten were equipped with motor engines.

AMERICAN PIG IRON OUTPUT

The American Iron and Steel Institute's statistical bulletin shows the production of pig iron in the United States to have been 38,647,397 gross tons in 1917, as compared with 39,434,797 gross tons in 1916.

PUBLIC UTILITY INVESTMENTS

No less than $14,500,000,000 is invested in public utility corporations in the United States. Of the capital invested, $5,000,000,000 is in electric railways, $4,500,-000,000 in electric power plants, $3,500,000,000 in gas plants, and $1,500,000,000 in telephone and telegraph equipments.

SWEDISH CHAMBER OF COMMERCE REPORT

In his annual report of the Swedish Chamber of Commerce of the United States, General Manager Oscar G. Marell comments on the fact that even while the war has necessarily curtailed the activities of the organization in certain directions, there has been a gradual and satisfactory increase in memberships. The item in the income account which shows the largest increase as compared with previous years is that of the Chamber's *Trade Journal.*

New York Forwarding Co., Inc.

Agents OSCAR A. OLSEN *Branch Offices*
GOTHENBURG General Manager CHRISTIANIA, Kirkegaten 6 B.
STOCKHOLM   COPENHAGEN, Peder Skramsgade 28

LICENSES: Applying for American and British Licenses.

WAREHOUSE: Storing all kinds of goods.

INSURANCE: Marine, War, Fire, and all risks.

FINANCING: Value of merchandise, freight and charges payable against surrender of documents upon arrival at destination.

SWEDISH IRON AND STEEL CORPORATION

THOMAS TOWNE,
Vice-President and General Manager

General Offices,
12 PLATT STREET, NEW YORK CITY

"SISCO" PRODUCTS

FINE TOOL AND ALLOY STEELS

in Billets, Bars, Discs, Blocks, and Sheets

Common and Deep Drawing Steel Sheets
High Speed Steel *Cold Rolled Strip Steel*
Drill Rods   *Drawn Bars*
Swedish Iron   *Sisco Welding Wire*
High Grade Specialties

Catalogues and information on request

BRANCH OFFICES AND WAREHOUSES

BROOKLYN	CLEVELAND	NEW ORLEANS
BOSTON	CHICAGO	DENVER
PHILADELPHIA	DETROIT	MONTREAL, Can.
	STOCKHOLM, Sweden	

Phone Greeley 4354

M. WAIN—Tailor

Some of the best dressed men are amongst my customers. H i g h - g r a d e clothes made at moderate prices.

366 FIFTH AVENUE

Above 34th Street   10th Floor

NORWAY PLANNING WATER-POWER COÖRDINATION

Plans are being considered by leading Norwegian engineers for constructing south of Trondhjem a great power plant to carry electric current far into the northern sections and utilize the boundless water resources of the country for this purpose. Such experts as Gregussen Vogter, Norberg-Schultz, and Director Kloumann are engaged in working out plans.

LIMITATIONS OF THE EMBARGO

One of the limitations of the embargo is that it applies only to goods brought in by ocean-going vessels. No ban is put on products that may come to the United States by rail from Canada and Mexico, and this fact of itself will permit the importation of many minerals, foodstuffs, and other articles. J. M.

Keep Down Fuel Costs

HERE is a product guaranteed to increase power and mileage per gallon, to clean out carbon, to save fuel. Owners of automobiles, motor trucks, motor boats, and kerosene or gasoline engines are asked to write for information.

Better still, send $2.50 for a quart can, enough to mix with 200 gallons of gasoline, and save 20 per cent. of your fuel bill.

Motor Department
WILLIAM H. SCHÜTZE, 13 Water Street, New York

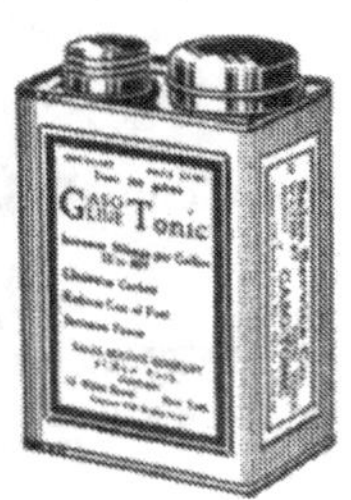

FINANCIAL

*Notes About Issues in the Financial World
Most Interesting to Readers of the Review*

WAR SAVINGS STAMPS AS INVESTMENT

For the purpose of explaining the exact relations of War Savings Stamps and Liberty Bonds, Frederic W. Allen, Director of War Savings for Greater New York, has issued a statement, which says in part: "There can be no conflict and no competition between Liberty Bonds and War Savings Stamps. They are both issued by the same department of the government and, from the standpoint of a public offering, for the same purpose. The War Savings Stamps committee will remain active, particularly in forming War Savings Societies, enlisting Liberty Bond buyers in these organizations in the same spirit in which owners of War Savings Stamps are enrolled, to refrain from competing with the government for the labor and materials needed to carry on the war and to lend their savings to the government to assist in the prosecution of the war, either through the purchase of Liberty Bonds or War Savings Stamps. This represents the fundamental purpose of the War Savings campaign and is just as applicable to those who invest their savings in Liberty Bonds as those who invest in War Savings Stamps."

FOREIGN TRADE BANKING CORPORATION

The Foreign Trade Banking Corporation, of which George A. Gaston will be the president, and Max May, managing director, has a capitalization of $2,000,000 and will deal in bankers' and trade acceptances. Connections are to be made with foreign banks and the new concern should be of particular interest to Scandinavian banking houses.

POULSEN WIRELESS

A Danish invention, the Poulsen wireless system, dates back to a time when few considered the extensive use of the wireless telegraph a possibility. Recent rumors regarding a possible consolidation of the Poulsen wireless with the American Marconi and the British Marconi companies call attention to the Federal Telegraph Company, which is the operating company of the commercial business of the Poulsen Wireless Corporation. The Poulsen Company owns about 25 per cent. of the Pan-American Company stock, which company was formed to do business in South America and Mexico. The president of the Poulsen Company is Dr. Washington Dodge, and the head office is in San Francisco. The New York Stock Exchange firm of Macquoid & Coady represents the investment interests of the Poulsen Wireless Corporation.

Buy U. S. Government Bonds

of the

THIRD LIBERTY LOAN

4¼ PER CENT INTEREST

Beginning May 9, 1918. Is paid on September 15 and March 15 of each year.

Bonds are issued in amounts of $50.00, $100.00, $500.00, $1000.00 and upward, and mature September 15, 1928.

For additional details see your banker, employer, pastor, priest, president of your club or society, or the local Liberty Loan Committee.

IT IS A DUTY TO BUY!

To keep your money in safety deposit boxes is unpatriotic and not profitable.
To hide your money is dangerous, unpatriotic and not profitable.
To invest your money in the Third Liberty Loan is PROFITABLE, SECURE and PATRIOTIC.

It contributes toward VICTORY!   It will bring PEACE!

Empire Trust Company

120 Broadway   New York   580 Fifth Avenue

London Office, 41 Threadneedle Street

Resources Over $50,000,000

The Fifth Avenue Office of this Company, corner 47th Street, is accessibly situated for anyone desiring the services of an Uptown Banking Institution.   Careful and courteous attention given to any business entrusted to it.

Interest may be arranged upon accounts subject to check.

Certificates of Deposit, maturing at a date to suit the needs of the depositor, issued at favorable rates of interest.

Empire Safe Deposit Company

Safe Deposit Vaults

AMERICAN SECURITIES FOR SCANDINAVIA

In line with the concern's customary important interpretation of securities values here and abroad, A. B. Leach & Co. now call attention to the exceptional opportunities presented the people of the Scandinavian countries to invest in American bonds. With the American dollar at a discount in practically every neutral country, its purchasing power is so much reduced that an American bond quoted at 100 per cent. in New York would cost only 84.7 per cent. in Sweden; 87.9 per cent. in Norway and 93.8 per cent. in Denmark. The many Scandinavian business men in the United States at the present time cannot fail to appreciate the chances presented in acquiring gilt-edged American securities under such especially favorable circumstances.

SWEDISH BANKING DEVELOPMENT

The Swedish Bureau of Statistics has prepared a survey which shows the progress of Swedish banking during the past forty years. During the past year Bergslagsbanken has been absorbed by Mälarbanken, Jämtlands Kreditbank by Stockholms Handelsbank, Mellersta Halland and Varbergs Bank and Herrljunga Landtmannabank by Beråsbanken, and Bergsjö Folkbank by Sundsvalls Handelsbank. Finally, Kristdala Folkbank has disappeared. In a general way, consolidation has been a marked feature of Swedish banking during the past year.

NORWEGIAN-AMERICAN SECURITIES CORPORATION

In view of the prominence of Norwegian enterprises, both industrially and as concerns shipping, the appearance of the Norwegian-American Securities Corporation in New York marks a new period in financial transactions between here and Norway. J. M.

NORWEGIAN AMERICA LINE

Modern Twin
Screw Steamers

16,000 tons displacement, 530
feet long

16½ knots speed

Accommodations:

The steamers are new, modern and efficiently equipped for the utmost safety and comfort of passengers. First-class staterooms are situated amidships on the Promenade and Shelter Deck. Cabins De Luxe on upper promenade.

For further particulars apply to

NORWEGIAN AMERICA LINE PASSENGER AGENCY, Inc.

8 and 10 Bridge St., New York   General Passenger Agents for United States and Canada

HOBE & CO.	BIRGER OSLAND & CO.	REIDAR GJÖLME
General Northwestern Passenger Agents	General Western Passenger Agents	General Pacific Coast Agent
123 South Third Street	115 South Dearborn Street	Arctic Bldg. Third & Cherry Streets
Minneapolis, Minn.	Chicago, Ill.	Seattle, Wash.

NORWAY MEXICO GULF LINE AND SWEDISH AMERICA MEXICO LINE

Regular service between GÖTEBORG, CHRISTIANIA and STAVANGER and NEWPORT NEWS, VA., HAVANA, CUBA, GALVESTON, TEX., and NEW ORLEANS, LA.

Passengers Carried   Wireless Apparatus

AGENTS

FEARNLEY & EGER, Christiania   SANDSTRÖM STRANNE & CO., Ltd., Göteborg

FURNESS WITHY & CO., Ltd., New York, N. Y. and Newport News, Va.

32 BROADWAY

JAS. P. ROBERTSON	FOWLER & McVITIE	LYKES BROS.	GEO. PLANT
111 West Jackson Boulevard	Galveston, Tex.	Havana, Cuba	1119 Whitney Central Bldg.
Chicago, Ill.			New Orleans, La.

Recommendation for Associate
of the
AMERICAN-SCANDINAVIAN FOUNDATION

I nominate..

Address..

GENERAL OFFICES: Passenger Department

117 N. Dearborn Street, Chicago, Ill.		544 Market St., San Francisco, Cal.
236 Nicollet Ave., Minneapolis, Minn.	**1 BROADWAY, NEW YORK**	
248 Washington St., Boston, Mass.		702 Second Ave., Seattle, Wash.

SWEDISH AMERICAN LINE

(SVENSKA AMERIKA LINIEN)

Direct Passenger Service between New York and Gothenburg, Sweden

Short Route to Sweden, Norway, Denmark, Finland, Russia and other parts of the European Continent

Twin-Screw S.S. "Stockholm"

Length 565 Feet. 22,070 Tons Displacement

Largest Steamer in Service between America and Scandinavia, is provided with all modern safety appliances, and every care is taken to give the passengers a safe and comfortable journey.

Unsurpassed passenger appointments in First, Second and Third Classes.

NIELSEN & LUNDBECK, General Passenger Agents, 24 State Street, New York.

MARTIN MAURD, General Western Agent, 183 N. Dearborn Street, Chicago.

NILS NILSON, General Northwestern Agent, 127 S. Third St., Minneapolis, Minn.

BRATTSTROM & CO., General No. Pacific Agents, 117 Cherry St., Seattle, Wash.

A. HALLONQUIST, General Agent, 396 Logan Ave., Winnipeg, Man., Can.

The American-Scandinavian Review

VOLUME VI   JULY-AUGUST, 1918   NUMBER 4

Published Bi-Monthly by THE AMERICAN-SCANDINAVIAN FOUNDATION, 25 West 45th Street, New York

Yearly Subscription, $1.50.   (One dollar to Associates of the Foundation.)   Single Copies, 25 cents

Entered as second-class matter, January 4, 1913, at the post-office at New York, N. Y., under the act of March 3, 1879
Copyright, 1916, The American-Scandinavian Foundation

HENRY GODDARD LEACH, *Editor*   HANNA ASTRUP LARSEN, *Literary Editor*

Advisors

New York, HAMILTON HOLT   Copenhagen, HARALD NIELSEN
Stockholm, CARL LAURIN   Christiania, CHRISTIAN COLLIN

CONTENTS

FOUNDED BY NIELS POULSON, IN 1911

ROYAL COPENHAGEN POR-
CELAIN AND DANISH ARTS
beg to announce that they have received a collection of Old Copenhagen
Figures, revival of porcelain in the style
of Juliane Marie, modeled and decorated from old and very rare examples.

LOVERS WITH CUPIDS
BY ANDREAS HALD

1781

Original at Kunstindustri Museum
Copenhagen

This is a charming group and must
be seen to be appreciated. It will be
a constant inspiration to the owner.

THE FLUTE PLAYER
BY SOREN PREUS

1784

Original at Dansk Folke
Museum, Copenhagen

LADY AT TEA TABLE
BY ANTON CARL LUPLAU

1776

Original at Fredericksborg
Castle, Copenhagen

THE HOLY CITY
JERUSALEM II
By SELMA LAGERLÖF
Translated by Velma Swanston Howard

Recent military events about Palestine add new interest to this latest book, "Jerusalem II," by the distinguished winner of the Nobel Prize. It is a continuation of her already famous epic, "Jerusalem," and yet it is complete in itself.

The religious upheaval that took the Dalecarlians to Jerusalem places them in the colony founded there by the Gordons, Americans. The highest level of this writer's genius is touched in this story of persecution and physical hardship. *Net $1.50.*

The Northland edition, leather. $1.75.

DOUBLEDAY PAGE AND COMPANY
GARDEN CITY, NEW YORK

D. B. UPDIKE
The Merrymount Press
232 SUMMER STREET
BOSTON
. . .
PRINTERS OF FINE BOOKS FOR
BOOK CLUBS, INSTITUTIONS, AND
PRIVATE PERSONS
&c. &c. &c.

The Series of *Scandinavian Classics*, and Hust-vedt's "Ballad Criticism" and Hovgaard's "Voyages of the Norsemen," in the *Scandinavian Monographs*, were printed for the American-Scandinavian Foundation by this Press.

If you are looking for color—visit

THE SCANDINAVIAN
ART SHOP
728 MADISON AVENUE
Near 64th Street
NEW YORK

The Shop removed to
Bar Harbor, June 15
to October 15

Orders for Carl Larsson Nurseries Executed
Painted Furniture for Country Homes
Wool-embroidered Smocks

THE HOTEL McALPIN has long been the favorite rendezvous in New York City of Scandinavian-Americans. Their patronage is valued as a privilege by the management.

Room and restaurant tariffs remain moderate.

HOTEL McALPIN

Broadway at 34th Street · · · · L.M.Boomer - *Man. Director*

The Only High-Class Scandinavian Restaurant in New York

NEAR HERALD SQUARE
Phone: Greeley 4782

Rendezvous for Scandinavians from all over the world when visiting New York

Dinner with famous "Smörgåsbord." American and Scandinavian Dishes.
HENRY MALGREN, Prop.

CLARX 100% PURE Whole Wheat Flour

Whole Wheat Graham Flour
Whole Rye Flour
Corn Flour and Other Substitutes

CLARX MILLING COMPANY
Minneapolis

Phone Greeley 4854

M. WAIN—Tailor

Some of the best dressed men are amongst my customers. High-grade clothes made at moderate prices.

366 FIFTH AVENUE
Above 34th Street   10th Floor

THIS PAGE IS DONATED BY NEW YORK LAWYERS

BUY
WAR SAVINGS
STAMPS

AUGUST REYMERT, 17 State Street
CHARLES A. OGREN, 149 Broadway
EDWIN O. HOLTER, 60 Broadway
H. E. ALMBERG, 124 East 15th Street
OLAV J. S. DE BRUN, 1275 Broadway

COUNSELORS AT LAW

CONTRIBUTORS TO THE JULY-AUGUST NUMBER

The most spiritual interpretation of Lincoln is still the bust by GUTZON BORGLUM, the Danish-American sculptor, who thereby has rendered his country as great a service as by any of his public activities.

ROGER NIELSEN, of Omaha, is the author of a remarkable book on the foreign policy of our President, which, published in Denmark, has been the means of clarifying Danish opinion regarding the unselfish purpose of our entrance into the war.

After writing the message that appears in this number, DR. MAURICE FRANCIS EGAN has announced his resignation from his post as American minister to Denmark, owing to continued poor health. The news will be received with deep regret. Dr. Egan's generous, sympathetic understanding of Denmark's difficulties has contributed greatly to our friendly relations with that country. Fortunately, we may hope that he will go on interpreting America and Scandinavia to each other by the work of his pen.

KNUTE NELSON of Minnesota will soon enter upon his fifth term in the Senate, at the request of the President of the United States, and as the practically unanimous choice of his state regardless of party. His American ideals found beautiful expression in his tribute to "The Life and Character of Lincoln," delivered in the Senate last 22nd of February, and it is significant of the position he holds that he should be chosen for this task. The Senator was born in Norway and still speaks his native "Vossing."

REV. J. A. O. STUB is executive secretary of the National Lutheran Commission for Soldiers' and Sailors' Welfare. In this capacity, and as field representative of the Lutheran Brotherhood, he has traveled 31,000 miles and visited most of the camps. He is now in charge of the New York office of the Commission.

ERNST W. OLSON is the editor of *Ungdomsvännen*, a Swedish magazine published in Rockford.

CARL NEUMANN was born in Denmark and went to sea as a youth, but has now lived in this country for more than fifty years. His home is in Chicago, where he plies his trade as a painter. He has written many popular poems both in Danish and in English.

THORA GRÖNVOLD has appeared in the REVIEW before as a translator of selections from Arne Garborg's poems. She is a teacher in the high schools of Faribault, Minnesota.

RASMUS R. SABY is instructor in political economy at Cornell University.

LOLA RIDGE is an American poet of Australian extraction who has recently become known through her long poem "The Ghetto" in the *New Republic*. A volume of her poems will appear in the early fall with the imprint of Huebsch.

WOODROW WILSON

"We Have No Selfish Ends to Serve. We Desire No Conquest, No Dominion. We Seek No Indemnities for Ourselves, No Material Compensation for the Sacrifices We Shall Freely Make. We Are but One of the Champions of the Rights of Mankind. We Shall Be Satisfied When Those Rights Have Been Made as Secure as the Faith and the Freedom of the Nations Can Make Them."

THE
AMERICAN-SCANDINAVIAN
REVIEW

VOLUME VI   JULY-AUGUST · 1918   NUMBER 4

A Message from the President

THE REPRESENTATIVES OF TWENTY-FOUR NATIONALITIES WROTE TO THE PRESIDENT ASKING HIS APPROVAL OF A PLAN FOR SPECIAL FOURTH OF JULY CELEBRATIONS ORGANIZED BY THE VARIOUS FOREIGN GROUPS TO SHOW THEIR LOYALTY. THE PRESIDENT'S ANSWER FOLLOWS:

TO OUR CITIZENS OF FOREIGN EXTRACTION:

I have read with great sympathy the petition addressed to me by your representative bodies regarding your proposed celebration of Independence Day, and I wish to convey to you, in reply, my heartfelt appreciation for its expressions of loyalty and good-will. Nothing in this war has been more gratifying than the manner in which our foreign-born fellow citizens and the sons and daughters of the foreign-born have risen to this greatest of all national emergencies. You have shown where you stand, not only by your frequent professions of loyalty to the cause for which we fight, but by your eager response to calls for patriotic service, including the supreme service of offering life itself in battle for justice, freedom, and democracy. Before such devotion as you have shown, all distinctions of race vanish, and we feel ourselves citizens in a Republic of free spirits.

I therefore take pleasure in calling your petition, with my hearty recommendation, to the attention of all my fellow countrymen, and I ask that they unite with you in making the Independence Day of this, the year when all the principles to which we stand pledged are on trial, the most significant in our national history.

As July 4, 1776, was the dawn of democracy for this Nation, let us on July 4, 1918, celebrate the birth of a new and greater spirit of democracy, by whose influence we hope and believe what the signers of the Declaration of Independence dreamed of for themselves and their fellow countrymen shall be fulfilled for all mankind.

I have asked the Committee on Public Information to coöperate with you in any arrangements you may wish to make for this celebration.

WOODROW WILSON.

President Wilson

By ROGER NIELSEN

THE mightiest man in the world, they call him. And still nobody thinks of him as a superman. Why? Is it because he, unlike the *Uebermensch* of Nietzsche, has become more and more human as his power has grown? Is it because he never forgets that power and might are nothing in themselves, but great only as means to the greater goals?

No overman, but who can name a career more remarkable than Woodrow Wilson's? Ten years ago, he failed to democratize a university. Five years ago, he started falteringly to democratize his country. To-day, he is successfully democratizing the world. History has seen nothing stranger.

And men ask: How has he accomplished it? How does he compare with other great men? What is the secret of his success?

Gladstone's greatest gift was his fascinating rhetoric. When he introduced the budget, even dry facts and figures became glowing romance in his mouth, and he held Parliament spellbound for hours upon hours. No such talent is Wilson's. He is eloquent, but he can not sway men as Gladstone could or Gambetta.

Napoleon never stopped working. If he woke up at night, he called his secretaries at once and began to dictate. Work was his life and soul. Wilson has not the same passion. Though no man has worked harder than he has for the past five years, he really likes to loaf and sleep late in the mornings.

Richelieu always impressed everyone as the master. His stately bearing, his stern and piercing eyes, his imperative gestures never failed to tell that his will was law. There is no atmosphere of willed masterfulness around Wilson. He has poise, dignity, and determination stamped all over his person, but he is inclined to keep down this side of his nature rather than to emphasize it.

It is said of nearly all the great commanders in the present war, Joffre, Haig, Pétain, and Hindenburg, that they were born taciturn. They can keep silent in more languages than Mithridates could speak. But, though Wilson has become the best listener that ever occupied the White House, he is not so inclined by nature; for he enjoys nothing better than a real talk, and his love of a good story is just as great as was Lincoln's.

Lloyd George is a man of instantaneous decisions. Instinct, intuition tell him what to do, and he acts at once, never hesitating. Wilson has not the same faith in his first judgments. He seldom reverses a decision once made, but he takes his time in reaching it. Passion shook him so when the *Lusitania* was sunk that he had to walk the streets of Washington most of the night; but he fought it out and returned in a spirit that allowed him to view the case unhampered by his feelings.

The personality of Roosevelt is all-conquering. He squeezes a man's hand, he smiles, he steps out on a platform and shows the crowd his teeth in that engaging grin, and—they are all his, body and soul. Wilson could never do it. Nobody has truer, more devoted friends than he, nobody impresses an audience as more sincere or worthier of their trust; but he cannot help keeping people at a distance, he is shy, he shrinks from too much intimacy.

Power was to Bismarck his very existence. Forced to resign, he lost interest in everything, became morose and morbid, and ceased to care for life itself. Wilson would possibly not feel the slightest personal regret, if he had to step out of the White House to-day. That fateful night in November, 1916, when it seemed that Hughes had been elected, there was no more cheerful person in Long Branch, New Jersey, than Woodrow Wilson. He showed no impatience, he smiled, he talked unconcernedly over the telephone, while victory after victory was announced for his opponent.

Wilson has few of the eccentricities of great men. As a matter of fact, he is a very plain, every-day person. One might even call him a little commonplace; for he prefers detective stories to problem novels, he goes regularly to vaudeville shows, and—worse still—his greatest pleasure is an old-fashioned family picnic with lunch under a shady tree and a nap afterwards.

But when all this is said, how much do we know of Woodrow Wilson? Did we find, did we even touch his real self? Surely the man who has attained his commanding position in the council of nations can be no ordinary man.

Long before America entered the war, he was hailed as the moral leader of the world. To-day he is more. He is the very conscience of the world. For he has proved himself the man of action and still kept the faith. In becoming the doer he has not thrown the idealist overboard. He had the courage, vision, greatness of thought to make this war a war of pure principles, morality against expediency, idealism contra egotism. He bound America to fight to the end for humanity and international justice, to make the world safe for democracy, and to ask nothing for itself, no matter how great the cost in men and money. The cause of the Allies was from the first the cause of right, but he made it the cause of unselfish right, and his messages have become their greatest source of inspiration and moral strength. His extreme fairness and ever-vigilant sense of justice have impressed even his enemies. There is no one in the world to-day able to dispute his supreme leadership in international affairs.

What is it, then, in this man, seemingly so plain and common, that

at times raises him to heights seldom, if ever, attained by other men?
Is there a side to him that we can not see? Has anybody really
penetrated to the man himself, the soul behind the mask? Maybe
a very few, his most intimate friends. Certainly not the public at
large. For Wilson knows nothing harder than to disclose himself.

In the greatest of all his speeches, his Lincoln address of
September, 1916, he said:

". . . I have nowhere found a real intimate of Lincoln's.
I nowhere get the impression in any narrative or reminiscence that
the writer had, in fact, penetrated to the heart of his mystery, or
that any man could penetrate to the heart of it. That brooding
spirit had no real familiars. I get the impression that it never spoke
out in complete self-revelation, and that it could not reveal itself
completely to any one. It was a very lonely spirit that looked out
from underneath those shaggy brows and comprehended men without
fully communicating with them, as if, in spite of all its genial efforts
of comradeship, it dwelt apart, saw its visions of duty where no man
looked on. There is a very holy and very terrible isolation for the
conscience of every man who seeks to read the destiny in affairs for
others as well as for himself, for a nation as well as for individuals.
That privacy no man can intrude upon. That lonely search of the
spirit for the right perhaps no man can assist. This strange child
of the cabin kept company with invisible things, was born into no
intimacy but that of its own silently assembling and deploying
thoughts."

In these beautiful words on Lincoln we have the best picture of
Wilson himself. They may be too spiritual, too subtle as applying
to the great Emancipator. But nobody can doubt that they are
wrung from Woodrow Wilson's heart, that they come from a man
who seeks his own inspiration in this holy and terrible loneliness
of the soul.

America

The hope of all who suffer,
The dread of all who wrong.

—John Greenleaf Whittier.

Freedom, Christianity, America

*A message through the AMERICAN-SCANDINAVIAN REVIEW from the
American Minister to Denmark*

By MAURICE FRANCIS EGAN

I HAVE only three words to say to my many American friends of
Scandinavian blood in this country.   One is Freedom: our fight
to-day is for the right to *be* ourselves, to exercise the free will
God has given us, to be men or to be machines controlled by absolut-
ism.   Think of Schleswig-Holstein, a monument of the broken pledges
of Prussia—struggling since '63 for the mere right to have the word
of God preached in the language of her Danish forefathers.   Read
Machiavelli's *Prince*, and you will see the inmost intentions of the
Kaiser.   No nation, according to the definition of Prussia, which
to-day treats Bavaria and Hanover and Saxony as subjects tied to
her chariot wheels, has a right to a national life of her own.   He who
would be free must fight for freedom and endure much.

My second word is Christianity, the essential teaching of which
is that the will is free.   Machiavelli held to the principles of anti-
Christ; he denied all that Dante and the lovers of freedom in Christian
ages had asserted.   If Christianity can submit to the dogma that
Might is Right, that all crimes are excusable in order that one tyrant
shall rule, then Christianity has been Prussianized, as Nietzsche
Prussianized philosophy.   "St. Paul says," a Lutheran Swedish divine
said to me recently, "that all power comes from God! but," he added,
"rulers like the Kaiser are the scourges of God, as Attila was."

And my last word is America, sacred to all of you who have chosen
it .as your home.   We who have been born here are less American
than you—for you chose your country, while we only inherited it—
America, which must flourish or perish in principle, if we do not win
this war.   But we shall win!

Long, Too Long, America

By WALT WHITMAN

Long, too long, America,
Traveling roads all even and peaceful you learn'd from joys and pros-
perity only,
But now, ah now, to learn from crises of anguish, advancing, grappling
with direst fate and recoiling not,
And now to conceive and show to the world what your children en masse
really are.

Norse Legions of Democracy

By Hanna Astrup Larsen

A HUNDRED THOUSAND strong and more the Norse legions of democracy are marching on from the prairies. They came at the first call to arms, taking their places as Americans, falling into step with Yankee and Celt and Slav and Latin. There is no Scandinavian regiment in this war resembling the Fifteenth Wisconsin in the War for the Union, and, even if one had existed, the young men from the "Scandinavian states" would not have cared to join it. Our Government has not encouraged the formation of regiments on lines of nationality; the time for such passed decades ago, and the young men of to-day train and fight as Americans and nothing else. Here and there, we find foreign groups, as in a regiment of the National Guard, where four hundred Finns, speaking no language but their own, had enlisted in a body, but nothing similar is recorded of the Scandinavians, and indeed it would be hard to find anywhere in the length and breadth of the land a solid group of Swedes, Danes, or Norwegians unable to speak English.

The estimate we can make of the actual number of men of Scandinavian birth or parentage in the army and navy is therefore based almost entirely on their names and their religious faith. We learn, for instance, from the postmaster at the Great Lakes Training Station near Chicago that the predominant nationalities among the thirty thousand men training there are the Norwegian, the Swedish, and the Irish. The secretary of the National Lutheran Commission for Soldiers' and Sailors' Welfare is authority for the statement that 225,000 men have registered as Lutherans, and it is roughly computed that Scandinavians constitute rather more than one-half of these, while a few would naturally be found in other denominations. I am therefore well within the facts in giving the actual number of Scandinavians in the service as 115,000.

Occasionally a flashlight falls on some high peak of patriotism and hints of the wide fields of unrecorded action. If every county in the United States had done as well as Chiago—the most Swedish county in Minnesota, if not in the Union—Bryan's famous prophecy that "a million men would spring to arms between sunrise and sunset" would not have been drowned in ridicule; for, on the very day war was declared, sixty-five young men enlisted from the county. A Swedish Lutheran congregation there, which numbers two hundred souls, counting babes in arms, has given thirty-two of its members. In numerous small towns throughout the Northwest, Governor Burnquist tells us, the draft was not put into operation because they had already more than filled their quota with volunteers. Among

THE AUGUSTANA COLLEGE BAND, WHICH ENLISTED IN A BODY

the first of these was Lindstrom in Minnesota, a city with an almost purely Swedish stock, and its record of eleven per cent. of the population enlisted is probably still unequaled. Winneshiek County, Iowa, the seat of Luther College, has a population only thirty per cent. Norwegian, but the volunteers from the county were seventy-five per cent. Norwegians. In the University of Minnesota, the proportion of Scandinavians in the service is slightly more than the normal ratio for the whole student body. At a recent meeting of the Red Wing Conference of the Augustana Synod, the pastors present were asked to report on how many of their church members were in the army and navy, and the total number was found to be 15,000, a proportion of the entire membership which, if carried out through the whole population of the country, would give us five million men under arms at this moment.

While the Danes are less numerous and more scattered than the other two races, no one with the slightest knowledge of Danish sentiment can doubt that the countrymen of *den tapre landsoldat* have done their duty bravely. The Norwegians have always been strong in our navy, a large number of the older non-commissioned officers being Norwegians; and their young men, even when born on the prairies, have preferably enlisted for sea service. In the Swedes, the old military spirit has reasserted itself with a vigor and spontaneity natural in a race brought up on traditions of great warrior-kings from the time of Sweden's greatest expansion. They seem to have furnished an especially large quota of officers, judging from the

Ensign Thor Norberg, Who Helped Introduce the Ling System of Gymnastics into the Navy

lists that fill column afte[r] ~~~~ in the Swedish-American week[lies] ~~~~ tan; and Gustavus Adolphus, the tw[o] ~~~ [lar]gest of their colleges, have respectively twenty and twenty-two officers represented on their service flags. The first two American officers to fall in the war were both born in Sweden and both men with splendid records. One was the aviator, Lieutenant Victor Carlström, killed by the collapse of his machine while instructing an army pupil at Newport News. The other was Lieutenant of Marines Fredrik Wahlström, who was with Pershing's Expeditionary Forces, and was killed in a motorcycle accident in France. On the other hand, the Scandinavian of highest rank now in active service is a Norwegian, Colonel Alfred W. Björnstad, of St. Paul, who is at present in France organizing the Third American Army Corps as chief of the General Staff.

The record for Scandinavian colleges is held by Augustana, whose service flag with 201 stars represents two-thirds of the male attendance. The Augustana men flocked early to the colors; the band enlisted in a body to form, with slight reorganization, a regimental band, and the college has furnished four chaplains and twelve camp pastors and Y. M. C. A. workers. The other colleges have also done well.

At Camp Cody and Camp Dodge, whole regiments show the complexion inherited from their Norse ancestry. In height and brawn they keep up the reputation gained in the War for the Union, when the Norwegians were the tallest Europeans in the army of the North, surpassed only—and that by a mere fraction of a centimeter—by the Colonial Americans. To-day North Dakota, with a population about half Norwegian, boasts the crack regiment of the army, the 164th U. S. Infantry, which, it is claimed, tops every other regiment in the service by two inches in average height and twenty pounds in average weight! South Dakota, also a strong Norwegian state, is the only one where over eighty per cent. of the young men examined were found fit for service, while next in order followed the other Middle Western and Northwestern States. Prairie spaces and Norse blood have made a race that is long-limbed and deep-chested.

PROFESSOR W. H. SCHOFIELD, PRESIDENT OF THE AMERICAN-SCANDINAVIAN FOUNDATION

PROFESSOR WM. HOVGAARD, WHO HAS JUST BEEN AWARDED THE GOLD MEDAL OF THE LONDON INSTITUTE OF NAVAL ARCHITECTS

CAPTAIN OSCAR H. HAUGAN, FORMER NORWEGIAN CONSUL IN CHICAGO, NOW INSPECTOR OF ORDNANCE IN THE ARMY

Nor is the spirit found wanting. Scandinavian boys have not the impassioned gallantry of the young French officers who went to meet the Germans with white gloves and red waving plumes. Their feeling is more akin to the cool pluck of the Anglo-Saxon, but sometimes they startle us with an expression that is all of the North; for now and then we see a familiar young face transformed, redrawn in lines of fierce strength; and we meet the glance of an eye that has changed overnight, kindled with the hard light that belongs to the fighting races. Then we remember that these are sons of a people who went into battle laughing. From the casualty lists we know that many of them have already made the supreme sacrifice.

The heavy enlistment from the "Scandinavian states" is not all due to inherited roving blood and love of hard blows. We shall not get many protestations of patriotism from the boys, but now and then a word, dropped carelessly, betrays a spirit of devotion as deep and strong as that in the older men. And what of these older men, many of them born on the other side, who leave large affairs to train in camp with the youths, men of subtly adjusted brains and wide experience, who are giving themselves to stop gaps in the trenches? And what of those who must stay at home and who are giving freely of their time, their money, their brain-power to less exciting tasks of feeding the furnace of war at home?

When we come to these latter activities, we can marshal at least some figures, since much of the work has been done through organizations already existing or organized for the purpose.

In the Liberty Loan drives, we find Scandinavians always measur-

Underwood Photo

Dr. Julius Lincoln, Who Has Resigned His Pastorate at Jamestown After Twenty Years' Service to Lecture for the U. S. Food Administration

Irvine L. Lenroot, Elected to the U. S. Senate from Wisconsin, the First Swede to Attain that Honor

Captain C. S. Peterson, Organizer of a Company of Reserve Militia Formed Chiefly by Members of the Swedish Club of Chicago

ing up to what is required, and in many localities distinguishing themselves by exceptionally solid and brilliant work. The states of Minnesota, North Dakota, South Dakota, Montana, upper Iowa, and upper Michigan—all strong Scandinavian states—are comprised in the Ninth Federal Reserve District, in which the Third Liberty Loan drive was organized with an efficiency that resulted in heavy oversubscription. Every man in every township in every state was allotted a certain amount, and when Swan Swanson or Ole Olsen came to town, the local representative of the committee would tell him how much he was expected to take and at the same time "pass the word" that the neighbors had decided to meet at a certain time and place to put in their subscriptions. On the appointed hour, the street outside the bank or opera house or whatever place had been designated, would be lined with automobiles, and the whole business would be finished in less than an hour. No distinction of nationality was made, but I am indebted to Professor A. A. Stomberg, a member of the central committee, for statistics which show that in seventy-five townships with a population from eighty to ninety-eight per cent. Swedish the oversubscription was forty-seven per cent.

In other districts a suggestion of the Government was carried out by the forming of foreign-language committees. While the amounts gathered by this means are not always impressive in themselves, they become so when we remember that they represent small amounts personally solicited by members of the committees. To swell them, servant-girls have taken of their slow savings deposits to

DR. MAX HENIUS, PRESIDENT OF THE JACOB A. RIIS LEAGUE OF PATRIOTIC SERVICE

BARONESS ALMA DAHLERUP, ORGANIZER AND PRESIDENT OF THE DANISH WOMEN'S CIVIC LEAGUE

HAGBART BRASE, CONDUCTOR OF THE GREAT ORATORIO CHORUS AT LINDSBORG

give to the land of their hopes, and housewives, in these days of mounting prices, have pared their expenses to the bone. Moreover, these small depositors have all contributed in other ways, through the various societies to which they belong, or through the schools where their children are vying with one another in buying Thrift Stamps. Looked at in this way, the $5,100,000 subscribed by Scandinavians in Chicago in the Third Liberty Loan drive becomes truly stupendous. Of this amount the Swedes have contributed $3,000,000, the Norwegians $1,500,000, and the Danes $600,000. If we accept as correct the estimate that there are 18,000 Danes living in Chicago, this means $33.33 for each person, exclusive of larger investments by business firms, which have not passed through the hands of the Danish committee.

By sanctioning the foreign-language committees for the Liberty Loan drive, the President set the stamp of his approval on patriotic work carried on within lines of racial grouping. Two organizations with a nation-wide scope have been formed by Scandinavians for such activities. The John Ericsson League of Patriotic Service came into being as an answer to those who questioned the loyalty of the Swedes. Now the Danes have undertaken to aid the Government by putting at its disposal a complete machinery for reaching every citizen of Danish descent in the country. The Jacob A. Riis League of Patriotic Service grew out of the efficient committee that managed the Third Liberty Loan drive in Chicago, and its headquarters will remain in that city, though it will have a National Council of prominent men all over the country.

The women of the North have never quite lost the art of knitting;

the demand for socks and sweaters found them not only willing, but skilled.   The first to organize for systematic work along this line was the Danish Women's Civic League in New York, formed early last year with the aim of showing the loyalty of the foreign-born to the American cause.   It has now four hundred members. Among the thousand or more garments knit from wool provided by the League, some are the work of the old ladies in the Danish Home for the Aged in Brooklyn.   It is the second time these good ladies are fitting out men to fight the Germans; for some of them can remember knitting for the soldiers in Slesvig in 1864.

In the nursing profession, Scandinavian women are well repre-sented, and at least one Red Cross unit, Chicago No. 11, is composed almost entirely of Scandinavian women.   In the coeducational colleges, the women of the faculty have conducted classes in food conservation on lines advocated by the Government and have supervised the making of surgical dressings.   At St. Olaf College in Northfield a War Service Institute is being held during summer vacation for intensive training in various kinds of home work.

I should like to tell of the women in every walk of life who have contributed in some unique way.   Ane Marie Jensen has her own page in the REVIEW.   There is Mrs. David Kindleberger in New York, who leads the army of trained knitters with ten sweaters a week made by her own hands; and there is another Norwegian woman, Mrs. Ole Schulberg of Dunn, North Dakota, who has given her farm to the Red Cross.   There are the clever organizers like Mrs. Othelia Myhrman, president of the Swedish-American Women of Chicago Club, which raised enough money by a sale of buttons to buy an ambulance for the Red Cross.   And I could tell of the artists, of Olive Fremstad singing in training camps, Marguerite Leslie giving all her time to the Red Cross, and Carlotta Nilsen selling Liberty Bonds.

I should like, too, to tell of the visit of the Great Oratorio Chorus of Lindsborg to Camp Funston to sing to eight thousand soldiers. "Never was there such singing in the history of Kansas," writes a local paper, describing how "The Battle Hymn of the Republic" rolled out over the moonlit prairie, sung by the Chorus and assembled soldiers.   In these days, when all are giving of their best to the country, it fell to Lindsborg's lot to give the crowning gift of a great and noble inspiration.

Why We Are at War

By Knute Nelson

An authorized interview written by R. S. N. Sartz

GERMANY wanted war, and she has it. That fact has been so well proven that further discussion of the question of responsibility for the war is unnecessary. How the war has been carried on by Germany is a matter of history. She began by

Underwood Photo

Senator Knute Nelson

declaring treaties "mere scraps of paper," violating all rules of international law, invading neutral territory which she was pledged by solemn treaty to defend, and leaving murder, atrocities, and piracy in her wake. Women and children, old and young, by the hundreds, were indiscriminately slaughtered with fire, gun, and sword, in a manner resembling the raids of the Indians upon our frontier settlers in pioneer days. Towns and villages by the score, with churches, libraries, museums, and works of art, were ruthlessly destroyed. But for the great generosity of the people of the United States and of Great Britain, the Belgian people would have slowly perished from starvation in the fangs of the German army of occupation.

How the submarine campaign against ships of commerce, which in itself is a violation of the rules of all civilized nations with respect to visit, search, and capture at sea, has been carried on ruthlessly since the first of February, 1917, is likewise a matter of record. At that time, a submarine zone was prescribed around the British Isles, in the English Channel, the waters of France, and the inner part of the Mediterranean Sea, in which zone all neutral shipping, including that of the United States, was forbidden to enter under the threat of an intensive, indiscriminate, and destructive submarine campaign.

The plan and purpose of the German government, if it could have been carried out successfully, would have amounted to a total embargo on all our trade with Great Britain, France, Italy, Holland, and Greece. This would have destroyed upwards of three-fourths of our commerce, as the chief markets for the products of our farms, our factories, and our mines are in the countries within the scope of the German submarine zone. Could our country tamely submit to an embargo by German submarines on nearly all our foreign commerce? But more than all this, could we tamely submit to the indiscriminate, ruthless, and cruel destruction and slaughter of our citizens and sailors at sea bound on peaceful missions?

As further evidence of German submarine methods, take the case of the small neutral country of Norway. She has aimed throughout the war to preserve a strict neutrality, and the scantiness of her natural resources has helped her in this purpose. Yet she fared almost as badly on sea as Belgium on land. More than eight hundred of her ships, about 1,500,000 tons in all, have been sunk by German submarines, and over a thousand Norwegian sailors have lost their lives in consequence, many of them killed by German guns after they had succeeded in entering the life-boats. In some instances, the officers of these ships were accompanied by their wives, but these women were no more than their husbands immune from German shells even in the life-boats, and thus suffered as cruel a fate as many of the poor women in Belgium. What has been said about Norway holds good also with regard to the other two Scandinavian countries. Though the actual losses of Denmark and Sweden have been smaller, it is only because they have not had so much to lose.

Long before Congress declared war against Germany, that country had made war upon us by invading our country with her army of spies, plotters, strikers, and other paid emissaries. What these more than undesirable invaders have accomplished, or rather in vain have tried to accomplish, is again a matter of record, and I shall not go into details here. It is sufficient to call attention to the fact that many of them have been tried and convicted, and are now in prison.

All these various schemes and plots were carried on, or inspired, by von Papen and Boy-Ed, official attaches of the German ambassador, von Bernstorff. The German government, during the period of our neutrality, seemed utterly oblivious of our rights and duties as a neutral nation. It acted as though our country were a province of the German Empire, where it could carry on its nefarious schemes with perfect immunity. Had American citizens carried on such operations in Germany, under the direction of our ambassador or otherwise, they would undoubtedly have been shot or hanged without a moment's delay. We have simply tried the plotters in our own civil courts and given them short prison terms, which serves to illustrate the benignity of our system of government compared with that of Germany.

Germany, no doubt, expected that her submarine campaign against our commerce and her plottings and schemings in this country would ultimately extinguish our great patience and forbearance. So, to be prepared for this contingency, she sought through her Foreign Minister, von Zimmermann, to secure Mexico's help in an attack upon our nation.

There is no doubt in my mind that, if Germany should succeed in vanquishing the Allies in this war, our country would be the next victim. With all Europe at her feet, the United States would seem Lilliputian to her, and she would soon reach out for us. To me it seems the part of wisdom to meet her now with the aid of our Allies, instead of waiting for them to be vanquished and our country invaded.

Aside from this consideration, however, the conduct of Germany toward our country in this war, both on land and sea, in our own domain and abroad, has been such that it more than justifies us in carrying on a war against her. She has rudely and defiantly trampled upon our rights and we should be a craven among nations if we silently submitted. What loyal and patriotic son or daughter of America can honestly say, or in his or her bosom cherish the idea, that we have not good and valid ground for war? Nay, more than this, does not the welfare of our common humanity warrant and demand it?

The war will undoubtedly be a considerable burden to us, but in the end it will prove to be the moral regeneration of our country. We shall now know "who is who," who is for our country and who is against it, who loves some other country more than ours—the country in which he lives.

Before concluding, I should like to call attention to one more point, namely, that this great war which our country and the Allies are carrying on in Europe will be of as much value to the small neutral nations as to our own land, for if Germany should succeed in conquering France, England, and Italy, she would be paramount in Europe and throughout the world; little countries like Norway, Sweden, Denmark, Holland, and Belgium would then be mere vassals of Germany and would have to dance to her fiddle. Therefore, as far as possible, these small countries ought to sympathize and co-operate with that country which is now the only supply and commissary they have left, the United States.

In Camp with the Brotherhood

By J. A. O. Stub

WHEN the boys from the great Scandinavian states in the West were called to the colors, the Church desired to follow her sons. She had given them gladly to the country, and she wished to provide for their welfare while they were in the service. This is being done through two organizations: the Lutheran Brotherhood, now engaged in a campaign for a hundred thousand new members, and the National Lutheran Commission for Soldiers' and Sailors' Welfare, which, together with the Brotherhood, has recently collected a fund of more than a million and a quarter dollars.

The inception of the Lutheran Brotherhood was at Camp Dodge last summer. While the camp was in process of construction, the Iowa district of the Norwegian Church, President H. C. Holm, purchased a plot of ground and authorized a committee to go ahead with the erection of a suitable church and recreation building for the Norwegian boys who would soon be pouring in. About the same time, the Iowa Conference of the Swedish Augustana Synod took similar steps, and the two committees soon decided to combine their efforts. To take care of the work, the Lutheran Brotherhood, an organization of men something on the order of the Y. M. C. A., was formed, its first president being a Swede, Rev. A. Norrbom. While the organization includes twelve Lutheran church bodies, it is but fair to say that the Scandinavians, who took the initiative, have also given the larger measure of support.

EBRASKA, AND THE DAKOTAS, ASSEMBLED AT CAMP CODY, NEW MEXICO, FOR EASTER SERVICE

The building erected by the Brotherhood in the heart of Camp Dodge is the finest of its kind in the country, steam-heated throughout, and completely equipped in every way. As many as twelve hundred men have attended the Sunday morning services, and as many as two thousand have been present at the social gatherings held twice a week. Two pastors are in charge of the work. Similar buildings are in course of construction in other camps. The slogan of the Brotherhood is: Loyalty to home, loyalty to church, loyalty to country.

Meanwhile the direct work of the church bodies grew by leaps and bounds. Our Norwegian Church authorized an expenditure of $100,000. It became evident that only by united effort, avoiding duplication, and husbanding of resources, could our church in any measure care for the Lutheran boys in the Army and Navy, estimated at about two hundred thousand. The National Lutheran Commission for Soldiers' and Sailors' Welfare was therefore formed at a meeting in New York, called last October, by President Schmauk of the General Council. About two-thirds of the Lutheran churches in the United States, including practically all the Scandinavian synods, are now formally affiliated with the Commission, while the remaining one-third coöperate in some external matters. It is no injustice to say, however, that Scandinavians have been the backbone of the Commission, and that their vigor and enthusiasm inspired all to undertake a work that, a year ago, would have seemed impossible.

To-day the Commission supports about one hundred camp pastors or volunteer chaplains, who devote their energies to ministering to

An Assembly in the House of the Brotherhood at Camp Dodge

our boys in various ways. They call on them in barracks, comfort and encourage them, and strengthen their determination to give their best to the country. They hold religious services. They speed those who are about to leave for overseas, write to their parents, and look up boys who are slow in writing home. These men wear a dark gray uniform and are now pretty well known in most of our camps. Furthermore, the Commission tries to keep in touch with the boys through its headquarters at 437 Fifth Avenue, New York. If correct military address is sent in, the workers there will endeavor to look after your boy.

A number of men are devoting their time exclusively to hospital work, and, although primarily working in the interest of our Lutheran Church, the representatives of the Commission try to minister to all who are in need of their services, and it is doubtful if any boy with a Scandinavian name is ever overlooked in a hospital. Among its other activities is the publication of literature, and it is endeavoring to place a practical Army and Navy Service Book in the hands of every Lutheran boy.

Last February, the Commission and the Brotherhood conducted a joint campaign to

The House at Camp Dodge, the First to Be Erected

raise $750,000 for the prosecution of the work. When the campaign closed, $1,300,000 had been raised, and money was still coming in! Many of our Scandinavian states in the Middle West doubled and quadrupled their quota, thanks to the splendid work of their state chairmen, often carried on at great personal sacrifice. Thus S. H. Holstad of Minneapolis gave up his business entirely to carry on the campaign in his state. Minnesota's quota was $89,000, but it raised $258,000. A single county, Hennepin, under the chairmanship of President Frank Nelson of Minnesota College, collected $50,000. Mr. J. K. Jensen of Janesville left his thriving business there and moved to Milwaukee in order to devote himself to the work in Wisconsin. The quota of his state was $64,000, and it raised $168,000. Mr. A. O. Hauge of Des Moines quadrupled Iowa's quota. Mr. Nestos of Minot sent in a cheque for $49,614.41 as the contribution from North Dakota. The chairman of practically every Middle Western and Northwestern state was of Scandinavian origin.

Much money was raised, but the work has grown to such gigantic proportions that the original estimate of $750,000 will not suffice to carry it on even for one year. Yet we are confident that when the call goes out again our devoted and loyal people will surpass our most sanguine expectations.

The Patriot's Prayer

By Ernst W. Olson

This Patriotic Air, Based on C. W. A. Strandberg's "Stridsbön," Has Been Sung by the Wennerberg Male Chorus of Augustana College at Several Training Camps as Well as at Patriotic Meetings

Lord of realms and spheres unnumbered,
Mighty Ruler evermore!
Hear our prayers, bestow Thy blessings
On us from Thy bounteous store.
Thine the power, Thine the glory,
Grant that freedom e'er be ours;
Lord Almighty, stand Thou with us,—
Then we fear no earthly powers.

Yet, if in our country's story,
Blazoned with Thy deeds, O God,
There's a page to fill with glory
Which must needs be writ with blood,
Grant us grace to fight with honor,
Else for us no sun must rise,
And the stars that saw us falter,
Cast them, Lord, from out the skies.

Interpreting America

NO policy could be more short-sighted than the suppression of the foreign-language press now advocated by some apostles of Know-nothingism. The newspaper in the immigrant's own language does more than any other one agency to acquaint him with the ideals and institutions of his new country. The Scandinavian press has from the beginning been an exponent of Americanism. The men who fought in the Fifteenth Wisconsin, many of them, could not read English, but learned the issues of the war from a little Norwegian sheet published in a hamlet in Wisconsin. The immigrant of to-day has a better education. He often knows English before he comes here, and in any case absorbs it with avidity as soon as he sets foot on American soil. Yet he needs a newspaper in the language of his homeland. It carries to him a more intimate message; it speaks in a voice he knows, and therefore inspires confidence.

During the first two years of the war, the Scandinavians in the West were lukewarm, inclined to blame both sides in the conflict equally. They were on friendly terms with their German Lutheran neighbors and slow to believe that the kinsmen of these people could be guilty of the atrocities they heard of. At that time, the press, with greater knowledge, was in advance of its constituency. As early as July 29, 1914, *Skandinaven* uncovered the intrigues of Austria against Servia, and, on August 18, *Decorah-Posten* wrote:

> The German emperor seems to be master of the situation. At a word from him, Austria would probably have accepted Servia's apology for the murder of the heir to the throne. . . . If the emperor had said this word, there would have been no war, but he did not say it. Therefore he now stands before the world as the one who is chiefly responsible for the war. If, furthermore, we ask why Germany wanted a world war, the only answer is: expansion of German power and military rule.

Minneapolis Tidende likewise blamed Kaiser Wilhelm for the war, while at the same time pointing out the failure of the whole "balance of power" system, and expressing what is now the one great hope of liberals the world over, saying:

> One consequence of this war, it is to be hoped, will be that a few rulers shall no longer have power to plunge the nations into war. The executive power must be so lodged that it is fully responsible to the men chosen by the people and thus forced to do the will of the people and nothing else.

The Danish papers were, of course, intensely anti-German from the beginning. *Nordlyset, Revyen, Ugebladet,* and *Den Danske Pioneer* have constantly printed violent attacks on the Kaiser and all that he stands for. *Revyen*, in 1914, expressed a fervent hope that he and his accomplices would hang from the lamp-posts of Unter den

Linden, and *Nordlyset* published some very unflattering cartoons of him.

Svenska Amerikanaren, among the Swedish organs, came out squarely against Germany from the first, saying:

> The fact that Germany began the war is beyond question. To be sure, it was Austria who first declared war against Servia, but we may be very sure that this happened after an agreement with Germany regarding the consequences. Germany could easily have prevented war by refusing her aid to Austria in case the declaration of war against Servia should provoke action from Russia. By not preventing the declaration of war, although the consequences could easily be foreseen, Germany incurred responsibility for the great war. History will without a doubt place this fearful responsibility on Germany.

Not all Swedish-American editors had an equally clear perception at that stage. Most of the Swedes in the United States belong to a generation that had the fear of Russia bred in their bone. They or their fathers left Sweden before the rise of Prussianism, and before the liberal development which shifted the foreign alignment of their mother country. To them, Russia was the hereditary enemy of western democracy, and they could not understand how liberal France and England could fight on the same side with the Czar. But as soon as Germany stood revealed the enemy of their adopted country, the Swedes in America knew no divided allegiance. The test of their loyalty came with the Luxburg revelations, which threatened serious misunderstanding between the country of their birth and that of their adoption. Then the Swedish-American press with one accord testified to the "one hundred per cent. Americanism" which has since become the slogan of Scandinavian-Americans. Among the numerous editorials breathing absolute loyalty, we choose a paragraph from *Nordstjernan*:

> Swedish-Americans honor their homeland, but the new land to which they have given their fealty and their oath must stand and always has stood first. They are ready, if fate demands it of them, to give their blood (*kläda blodig skjorta*) for their adopted country, even against the land where they were born and bred, or where their parents were born and bred.

This article was attacked as "traitorous" by the Conservative organ, *Nya Dagligt Allehanda* in Stockholm, whereupon *Nordstjernan* reaffirmed its American loyalty in even stronger terms, saying:

> It is inconceivable to us how any Swedish newspaper editor can fail to see that in the moment when we took our oath as citizens of this country we bound ourselves to defend it with our heart's blood, and this means that we might even have to fight our old homeland, if—which God forbid . . . there should be war between the United States and Sweden.

Our entrance into the war was accepted by the Scandinavian-language press with a sober realization of the struggle ahead of us, but in a spirit of absolute loyalty. The pacifist organ, *Reform*, still believed that President Wilson's ideal of a League of Nations could have been realized without war, but bowed to the will of the people as expressed through Congress, counselling all citizens of Norwegian blood to stand solidly with the country, and to bear their share of the burdens faithfully. *Veckobladet*, which on the very eve of war had pleaded for peace, wrote that "we must each and all be ready to make sacrifices in whatever manner the welfare of our country demands, and must show in word and deed that we are worthy of our citizenship." A more belligerent note was struck by the larger newspapers. Thus *Svenska Amerikanaren*, before the declaration of war, wrote:

America did not want war and does not want war. If the matter rested with America, there would be no war between us and any other country. If America were to renounce all rights as a neutral, war might be avoided, but that would be the most contemptible position any one could take, and such a course would soon bring its own punishment.

On the day war was declared, *Ugebladet* wrote:

America is now in the war. That is no cause for rejoicing—on the contrary, it is to be regretted that it should be necessary to go so far. But the step has been taken, and now all Americans, native-born or immigrant, have but one duty: to be loyal to our country and our Government.

Skandinaven expressed unqualified approval of the action taken by Congress:

No one who has read the President's message to Congress can doubt that Germany, through a long series of lawless acts that lack a parallel in history, has forced the United States into the war. It had to come. The United States has been compelled to take up the gauntlet thrown us by Prussian autocracy, the natural enemy of democracy.

Turning from the press comments at the time of our entrance into the war to those of a year later, we find a remarkable consolidation of patriotic purpose. All papers without exception give generous space to the Liberty Loan, the Red Cross, and other national service. All record with pride the part taken by Scandinavians, the flocking of young men to the colors, the dedication of service flags, the loyalty meetings, the innumerable activities to aid the Government in its prosecution of the war. Among the editorials urging subscription to the Liberty Loan, we note one in *Washington-Posten* reminding its readers that liberty was "often the only heritage they brought with them from Norway," and they, to whom liberty had always been the very breath of life, ought to be the first to contribute.

It might perhaps be expected that Scandinavians, being proverbial "kickers" and haters of graft, should be the most loud-voiced critics of the Government, but their press is singularly moderate, slow to believe in "exposures," strong in demanding fair play for the Government. Thus *Svenska Kuriren* urges everybody to "drop all discussion and cease all criticism" that might "breed dissension and create division, thus discouraging people from the sacrifices necessary to win the war." Similar pleas are made by *Minneapolis Tidende, Decorah-Posten, Veckobladet,* and others.

While the moral loyalty of the Swedish-American editors to their country has always been beyond cavil, it might perhaps be said that their intellectual enlightenment was completed with the German occupation of Finland. *Svenska Tribunen Nyheter* writes:

> What does all this mean except that Germany is carrying on a war of conquest, and that Prussian autocracy is a real danger threatening the world? That danger is imminent for little Sweden, which is now in a much more dangerous position than in the days of the mighty Russian Czarism. Any one with open eyes can now see that a German victory would be fatal to all democratic nations, and not least to Sweden and the other Northern countries. Therefore it seems to us that the Swedes and their nearest neighbors should be especially thankful to America, which has entered the war, not for gain, but in order to help the weaker nations, to destroy German autocracy and militarism, and protect the freedom of the world. From America help must come, and America will win.

Minnesota Stats Tidning, while admitting that "the war was not at first popular," thinks that "there are surely few who do not now see the necessity of America's entrance into the war in order to crush German insolence."

Nordisk Tidende, published in Brooklyn, is in a position to reach a large number of unnaturalized Norwegians. Last November, the paper printed an article explaining the rules for exemption of foreign citizens from military service, and in doing so gave special typographical display to the following paragraph:

> We hope that no Norwegian citizen will claim exemption unless absolutely compelled to do so. Norwegian citizens should remember that America is fighting for the right of small nations, and that a victorious ending of the war is just as important for Norway as for America itself.

In conclusion, we quote from a fervently patriotic editorial in a recent number of *Duluth Skandinav:*

> Perhaps some of us feel a little depressed because duty lays upon our shoulders a burden which is a thousand times easier to bear than that borne by the soldier's mother or father. Perhaps we think times are hard, and we complain that we are not getting out of life all the pleasure and happiness that is our due. And yet—think for a moment of what is happening in the various training camps in this country—think of what is happening in Europe—think of the suffering—think of the privation—of the losses and of the pain and anguish, physical and mental, endured by the men in the trenches, and you will wake up to a new understanding—an understanding that will make you sacrifice everything to be of the greatest help, that will make you unfold all your powers to help not only our own community, but the entire world. Then duty will become a precious burden to you. You will sit down and think of what you have left undone that you might have done. You will feel small and weak and miserable when you measure yourself with your own great desire to work wonders, and you will feel what a great debt you owe to those who are pouring out their hearts' blood on the soil of France.

For Liberty and Right!

By CARL NEUMANN

THE AMERICAN PARAPHRASE OF "DEN TAPRE LANDSOLDAT" IS OFFERED BY MR. NEUMANN IN THE HOPE THAT THE MAGIC THIRD TIME WILL HAVE ITS EFFECT WHEN THE OLD TUNE IS SUNG BY AMERICAN BOYS ON GERMAN SOIL. THE ORIGINAL DATES BACK TO THE WAR BETWEEN DENMARK AND GERMANY IN 1848. IT WAS SUNG AGAIN IN 1864. THE POPULARITY IT HAS ALREADY GAINED IN OUR CAMPS PROMISES THAT IT WILL GO ACROSS WITH OUR BOYS AND BE ONE OF THEIR FIGHTING SONGS

I heard my Country's call, I heard my Country's call,
A summons to us all, Yes, a summons to us all;
I shook my Daddy's fist, my Mother dear I kissed,
And told her how it was, I felt that now I must enlist.
But when I said good-bye to my girl so sweet and true,
She told me that, as nurse, she of course was going too;
So I am off to fight—for Liberty and Right,
Hurrah!   Hurrah!   Hurrah!

I heard my Father say, I heard my Father say,
In his old-fashioned way, Yes, in his old-fashioned way,
When those who work and toil go off to war and spoil,
Who then shall do the harvesting and who shall till the soil?
Well, that is just the reason we all must hurry up
Or Teutons will come over and try to boss the job—
So I am off to fight—for Liberty and Right,
Hurrah!   Hurrah!   Hurrah!

If the junkers should come here, if the junkers should come here,
They sure will domineer, Yes, they sure will domineer;
They meet you with a scowl, and tell you "Du bist faul,"
And if you talk United States, at once they yell "Halt's Maul."
For people who are linguists it may not signify,
But it makes quite a difference to chaps like you and I.
So I am off to fight—for Liberty and Right,
Hurrah!   Hurrah!   Hurrah!

The Kaiser hates our flag, the Kaiser hates our flag,
Considers it a rag, Yes, considers it a rag,
But he and all his tribes, despite Teutonic jibes,
Will have to bow and bend the knee before the Stars and Stripes,
And proudly shall Old Glory wave on the battlefield,
Until the Hohenzollern shall bite the dust and yield;
So I am off to fight—for Liberty and Right,
Hurrah!   Hurrah!   Hurrah!

Our fathers fought before, Our fathers fought before,
And we will fight some more, Yes, and we will fight some more,
They fought for Liberty, and so indeed shall we—
And also strike an extra blow just for humanity;
When autocratic rulers they try to run amuck
It's up to us to show them their hour of doom has struck.
So I am off to fight—for Liberty and Right,
Hurrah!   Hurrah!   Hurrah!

Current Illustrations

MEN WHO FOUGHT IN THE CIVIL WAR THINK THE SOLDIERS OF TODAY ARE BEING SPOILED WITH "MOVIES AND SUCH NONSENSE." HERE IS A SAMPLE: TWO SILHOUETTES FROM THE COLLECTION OF MISS MAUDE I. G. OLIVER, WHO MAKES A PRACTICE OF CUTTING OUT PORTRAITS OF THE BOYS AT THE PARTIES GIVEN ON SUNDAY AFTERNOONS AT THE GREAT LAKES TRAINING STATION BY THE CORDON CLUB OF CHICAGO. MISS AGNES FROMEN CONTRIBUTES HER SHARE TO THE FROLIC BY MAKING MINIATURE BUSTS OF THE MEN

WHEN PRESIDENT ANDREEN VISITED HIS AUGUSTANA BOYS AT CAMP LOWDEN, THEY HAD MISGIVINGS ABOUT HIS ABILITY TO MOUNT A HORSE. ONE EAGER YOUTH WOULD HAVE BROUGHT A STEP-LADDER, AND ANOTHER SUGGESTED A FENCE, BUT "PREXY" ASTONISHED THEM BY VAULTING INTO THE SADDLE AND SITTING HIS HORSE LIKE A VETERAN. THE RIDE WAS LONGER THAN HE HAD EXPECTED, FOR THE BOYS INSISTED ON LEADING HIM IN TRIUMPH THROUGH THE CAMP

Courtesy of Augustana Book Concern

Madame Signe Lund, Who Won the Prize Offered by the National Arts Club for Her Composition "The Road to France" to the Words of Daniel M. Henderson

Dean of Women, Gertrude M. Hilleboe Has Established a Splendid Record for Red Cross Work at St. Olaf College. Not Only Is Every Student Enrolled as a Member, but the College Has Its Own Red Cross Auxiliary and Its Own Work-room. There Surgical Dressings Are Made Under the Direction of Twenty Upper Class Women, Who Have Taken the Supervisors' Course. Most of the Young Women Have Enrolled in the Red Cross Preparedness Classes in "First Aid" and "Home Care of the Sick." The Parade Through the Streets of Northfield Marked the Conclusion of a Month in Which 3,600 Bandages Had Been Made at the College.

"THE CHARGE" AND "RECONSTRUCTION" ARE TWO OF THE FOUR BRONZE RELIEFS ON THE SOLDIERS'
MONUMENT BY DAVID EDSTRÖM JUST COMPLETED IN OTTUMWA, IOWA. THEY DECORATE THE BASE,
WHICH SUPPORTS A GRANITE PILLAR SURMOUNTED BY AN EAGLE WITH WINGS SPREAD. THE FOUR
RELIEFS CONSTITUTE AN EPIC OF WAR. THE FIRST SHOWS THE DEPARTURE OF THE SOLDIER FROM
HIS OWN HOUSEHOLD. THE SECOND IS A POWERFUL REPRESENTATION OF THE FORWARD THRUSTING
PASSION IN THE BAYONET CHARGE—THE "CARRYING ON," AS THE BRITISH CALL IT. THEN COMES
THE DEATH OF THE SOLDIER IN THE FOREST WITH THE BATTLE RUSHING MADLY ON. THE LAST IS
THE QUIET PATHOS OF THE RECONSTRUCTION, THE REHABILITATION OF THE LAND BY WOMEN AND BOYS.

The Service Flag

By THORA GRÖNVOLD

THE occasion was the dedicating of a service flag. The particular place I need not mention, for what I have to relate is true of most, if not all, Scandinavian communities of the Middle West. I walked up the broad aisle formed by two rows of majestic elm-trees to the large white church. About it were the graves of the pioneer settlers who had been its first members. The trimness of the lots and the dignity of the white tombstones bespoke the veneration with which the community had buried its dear dead.

Within the church, spacious though it was, the very aisles were crowded. We were ushered up to the benches beside the old-fashioned altar, and from that vantage point I had an opportunity to study the audience: faces familiar to my childhood, and yet unfamiliar. Some were aged, others but matured; all had a look of calm, strong determination, and bore the marks of character growth seen in those who have fought a battle and won; in those who have beheld a high vision and followed it.

With a feeling almost of awe, I watched the play of expression on their frank, kindly faces during the programme of speeches and songs. Weatherbeaten, graying fathers and stooped, toilworn mothers were there; younger men and women, some fairly beginning their life-work; young girls and children, their serious faces alight with enthusiasm over the beauty of the service.

The boys who were about to leave their homes to defend the Great Cause, were there for the last time. I saw no manifestations of regret or grief at leaving their beautiful homes and their chosen life-work. Brave smiles, erect heads, and eyes fastened on their own stars in the service flag told more eloquently than words that they realized the worth of their privilege: to give themselves to their country, that their loved ones might live in happiness.

The community is a prosperous one. In fifty odd years, large, modern farms have sprung up where Minnesota forests once grew. The people show the signs of affluence. Their dress is tasteful and modish. Their bearing has the self-confidence that comes with success. Their sons and daughters are given a good education. Their farm labor is lightened by modern inventions. Automobiles conserve their time. America has given them bounteously, and now they stand with open hands, eager to give to America in her time of need.

The progressive farmer of to-day keeps his money working. His income is put into additional land, into labor-saving implements, and into all modern improvements. In spite of the fact that the farmer's money is "tied up" in this manner, the response in the community to the Liberty Loan drives, the Red Cross, and all other patriotic work has been hearty. The township I have in mind subscribed $61,250 to the third Liberty Loan. The whole county, which has a large percentage of Scandinavian people, went far over its allotment by subscribing one and one-half million dollars.

The busy farm-wife does her direct share of Red Cross work. Up at four or five o'clock in the morning, she has her house in order, her bread baked, and her evening meal planned in time to spend the afternoon in the nearest church basement sewing for the Red Cross. She is capable, cheerful, and energetic. She sends her sons away with a smile, and lets the still, dark watches hide her grief.

Every church has its service flag, one with fourteen stars, one with thirty, and still another with fifty-five. Each star means not only a sacrifice of love, but also the re-shouldering of the burden by a father who has already done a life's work, and who has been looking forward to spending the afternoon of his life in the enjoyment of the fruits of his strenuous labor.

"What will you do without John on the farm?" I asked the gray-beard owner of a large, well-kept farm. His son was to leave for the army on the morrow.

"Oh, we'll manage somehow," was the answer. "Mary and Agnes will have the dairy with its twenty cows. Mary will take the cream to town in the truck, while Agnes helps her mother. Little Alfred will drive the horses in the field, run the tractor, and do the chores. If the Lord gives us health and strength, we can manage."

"John could have claimed exemption on the ground of truly necessary farm work," I suggested. I received a direct look from the clear, gray eyes of the good man.

"It is our privilege to release a brave son that he may do his duty to his country," came the quiet reply. "My father fought in the Civil War, though he had been here but a short time. His grave is yonder by the church. He gave us as a legacy a deep love for the country of our birth—of his adoption."

I looked in the direction he designated, and my thoughts overwhelmed me for a moment. That generation of stanch Norse men and women came to this country, bringing their dreams with them. They lived to see their dreams come true. But those visions, strong and worthy though they were, were but forerunners of other visions. In the brave faces of those people, I read the wonder-dream that is transforming this young country of many strains and welding it into one mighty brotherhood with an unswerving ideal: World Democracy.

One of the Knitters

A T the edge of the prairie town Dell Rapids in South Dakota
lives Ane Marie Jensen of Aalborg (Mrs. Chris White), a
splendid representative of thrifty, healthy Danish woman-
hood.   When I entered her well-kept home, a savory odor of freshly

fried doughnuts greeted me, but I had to cross the road in order to find the maker. Briskly she stepped out of the neighbor's house explaining that she had just brought over a few dough-nuts for the "old lady"—who hardly claims more years than Ane Marie herself, but Ane Marie is only seventy years young.

I explained that a New York magazine wanted to publish the story of the socks she had knit from the wool of her own sheep, sheared, carded, and spun by her own hands.

"Oh, so much fuss about those socks! Why, I've all my life raised sheep and knitted— that's nothing new nor extra-ordinary," and she displayed sweaters, socks, shawls, all the fruit of her labor for her im-mediate family. "In Denmark I raised sheep and made my liv-ing by knitting," she continued, "and when we came to Dakota forty-two years ago, of course we kept sheep. I was young then and had strong hands, and the farmers used to have me shear their sheep. I have done as many as thirty-five in a day. I remember once, when one of my children was a baby in arms, a farmer called for me to help him, and as I couldn't leave my baby, he lifted the cradle, baby and all, into his wagon. Yes, those were busy and happy days," and a soft light came into the snapping brown eyes. "I have had ten children and raised seven of them, and my second husband also had seven children, so you see I have had a large family to care and work for, and now I think I should have a rest."

As I looked at the strong, fine face, I said impulsively: "Oh, you can do much yet."

"I can do some," she said, with sparkling eyes. "Now the children are married and scattered, I have plenty of time to spin and knit, and I want to help keep the boys warm. I have a grandson in the army myself, Harvey Pedersen in Spokane"—she showed me a snapshot of a young soldier saluting—"and I want to do my little share for Uncle Sam who has done so much for me and mine."

A. S. S.

Beat! Beat! Drums!

By WALT WHITMAN

Beat! beat! drums!—blow! bugles! blow!
Through the windows—through doors—burst like a ruthless force,
Into solemn church, and scatter the congregation,
Into the school where the scholar is studying;
Leave not the bridegroom quiet—no happiness must he have now with
*   his bride,*
Nor the peaceful farmer any peace, ploughing his field or gathering
*   his grain,*
So fierce you whir and pound you drums—so shrill you bugles blow.

Beat! beat! drums!—blow! bugles! blow!
Over the traffic of cities—over the rumble of wheels in the streets;
Are beds prepared for sleepers at night in the houses? No sleepers
*   must sleep in those beds,*
No bargainers' bargain by day—no brokers or speculators—would they
*   continue?*
Would the talkers be talking? Would the singer attempt to sing?
Would the lawyer rise in the court to state his case before the judge?
Then rattle quicker, heavier, drums—you bugles wilder blow.

Beat! beat! drums!—blow! bugles! blow!
Make no parley—stop for no expostulation,
Mind not the timid—mind not the weeper or prayer,
Mind not the old man beseeching the young man,
Let not the child's voice be heard, nor the mother's entreaties,
*   *   *   *   *
So strong you thump, oh terrible drums—so loud you bugles blow.

Editorial

Loyalty of Scandinavians "Are the Scandinavians loyal?" To us the question seems absurd, and yet we must accept the fact that it is now and then asked. *The Bellman,* a Minneapolis weekly of purely American affiliations, calls the question of Scandinavian loyalty "in itself almost an insult," and proceeds to answer it so much better than we could have done that we have asked permission to quote a few paragraphs.

"One of the most admirable traits of the Scandinavian is the quiet deliberation with which he forms his judgments. He is not to be stampeded into ill-considered action by flamboyant and superficial appeals. He makes up his mind on any given subject, not lightly, but soberly, considering it carefully in all its aspects. He is not satisfied with ready-made opinions, but must think out conclusions for himself; he is not given to precipitate decisions, but must fully understand before he will commit himself openly. . . . The Scandinavian judgment, conscientious in its desire not to be swayed by prejudice or hatred, but to arrive at its conclusion through knowledge of the truth and a sane, calm process of reasoning, has been formed, and it is not vacillating. A just and righteous wrath against the military aggression which has its exponent in Germany is aroused, and a patient, peace-loving people has fully determined on its course."

The Bellman goes on to speak of the Scandinavian element in the army and navy, and concludes: "In view of the exceptionally notable response of the Scandinavians to the calls made upon them by the Government, in acts of patriotism that count so much more than high-sounding, glib, and inexpensive language, those who, from ignorance or preconceived notions of race sympathies, would question their loyalty are put to shame. If all native-born Americans were doing their duty half as well as the Scandinavians, the country might well congratulate itself. In this great fight, by land and sea, in the service that goes to war and the service that helps at home, the American born in Scandinavia or of Scandinavian ancestry will be found among the foremost in strength, endurance, sincerity, and courage."

Food for Norway The treaty between our Government and that of Norway, which went into effect May 10, is gratifying in every way. It inaugurates an era of good feeling between ourselves and a friendly nation, and is entirely in keeping with the principles which our President laid down at the beginning of the war for our dealings with small neutrals. In providing generously for Norway's wants, our Government recognized the splendid service rendered our cause by Norway's brave seafaring men and enterprising shipowners. The War Trade Board, in its public statement, spoke of the amicable and conciliatory spirit in which the negotiations have been carried on and paid a tribute to the eminent qualities of Dr. Nansen, the head of the Norwegian Special Mission.

The agreement confers substantial and, so far as we can see, nearly equal benefits on both parties. The Norwegian representatives were able to send at once the seed and motor plows needed for the spring plowing, and these shipments were quickly followed by supplies of corn and barley stored here by the Norwegian Government. Further purchases will be made in coöperation with Mr. Hoover's office, and it is expected that wheat and rye may be obtained from Argentina. The amount which Norway is allowed to import annually includes 300,000 tons of bread grain, 200,000 tons of fodder, besides other food, textiles, metals, fertilizers, and various miscellaneous articles.

Guaranties are, of course, given that none of these imports will benefit Germany directly or indirectly. The bulk of Norway's own products will go to our Allies, and, while the exports to Germany are not absolutely stopped, they are so curtailed that they will, in fact, be negligible. It is unofficially understood that the exportation of nickel will not be resumed during the war. Norway possesses certain rare and almost invaluable minerals used for lighting and in the manufacture of ammunition, and these will go chiefly to France, together with timber, fish, nitrates, and wood pulp. No disposition is made of Norwegian tonnage, since that has for a long time been used chiefly in the service of our Allies.

SCANDINAVIAN STUDIES   The war cannot be won by men in khaki alone. Some of us must possess our souls in patience and take our places thousands of miles behind the fighting lines. Our high schools and universities must be supported and a reserve of brains maintained, particularly in the chemical and engineering sciences. Nor can the study of languages be neglected. Even German will be needed if the war continues several years, and our armies find themselves, as we hope, on German soil. The fact remains, however, that German studies have received a permanent setback. Our children will prefer hereafter to study the languages of free peoples, and no literature has contributed to the democratic thought of the world in richer proportion than the Scandinavian. Happily, we have had in this country since 1911 a Society for the Advancement of Scandinavian Study. Its publication, *Scandinavian Studies and Notes*, edited by Professor George T. Flom, with Professor A. Louis Elmquist as associate editor, serves the double mission of providing scholars with an organ for their investigations in Northern fields and of encouraging the introduction of Swedish and Norwegian into our high schools. Thus the latest number contains a complete schedule of four-year high-school courses in Norse and in Swedish with text-books and supplementary reading. It is hoped that the Society will continue to concentrate in these two fields and not dissipate its energy. At the annual meeting on May third and fourth at the University of Chicago, Professor A. A. Stomberg was again made president, and most of the officers were reëlected. Application for membership should be made to the Secretary-Treasurer, Professor Joseph Alexis, University of Nebraska, Lincoln, Nebraska.

ABSENT VOTING Legislators have busied themselves, recently, in devising some means by which the voter who happens to be unavoidably absent from the polls on election day shall not be deprived of his vote. Nineteen of our states have passed laws in the past five years adopting some form of absent voting for civilians, whereas before 1913 only two had any such laws. In Norway, on the other hand, "absent voting" is an old, well-established institution, provision being made for it in the Eidsvold constitution of 1814, which with amendments is the constitution of Norway to-day. It is permissible both in national and in local elections, where absence is due to sickness, military service, or other valid excuse.

There is but little red tape connected with the practice. No official ballots are furnished. The "absent" voter makes out his ballot privately, and places it in an envelope, which he seals. If unable to help himself, he may have it made out for him. If outside the territorial limits of Norway, he may vote for his political party without naming candidates. He sends this ballot, together with a letter giving the reasons for his absence, to the election officers of the precinct in which he is a registered voter. He must affirm that the reasons given for his absence are true, but no further proof is required by law. Ordinarily, however, the statements will be confirmed by witnesses. Within the kingdom, his signature must be witnessed by some person of legal age; if outside the kingdom, by a Norwegian consul or Norwegian ship's officer.

After sending in a ballot, a voter may change his vote at any time before election by sending in another ballot. A voter may cast his ballot before leaving home if he so desires.

When the polls are closed, the election officers first pass on the validity of the excuses submitted by the absent voters. The tendency is toward liberality, particularly in local elections, but, since the voters throughout Norway are quite generally known personally to the election officers, there is little likelihood of fraud.

Five per cent. of the valid ballots cast in the parliamentary election in 1912 were sent in by letter. 619 were sent in from outside the realm. Of the 32,541 ballots sent in by letter, twenty-three per cent. were rejected. In the local elections of 1913, nearly eight per cent. of the valid ballots were cast *in absentia*, and of the 37,977 ballots so cast, 13.2 per cent. were rejected. In Finmarken, a sparsely settled northern county, nearly half as many men and more than four-fifths as many women voted by letter as voted personally at the polls.

Absent voting is used to a greater extent in rural districts than in cities, and is used more freely by women than by men. The institution originated as an accommodation to fishermen, sailors, and members of scattered rural communities. It continues to serve great numbers who otherwise would be virtually disfranchised.

RASMUS S. SABY.

OVER THE TOP   The REVIEW likewise has "gone over the top": more than four thousand new Associate subscribers since October 26, when we fired the first blast in Uncle Sam's mail-bag for our Friendly Aid Campaign. On May 17, the anniversary of Eidsvold, we registered our farthest advance into the territory of international indifference—8,274 subscribers. Thank you, good friends, one and all! If you wish to know the names of those who sent us most new Associates, here are a few of them:— fifty or more: J. G. Bergquist, O. Dorff, C. S. Haight, H. G. Haugan, E. O. Holter, H. G. Leach, Frederick Lynch, Tinius Olsen, W. H. Schofield, H. Björnström Steffanson, and A. A. Stomberg; twenty-five or more: John Aspegren, P. T. Berg, Mrs. J. A. Gade, J. W. H. Hamilton, H. J. Krebs, A. E. Paulson, J. P. Seeburg, H. W. Sibley, and C. A. Smith.

PRESIDENT SCHOFIELD   The President of the Foundation has had an active semester, lecturing at five Western colleges and to communities round about. He represented not only the American-Scandinavian Foundation but Harvard University and the National Security League, and, none the less, his own strong personality. In his college lectures he endeavored to explain the origin of chivalric ideals in medieval France and England, showing how they were definitely animating the Allies in the present world war, in glaring contrast to the standards of the Central Powers. From all accounts Professor Schofield enjoyed the Middle West as heartily as it enjoyed him. He achieved four lectures in one day, and delivered fourteen addresses in the Twin Cities. Immediate fruits of his trip are Societies of Associates of the Foundation, with duly elected officers, in Galesburg and Rockford, Illinois; in Beloit, Wisconsin, and Northfield, Minnesota; in Wisconsin a strong Council of five of the most forceful men of the state, with Professor Julius E. Olson as Secretary. Professor Schofield has done yeoman service in urging the Yankee element to welcome with open arms the loyal and hearty coöperation of their liberty-loving fellow citizens of Scandinavian blood. Likewise he encouraged the latter to respect and preserve their heritage as a glorious asset given to America in her hour of need. In Professor Schofield's work the heat of patriotism is accompanied by light and illumination. And no class of citizens, we take it, is better able to appreciate the rich learning and fine ideals of this American scholar than those of us who have learned our love of books and scientific self-analysis from the nursery of the North. Such is the testimony of the many letters attesting to Professor Schofield's work which have come to the editors of the REVIEW. "He has done wonders out here," says one. "He has shown us that the Foundation and its ideals of intellectual brotherhood are something which we must support now of all times; to become an Associate of the American-Scandinavian Foundation is a patriotic privilege."

H. G. L.

BECH TRUSTEE   The Trustees of the American-Scandinavian Foundation, at their regular meeting in New York, June 8, elected two new Trustees. The choice of Mr. Georg Bech, formerly Consul General for Denmark in New York, and now engaged in export and import trade in that city, will be acclaimed by Danes the world over. He was elected to succeed Mr. Eskesen, and was, moreover, elected treasurer of the Foundation in place of Mr. Short, who resigned after six years of service. Mr. Charles J. Rhoades, formerly Governor of the Federal Reserve Bank in Philadelphia, and now in France in Y. M. C. A. service, was elected as the seventeenth Trustee. Mr. Rhoades is an American of English descent. At the same meeting the following nominations of Fellows for the academic year 1918-1919 were confirmed:

FROM NORWAY

DITLEF HALD, engineer, state railways of Norway, to study railroad technique, particularly signaling.
JOHN ANSTEINSSON, librarian, to study at the New York State Library School.

HONORARY (without stipend)

HERMAN DEDICHEN, chemist, to do research work in the by-products of cellulose at the Massachusetts Institute of Technology.
MARTIN L. REYMERT, doctor of philosophy, Foundation Fellow 1916-17, to study psychology at the University of Iowa.

FROM DENMARK

HARALD TRAP FRIIS, electrical engineer, to study wireless telegraphy and telephony at the College of the City of New York.
JOHANNES MICHELSEN, master of arts, to study the theory and practice of library work at the New York State Library School.

HONORARY (without stipend)

ELISABETH NORDENTOFT, dentist, to study orthodentistry at the University of California and the University of Pennsylvania.

FROM SWEDEN

PER ENGSTRÖM, dentist, to study at the Dental College of the University of Minnesota.
GÖSTA LANGENFERT, master of arts, to study American literature.

On account of war conditions, no Scholarships were awarded to American students for study in Scandinavia. The usual subvention was granted the *Publications* of the Society for the Advancement of Scandinavian Studies, and a number of smaller stipends for study in America.

Books

THE HOLY CITY. By Selma Lagerlöf. Translated by Velma Swanston Howard. Doubleday Page & Company. Price $1.50.

There seems to be no particular reason for the tedious controversy in the prologue to this book. All that it demonstrates is brought out in succeeding pages. And in spite of the witchery of the "pale-green moonlight" over Palestine —"the Old World's haunted chamber"—one tires of the weakened rushes of those dry husks of faiths, advancing and crumbling upon one another.

The story paints vividly the sufferings of the Swedish pilgrims in the little communistic colony. With a curious other-worldliness that seems incompatible with their sturdy peasant earth-hunger, they endure privation and persecution. The pale flame of their faith throws a weird and flickering light over the cesspool that is Jerusalem. We seem to be looking at the ancient city through green glasses. They are particularly hated and traduced by their American neighbors, who exhibit a refined manifestation of the mob spirit. Here, however, the author shows a misconception of American psychology. It is true, the American spirit can be cruel, brutal, and destructive—savage beyond belief; but it is rarely underhanded or treacherous. It does not maintain a fair front while slowly eating at foundations. Rather it mounts in hot rushes with a tidal fury and subsides —leaving hardly a ripple.

I do not think the *form* of this book equals that of *Jerusalem* or some of the early masterpieces. Having read and laid it aside, I see it in brilliant flashes rather than as a perfect and rounded whole. Technically it is an advance. The author has done nothing finer than the killing of Gunhild by the sun. Here is no interpretation of the sun by one who has tossed under his love-bites on yellow beaches. Only one whose child eyes had opened on snowed-in places and whose young flesh had been stroked by icy winds could have given this bitter and alien aspect of the sun.

The episode opens like the tolling of a bell. When Gunhild steps out into the blazing noon, with the fanged letter like an asp clutched to her breast, we feel the inevitable end. Here Slander seems to have attained a deadly and conscious entity. It is the first assassin. The vulture sun, over-hovering, only strikes deeper into the yet living prey. The style coruscates like a malign jewel. "Tiny sharp arrows seemed to shoot up from the glittering granules of the road-stones; the green window-panes of a convent at the wayside sparkled so that she dare not glance up at them; the steel key in a door sent out little threatening rays." When at last, maddened, she faces about and looks full at her torturer—"And there rolled the sun, like a great bluish-white flame! As Gunhild stood blinking at it, the whole sky turned black, and the sun shrank to a mere spark, with a malevolent glint. Suddenly it seemed to break away from the heavens and come shooting down." This is great art, and Lagerlöf walks with the masters.

The situations between Gertrude and Bo are treated with delicacy and charm. We feel and share the writer's intimacy with both. It is different with Barbara. We feel the latter's travail—vaguely. But when we catch a glimmer of her mind, it is as though one glimpsed a witch's eyes through wind-blown leaves on a grey day. But Ingmar Ingmarsson's weighty, unmagnetic personality is always overpoweringly with us—his great hands seem to paw the pages. When Gertrude seems likely to float away on her ecstatic fancy, it is fitting that he should be the ballast to bring her unerringly back to earth.

The end is unconvincing. When art tries to pick up life's dropped stitches, the result is likely to approximate patchwork—even in the hands of so gifted an artist as Selma Lagerlöf.

It is not necessary to understand Swedish to see that the translator has lost as little as is possible in a shuffle of languages. The wonderful individuality of style —a style unlike that of any other writer I know of—has been perfectly preserved. Everywhere the meaning has been conveyed not only by the good but by the magic word, so that there is a complete collaboration between sense and sound.

LOLA RIDGE.

ASGARD AND THE GODS. The tales and traditions of our Northern ancestors. Adapted from the work of Dr. W. Wägner by N. W. Macdowell and edited by W. S. W. Anson, with illustrations. 326 pp. E. P. Dutton & Company, New York. Price $2.00 net.

During the early creative period which brought forth the old Norse literature, the peoples of the North were yet pagan in spirit, though nominally converted to the Christian faith. Their literature is to such an extent the product of pre-Christian views that it can be understood only in the light of the myths and folkloristic popular beliefs in which their religious and moral conceptions are embodied. No one could attempt to unravel the intricate web of their poetry or seek to understand Teutonic intellectual and social life without knowledge of so important a branch as mythology. Even in modern life and art, the old conceptions are firmly enough imbedded. The familiar coils of Fafnir still enliven the finest work of jeweler and woodcarver, the melancholy *nök* sobs in our songs and through our melodies, valkyries storm in our operas, and the nightmare troubles us in our dreams. If we wish to know somewhat fully our own art and ideas, we must study the old myths which in one form or another have become our intellectual heritage. Dr. W. Wägner greatly facilitates this work by placing in our hands a well-written book on Teutonic mythology and popular beliefs, *Asgard and the Gods*. He has sought to present a general survey of the subject by adding to the more prominent features of Norse mythology the mythical traditions still found especially in Germany. The stories of Kyffhäuser, Berchta, Holda, and the Lorelei are placed with the myths connected with the chief deities, an arrangement which is justified in so far as the more recent popular tales have grown out of the older myths. It gives the book the character of a collection of romantic narratives, but makes it also a rich depository of traditions frequently met with even in modern literature. Now and then the author goes rather far afield, as when he speaks of Chinese and Indo-Chinese languages, of the Phenicians in the North, or when he draws comparisons between Teutonic and Hindu myths. These features might with advantage have been omitted, as they are out of keeping with the popular tenor of the work. They are too cursory to be of much aid to the scholar, and too obscure and remote to be of interest to the general reader. The work is written from the romanticist's and folklorist's point of view, in a form which naturally lends itself to a popular presentation of the subject. The poetic features of the myths become especially prominent under this mode of treatment, which appeals to the imagination, awakens sympathy for the heroes of the narrative and sustains interest in its dramatic events. It is a form of presentation which appeals especially to the young reader. But it has the disadvantage that it never penetrates deeply. It does not show the inner coherency of the myths; the efforts to express through them a solemn and somber view of man's life and his ultimate destiny. The deeper meaning of mythology finds no interpretation; nor could this be done in a book of so popular a character. The work is ably written and well illustrated. It will be a welcome addition especially to college and high-school libraries.

K. G.

Brief Notes

The Augustana Book Concern has added two more volumes to its Swedish texts, *Svensk Diktning* (Selections from Swedish Poets), arranged by Mauritzen and Olson. The books will be most welcome to all teachers of Swedish. They include specimens of lyric poetry from Dalin to Heidenstam and Karlfeldt, the two latter being the only living authors included. The biographical sketches, notes, and vocabulary make a very complete apparatus for the students. The text seems brief in proportion, but is sufficient to stimulate the reader to further investigation. Bellman, Lidner, Runeberg, and Topelius are not represented; we hope they are but held over for a separate volume.

J. A. Jakobsen's *The Crank* is a début with a promise. It is a political play with a plot based on the various intrigues and surprises incidental to a gubernatorial campaign, and the denouement discloses the comforting truth that honesty is the best policy. The characters are well drawn, and, in spite of some monologues savoring of the platform, the action moves with increasing speed and interest to the climax in the last act. Russell Pike is a type new to the American stage, the gamin-gangster. The women, as might be expected in a political play, are little but decorative setting. The play is brought out by Nordmanden Publishing Company in Grand Forks.

Forty-two Swedish artists exhibited 116 paintings, miniatures, and sculptures at the annual art exhibit of the Swedish Club in Chicago, which was held from April 28 to May 5. This year the prizes were either Liberty Bonds or Thrift Stamps, and were awarded to Alfred Jansson, Chicago; Helge Anderson, Boston, and Karl F. Skoog, Cambridge, Mass. Einar Bergstein and Edwin Pearson, both of Chicago, received honorable mentions. The show was largely attended, not only by Swedes, but by art-lovers generally throughout Chicago.

Under the general title *Bibliothèque Scandinave*, a series of publications analogous to the translations into English published by the American-Scandinavian Foundation has been instituted in France under the direction of M. Lucien Maury. This carefully edited collection of French translations from Northern authors is being inaugurated by an edition of *The Logic of Poetry* by Professor H. Larsson of the University of Lund. It is planned to bring out two volumes a year, and to subscribers of the *Bibliothèque Scandinave*, who pay an initiation fee of five francs, there will be a uniform price of four francs per volume. Subscriptions may be sent to the general secretary, Mr. Paul Desfeuilles, "Editions Ernest Leroux," 28 Rue Bonaparte, Paris (VI).

As a further proof of the interest in Scandinavia which seems growing in France, we note the following recent publications:

Jacques de Coussanges: "La Scandinavie et la Guerre," *Revue de Paris*, July 1, 1915. Jacques de Coussanges: "Verner de Heidenstam," *Revue des Deux Mondes*, May 1, 1917. Paul Verrier: "Le Slesvig," *Revue de Paris*, May 1, 1917. F. Baldensperger: "De Descartes à Gobineau," *Revue de Paris*, June 1, 1917. Edouard Soulier: "Les Pays du Nord et la France," *Correspondant*, August 10, 1917. S. Rocheblave: "Chez les Neutres du Nord, II: de Hollande en Scandinavie," *Revue des Deux Mondes*, October 15, 1917. P. G. La Chesnais: "La Paix de Stockholm," *Grande Revue*, January, 1918.

A magnificent Campanile dedicated at the University of California on the Charter Day of the institution, last March, was the gift of a Norwegian woman, the late Jane K. Sather. It is made of granite and marble and towers high above all the other buildings of the campus. A remarkable system of bells brought from England plays chimes three times a day and has a repertoire including some Norse folk-songs. The Campanile is not the only gift of Mrs. Sather to the University. She had previously presented it with the Sather Esplanade and the Sather Gate, besides endowing two professorships, one in classical literature and one in history.

In the midst of war activities, Lindsborg has not neglected its usual art exhibition held in connection with the Messiah Festival. Besides the "Lindsborg School" there were artists from Chicago and San Francisco represented. Among the visitors were Madame Olive Fremstad, who showed her interest in Western art by purchasing two paintings and three lithographs by Birger Sandzén. Other works by Sandzén were acquired by Professor Schofield and Mr. Reed Miller.

FINANCIAL

*Notes About Issues in the Financial World
Most Interesting to Readers of the Review*

OWN HOME FOR FEDERAL RESERVE BANK OF NEW YORK

The Federal Reserve Bank of New York is to have a building of its own, and for this purpose has acquired the entire block front on the easterly side of Nassau Street, from Liberty Street to Maiden Lane. The cost of the property is more than $3,000,000.

DANFORTH CARDOZO MADE SECRETARY

The Scandinavian Trust Company announces the election of Danforth Cardozo as secretary of this financial institution which is doing so much to further business intercourse between the United States and Scandinavia. Mr. Cardozo formerly was assistant secretary of the company.

COPENHAGEN BANKS PROSPEROUS

The present capitalization of Copenhagen banks is placed at 260,000,000 kroner, with a reserve amounting to more than 76,000,000 kroner. The increase during the past ten years in bank capitalization is no less than 60,000,000 kroner.

TRANS-ATLANTIC COMPANY REPORTS

Organized in September, 1916, the Trans-Atlantic Company, with headquarters in Copenhagen, is gradually extending its operations throughout the world. This company operates on a unique plan in that it strives to make connections with the most representative house in a given locality and thus participates in business transactions that indirectly profit the head office in Denmark.

METROPOLITAN CANVASS COMMITTEE

At the conclusion of the Third Liberty Loan campaign, Chairman A. B. Leach announced that subscriptions amounting to almost $139,000,000 were obtained by the workers of the committee. Among those active in the campaign was Niels Frode Holch, whose labors in a district of the less well-to-do resulted in innumerable small subscriptions that helped to swell the grand total.

NORWEGIAN BANK EARNINGS

The net profits of twenty leading Norwegian banks during 1917 was 63,000,000 kroner. Of these banks, Norges Bank earned 12,693,509 kroner; Norske Handelsbank, 6,457,522 kroner; Bergen's Kreditbank. 6,144,865 kroner; and Bergen's Privatbank, 5,830,600 kroner.

INTERNATIONAL NICKEL COMPANY EARNINGS

The International Nickel Company's earnings for the last fiscal year amounted to $16,181,501, which, after deducting all expenditures, left a balance of $10,129,988 for dividends.

NORWEGIAN CUSTOMS RECEIPTS

For the twelve months ending March 31, 1918, the total Norwegian customs receipts amounted to 62,-471,542 kroner. This compares with 66,255,731 kroner in 1917, and 54,482,852 kroner in 1916.

RISE IN SWEDISH RAILWAY RATES

The board of managers of the State railways has filed with the Government a proposition for the increase of the temporary additional railroad rates now in force.

J. M.

The National City Bank of New York

has correspondence relationships with the strongest banks in Scandinavia and maintains a representative in Copenhagen to facilitate their business in the United States.   It is able to offer unusual facilities for the transaction of commerce everywhere. Its Travelers' Letters of Credit and Commercial Credits command funds in all accessible countries.

Condensed Statement as of May 10, 1918

ASSETS

CASH on hand, in Federal Reserve Bank and due from Banks and Bankers and United States Treasurer	$151,779,713.92	
Acceptances of Other Banks	35,397,183.63	
UNITED STATES TREASURY CERTIFICATES Maturing in less than 90 days	140,512,500.00	$327,689,397.55
UNITED STATES BONDS	25,449,526.20	
Loans and Discounts	310,702,357.99	
Other Bonds	39,291,806.09	
Stock in Federal Reserve Bank	1,500,000.00	376,943,690.28
Due from Branches		14,058,790.31
Banking House		5,000,000.00
Customers' Liability Account of Acceptances		20,637,939.26
Other Assets		2,911,280.35
Total		$747,241,097.75

LIABILITIES

CAPITAL, Surplus and Undivided Profits	$ 74,994,970.02
DEPOSITS	628,196,322.63
Reserve for Expenses, Taxes, and Unearned Interest	4,605,767.41
Circulation	1,756,300.00
Rediscounts and Foreign Bills of Exchange Sold	9,963,889.69
Acceptances, Cash Letters of Credit and Travelers' Checks	22,181,039.01
Other Liabilities	5,542,808.99
Total	$747,241,097.75

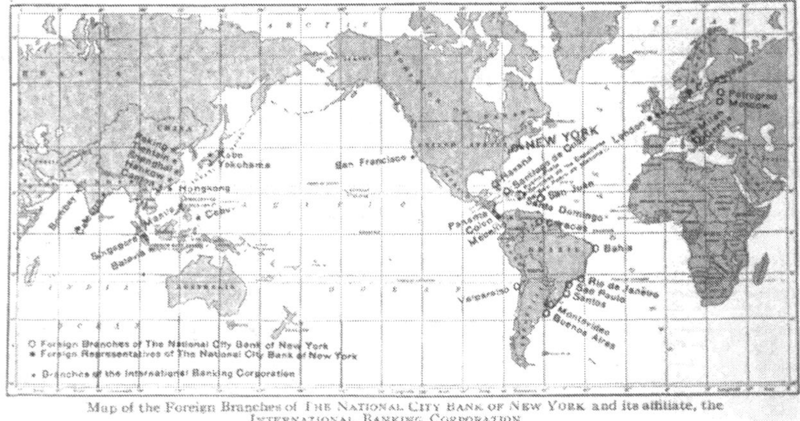

Map of the Foreign Branches of THE NATIONAL CITY BANK OF NEW YORK and its affiliate, the INTERNATIONAL BANKING CORPORATION

FINANCIAL

Notes About Issues in the Financial World
Most Interesting to Readers of the Review

FINE BANK RECORD

Few financial establishments in the United States can equal the record of the Scandinavian Trust Company of New York, which at the conclusion of the first year of its existence, in June, showed deposits of more than $26,000,000 The loans and discounts in the semi-annual statement figured $20,972,846. The growth of the business is evidenced by the fact that an assistant secretary has been appointed, C. C. Kelley joining the Scandinavian Trust Company in that capacity.

STOCKS LOOKING UP

According to *Bradstreet's*, the stock market during the half-year ended July 1 had a "substantial but irregular advance." The movement, to quote once more, "represented a recovery from the semi-panicky conditions into which the securities market fell during the latter months of 1917." *Bradstreet's* appears of the opinion, concurred in by other authorities, that Government control of railroads has had a good effect from the investment standpoint.

HANNEVIGS ENLARGING BUSINESS QUARTERS

With the removal of Hannevig & Company to larger quarters at 32 Broadway, the banking facilities of the Hannevig interests remain at 139 Broadway, in charge of Andreas Stolt as manager, while the shipping division is at the new address, under the management of Finn Hannevig.

WAR THRIFT URGED

The War Loan organization of the Treasury Department continues its appeal to the people of the United States to aid in the prosecution of the war by liberal investment in War Savings Stamps. Congress has authorized an issue of $2,000,000,000 for 1918. The purpose is twofold: (1) to get money for the Government for war needs; (2) to instill the habit of thrift into the American people and by the practice of thrift to save labor and material for the Government. The REVIEW trusts its readers will see the wisdom of giving heed to what the Government has to say in this matter.

SEPTEMBER 28, 1918

The Fourth Liberty Loan is announced to begin September 28. We count on the readers of the REVIEW to respond as generously as they have in the past. Meanwhile War Savings Stamps are within the reach of everyone who conscientiously wishes to save.

AMERICAN-NORWEGIAN FINANCIAL LINK

The Norwegian American Securities Corporation, under the presidency of T. Barth, continues to prove its value to Scandinavian interests in America. The difficulty of corresponding under the present abnormal conditions is to a considerable extent overcome when a financial and investment organization like the Norwegian American Securities Corporation is at hand to facilitate business. Many Norwegians with extensive interests here have found this service invaluable in recent months, and as the Norwegian importations increase with the lifting of the embargo still greater need will be found for such an international medium.

J. M.

Scandinavian Investors

should be particularly interested in a publication which has been issued by my firm,

A. B. LEACH & CO., Inc.

62 CEDAR STREET
NEW YORK,

and which explains the great advantage which to-day they have over any other investors.

Please write for copy, which will be mailed free of charge.

NIELS FRODE HOLCH

ESTABLISHED 1879

STATE BANK OF CHICAGO

MEMBER FEDERAL RESERVE SYSTEM

CHAMBER OF COMMERCE BUILDING, CHICAGO, ILL.

CAPITAL.. $1,500,000.00
SURPLUS.. 3,000,000.00
UNDIVIDED PROFITS.................................... 1,094,571.00

OFFICERS

LEROY A. GODDARD
President

HENRY A. HAUGAN
OSCAR H. HAUGAN
Vice-Presidents

HENRY S. HENSCHEN
Vice-Pres. and Cashier

C. EDWARD CARLSON
WALTER J. COX
Vice-Presidents

FRANK I. PACKARD
AUSTIN J. LINDSTROM
JOSEPH F. NOTHEIS
Assistant Cashiers

SAMUEL E. KNIGHT
Secretary

WILLIAM C. MILLER
Assistant Secretary

CHECKING ACCOUNTS

of individuals, firms and corporations are solicited. Loans made on approved names or collaterals.

WILLS AND TRUSTS

This bank's Trust Department is equipped to handle with skill and experience its clients' wills, estates, agencies, trusteeships, etc., and is authorized by law to act in such matters.

INVESTMENTS

Clients wishing to avail themselves of the bank's experience in selecting safe investments are invited to call on or write our Bond Department or Real Estate Loan Department for choice bonds and mortgages yielding 5½ and 6 per cent. interest. These can be had in amounts of $500 and upwards.

DIRECTORS

DAVID N. BARKER

J. J. DAU
Chairman, Reid, Murdoch & Co.

LEROY A. GODDARD
President

HENRY A. HAUGAN
Vice-President

H. G. HAUGAN
Retired

OSCAR H. HAUGAN
Vice-President

A. LANQUIST
President Lanquist & Illsley Co.

WM. A. PETERSON
Proprietor Peterson Nursery

CHAS. PIEZ
President Link Belt Co.

MOSES J. WENTWORTH
Capitalist

HANNEVIG AND COMPANY

Bankers

139 Broadway, New York

SPECIALIZING IN

SHIPPING and FOREIGN EXCHANGE

HANNEVIG AND COMPANY

139 Broadway, New York

Empire Trust Company

120 Broadway   New York   580 Fifth Avenue

London Office, 41 Threadneedle Street

Resources Over $50,000,000

The Fifth Avenue Office of this Company, corner 47th Street, is accessibly situated for anyone desiring the services of an Uptown Banking Institution. Careful and courteous attention given to any business entrusted to it.

Interest may be arranged upon accounts subject to check.

Certificates of Deposit, maturing at a date to suit the needs of the depositor, issued at favorable rates of interest.

Empire Safe Deposit Company

Safe Deposit Vaults

Norwegian American Securities Corporation

74 BROADWAY, NEW YORK CITY

Capital, $1,000,000

TRYGVE BARTH, President

LEIF H. STROM, Vice-President   GEORGE REITH, Vice-President
B. KROEPELIEN, Sec'y and Treas.   LEROY JONES, Assistant Secretary

DIRECTORS

T. BARTH, President
T. LANGLAND THOMPSON, Attorney
W. K. FRIMANN, Shipowner
B. KROEPELIEN, Treasurer
WILHELM ALME, Man. Dir. Bergen Agent a/s
TH. JULLUM, Gen. Agt. Norw'g'n Marine Ins. Co's
P. HARSEM, Merchant

L. H. STROM, Vice-Pres. New York Oversea Co.
GUNNAR HARTMANN, Pres. Hart Trading Co.
GEORGE REITH, Vice-President
C. STEENDAL, Pres. Jefferson Insurance Co.
WM. SCHENSTROM, Pres. Electric Welding Co.
of America
KARL KROGSTAD, President S. O. Stray & Co.

The Norwegian American Securities Corporation was formed for the purpose of facilitating business transactions between Norway and the other Scandinavian Countries and the United States of America.

Members of
New York Produce
Exchange

Cable Address:
"Norameric" New York
A.B.C. Code Fifth Edition,
Watkins Scotts and Private

Norwegian American Trading Co.

INCORPORATED

25 Broad Street, New York, U. S. A.

and Kristiania, Norway

EXPORT:

Food Products, Metals and Machinery, Drugs, and Chemicals, Manila Rope, and Cotton Yarns

Flour. Lard, Oleo, Oil, Hams, Bacon. Beef. Pork, Sugar, Syrup, Molasses, Apples, Coffees, Peas and Beans.   Steel Wire, Coke, Tin Plate. Galvanized Steel Plates, Plumbers' Supplies, Motors, and all kinds of Machinery.   *Write for Catalogue*

IMPORT:

Canned, Salt, and Dry Fish, Fertilizer, Fish Oils, Wood Pulp, and Sulphites

GENERAL REPRESENTATIVE IN NORWAY:

BIRGER GRAN, Kristiania   JENS GRAN & SÖN, Bergen

References: National City Bank of New York; New York Produce Exchange Bank, N. Y.; Kristiania Bank og Kreditkasse, Kristiania; Centralbanken for Norge, Kristiania; Bradstreet's Commercial Agency

---

When the Foreign Business Man Comes to the United States

He will always find a cordial welcome from The New York Evening Post.

He comes to our shores bringing a greeting and a message from his native land. His mission is in the interest of international commerce.

His commissions are many; his time is limited. Strange surroundings and unfamiliar customs oftentimes make his task difficult.

He brings excellent introductions which place him in touch with small groups of our business men who are glad to assist him. But often he confronts them with questions which they are not prepared to answer immediately and accurately. In such a case an enterprising newspaper may perform a service of special value.

The International Bureau

will undertake to render any assistance within its power. Its facilities are cheerfully placed at the disposal of persons interested in world trade.

By aiding business men who come to us from foreign lands The New York Evening Post stimulates international trade and thus renders also a genuine service to *American* business.

The New York Evening Post

More Than a Newspaper—A National Institution

Founded 1801

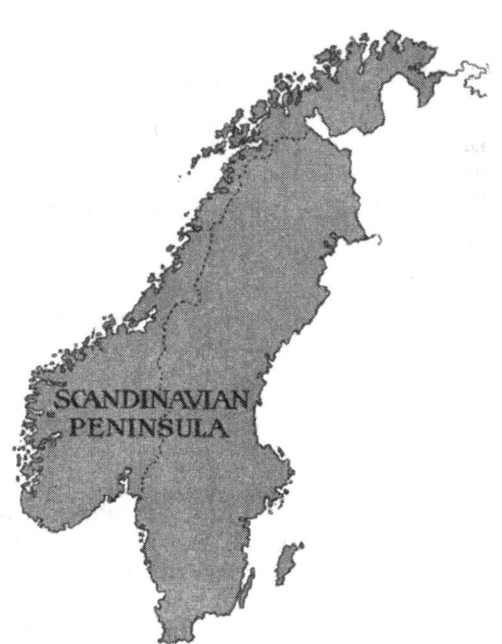

AN intimate knowledge of commercial conditions in Norway and Sweden is obtained by this bank through personal contact with the executives of its long established Scandinavian connections.

IRVING NATIONAL BANK

WOOLWORTH BUILDING   **NEW YORK**

Strictly a Commercial Bank

CONTRIBUTORS TO THE SEPTEMBER-OCTOBER NUMBER

THE cover illustration is a photograph of the stone mentioned in Mr. Bodholdt's article which was placed by Christian V at the Eider River to mark the boundary between Slesvig and Holstein.

IVAR KIRKEGAARD will be remembered by readers of the REVIEW as the author of the article on "The Fall of Dannevirke and Dybböl" in our Yule Number. A Dane by birth and for many years a resident of this country, he has visited the old battle grounds in Slesvig, interviewed the people who still remember the days of 1864, as well as their descendants who now live under the German rule. His book *My South Jutland Days* appeared serially in a Danish magazine, in 1909.

K. C. BODHOLDT is the president of the United Danish Church of America. He was born in Slesvig, in 1855. As a young man he followed the sea, but came to America, studied at the Danish schools in the West, and entered the ministry, in 1882. His present parish is in Racine.

JENS JENSEN, the noted landscape architect of Chicago, was the subject of a sketch by Miss Eskil in the REVIEW not long ago. He is a South-Jutlander by birth and knows the people of Slesvig intimately.

HANS PETER HOLST is one of the older generation of Danish poets who have written on the Slesvig tragedy.

KAREN LARSEN is instructor at Mount Holyoke. During the past academic year she did research work at Columbia University on the part played by Danish representatives in the German Reichstag and the Prussian Landtag.

KARL GUSTAF DERNBY was Swedish Fellow of the American-Scandinavian Foundation for the academic year 1917-18. He recently published an article in *The Nation* on "The Tragedy of Finland."

Gottorp Castle in Slesvig, Birthplace of Christian IX

THE
AMERICAN-SCANDINAVIAN
REVIEW

VOLUME VI   SEPTEMBER-OCTOBER · 1918   NUMBER 5

Essential Justice

THE time is drawing near for the great international adjustment in which, as President Wilson said, "every territorial settlement must be for the benefit and in the interest of the populations concerned," in which "all well-defined national aspirations shall be met with the utmost satisfaction consistent with the future peace." "Final settlement," said the President further, "must be based on essential justice."

No people have better reason to look forward to that day with the highest hopes and the fullest confidence than the Danes in North Slesvig. They have suffered under the Prussian regime for more than fifty years—suffered with resignation, without whimpering. They have offered all the resistance possible under the law and without dragging the mother country into another disastrous war. The Slesvig Danes have stood like men, faithful to their language and traditions, and, amidst persecution and oppression, they have remained the most Danish of the Danes. They have been waiting patiently for the day when "essential justice" should again reign in the world and when such principles as those enunciated by President Wilson should regulate national aspirations. The words quoted from the President's address to Congress on February 11 were addressed to the whole world, and were so understood everywhere. They have awakened fresh hopes among oppressed races and not least in North Slesvig, where the people look with firm faith and warm admiration to the great statesman and the country whose spokesman he is.

That the mother country will welcome her lost children, when they are some day allowed to return, goes without saying, but Denmark recognizes that it is for the Danes of North Slesvig to declare where they wish to belong; nor has she any desire to rule over unwilling German elements in the southern part of the province. The principle of self-determination is the only one that can lead to a permanent and stable solution.

Fifty Years Under German Rule

By Ivar Kirkegaard

IN a village by the smiling Flensborg Fjord, a little girl came home
from school one day, more than twenty years ago, with red cheeks,
bearing evident marks of a drubbing just received. Her father,
a prosperous farmer, questioned her, and found that she had been
whipped for refusing to sing *Ich bin ein Preusse, will ein Preusse sein*.
Little Marie made it *kein Preusse*, and no amount of cudgeling could
move her. The teacher finally had to order the German children
to sing so loud that they drowned Marie's *kein*. This little girl who
could not be cowed by a brutal teacher is typical of South Jutland,
held in the iron claws of Prussia, its Danish people harassed and
persecuted simply because they have refused to break with their
past and renounce their nationality.

The battle is waged along various lines: political, national,
religious, and economic. The political struggle may be traced in
the elections, and in order to understand the fluctuations of Danism
and Germanism it is necessary to remember that the Treaty of
Prague, by which Austria, in 1866, ceded her part of the booty to
Prussia, contained the famous Article 5, inserted through the influence of Napoleon III, stipulating that the northern district of
Slesvig should be returned to Denmark in case the people, by an
unhampered plebiscite, expressed themselves in favor of it. This
provision was confirmed by the Prussian King, William I, with a
solemn oath in the name of the Triune God. It was never carried
out. After defeating France, Prussia felt powerful enough to do as
she liked, and simply canceled Article 5 by an agreement with
Austria, in 1878.

Such treachery was unbelievable to the people of South Jutland.
They had rested their faith on Article 5 as on a rock, believed in it
as in the Bible. Taking for granted that they would soon be reunited
with the mother country, many of them had made use of the option
given them by the Treaty of Vienna, in 1864, to remain Danish
citizens. They became what is known as "optants for Denmark,"
but thereby they lost all rights of citizenship within German boundaries, and were henceforth aliens in the land of their birth. Others
emigrated, particularly young men of military age, who were naturally
loath to put on the hated Prussian uniform. In this way South
Jutland lost about 60,000 people.

The first election to the German Reichstag, in 1867, was looked
upon by the South-Jutlanders as an expression of their firm purpose
to return to Denmark. In all the districts above a line drawn to the
south of Flensborg and Tönder, the Danish majorities were so large

that, in some places, they amounted to unanimity. In the years that followed, the vote declined very much, owing to emigration and the disfranchisement of the "optants," and in 1886 it was at its lowest ebb. After that it rose again steadily. When it became evident that the provisions of Article 5 would never be carried out, the resistance of the people to Prussianism began in earnest. Emigration ceased, and preparation was made for a long struggle. Unfortunately, much had been lost in the meantime; the people were weakened; the youth of the country was gone, and a new generation had to grow up to fill the ranks. But a well-organized campaign soon had its effects. A large Electoral Society was formed, besides many smaller local organizations, and in 1912 the number of Danish votes had increased by several thousand.

The German administration has, of course, used every possible means, even the most unscrupulous, to stop this Danish advance. Ever since the first election to the Reichstag, when the Danes captured two out of the four election districts, the Germans have practised a system of electioneering geometry (gerrymandering) by which they have neutralized as far as possible the Danish vote. Nor have they shunned coarser methods. They have marked with pin-pricks the ballots in the "secret" elections so as to control the vote of Government employees, such as postmen and railroad workers, who would, of course, be dismissed if they did not vote as ordered. One man who voted for the Danish candidate was denied permission to rebuild his chimney or to engage a shepherd boy for the summer. People receiving sickness, accident, or old-age pensions have been intimidated by veiled threats. Thus, in the election of 1898, all the men in Aastrup, in Haderslev, drawing old-age pensions were given a ballot marked for the German candidate with a note saying: "On account of your old-age pension, a ballot is enclosed which is to be used on election day."

One of the most flagrant instances of election fraud is that of the district judge, Winther von Adlersflügel, in Skaerbaek, who prepared for the election in 1903 by falsifying the tax lists and the lists of voters so that the Germans secured a better representation than they were entitled to, and the election had to be decided by drawing lots. And Herr von Adlersflügel could well manage the drawing of lots— that he had promised his partisans beforehand. He was surprised in his home in the midst of a rehearsal; his method consisted in making a little fold in a corner of the "right" ballot before dropping it into the box and feeling his way round until he found the one with the fold. No wonder that in more than twenty elections which were decided by lot and were presided over by Adlersflügel the Germans never failed to win.

The struggle in its national phase has been fought chiefly over the language. Soon after 1864, German was made the chief language in the schools, and Danish was gradually forced out, until, in 1888, it disappeared from all except a few schools in the northern districts, where the children were still to be allowed two hours a week of religious instruction in Danish, provided the parents demanded it. These Danish lessons, however, were put at the most inconvenient time, and the children who attended them were refused dispensation from summer school—a severe blow to people of small means who would often let their children take service as shepherd boys or goose girls. While the state schools were being Germanized, the war was also carried into the domain of the private schools, and finally the Danish schools were closed altogether "because there was no demand for them"—though they were overflowing with pupils. Parents were also forbidden to engage Danish tutors for their children.

The remarkable fact is that the South-Jutlanders write Danish, if anything, better than the average graduate from the renowned public schools of Denmark. Parents and elder sisters and brothers teach the little ones in their homes and help them with their compositions. Later they are often sent to one of the Danish folk high schools that have sprung up right across the border especially for their benefit.

But what do the children learn in the state schools? They learn that they are Germans, that in 1864 they were "freed from the Danish yoke," and that Germany is their fatherland. And Danish children coming to school from homes where nothing but Danish is spoken have been whipped for speaking Danish among themselves in recess. In the school at Tönder the teacher would begin the day with a German hymn, after which one of the children would say the *Vaterunser*, adding the words: "Slesvig is my home, Germany my fatherland." But one morning a bright little curly-head, whose turn it was to say the prayer, ended with the words: "Slesvig is my home, Denmark is my fatherland." The teacher went toward him with hand lifted for a blow, crying, *"Verfluchter Dänenjunge!"* but the boy stood his ground so well that involuntarily the teacher's hand fell, and after that day the appendix to the Lord's Prayer was dropped.

Such schooling does not produce a gentle and carefree childhood; it develops defiance and hardness, but it strengthens the will and sharpens the faculties. The children come to feel the fight between Danism and Germanism, not as something they have merely heard of, but as a struggle in which they themselves take part and which involves their deepest and most sacred feelings. They are proud of their post as guards of the frontier, and the sense of their own strength gives them joy and confidence.

The South-Jutlanders receive their intellectual stimulus from

Denmark. The Germans have therefore tried to prevent the current of Danish thought and literature from crossing the border. Lecturers from the kingdom have for years past been forbidden in South Jutland, no matter on what subject they wished to speak. Danish actors have shared the same fate, and it soon became evident that the prohibition would even be applied to their kinsmen, the Norwegians. Fru Dybwad of the National Theatre in Christiania was refused permission to fill a two weeks' engagement in the cities of South Jutland at the same time as a German traveling company was advertising Ibsen's and Björnson's plays in German. Roald Amundsen was not allowed to speak in Flensborg on his expedition to the South Pole, though the same lecture, given in Berlin, was highly praised.

All this has only strengthened the determination of the Slesvigers to remain, culturally, a part of the North. Young people have flocked across the border to the folk high schools, where they have been imbued with Danish democratic ideals and have learned to keep in touch with the progress of Danish scientific farming. Gifted men and women have been sent to Denmark to take courses in reading and music and have returned to spread their knowledge through popular entertainments. A network of lecture societies throughout the smaller communities has been organized. But all such intercourse with the mother country has been looked upon with disfavor. The societies have been declared "political," the meetings broken up, and the members persecuted in various ways. Private theatricals, singing societies, athletic clubs, agricultural and loan societies—all have come under the ban of the authorities, who well know that solidarity is the great armor of Danism. For a while athletic clubs were under special disfavor, and one pastor was known to warn his candidates for confirmation against card-playing, drunkenness, and *athletics!* All public meetings, whether political or not, have to be reported in advance to the authorities and receive their sanction. They are always attended by at least one gendarme, who has power instantly to dissolve the meeting; the slightest word that jars on the sensitive ears of the Prussian police is enough. It has often happened that they have forced their way into private gatherings in the homes of Danish-speaking citizens and fined the host for not reporting a "public meeting."

The Church, too, has been taken into the service of Prussianism. The pastors of the State Church are all Germans. Yet this could be borne if they were really spiritual guides of their flock. Unfortunately, most of them devote their time to uprooting the Danish language and Danish nationalism.

The South-Jutlanders are a religious people, and finally their patience with the German clergymen was at an end. In many localities they withdrew from the State Church, which they nevertheless had to support by taxes and dues, and formed their own free congregations; they built churches and paid pastors exactly as their American brothers do. The first two Free Churches were completed in Bovlund and Haderslev in 1896 and 1897. When that at Bovlund was finished the Government issued an injunction against its being taken into use. In Haderslev the people were allowed to gather for the dedication, but when they had assembled, a gendarme suddenly appeared from behind the pulpit, announced that the meeting was forbidden, and ordered the people to leave the "hall." It took three and a half years of battle against the most absurd legal technicalities before the people were allowed to take into use the churches which they had built with their own money to satisfy their own spiritual needs.

The judges as well as the clergymen look on themselves as champions of Prussia against the South-Jutlanders, and there is no such thing as equality before the law. Danes are always discriminated against. Yet even the decisions of these unjust courts are not always respected by the police: An aged, highly respected farmer in Haderslev was illegally declared, in 1902, to be an "optant," and was deported by the police. He returned and thereby managed to bring his case before the Supreme Court, which declared him to be a citizen. Meanwhile his son had also been banished, and in his case the court ruled that his father was an "optant." On the strength of this, contrary to the ruling of the Supreme Court, the father was again banished, and had to leave the home where he had passed his whole life.

Incidentally, this episode throws light on the means employed by high Prussian officials to get rid of a political opponent. The decision by which this venerable gentleman had to go into exile was based on the testimony of two witnesses. One of these was a gendarme who afterwards admitted that he had sworn to something which he "remembered wrong," and that he had not even been in the neighborhood at the time the events occurred. The other was an old woman who later confessed that the *Landrat*—the highest official in the district—had promised her 2,000 marks if she would give testimony that would lead to the conviction of the old gentleman. When H. P. Hanssen, delegate to the Reichstag, called attention to these undeniable facts, he was sentenced to three months' imprisonment for contempt of court.

Such administrative expenses as the bribe to the old woman are probably covered by the "black fund" which the Prussian Chief President of South Jutland has at his disposal, and for which he does not have to render any account. It might be a little unpleasant to enter in the official ledger: One perjury—2,000 marks.

Gradually the authorities realized that they could not browbeat, threaten, nor cajole the Danish South-Jutlanders into becoming

German. So they tried to drive them out or render them harmless by depriving them of their property and civil rights. The "optants" were completely at their mercy. These people, who in 1864 had declared their intention of remaining Danish citizens, were in the position of aliens, liable to expulsion from the German Empire for any offense. And it was easy to find an offense. Many deportations took place in the eighties, but the movement ceased when Denmark's good friend, Czar Alexander III, retaliated by expelling a corresponding number of Germans from Russia. In 1898, it was resumed again in a more brutal form. Many prominent men were declared "optants," though their option had never been executed, and some of them had served loyally in the Franco-Prussian War. Wealthy business men were favorite victims of Prussian tyranny. Aged men and women were driven across the border; the young were torn from their life-work; the sick were not spared, and for some of these exile meant death.

America has been the gainer by these deportations, for practically all the banished South-Jutlanders who did not remain in Denmark have come here. In California they are so numerous that the Society Dania, an American organization of Danish-born citizens with a membership of 2,500 men, has several lodges almost entirely composed of Slesvigers.

Appropriations for buying up land in Slesvig are a regular part of the Prussian budget. Abnormal prices are offered for Danish farms, and when the Government succeeds in acquiring a bit of property it is leased to Germans at a ridiculously low rate. But the South-Jutlanders cling tenaciously to their farms, many of which have been in one family for hundreds of years. They have protected their ancient heritage by forming an association to take over any threatened piece of land and hold it until a Danish owner can be found.

When the war broke out, the South-Jutlanders had a strong national organization. They were regaining possession of the soil and steadily advancing in political influence. Their religious and intellectual life was flourishing. Let me quote from a speech by the Danish delegate to the Reichstag, H. P. Hanssen, at the annual national meeting in Haderslev, in the summer of 1914, where ten thousand people were assembled. He said:

"Our fathers were contented in their thousand-year-old union with the mother country. They lived under happy conditions; our culture and our prosperity bear witness to that. They enjoyed great personal liberty; our stiff backs, our sturdy wills, and our high courage are the heritage of freemen. And we ourselves will testify that our fathers felt the breaking of the Danish bonds as the greatest calamity that could befall our people. . . . The year that is just passed has been one of struggle. Police rule has been made more stringent.

Young people's societies have been placed under a ban, athletic clubs harassed, lectures prohibited.   The Prussian ideal of a gendarme at every meeting has been well-nigh realized.   The State's attorney has been ordered to keep a close watch on the Danish press, and the prison doors yawn for Danish editors.   The muzzle has been strapped more tightly over the mouths of the pastors. . . . Our great national organizations have sprung to life under the onslaughts of the Government upon our rights.   Von Köller closed the public halls to us; we have answered by erecting fifty private clubhouses.   Count Rantzau tried to build a wall of German farms right across North Slesvig; our reply is the North Slesvig Loan Society.   Last year the attacks on our ancient freehold farms were strongly organized; we met them with our Yeomen's Society.   Thus we have parried every blow, and we shall do so in the future.   For more than a thousand years we have stood against the German flood, and we still stand firm. We have love for the cause and strength for the fight.   We have energy and enthusiasm.   We have faith in the future of our race!"

A few weeks later the World War broke out.   Since then the struggle of South Jutland has been carried on quietly, in the midst of terrible sorrow and suffering, but it has never been abandoned.

They still "stand firm against the German flood," these frontier-fighters of ancient fame, these guardsmen of Denmark's Alsace-Lorraine —firm in their fight against oppression, firm in their Lincoln-faith that right makes might and that government of, by, and for the people shall not forever perish from the earth.

May their fight win victory, their faith reward!

Slesvig Before 1864

By K. C. Bodholdt

LORD PALMERSTON, we are told, used to say about the Slesvig question that it was so complicated and obscure that only three European statesmen had grasped it thoroughly; one of these, Prince Albert, was, unfortunately, dead; another, a foreign politician, had lost his reason, and the third person was Palmerston himself, and he had forgotten it.

Yet there is no question in the world which is simpler than that of Slesvig. The history of Slesvig can be told in a few lines: From the beginning of history down to 1864, this region was a part of the kingdom of Denmark. Then a Prussian statesman, Prince Bismarck, said to himself, as he later admitted,* in his Low German, "*Dat möt wi hebben.*"

With the aid of Austria, Prussia then attacked Denmark, and, after half a year's struggle against the same powers that now have set the whole world in flames, the little kingdom was forced to relinquish this ancient land. But the "conquerors" came to blows about the spoils, and, after the war of 1866, Slesvig was incorporated into victorious Prussia.

This is the story in a nutshell.

Thus the matter stands.

If we wish to know more about it, the same story might be told a little more fully in this manner: Denmark is the oldest of the European states now in existence. From the tribes that, in the Stone Age, thousands of years before Christ, took possession of the virgin soil and cleared homes for themselves in its woods the people are descended who to-day own and inhabit the land. Here they were welded together into a nation; here they formed, in the course of time, a united kingdom. When this kingdom came into existence is not known accurately. It had stood for centuries when the expeditions of the Vikings, about the year 800, awakened the interest of the Anglo-Saxon and Frankish chroniclers in this realm. At that time, as a protection against the newly formed empire of Charlemagne, the Danes under King Godfred built Dannevirke, the southern rampart of the kingdom, *Opus Danorum*, the old wall which still stands, though in the power of the enemy. A few miles south of Dannevirke flows the Eider River. Here the representatives of the king and the emperor met and determined that it should form the boundary line between their realms. The region on both sides of the Eider was then clad with forests and almost unpeopled. Only here and there, in the little strip of land between the river and the

*Speech by Bismarck at Friedrichsruhe, May 26, 1895.

One of the Gold Drinking Horns Found in Slesvig and Bearing the Oldest Known Danish Inscriptions

nationality of the people in the country as far south as Dannevirke and the Eider—in other words, of the whole region which is now called Slesvig. The original names of places are Danish, the manner of building houses is Danish, and all the inscriptions that have been found are also Danish. In fact, the oldest known inscription in the Danish language was found in Slesvig. It is written on one of the famous gold drinking horns, dating from about 500 A.D., which were found in the seventeenth and eighteenth centuries near the town of Mögeltönder. The runic stones from about the year 900, some of which were found in the neighborhood of Dannevirke, also speak the

rampart, were Danish dwellings. Where continuous Danish settlement ended, and the lay of the land was suitable for defence, the Danes built their wall. Down through the ages, it was improved and strengthened by the best rulers of Denmark, such as Tyra Dannebod and Valdemar the Great. A thousand years after the time of King Godfred, the Danes again took their stand by the same wall to protect themselves against enemies from the south.

These are all incontestable historical facts. The results of all research concerning these ancient times bear indisputable witness to the Danish

Runic Inscriptions Found in Slesvig, Testifying to Early Danish Occupation

Danish language. After Dannevirke was raised—just at what time is not known—a little Friesian tribe moved in and settled in the uninhabited marshy region in the southwestern corner of Slesvig. These people lived there, down through the centuries, as faithful subjects of the Danish king; but they kept their own language, which is closely related to the Dutch, and retained the customs of their ancestors without being molested until they came under German rule. For centuries Friesian was the only non-Danish tongue north of Dannevirke.

THE COAT OF ARMS OF SLESVIG, RESEMBLING THAT OF THE DANISH KINGS

Possibilities for the Germanization of Slesvig began in the thirteenth century, when Slesvig was given as a fief by the Danish Crown to a younger branch of the royal house. At this time the separate coat of arms of Slesvig originated. The Danish kings have as their device three blue lions; the dukes of South Jutland, two. So this coat of arms also shows to what country the region belongs. Another evidence from the same age might be mentioned in this connection. Immediately before granting the fief, King Valdemar the Victorious issued "King Valdemar's Jutland Code," founded on the old common law and applying to the whole peninsula of Jutland, both North Jutland and South Jutland, the original name for Slesvig. This code continued to be the legal law of the land in Slesvig down to the year 1900. Not until that year did the consolidated German Empire establish a civil code which took the place of that old Danish law.

Under a succession of weak kings, the members of the ducal family of South Jutland were trying to become more independent of Denmark. In these efforts they allied themselves with the neighboring German counts of Holstein, an estate under the Holy Roman Empire. Like the Prussians, the people of Holstein are of mixed German and Slavonic blood—a warlike and disciplined race. Their rulers were politic and unscrupulous. At last the counts of Holstein of the house of Schauenburg acquired by force the control of Slesvig, recognizing, however, the suzerainty of the Danish Crown. Thus the boundary of the kingdom remained the same. Under the Schauenburg rule, the Germanization of Slesvig began. The forests south of Dannevirke were cleared by German colonists, and the scattered Danish population in this narrow strip of land was absorbed by the German colonization. In the region between Dannevirke and Flensborg Fjord, the nobles of Holstein acquired estates. But there the original inhabitants faithfully preserved their Danish language.

During the feudal controversies between the Danish kings and the German lords, the matter was on one occasion referred both to Danish and to German tribunals. That the Danish court gave a decision in favor of the king may be natural enough. But it is of considerable interest that the German Emperor Sigismund (1411-37) pronounced this verdict: "The whole of South Jutland, in which are located Slesvig, Gottorp, and other towns belonging to this same Jutland, and also the Danish Forest, the Island of Als, and Friesland, with all their prerogatives, and the adjacent lands have been, are, and shall be an estate of the Danish king and realm, with all the rights of usufruct and suzerainty; and that this same shall be and by right ought to be incorporated into the tenure of the aforesaid duchy and lands with their above-mentioned appanages; and furthermore that the counts have as holders of the fief acquired no claim to the duchy and its appanages." That the German counts did not submit to this verdict will astonish no one who knows German respect for law and justice.

In the middle of the fifteenth century, the house of Oldenborg succeeded to the Danish throne (1448). About this time the Schauenburg line died out, and there was an opportunity of canceling the feudal relations of Slesvig. But the nobles of Holstein, who had acquired estates in Slesvig, wished the connection between Slesvig and Holstein to be continued. They offered to choose the Danish king as their count, or, as the title soon became, their duke, on condition that he would not seize Slesvig as a fief reverting to the Crown. Consenting to this, King Christian I, in 1460, became the duke both of Slesvig and of Holstein—granting the first as a fief to himself and receiving the latter as a fief of the empire. Each duchy was to retain its own ancient laws, and the two should constitute a joint inheritance in the family of King Christian. The king on this occasion declared that the two duchies should remain forever united—"*up ewich tosammende ungedelt!*" Although the districts have repeatedly been divided and parceled out, this old, long-forgotten clause was resurrected, about four hundred years later, and was destined to play a prominent part in the German agitation. A remarkable logic indeed! A declaration which has never been kept and which was made when a German duchy voluntarily placed itself under the sovereignty of the Danish king was to be used, four hundred years later, by the German state of Prussia, which did not at that time exist, to justify the conquest not only of the German duchy but also of the old Danish domain of Slesvig. Not before the outbreak of the great catastrophe of the present time has the world at large appreciated the true character of "just German claims." Denmark has long understood.

To the landed aristocracy the joint rule of the Danish and the German duchies brought great advantages, but for the common people it was a disaster. When the Lutheran Reformation was introduced, German was, to the joy of the nobles, made the language of the Church in half of Danish Slesvig, the region south of the Flensborg Fjord. Touching letters of complaint have been preserved in which the parishes beg the king of Denmark for pastors whose language they can understand. It was of no avail. The German lords knew how to thwart their wishes. In spite of this, the people preserved their Danish speech.

The Oldenborg family was later divided into several branches. One of these, the house of Gottorp, shared with the royal line the rule of the two duchies. They were so divided that each family had a part of both duchies. Still the difference in the status of the two was maintained. Over the portal of the fort at Rensborg on the Eider River, which marks the boundary between the duchies, King Christian V (1670-99) placed the noted stone with the legend: "*Eidora Romani Terminus Imperii.*" The stone is now preserved in the arsenal in Copenhagen.

The relations between the royal house and that of Gottorp soon became very strained. The latter entered into treasonable connections with the enemies of Denmark, and thus forfeited its rights to fief in Slesvig. King Frederik IV (1699-1730) confiscated this land and reunited it with the royal part of Slesvig "as an appurtenance of the Crown of Denmark unrighteously torn away in grievous times." The application to the recovered regions of the law of succession to the Danish throne was formally established in 1721. A year earlier both England and France had, by the treaties of July 26 and August 18, guaranteed to Denmark the "permanent possession" of this land. Had the obligation of this guarantee been remembered at the proper time, it seems as though the world might have been spared many calamities; for it was only through the possession of Slesvig that Prussia became an important naval power.

Half a century later, the family of Gottorp, which through marriage had succeeded to the Russian throne, resigned its fiefs in Holstein to the king of Denmark. Thus the king once more gained possession of all Holstein, yet always recognized that this duchy was a part of the German Empire. When the German Confederation was formed, in 1815, Holstein, as well as the little duchy of Lauenburg, which stood in the same relation to Denmark, were admitted as members of the Confederation.

But the difference between the two duchies was not maintained in the administration. On the contrary, as has been mentioned, a

Christian IX. Himself a South-Jutlander by Birth, Took Part in the War Against Germany in 1848, and Had Become King of Denmark Only a Few Months Before the Prussian Attack of 1864. He Mourned the Lost Provinces Till the Day of His Death

common administration was in the interests of the landed proprietors. To please them, an administrative union between the two districts was maintained to the detriment of the Danish people of Slesvig. The aristocracy and bureaucracy of the duchies made use of this union to carry on active Germanization. When the Danish school law of 1814 introduced compulsory school attendance, German became the language of the schools, as it was already the language of the Church, south of Flensborg Fjord. The Danish language had successfully defied the attack of landlords, officials, and pastors, but it wavered before the onslaught in the schools; at last German won a partial victory, and in the nineteenth century it became to some extent the spoken language of the people. When the Danish Government, after the war of 1848-50, tried to remedy the matter somewhat by a new language regulation, a cry of "righteous wrath" arose from all Germany. The strong national sentiment which developed in Germany in the early part of last century spread to Holstein and thence, to some extent, to the academic youth of Slesvig. There developed a powerful German movement of the upper classes, supported by officials, by the landed aristocracy, and university circles, which had as its aim the separation of Slesvig from its ancient connection with Denmark and its incorporation into Germany. No consideration was paid to the Danish nationality of the people. The leadership of this movement was taken by members of the family of Augustenborg, a branch of the royal family which had originated at the time of the Reformation. They dug out some obsolete rules about inheritance which had been buried for centuries, among them that oft-quoted "*up ewich tosammende ungedelt,*" and on this basis demanded recognition as the heirs of Slesvig and Holstein when the male line of the royal house should become extinct, as seemed imminent. An armed rebellion, supported by Prussia and other German states, led to a war of three years, 1848-50. With pride the Danish army calls to mind the battles of Bov, of the city of Slesvig, of Dybböl, Fredericia, and Isted. Once more Denmark's possession of Slesvig was upheld.

With the coöperation of the European powers, the Danish succession was so arranged that, when the ruling male line became extinct, the entire kingdom, including the German duchies of Holstein and Lauenburg, should fall to Prince Christian of Glyksborg, a castle near

The Ancient Rampart Dannevirke, Now in German Hands

Flensborg. He was born at Gottorp, near the city of Slesvig, and was thus a Slesviger by birth. This arrangement was ratified by the treaty of London of May 8, 1852, and among the signers were France and England, as well as Prussia and Austria.

In 1863, Prince Christian ascended the Danish throne as Christian IX. Under the leadership of Bismarck, Prussia now found a pretext to dispute his claims, in spite of her signature to the London protocol— what matters a scrap of paper? With Austria she attacked Denmark, and on the first of February, 1864, the allied powers crossed the Eider. The Danish army stood at Dannevirke, but had to retire before the superior force. At Sankelmark the German pursuit was delayed so long that the Danish army reached the weak fortifications

The Battle of Sankelmark

The Mill on Dybböl Hill Where the Danes Made Their Desperate Stand Against the Invaders in 1864

at Dybböl. Here they withstood a siege of ten weeks, and when the ramparts had been shattered by the superior German artillery, Dybböl was stormed on April 18. Inch by inch, the Danish army retreated, fighting continually, and crossed to the island of Als. A naval encounter near Helgoland, though favorable to the Danes, had no material results. Because of Prussia s greed, a conference at London which discussed the possible partition of Slesvig led to nothing. Finally Christian IX had to cede not only the two German duchies, but also the old Crown land of Slesvig to enemies who a few years earlier had recognized him as the rightful heir to them all.

This war was followed by a singular after-play. Austria was at least so honest that she wished the captured lands to be turned over to the house of Augustenborg, whose injured rights "had raised loud protests in Germany." But Bismarck declared cynically that "the chickens you have hatched yourself, their necks you can also wring." On September 12, 1865, he had the royal jurists make the ruling that the house of Augustenborg had no claim whatever to the duchies. The only rightful owner had been Christian IX, and Bismarck concluded that, as Christian IX had been the rightful owner, the ownership had now legally passed to those to whom he had ceded it.

Ay, so "complicated and obscure" is the question of Slesvig! The world has scarcely been willing to believe it. Only the past four years have opened the eyes of all to the bottomless depth of Prussian intrigue.

Some words of Thiers, however, deserve to be called to mind, which he uttered May 3, 1866, in the French Parliament, while speaking about the ruling of the Prussian crown jurists on the Slesvig question:

You see what has been decided: "The Duke of Augustenborg has no claims. King Christian has the only right to the duchies; he alone can cede them. And now since, as a result of the war which we have waged, he has by treaty resigned his claims to us, we are in turn the only owners, having become so by the wish and the act of the legitimate owners." (Exclamations and prolonged stir.)

Emilie Olivier: It is abominable!

Thiers: Yes, indeed, gentlemen, in a matter so grave, I may not seem serious in making the report ("Yes, Yes!"), but it is the very truth that I relate to you. ("Yes, yes, it is only too true!") Yes, gentlemen, this burlesque spectacle, pardon the word, is the very truth. (General expressions of approval and assent.)

Emilie Olivier: It is as loathsome as it is burlesque.

Thiers: Yes, indeed! The duchies rightfully belong to the king of Denmark. Nevertheless you do not give

THE PRUSSIAN EAGLE TRIUMPHING OVER DENMARK'S BROKEN GUARD

them to him, but you claim that they have become your property. By what right? By the right of an unjust war which you have waged on the legitimate owner. (Renewed expressions of assent.)

Gentlemen, read well this story! Has anything like it ever happened? We were shocked at the partition of Poland; but where was ever the loathsome and the burlesque mingled and combined to such an extent as here? ("It's true, it's true!"—Bravos and applause.)

We know how Bismarck carried his war through, and how Austria succumbed in 1866. The booty remained in the hands of Germany, and the whole of Danish Slesvig was incorporated into Prussia. There followed half a century of oppression and proud resistance to tyranny, and then came the past four years of horror.

But the last chapter of history has not been written—nor the last word on Slesvig.

Are the Slesvigers Danes or Germans?

By JENS JENSEN

THERE is not a doubt as to which of the two adjoining peoples the Slesvigers belong to racially. The original inhabitants of South Jutland were Danes, and although there has been some German migration into the southern section, this has had no material influence on the race as a whole.

In their usages and mode of thought, the Slesvigers—even those who speak the German language—are true Danes. They are plain folk and democratic in the best sense of the word; they look with disfavor on class distinction and feel on a par with anyone. They respect a man for what he has done, not for his fortune or his birth, and snobbishness, which among the Germans has developed into an elaborate system, is foreign to them. The South-Jutlander thinks for himself, forms his own opinions, and clings to them. In a sense, he is superior both to Dane and German. The latter, uncritical and unreasoning, thinks what he is ordered to think, as he does what he is commanded to do. The Dane, going to the other extreme, is inclined to answer every warning with an indulgent shrug. But the Slesvigers have learned that nothing, however unreasonable or distressing, is impossible, and therefore they scorn no warnings, but obey orders. Yet they yield no unthinking submission. They follow most willingly their own chosen leaders. And these leaders, regardless of birth or station, are elected on account of fitness only; for a noble name, which gives power and prestige in Germany, is of no

VETERANS OF 1864

avail in South Jutland, unless it is brought forward through the ability of its owner.

The character of the South-Jutlanders is emphatically Danish. As their appearance is Northern, so is their manner. Gentle and placid, yet tenacious and energetic, they are typical of all that is best in the Danes. Constant struggle has brought out their finest qualities, has pruned away their selfishness, and developed a strong group consciousness. They are simple and unpretentious in their speech, free from all German slush and bombast. But back of their plain speech stands a firm will; behind their quiet manner is a strong faith in themselves and one another and a spirit of mutual helpfulness which has done much to weld the people together.

DANISH-SPEAKING PEOPLE
FRIESIAN-SPEAKING PEOPLE
GERMAN MIGRATION IN THE NINETEENTH CENTURY
GERMANS

1 : 750000

LINGUISTIC CHART OF SLESVIG

Language, while it is not the only decisive factor, is generally an important element in nationality. In the greater part of Slesvig, the original Danish is still the only language. Into the little strip between the Eider River and Dannevirke, Germans migrated in early medieval times and cleared the primeval forests. Even north of this, Low German is the preponderant language on the east shore as far up as to the Flensborg Fjord, while in the middle of the country Danish extends far down toward the Dannevirke line. In the west German came into conflict with the Friesian language, which had for centuries held its own on the coast of Holstein and Slesvig.

Where there are Slesvigers who speak German, it is noteworthy that the change in speech occurred early in the nineteenth century, before the value of language as an element in nationality was realized. Since 1864 the language frontier has not changed, but Danish has held its own in spite of violent onslaughts of German backed by a powerful and unscrupulous government. And the Danish that is spoken in Slesvig is purer and freer from foreign admixture than the language of any other Danish section. The German, on the other hand, especially near the frontier, is largely not German at all, but simply Danish transposed. The structure of sentences and the order of words, the vocabulary and inflections are so pronouncedly Danish that when the *hjemmetyskere* (pro-Germans born in Slesvig) speak what they imagine to be German, the result is often ludicrous.

The "Free Church" at Haderslev, Closed for Three Years by Prussian Orders

In short, the greater part of Slesvig is Danish in language; a smaller section at the south speaks German, and in a little region between these two both languages are used.

But there are other factors of a national civilization which are of nearly as great importance as the language. Where do the South-Jutlanders get their knowledge, their books and songs, their arts and customs? Go into the humble cottage or the prosperous farmhouse. Everywhere you will find Danish books on the shelves: the history of Danish literature, Danish reference books, and the great Danish and Norwegian poets. Danish agricultural papers lie on the table, and on the walls hang good reproductions of Danish paintings, far different from the German chromos seen farther south. The babies are rocked to sleep to old Danish lullabies, the larger children play the Northern games with their old rigmaroles, and later, as young men and women, they sing the same songs that echo throughout Denmark. In the Free Churches, the Danish hymns are sung as earnestly and devoutly as anywhere in Denmark, and the youth of South Jutland seeks an education in Danish schools.

If we examine the general status of the agricultural class, which constitutes by far the greater part of the population of South Jutland, we find that it bears all the Danish hall-marks. The rural population consists

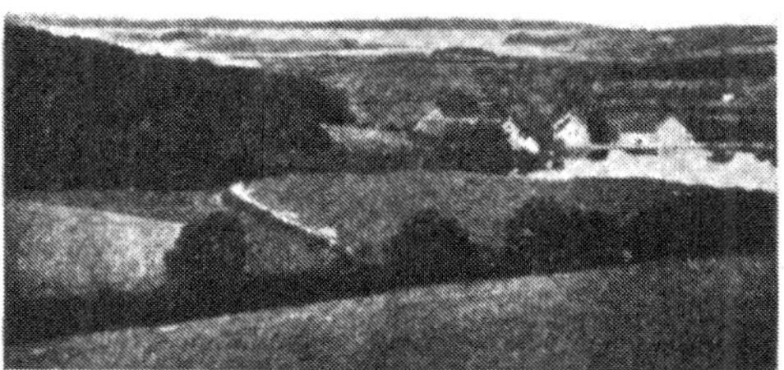

THE GJENNER FJORD, A TYPICAL EAST SLESVIG LANDSCAPE

principally of well-to-do independent farmers owning moderately large farms tilled by the family with the aid of hired hands. Only here and there is an estate with dependent tenants, and the crofters are also few. As in Denmark, the farmers are the mainstay of the people, while in Germany, especially in North Germany, the aristocracy owns the soil, and the peasant counts for naught. Only in a tiny isolated section of southern Slesvig have German conditions been established, and this region stands out in sharp contrast to the remaining Danish Slesvig.

If we finally examine the practical economic position of Slesvig, we cannot deny that Germany's artificial protection of agriculture has also, to some extent, benefited the South-Jutlanders. Yet the high tariff and many taxes and tolls have made living in the German Empire so expensive that the farmers would be as well off under Denmark. Besides the agriculture of Slesvig, especially the

export of butter and bacon, would have the same opportunities in the large markets of Europe as the Danish has, while under the Empire Slesvig is put in the peculiar position of a foreign country exporting to Germany. Thus Slesvig is closely bound to Denmark economically and

A WEST SLESVIG FARM OF THE TYPE THAT HAS DESCENDED IN DANISH FAMILIES FOR HUNDREDS OF YEARS

has no interest in common with Germany. The same is true of agricultural methods. The dairying is Danish; the powerful coöperative movement, which has taken as firm a hold in Slesvig as in the kingdom, is also Danish. So is the division between grain-producing and cattle-raising, and even the types of farms and of wagons and tools are Danish.

The whole vigorous life that has unfolded in rich and beautiful South Jutland is as Danish as the land itself, with its fields and hedges, with its wooded fjords at the east, the wide heaths of the midland, and the broad fertile meadows toward the west.

Two Monuments

On the Skamlingsbanke, Across the Danish Border, a Tall, Slender Monument Lifts a Defiant Finger Toward Those Who Think They Can Root Out the Memories of a Nation. It Was First Raised to Commemorate the Great Patriotic Meetings Held on the Site. In 1864, the Prussians Blew It up and Sold the Pieces for Crushed Stone, but the Farmers in the Neighborhood Bought Them Back and Rebuilt the Monument. At Its Foot, a Huge Dannebrog Waves a Message Across the Border to Those Who Are Forbidden to Show the Danish Red and White.

The Lion of Isted Has Gone to Grace the Military Academy at Berlin. The Picture Shows It When It Was in Its Place in Flensborg Churchyard, Where the Danes Had Raised It in Honor of Their Countrymen Who Fell in 1848. It Was Carried Away by the Germans in 1864. How Different the Spirit of the French, Who Left the Lion at Waterloo in Its Place, Only Filing off the Sharp Claws in the Paw that Was Lifted Against France!

Memory Song

Original Danish by HANS PETER HOLST

English verse by JANE CAMPBELL

Sweetly sleep in Slesvig's ground!
Though dear bought, naught does it matter;
Summer fair its sweetest flowers
O'er your grave will freely scatter.
As a bird will memory fly,
On to Slesvig its flight winging;
From the lonely hiding-place
Of the grave we hear its singing.

Lonely, for no friendly eye
Your last dying glance was meeting;
No friend heard your last-drawn sigh
Nor clasped hand in loving greeting!
But for Denmark was that sigh,
For the victory coming surely;
Rest then sweetly on earth's lap,
In the grave's shade rest securely!

Oft will memory fly afar
Where, dear ones, you now are lying,
Who with ardor fought and fell,
For old Denmark's honor dying.
But your death has brought reward;
Slesvig's land can be lost never.
Blood binds blood, and with your blood
It is bound to us forever!

Fairer death could not be found
Than yours for old Denmark falling;
So no tearful glances we
Cast when on your memory calling.
But where'er beat Danish hearts,
Where'er Danish blades are ringing,
They with pride to great and small
Thanks of motherland are bringing.

of North Slesvig, who to-day is championing the cause of his people with unsurpassed courage and eloquence—all these men have, in some form or other, kept up an open fight against oppression in the very home of the oppressor.

As a rule, purely German legislation has not interested them unless it has had some bearing on the welfare of North Slesvig. Yet they have strayed from this position of apartness long enough to enter repeated protests against all forms of Prussianism. They have opposed the anti-Catholic laws, the anti-Socialist laws, and above all the repressive measures against the other dissident nationalities, the Poles and Alsatians. From the time of Krüger till the present War, when Hanssen has refused to vote for the budget, they have been consistent protestants against the growing spirit of militarism in the empire. They have tried to show that the dangers which made increased armaments necessary were caused by Germany's expansion beyond her natural ethnic boundaries through the conquest of Slesvig and Alsace-Lorraine, and have pointed out that the Germans rouse enmity by disregarding in others the national sentiments which they exalt in themselves.

They have never recognized the abolition of the paragraph giving them the right to self-determination. With prophetic vision, Lassen expressed the conviction that "toward the close of the nineteenth century people and countries will no longer be treated as common merchandise." Johansson reiterated in the most unequivocal terms their stand on the Treaty of Prague and on their political status as defined therein. Nor have they been silent during the present war. Last spring Hanssen spoke in the Reichstag in favor of self-determination for Åland, and only a few weeks earlier Skrumsager closed a speech in the Prussian House with these words: "We have always been adherents of the doctrine of self-determination, and we hope that now when this right is being recognized by the German Empire [at Brest-Litovsk] we too shall have our most ardent wish fulfilled."

How much this untiring opposition has accomplished it is impossible to estimate. No one who has noticed how even the strongest liberal factions have broken their strength in vain against the intrenched government of Germany can wonder that this mere handful of Danes should not have accomplished any great tangible results. Yet their work has certainly not been in vain; it has served to rouse the national pride of their countrymen and to keep the cause of Slesvig before the world.

The Scandinavian "Bolsheviki"

By Karl Gustav Dernby

THE Russian revolution resembles in many respects the French. The forces that caused the latter were first considered shockingly radical, but when they were confronted with the great task of governing the country, they were modified, and, in their turn, ousted by still more radical elements, and so the movement went more and more to the left, until it ended in general anarchy. The great French revolution had a tremendous influence on all social movements in Europe. The question is: Will the Russian revolution exert a similar influence in these days?

Revolutions are like contagious diseases: they spread rapidly. The countries first to be infected by the Russian and Finnish revolutionary germs are those of Scandinavia, and dispatches therefrom have lately been printed with headlines such as "The Norwegian Bolsheviki," "Revolution Feared in Sweden," or "Serious Riots in Copenhagen." It must be remembered, however, that the bourgeois papers are always a little prone to exaggerate social movements or, as we say in Sweden, to "paint the devil on the wall." It should also be borne in mind that, under normal conditions, there are not at all the same premises for revolution in the comparatively democratic and wealthy Scandinavian countries as there were in Russia.

Let us first inquire what are the new truths that Bolshevism offers. It has not yet produced any great prophet who has given its doctrine classic form, though we may find hints of it in all the proclamations and newspaper articles emanating from Lenine and Trotzky. In part, it seems there is nothing either new or original in the ideas of the Bolsheviki. The main points seem to be the same as the original "catastrophe theory" of Marx, according to which the chief issue in modern society is an implacable strife between the "consuming" classes, the "oppressors," who constitute a minority, and the "producers," the "oppressed," who constitute the great masses. Marx thought a peaceful settlement of this problem impossible, and took for granted that it must of necessity bring on a catastrophe, a revolution, which would transfer all power to the masses and their chosen organs. He afterwards modified this idea, and his pupils, Engel and Bebel, were the fathers of the so-called "reformistic" theory, which holds that the same goal can be reached by lawful, that is parliamentary, means.

Other points in the Bolshevist programme are: complete internationalism, the breaking down of all national barriers, to be followed by total disarmament; abolishment of private property and the equal distribution of land among all; the closing of all industries not essential to the welfare and happiness of man; the abolition of bureaucracy by lodging all power, judicial as well as executive, in the workmen's councils chosen by the masses. There seem to be certain similarities here to the programme launched by the Industrial Workers of the World in this country.

When socialists first made their appearance in Scandinavia, people regarded them as dangerous anarchists, and predicted that they would wreck the country. Times changed, however. Labor unions increased in power year by year, and in Scandinavia the labor unions, unlike the American Federation of Labor, are closely affiliated with the Socialist party, which is now a most important political factor in all three countries. In Sweden it will perhaps not be long before the Socialists will have a majority in the Riksdag, and nowadays it is regarded as quite respectable for even an educated man to be a member of the party.

The Scandinavian socialists adopted the "reformistic" tendency that had the upper hand in Germany, while the syndicalist movement originating in France did not at first find a fertile soil among them. In Sweden, the Socialist party has been built up almost entirely by the will of one strong man, the world-famous Hjalmar Branting, and his personality has set its stamp upon the organization. He has always denounced sabotage and all illegal methods, urging upon his followers the use of parliamentary measures only.

It is always more convenient to be in opposition than to carry responsibility. So long as they were a powerless minority, the socialists could launch "maximum" programmes, including internationalism, total disarmament, the taking over of capital and all means of production by the State, the establishment of a republic, and so on. When they came into power, however, they found it impossible to realize all these demands at once, and the Swedish Socialist party has now adopted a modified policy differing only on some economic questions from that of the Liberals.

But this disappointed many people, who regarded the "parliamentary" or "salon socialists" as traitors to their holy ideals. In the early part of the century, a rather anarchistic movement was started by Hinke Bergegren. It was marked by many acts of sabotage and is remembered for the famous "Amalthea" case in 1908, when a steamer harboring imported English strike-breakers was blown up in the harbor of Malmö. As early as 1903, however, Branting's strong hand excommunicated Bergegren and his Young Socialists or *ung-hinkar*, and now this movement is practically dead.

Yet there are still within the party plenty of opponents against Branting personally and against his policy. The most prominent of these is the distinguished jurist, mayor of Stockholm, Carl Lindhagen, an idealist and a noble political personality, whose only fault is that his idealism sometimes drives him too far away in the blue. Other opposition leaders are: Z. Höglund, an editor who has served two prison terms for treason; Ture Nerman, the poet, and Fabian Månsson, an agitator who would match Billy Sunday.

The split in the party came on the issue of military preparedness. Face to face with the grim outlook in 1914, the majority Socialists voted for an increased army and navy. The extremists accused them of abandoning the cardinal principles of socialism and launched bitter attacks upon such men as Palmstjerna, now secretary of the navy, Rydén, now secretary of education, and many others. Finally, in 1916, Branting took the drastic step of excommunicating all his opponents, whereupon they formed the Left Socialist party and started their own paper, *Politiken,* famous in these days for its revelation of the Lichnowsky documents.

In the general elections of 1917, the new party was not successful. Out of the 230 seats in the second chamber, it secured only 12, while the majority Socialists had 86. The powerful labor unions, as a rule, vote with the majority, but some of the longshoremen and a number of the lumberjacks and miners in Norrland—many of whom are Finns—support the new party. They have also a stronghold in *Ungdomsklubbarna,* which are not regular labor unions, but discussion clubs with a membership of youths from fifteen to twenty-five years of age. The Left Socialists have a powerful apparatus for agitation, and it should be noted that among their leaders are educated men and trained politicians.

Which of these parties is right? Every observer must admit that in the present disturbed times the majority Socialists have acted in a sane and dignified manner; their determined stand against the Activists has saved Sweden from being dragged into the war. The policy of the Left Socialists, on the other hand, has been uncertain and perilous. They have swung between the extremes of Germanophobia and Anglophobia, and they are not free from the suspicion of having received subsidies from foreign governments, most recently from that of Russia. Yet, with all their mistakes, they have a certain mission to perform, as the salt that has not lost its power, in upholding the full programme of socialism.

When the old Internationale was shattered by the war, a new and more radical organization was formed, at Zimmerwald in Switzerland, at a congress where, if I mistake not, Lenine was present. The Left Socialists in Sweden have officially subscribed to the principles of the Zimmerwald Internationale, and, in the Russian revolution, they have sympathized with Trotzky and Lenine, whereas the majority Socialists sympathized with Kerensky. The "Lefts" may therefore not improperly be called "Swedish Bolsheviki."

These "Bolsheviki" have never, like the majority Socialists, taken a stand against the recent rioting due to food shortage and unemployment, but have rather incited to violence; yet they are by no means united on this point. If there should be more disturbances, the Liberal-Socialist ministry under Edén would, no doubt, put them down with a firm hand, and in this it would have the support of an overwhelming majority of the people. Besides, there is still Branting— a strong wall against which all anarchistic movements break their force in vain. If his influence for any reason should be removed, it might result in the collapse of the Socialist party into a number of small factions, as in France, and then the left wing might gain much in power.

In Norway, the Socialist party polled one-third of all the votes cast in the general elections in 1915. Nevertheless it is not so strong in the Storting as in the Swedish and Danish parliaments. This is due in part to a peculiar system of voting, by which the country districts are favored at the expense of the cities, and here we may perhaps trace one cause of the bitter radicalism shown by many Norwegian socialists. The movement has been headed by such pioneers as Chr. Holterman Knudsen, C. Jeppesen, a Dane, now mayor of Christiania, and Ole O. Lian, until recently secretary of the party. All are men who approve only of parliamentary methods of warfare, and their programme has been formed on the German "reformistic" ideas, but it has been a shade more radical than that of the Swedes. Within the party there has always been an important left wing, sometimes known as the Young Socialists, and this element has grown so in strength that the moderate leaders have never dared to risk an absolute break as Branting did in Sweden.

Even before the war, the sudden expansion of manufacturing created a large wage-earning class, and the radical socialists were recruited chiefly from the poorer and less educated workingmen— the proletariat in the truest sense. This faction is syndicalist in its doctrine, and has for its slogan sabotage and anti-militarism. It found a fiery leader and agitator in Martin Tranmael, the editor of *Ny Tid* in Trondhjem. During the war, Norway, too, has seen hard times, and, naturally, the poor people have suffered most. Hunger is the cradle of revolution, and the extremists have gained a number of proselytes.

At the national convention of the party, last Easter, the radical faction, for the first time, had a majority. The conservative leaders, seeing their programme voted down at every point, retired from office, and Tranmael was elected secretary of the party. A resolution was passed in which the principle of class war and the right of revolution were openly proclaimed. The meeting furthermore decided to coöperate with the Left Socialist party in Sweden and to affiliate with the Zimmerwald Internationale. It endorsed the Workmen's

Councils formed by several large labor unions on the pattern of the Russian Workmen's Councils, with the ultimate aim of taking full control of all industries, agriculture, trade, transportation, and government.

It is yet too early to say what action these Norwegian Bolsheviki will take. Undoubtedly their movement should not be belittled, but, on the other hand, we may hope that the position of full control of a large and steadily growing political party will have a sobering effect on them. Recent accounts from Norway say that Tranmael has been sentenced to a short term in prison for treason, but the riots which the bourgeois papers feared in consequence do not seem to have taken place.

In Denmark, socialism made its entrance earlier than in the other countries, and its course has run more smoothly. The Danish socialists, recognizing the impossibility of their little country defending itself against Germany, have always had disarmament on their programme. Moreover, the Danish State has been perhaps more thoroughly socialized than any other; State care of the aged, the infirm, and the unemployed has been accepted in principle and carefully worked out in practice. Due perhaps to these two reasons, there has never been any radical faction of importance within the party. Sporadic syndicalistic movements have occurred sometimes, but have never been successful. The two chief party leaders, Frederik Borgbjerg, editor of *Socialdemokraten*, and Th. Stauning, until recently a member of the cabinet, have upheld a policy along German "reformistic" lines.

Quite recently, however, the failure of the raw materials formerly imported from America and other countries suddenly created a large unemployed proletariat, numbering perhaps 50,000 people. The socialist leaders supported the demand that the government should care for these sufferers, and the government took adequate measures to do so. But in the meantime, the masses had been stirred up by persons infected with Bolshevist ideas, and the movement got beyond the control of the conservative leaders. Official Social-Democracy then took its hand away from these agitators and denounced them in the strongest terms. A demonstration of 10,000 unemployed in Copenhagen last January was directed against Borgbjerg and Stauning as well as against the Rigsdag, but it dissolved in a mere farce. This was followed, a month later, by more serious riots in front of the stock exchange, which resulted in the arrest of Chr. Christensen, the editor of *Solidaritet*, and some of his companions. In other parts of the country, too, there have been sporadic riots, but well-informed Danes regard them as rather local and harmless.

What is the outlook now in the Scandinavian countries? Are they facing a social revolution like that in Russia and Finland?

The answer is reassuring. The workingmen in Scandinavia are too intelligent not to know that revolution never created a loaf of bread. They have too much political education not to take warning from the miserable conditions in Russia and Finland. We may trust them to keep their heads cool, provided the food scarcity and unemployment do not grow more acute than at present.

Much depends on the attitude of the bourgeois elements. In Sweden there was a tendency, in 1917, to form "protection guards" similar to the White Guards in Finland, but the project was nipped in the bud after a fiery speech by Branting in the Riksdag. If the bourgeoisie will meet the workingmen peacefully and in a conciliatory spirit, instead of irritating them, it will tend to stop any incipient uprising.

There is, of course, the possibility of crop failure and disastrous famine. With the nightmare of hunger torturing them, even wise and sane people may lose their heads, and in that case the very existence of Scandinavia might be threatened; for we know from the example of Finland that, in case of armed conflict, Germany would not for a moment hesitate to intervene to "restore order." At present, however, there seems no reason for pessimism. We may confidently hope that such a situation will never be created.

A Characteristic View of the Kiel Canal Shows One of the Four Railroad Bridges That Span It. This German Waterway Is Sixty Miles Long and So Wide That Two Large Ships Can Pass Each Other. Emperor William I Began the Construction in 1887, and the Present Emperor Opened the Canal in 1895. For a Third of Its Length, in the Eastern Part, It Touches the Slesvig Border; in Its Middle Course It Is Entirely Within Holstein Though Still Near the Border; Then It Turns Abruptly South to Enter the Mouth of the Elbe River.

Alexander E. Johnson

THE life of Alexander Edward Johnson, who died on June 11 after a lingering illness, is a fine example of a commercial career turned to public service. Not only that he gave liberally of a well-earned surplus, but his business activity had something of the wide outlook of the statesman. As immigration agent for the State

ALEXANDER E. JOHNSON

of Minnesota, and later as land commissioner for the Hill railway interests, he was instrumental in leading the stream of Scandinavian immigrants to Minnesota, North Dakota, and the far West. The Red River Valley, "the bread-basket of America," was settled by sixty thousand people, largely through his endeavors. Not content with securing sturdy tillers for the virgin soil, he took care to lead the newcomer to fertile land, showed him how to get his title in order, and helped him to become an American citizen.

Mr. Johnson had himself known what it was to be an immigrant. Born in Värmland, in 1840, he came to this country at the age of fourteen. His father died soon after, and the boy was thus confronted with the problem of supporting his mother and winning an education for himself.

Though his life-work was in the West, Mr. Johnson spent his old age in New York. Those who came in contact with him there remember the great kindliness and good-will that radiated from his personality. Many honors came to him. He was first Swedish consul in America after 1905, first president of the Swedish Chamber of Commerce, trustee of the American-Scandinavian Foundation, Commander of the Vasa Order, Knight of the Dannebrog, and honorary member of various organizations.

Editorial

  The President, in an address to both houses of
Congress, on January 8, enunciated the fourteen cardinal points of the peace programme
for which the United States is willing to fight until it is achieved.
In summing up, he said: "An evident principle runs through the
whole programme I have outlined. It is the principle of justice to
all peoples and nationalities and their right to live on equal terms of
liberty and safety one with another, whether they be strong or weak.
Unless this principle be made its foundation, no part of the structure
of international justice can stand." In conformity with this principle laid down by the President, the Editors of the REVIEW have
prepared the Slesvig Number, presenting the case of a small group
of Scandinavians living against their will under Prussian dominion.

The problem of Slesvig will undoubtedly come up at the peace
conference. Indeed, it has already been discussed in the British
Parliament, when the restoration of the lost province to Denmark
was suggested as the best means of internationalizing the Kiel
Canal. The Danish South-Jutlanders have stood out for half a
century against Prussianism. They have fought their battles in
the open and with fair weapons, and morally they have won. In
the face of organized German effort, they have not only preserved
their entity, but deepened and broadened their national character.
They speak Danish with greater purity than ever before, and are
more than ever imbued with Northern ideals. Though physically
a part of the German Empire, subject to its unjust laws and abominable military system, they have preserved their souls apart. They
have not been tainted by the moral blight that has fallen on the
German people. By their intrepid spirit, their splendid organization, their intelligent fight for justice, they have showed their ability
to guide their own destinies and earned the right to determine
their own fate.

Regard must, of course, be paid to the interests of Denmark.
The Danes have bravely accepted their defeat at the hands of a
brute power, and have refrained from all political intrigues against
Germany, although they have loyally helped the South-Jutlanders
to preserve their heritage of Northern culture. The possession of a
region coveted by Germany and inhabited by Germans would
undoubtedly expose Denmark to attacks in the future. The restoration of Slesvig should therefore concern only the northern region,
which is essentially Danish, and should be based on self-determination, thus carrying out, though tardily, the provisions of the Treaty
of Prague. We trust that wisdom may guide the peace negotiations
in the course that will insure liberty and safety for all concerned.

THE VALUE OF SLESVIG TO GERMANY
Slesvig, with its 8,734 square kilometers of territory and its 430,000 inhabitants, has an importance in European history that is out of proportion to its size. The beginning of German dominion is generally traced to the conquest of Alsace-Lorraine and the humbling of proud France; but if we go back a few years, we find that the acquisition of Slesvig and Holstein, through the defeat of little Denmark, in 1864, really laid the foundations of the modern German Empire. That was the beginning of the forceful assimilation of alien border peoples which committed Germany to her policy of blood and iron, and necessitated a huge army. A long strip of coastline was then added to her possessions, thus giving her added freedom for military operations in the Baltic, and therewith commenced the encircling of that inland sea, in which the occupation of Finland is the last link. The annexation of the two provinces forming the neck of the Danish peninsula made possible the construction of the Kiel Canal, which, together with the Kiel harbor, established the maritime power of the empire. The harbor with its fortification is the cradle of the German navy. The canal enables her to keep her battleships under cover, ready to slip out suddenly and secretly, and in this way she can tie up a large part of an enemy's fleet. Commercially the waterway has been of enormous importance, eliminating the tortuous route through the Öresund and giving Hamburg direct communication with the east. Before the war, Hamburg had become one of the greatest trading marts in the world, and an immense volume of American goods was transshipped there for Scandinavia, Finland, Russia, and Siberia. By the absorption of the Baltic provinces and Finland, Germany is now trying to block the future commerce between America and the countries of western Europe on one side and Russia and her former possessions on the other. She is threatening to mobilize the vast man power and inexhaustible resources of Russia to her own advantage. But all this presupposes control of the Baltic and its key, the Kiel Canal, and while the harbor and canal are both in Holstein, they are so close to the Slesvig border that the possession of that old Danish land is considered a military necessity from the German point of view.

IN THE WORLD WAR
Up to the end of July, 5,144 Danish South-Jutlanders had fallen in the war out of a total of 148,000. Many times that number are wounded and disabled. They have been forced to fight for the cause they abhor, against people whom they can only regard as fellow-victims, pitted against them by merciless fate. Prisoners of war bear testimony to the kindliness of the South-Jutlanders compared with German brutality. The

Germans themselves have abundantly testified to their bravery and have rewarded them with unwelcome iron crosses.

With all this, Germany's methods are unchanged. Never has oppression been harder in South Jutland than to-day; never has hatred and persecution of everything Danish been more violent. When the war broke out and the youth of South Jutland, obedient to the law, flocked to the German colors, and Danish men were even taken ahead of the Germans in their classes, then gendarmes, policemen, and soldiers with loaded guns were sent out through the country to seize and carry away to jail hundreds of prominent Danes. Not because they had done anything punishable, or even were accused of anything, but only to hinder any action they *might* commit prejudicial to the interests of the State—in other words, because the bad conscience of the Germans told them that a country which had been maltreated as South Jutland had been would, with full justice, employ every means to harm its tormentors. These men were kept prisoners for weeks, some of them under most miserable conditions, and when they were sent home from the distant points to which they had been taken they were themselves forced to pay the journey forth and back and their prison stay at hotel rates.

As an example of the brutal procedure of the Germans may be mentioned the arrest of the old editor, Mr. Mathiesen of Haderslev, by seven soldiers with fixed bayonets, who escorted him to jail through the crowded streets. He had for a long time been mortally ill with cancer; he was deaf and almost blind. In spite of this, he was taken to a little island far away off the Pomeranian shore. His wife tried repeatedly to obtain a little mercy for him, but the commandant answered her agonized prayers by saying: *"Es ist mir doch einerlei, ob so ein Kerl krepiert."* The sick man was kept in jail for weeks and died a few months after being released.

The South Jutland press is even now kept under the severest censorship, not only in that it can not write freely, but in that it receives orders what to print. The persecution of the Danish language continues unabated. At the annual meeting of a stock company in Flensborg the police refused to permit the directors to speak Danish. Danish Slesvigers in the Prussian army have likewise been forbidden the use of their own mother tongue.

All this goes on while the flower of South Jutland is giving its life in order to fulfill the duty demanded by the law and while the Germans themselves acknowledge that they are doing so.

It is the same old story. The Germans consider themselves the chosen people placed above all others, without respect or feeling for those who think otherwise. In South Jutland the hatred of Germany has never been more bitter than at present, nor the cleavage between German and Dane deeper. The storm is devastating the country; thousands of its best men are maimed and killed. But their purpose has not changed; hope is not abandoned, and, as one of their songs says: "Hope points toward Denmark."

A NEW FOURTH   In sanctioning the celebration of the Fourth of July by racial groups, all marching under the Stars and Stripes, President Wilson showed the way to that newer ideal of patriotism which must be ours if we are to attain full stature as a nation. Our national holiday was transformed from a day of boasting to a day of consecration. Instead of the old spread-eagle oratory, we had proclamations of freedom for all the people that dwell on the face of the earth. To the foreign-born it was a day for bringing all their pride of race and all their memories of the past as gifts to the country in which they have found happiness and freedom.

The inspiration of such a day was needed at this time. The abuse of our hospitality by German propagandists has naturally roused bitter resentment and suspicion. Many well-meaning people think that the only safeguard for such evils in the future lies in suppressing all individuality in the immigrant and imposing on him a standard Americanism as quickly as possible. Hence efforts that might better be directed to fostering good-will among our various groups of citizens are turned against a loyal press, against loyal churches and schools, because they employ another language than English.

This recrudescence of Know-nothingism would be more discouraging if we did not see, side by side with it, the growth of that larger Americanism which found expression on the Fourth of July. More and more people realize that love for this country need not imply the loss of that "backward vision" which is the heritage of the old nations. There is an increasing interest in the native culture of the immigrant groups that make up our population. It is seen that every human being is tied to the land of his birth by the subtle forces which the old Norsemen symbolized in the chain that bound the Fenris Wolf—forged of "the noise a cat makes in footfall, the beard of a woman, the roots of a rock, the sinews of a bear, the breath of a fish, and the spittle of a bird"—and the sudden snapping of this chain makes the children of immigrants intellectually barren.

Those of us who have always believed in retaining the spiritual bond between the immigrant and his mother country felt our faith justified by the splendid pageant on Fifth Avenue, where it seemed that the essence of all the beauty and color and poetry of the old nations was brought together to enrich America. May the spirit of that day stay with us! This country has already in a measure solved the problem of harmonizing different races. We know nothing of the national strife that is rending Slesvig and Finland and Austria. Here and here alone people of every blood, from every clime, dwell together in peace and amity. Freedom of language, of creed, of family custom, of thought and speech has contributed to this result as much as, perhaps more than, the right to vote and the opportunity to earn a fair wage. There should be no tampering now with the policy of broad tolerance that has made us a happy and united nation.

AMUNDSEN'S DEPARTURE   The New York *Times*, in its issue of June 30, comments editorially on Amundsen's departure for the North Pole as follows:

"If Roald Amundsen were not a Norwegian, and therefore an explorer by race and blood, one might wonder how he could set out for the North Pole, which everybody expects him to attain, when the world is ablaze with war and there is a hazard that he may have no country when he returns to Christiania. It is really a pity that a born leader of men like Amundsen is not in the fight against Germany. At forty-six he is in the prime of life, with a courage that no peril can daunt, and a frame proof against hardship. The driving power of the man is tremendous, and he has a magnetic personal charm that attracts heroic spirits to him. Venturesome as the enterprise was, the crew of the *Gjöa* that he took through the Northwest Passage was always a happy ship's company; and the South Pole was gained by men who found the way made easy by Amundsen's cheerful and sturdy leadership. His talents and character would tell in the Great War, but Fate decreed that he should be an explorer first, and then a neutral. A neutral, however, only in the national sense. Germany became odious to the man who returned the Kaiser's decorations as 'a personal protest against the German murder of peaceful Norwegian sailors in the North Sea.'

"Two, three, four years Roald Amundsen may be gone, and perhaps he will never come back from the polar silences, for this is his greatest venture. But he admits no such word as failure, and never was Arctic explorer better equipped with aids to success and native resources, or more staunchly backed by seasoned comrades. The War will probably be over when he sails into the home harbor, and civilization will have been saved. Imagine the thrill of the stoutest of Norwegian explorers when he sights his first ship in temperate seas, and the answer is made to his question, shouted across the surges, 'How's the War?'"

WAR SAVINGS   The REVIEW blew a strong blast for War Savings in our last issue. Three full-page announcements were contributed by loyal readers of the magazine. Let the good work continue. People of Scandinavian blood are taking the lead in the organization of War Savings Societies throughout the country. At the Swedish celebration of the Fourth in Chicago, the Swedish Division Illinois War Savings Committee combined with the John Ericsson League. Among the speakers were Governor Charles S. Deneen and Dr. Amandus Johnson. "From this time forward," says the Treasury Department, "emphasis should be laid upon the organization and continuation of War Savings Societies. There should be one or more of such War Savings Societies within every existing organization (civic or church)."

Current Events
Denmark

⁋ The Rigsdag was opened by the King in person, on May 28. It was a notable occasion in many ways. The legislators met for the first time in the rebuilt Christiansborg Castle, a splendid structure which it has taken nearly fifteen years to complete, and which includes under one roof the royal palace, the houses of the Rigsdag, and the rooms of the Supreme Court. It was particularly appropriate that the new halls should be opened with the Rigsdag which is the first to be elected under the new liberal constitution of June 5, 1915. It was the first time women voted in national elections, and four women took their places among the members of the Rigsdag. The first speech by a woman member was made by Fru Elna Munch, wife of the minister of defenses, who is himself also a member of the Folketing. ⁋ The parties are very evenly divided. In the Folketing the government party, a coalition of Radicals and Socialists, has a majority of only two over the combined strength of the other parties. In the Landsting the government has a minority of four of the new members elected, but the eighteen members of the former Rigsdag who still hold their seats help to swell the Conservative ranks, so the government has, in fact, a total strength in the Landsting of only twenty-eight against forty-four. Under these conditions, it can of course not count on forcing through any radical measures. An outstanding feature of the elections is the growth of the Socialist element in Copenhagen. Remarkably little interest was taken in the elections, probably due to the fact that there were no exciting issues. All parties agree in preserving the neutrality of the country and in trying to solve the problems of food shortage, unemployment, and other evils due to the war in the best possible manner. ⁋ In the matter of food Denmark is, perhaps, as well off as any country in Europe, but a strict rationing is maintained in order to husband the resources of the country and save enough for "compensation" goods to other countries. Denmark has put at the disposal of Sweden 15,000 tons of grain, and has also exported large quantities of butter in return for Swedish wares. The short rations of bread and butter led to serious riots in Copenhagen in June, but the government persisted in its plan for food conservation. The importation of Norway saltpeter to Denmark amounted to 20,000 tons in the month of May. ⁋ A delegation of four men headed by the minister of finance, Chr. Hage, left for Iceland in June to attend a conference at Reykjavik for the settlement of the differences between Denmark and Iceland. The Icelanders wish to use their own flag and be regarded as a sovereign state while remaining in a personal union with the kingdom of Denmark.

Sweden

¶ King Gustaf's sixtieth birthday, on June 16, brought him warm congratulations from Denmark and Norway, as well as from all parts of Sweden. He is recognized in the neighboring countries as the creator of the idea of Scandinavian coöperation which is steadily growing in importance. The large-minded manner in which the King laid aside all personal grievances to visit King Haakon recently has established his place in the affection and esteem of the Norwegians. ¶ The Riksdag of 1918 failed to pass two leading measures in the programme of the Liberal-Socialist government. Woman suffrage was again voted down by the first chamber after passing the second. The bill for liberalizing the communal suffrage and thereby the elections to the first chamber was likewise blocked by the Conservatives in that reactionary body, after a debate characterized by bitterness and a threatening tone on both sides. ¶ The session was marked by a great volume of legislation dealing with war conditions. In Sweden, as in the belligerent countries, the State is more and more taking over the management of production and distribution formerly left to private enterprise. It has been necessary to stimulate agriculture and to encourage the home manufacture of articles formerly purchased abroad. Furthermore, the state is interesting itself in the utilization of water power, and work will soon begin on one of the great falls of Lapland, partly in order to increase the supply of electricity available and partly as a measure against unemployment. As a consequence of all these government activities, the budget has increased to 1,582,700,000 kronor for 1918 as against 261,100,000 for 1913. ¶ By the agreement with the Allied governments, signed in London on May 29, the Swedish government has undertaken to facilitate the export to the Allied countries of wood pulp, steel, and iron ore, and has approved the chartering of 400,000 tons of Swedish ships to the Allies. In return Sweden will be allowed to import grain from Argentina and Australia, fodder, oil, leather, hides, and wool from South America, and raw materials for manufacturing, chiefly cotton and metals, in sufficient quantities. Some anxiety is felt in Sweden over the large amount of tonnage which is thus diverted from the Swedish trade. It is claimed that Sweden will have only 600,000 tons for her own disposal, of which only 150,000 can be used for transoceanic trade, an amount that seems inadequate for Sweden's own use. ¶ The good ship *New Sweden*, one of the two largest freight steamers owned in Sweden, has been torpedoed on the way from Naples to a North-American port. The vessel was the property of the Swedish East Asiatic Company. ¶ The Spitzbergen coal mines are expected to yield 10,000 tons this summer. Most of this will be used for the State railways.

Norway

❡ General satisfaction is felt with the treaty negotiated by the Nansen Commission with our government. It is true, some of the papers point out that Norway has really bound herself to export to our allies certain quantities of her products without absolute assurance that she will receive anything in return, since the United States Food Administrator promises only to release what can be spared. Nevertheless it is realized that our government is sincerely anxious to relieve Norway's want so far as possible, and the prevailing tone is one of optimism. The return of Dr. Nansen and his expressions of good-will toward the American people and administration have helped to increase the cordial feeling which is noticeable in the press comments. ❡ The Norwegian losses from submarines in the month of May were fourteen vessels with a total tonnage of 11,791. This unusually heavy toll was due to the war of destruction on the sealing and whaling vessels along the northern coast under pretense that they were supplying England with oil, though, as a matter of fact, the Norwegian government has laid an embargo on all oil and is even paying a high premium for it. The German operations were carried on in the customary brutal fashion. A few crews of torpedoed vessels managed to save themselves by rowing to the Russian port Vaida-Guba. While they were there, the Germans bombarded the village in order to destroy its wireless plant. Fourteen of the inhabitants were killed and fourteen wounded, some of the bodies being horribly mutilated. The Norwegian losses since the war began have now reached 769 ships and 1,008 seamen, besides 53 ships and 704 men missing. ❡ The Norwegian government has acquired the French interests in the Grong mines near Trondhjem with the stipulation that none of the pyrites mined there shall be sold to Germany for the duration of the war. The government is also taking steps to buy several large waterfalls in the same region. A commission is being formed to deal with the centralization and distribution of water power. ❡ A national collection is being taken up in order to enlarge the area of cultivated land. In Bergen 1,300 volunteers have planted 3,500 sacks of potatoes and hope to raise a crop of 30,000 barrels if the harvest is good. In Christiania the University students, men and women, are also busy in the potato patches. A consignment of 115,000 sacks of Australian wheat arrived in Bergen on June 9. ❡ The Christiania commune has laid in such large quantities of wood and coal that the fuel administration hopes to avoid rationing in the coming winter. ❡ A general system of old-age and invalid pensions is under consideration in the Storting. The plan includes all persons living in Norway or on Norwegian ships and all those employed by the government in foreign countries.

Books

Essay Toward a History of Shakespeare in Norway. By Martin B. Ruud. (Scandinavian Studies and Notes, IV, 2.) Urbana, Illinois: The Society for the Advancement of Scandinavian Study, 1917.

It is generally very instructive to trace the fortunes of a great poet in foreign countries. Such study is capable of shedding light in both directions. The reputation of Shakespeare abroad affords material especially suitable for such inquiry; the reactions when he is in question are likely to be particular and intense. To Jusserand's *Shakespeare in France* and Collison-Morley's *Shakespeare in Italy* it is now possible, by reason of the generous support of the American-Scandinavian Foundation, to add Martin B. Ruud's *Essay Toward a History of Shakespeare in Norway*. Dr. Ruud takes up his matter chronologically. He is tracing, be it noted, not the influence of Shakespeare on Norwegian literature, but the widening interest in the English poet as expressed in translations, criticisms, and performances of his plays. For the seventeenth century there is nothing to record; for the eighteenth very little; even in the nineteenth century Norway got its Shakespeare from Denmark. By 1818 a translation of *Coriolanus* had appeared (somehow appropriate, one thinks, that this should be the first play to be translated at the hands of a countryman of Ibsen's) and Niels Hauge translated *Macbeth* in 1855. Meanwhile, Ivar Aasen had experimented with Shakespeare in the *Landsmaal*, an effort very recently widely extended by Madhus, Egge, and Wildenvey. All of this material the author analyzes in detail; he seems to have some doubts about the suitability of the *Landsmaal* as a vehicle for Shakespeare. A version in the *Riksmaal* remains to be made. Chapter II deals with Shakespeare criticism in Norway. Björnson and Collin supply the most important matter. The record of performances, the subject of Chapter III, begins with a representation of *Macbeth* in 1844, and Johannes Brun's impersonation of Falstaff (1867) is probably its artistic climax. The performances are tabulated in an appendix.

If the material discussed by this monograph appears to be limited and relatively unimportant, it is in a measure due to the close dependence of literary Norway upon Denmark, and Shakespeare in Denmark the author expressly reserves for a later treatise. Meanwhile, he has our gratitude for taking us over the ground and showing us what there is; all a very necessary prelude to the more delicate task of assessing Shakespeare's influence upon the literature of Scandinavia.

Harry Morgan Ayres.

Sweden-America. Edited by Oscar G. Marell. The Swedish Chamber of Commerce of the United States of America. Produce Exchange Annex, New York. 1918. 144 pp. Price $1.00.

This annual of the Swedish Chamber is an ambitious book, as chock-full of information as an almanac. It is a practical publication for American business looking Sweden-ward, but its illustrations, crisp typography, and general articles appeal also to the layman. For a frontispiece we find the most attractive photograph that we have seen of Independence Hall, where a Swedish-American, John Morton, cast the deciding vote for the declaration of liberties on the Western continent—"turned the key" that made Pennsylvania the "Keystone State." Several vexed historical questions are answered in the annual. For example, how about Admiral Dahlgren of Civil War fame: was he born in Sweden? Major Machold tells the story of his life and that of his son, Colonel Ulric Dahlgren, likewise of Philadelphia. The subject of George Washington's Swedish ancestry is also discussed. Trade subjects, of course, and statistics form the core of this book. To our mind, the most vital contribution is a compact digest on "Wood Pulp in 1917," by Hans Lagerlöf, with suggestions for the future. America could use the entire wood pulp and iron output of Sweden, and it behooves us to be alert and study this business, and capture it. Many firms having Swedish houses have shown their vision by rallying to the annual with advertising. May the editor be forgiven for allowing the photographs of the directors of the Chamber to adorn three pages; they are handsome and distinguished men all of them, and the editor's pride is justified, but the exhibit is too reminiscent of senior class day albums. Turning the pages casually, the reader is impressed by the pictures of Swedish waterfalls interspersed throughout the book; he seems to hear the distant rhythm of the harmony and potentiality with which nature has endowed Sweden and becomes prayerful for renewed communications between our two lands after the war that shall be productive of art and literature as well as social and economic progress.

THE HISTORIC BASIS OF "THE HOLY CITY"

To the Editor of the REVIEW:

I have just read Lola Ridge's fascinating review of *The Holy City* a second time, and I am struck with her opinion that Miss Lagerlöf showed a misconception of American psychology. This leads me to recall the facts on which the book is founded. They are now an old story and may be forgotten by many readers of the REVIEW.

It is unfortunately true that the American Methodist and Presbyterian missionaries at Jerusalem circulated the most awful and deliberate slanders. The head of the Methodist Mission was also our American consul at the time, and he was one of those narrow intolerants who hate what they do not understand. The relentless persecution suffered by the members of the American colony (the Gordon colony of Miss Lagerlöf's story) at the hands of their compatriots is a matter of record. *Appleton's Magazine* published a graphic account, as did other periodicals. Miss Lagerlöf was commissioned by a Swedish society to look into the scandal in so far as it involved the Swedes. She went into matters pretty thoroughly, and, as a consequence of her report, the American consul was recalled by our Administration to answer to the charges, though he died, if I remember rightly, on the voyage. Miss Lagerlöf devoted months to the task, and her book *The Holy City* grew out of her investigations. However little we can reconcile it with our general conception of American nature—whatever the malign influences may have been that corroded the character of these missionaries in Jerusalem—we know that every incident recorded of Americans is founded on fact.

VELMA SWANSTON HOWARD.

Brief Notes

The Swedish Study Club in Chicago closed the first year of its activity, on May 31, with no less than fifty lectures to its credit. Five of these were given in the auditorium of the Chicago Academy of Sciences and were free to the public. As most of the work has been done by volunteers, the result has been accomplished with a minimum of expense. The president of the club is Mr. Axel G. S. Josephson.

Several attempts have been made lately to adapt Northern patriotic songs to American needs. Mr. J. A. Lengby, of St Paul, has made an American version of Nybom's *Fänsang*. Mr. Siver Serumgard of Devil's Lake, North Dakota, contributes paraphrases of *Hör oss Svea, Jeg vil vaerge mit land,* and *Björneborgernes marsch*. All are sung to the original melodies.

An Anglo-Norse Club has been founded in London with a view to promoting friendly relations and especially for furthering the Norwegian studies carried on by the London County Council and the University of London. Mr. William Archer and Mr. K. F. Knudsen are presidents of the club, which meets every other Wednesday evening. Mr. Illit Gröndahl, whose translations of Wergeland have appeared in the REVIEW, is active as teacher and lecturer. We hope the good work will be extended to include also studies of Danish and Swedish.

The commissioners of Fairmount Park in Philadelphia and the art jury have accepted the plaster model designed by Einar Jónsson, the Icelandic sculptor, of Thorfinn Karlsefni. The statue is now being cast in bronze. Mr. Jónsson has spent the past year in Philadelphia completing his model as the guest of Mr. J. Bunford Samuel, who personally presented the statue to the city of Philadelphia as the first in a series of historical statues to be erected along the river in Fairmount Park, the others being provided for by the will of the late Mrs. Samuel. Mr. Jónsson came to America at the suggestion of the American-Scandinavian Foundation. A number of the Scandinavian citizens of Philadelphia saw the statue at a private view held on the afternoon of Sunday, July 14.

A recent meeting of the Danmarks Amerikanske Selskab in Copenhagen was addressed by the President, Director H. P. Prior, on his impressions of America and the War derived from his recent visit to this country as a special commissioner. A considerable audience was gathered to hear Mr. Prior, including the Rector of the University of Copenhagen and the Director of the Polytechnic High School. The society plans to raise a fund to send Danish apprentice students in technical subjects to America, connections to be made by the American-Scandinavian Foundation.

Among the numerous accounts of patriotic work that have come to us since the National Service Number went to press, one deserves special mention in the South Jutland Number. Lutheran churches centering around San Francisco, including those of northern California and some scattered congregations in neighboring states, raised more than four million dollars in the Third Liberty Loan drive. The membership of these churches is chiefly Scandinavian, the South-Jutlanders forming a strong element. The chairman of the committee was Rev. E. M. Stensrud, pastor of an English Lutheran church in San Francisco.

To Mr. Viggo Eberlin, of New York, belongs the credit of having brought Carl Neumann's song, "I Heard My Country's Call," before a wider public. The text with the music may be ordered from him either in a small folder at ten cents or printed on post-cards ready for mailing. Mr. Eberlin's address is 305 East 206th Street.

Mr. David Edström has signed a contract for two statues, representing Isis and Nephthys, to be erected in the Masonic House of the Temple, one of the most beautiful buildings in Washington. The figures are to be cut in Swedish block granite.

Mr. Edwin Olaf Holter was chairman of the committee on organization for the great meeting held in Madison Square Garden on Bastile Day, July 14, as a tribute of admiration and sympathy for France.

The following have been elected corresponding members of the Society for the Advancement of Scandinavian Study: Professor W. A. Craigie for Scotland; Professor Halfdan Koht and Professor Gerhard Gran for Norway; Bredo Kristensen (instead of Axel Olrik, deceased) and Dr. Kr. Kaalund for Denmark.

In his review of William Morton Payne's translation of *Arnljot Gelline* (Volume VIII of the SCANDINAVIAN CLASSICS published by the Foundation) which appeared in the February number of *Scandinavian Studies and Notes*, Professor Flom erroneously states that this edition is a *reprint*. Professor Payne was engaged by the Foundation to translate the volume especially for this series, and it has never before appeared in English.

Mr. F. E. H. Velander, Swedish Fellow of the American-Scandinavian Foundation for 1917-18, has been appointed for the coming year research assistant in the department of electrical engineering at the Massachusetts Institute of Technology. Mr. Velander recently received the master's degree at Harvard, with the highest standing in all courses.

The personal misfortune which attended Professor Amandus Johnson of the University of Pennsylvania on the evening of June 25 was also a public loss. In the fire that destroyed his cottage the manuscript of the third volume of his *Swedish Settlers on the Delaware* was consumed, as well as another manuscript, the labor of years.

The faculty and students of Concordia College in Moorhead have chosen an excellent means of aiding the library of their institution—so often a weak point in small colleges—by pledging $1,800 in War Savings Stamps to be applied, when they fall due, to the purchase of books.

THE HOLY CITY
JERUSALEM II

By SELMA LAGERLÖF

Translated by Velma Swanston Howard

Recent military events about Palestine add new interest to this latest book, "Jerusalem II," by the distinguished winner of the Nobel Prize. It is a continuation of her already famous epic, "Jerusalem," and yet it is complete in itself.

The religious upheaval that took the Dalecarlians to Jerusalem places them in the colony founded there by the Gordons, Americans. The highest level of this writer's genius is touched in this story of persecution and physical hardship. *Net $1.50.*

The Northland edition, leather. $1.75.

DOUBLEDAY PAGE AND COMPANY
GARDEN CITY, NEW YORK

D. B. UPDIKE
The Merrymount Press
232 SUMMER STREET
BOSTON

· · ·

PRINTERS OF FINE BOOKS FOR BOOK CLUBS, INSTITUTIONS, AND PRIVATE PERSONS
&c. &c. &c.

The Series of *Scandinavian Classics*, and Hustvedt's "Ballad Criticism" and Hovgaard's "Voyages of the Norsemen," in the *Scandinavian Monographs*, were printed for the American-Scandinavian Foundation by this Press.

THE SCANDINAVIAN ART SHOP

NEW YORK and
BAR HARBOR

The present reaction from Period furnishings to Peasant art is interestingly treated in our shop.

Architects, decorators and home furnishers will find a visit both interesting and helpful.

STORM & BULL

(INCORPORATED)

2 RECTOR STREET, NEW YORK CITY

IMPORT

Specialties

South American and Scandinavian Products

EXPORT

Specialties

Iron and Steel Products, Paper, Chemicals, Machinery

Own Houses:

CHRISTIANIA · STOCKHOLM · BUENOS AIRES · MONTEVIDEO

VALPARAISO—LA PAZ

Active Representation:

Principal Cities:

AUSTRALIA—BRAZIL—SOUTH AFRICA—FAR EAST

CORRESPONDENCE INVITED

TRADE NOTES

News and Comment on Exports and Trade Conditions Between America and the Scandinavian Countries

NORWEGIAN SHIPBUILDING IN THE UNITED STATES

Critics of Scandinavian neutrality will have to admit that so far as concerns Norwegians in the United States those occupied with shipbuilding are giving their entire effort to aiding this country in the winning of the war. This applies in particular to Christoffer Hannevig, Inc., owners of the Pusey & Jones shipyards at Gloucester, N. J., and Wilmington, Del. The largest ship launched on the Fourth of July was a Hannevig product, the *Indianapolis*, which stands as a direct evidence of the manner in which the Norwegians are pushing the shipbuilding program of the United States.

SCANDINAVIANS IN SOUTH AMERICA

The Norwegian Commodoro Oil Fields, Ltd., is the latest Scandinavian concern to enter South America on a large scale. Argentina is now proving itself a valuable oil country, and among those interested in the Norwegian enterprise are Eilert Sundt, Consul General Rudolf Olsen, and Ole Thoresen, of Christiania, and Engineer Albert Schwartz, of Buenos Aires.

SWEDEN PREPARES FOR AFTER-WAR TRADE

A new central committee for Swedish export after the war has been formed to work in conjunction with the existing organizations, the Swedish General Export Union and the Swedish Chamber of Manufacturers. The object of the new committee is to take care of the Swedish export interests in a more complete way than is possible through any existing industrial corporation. The central committee is composed of twenty-two members, with Prof. Nils Wohlin secretary. Almost all the industries and trades in Sweden are represented in the new organization.

VALUABLE REPORT BY CONSUL BÖGGILD

The Copenhagen newspapers are quoting freely from the report of Consul J. E. Böggild at New York on America's war preparations and the manner in which the various interests here are coöperating to bring about victory. Consul Böggild has the faculty of presenting facts and figures in a way to make his report extremely readable, while his long familiarity with American institutions naturally gives weight to his opinions at home.

NORWAY HAS CABLE FACTORY

American Vice-Consul Carlson at Christiania informs the State Department that the plant of the first Norwegian cable company has just been completed. The home manufacture of all kinds of wire and cable should somewhat overcome the difficulties of importations and will be of great importance in a country where electrical energy is to play an ever-increasing part, owing to the development of the water power.

"EVENING POST" FOREIGN SUPPLEMENT

The third quarterly issue of the New York *Evening Post's* foreign trade supplement contained several interesting articles on Scandinavian trade, now and later. Norway and Sweden are making steady progress in adjusting themselves to the situation created by the War, and with the gradual lifting of the embargo there is every possibility that trade relations with America will return to a condition more nearly normal than is now the case.

New York Forwarding Co., Inc.

Agents   OSCAR A. OLSEN   *Branch Offices*
GOTHENBURG   *General Manager*   CHRISTIANIA, Kirkegaten 6 B.
STOCKHOLM   COPENHAGEN, Peder Skramsgade 28

LICENSES: Applying for American and British Licenses.
WAREHOUSE: Storing all kinds of goods.
INSURANCE: Marine, War, Fire, and all risks.
FINANCING: Value of merchandise, freight and charges payable against surrender of documents upon arrival at destination.

ANDREW GULICK & CO., Inc.

Exporters and Merchant Brokers

S. HENDRICHSEN, Agent   A. G. GULICK   **256 and 257 BROADWAY**
Fougstadgt .25, Kristiania   President   **NEW YORK, U. S. A.**

. . EXPORTING . .

Motor Attachment for Cycles	*Adding Machines*	*Hosiery*	*Tractors*
Truck Attachment to "Ford"	*Boots and Shoes*	*Raincoats*	*"Carbola"—White-washing*
Electric Lamps and Batteries	*Hide and Sole Leather*	*Folding Saw*	*Dyes*
Row Boat Motors	*Cotton Goods*	*Typewriters*	*Snap Fasteners*

JAMES ROSENBERG, President   L. W. BOWMALL, Vice-President and Treasurer

AMERICAN WOODPULP CORPORATION

CHEMICAL AND MECHANICAL WOODPULPS

RAGS, NEW CUTTINGS, BAGGING, ETC.

347 MADISON AVENUE   Telephone: Vanderbilt 3440-1-2-3   NEW YORK

Branches:

Dayton—R. R. Reed   Kalamazoo—F. D. Haskell   Holyoke—J. B. Woodruff Inc.

CLARX 100% PURE
Whole Wheat Flour

Whole Wheat Graham Flour
Whole Rye Flour

Corn Flour and Oat Flour

CLARX MILLING COMPANY
Minneapolis

SCANDINAVIAN BUSINESS MEN IN THE VAN

It was remarked during the great Fourth of July loyalty demonstration that the Danish, Norwegian, and Swedish divisions made a most unique appearance with their various floats representative of episodes in the development of the nationalities here. Scandinavian-American business men contributed liberally for the purpose.

———

AGRICULTURAL EXPORTS

The complete returns of the country's agricultural exports, as issued by the Department of Commerce for February, shows total shipments to have amounted to $180,271,457, as against $186,502,274 in January and $120,416,541 in February of last year.   J. M.

Telegraphic Address:
MATCHSTROM—NEW YORK

Telephones—BEEKMAN { 4470 / 3769

Stromborg Export & Import Co., Inc.

Tribune Building, NEW YORK

Swedish

Safety

Matches

Sole Agents

FOR

UNITED SWEDISH MATCH FACTORIES
STOCKHOLM, SWEDEN

EXPORT CHEMICALS IMPORT

SWEDISH IRON AND STEEL CORPORATION

THOMAS TOWNE,
Vice-President and General Manager

General Offices,
12 PLATT STREET, NEW YORK CITY

"SISCO" PRODUCTS

FINE TOOL AND ALLOY STEELS
in Billets, Bars, Discs, Blocks, and Sheets

Common and Deep Drawing Steel Sheets
High Speed Steel   Cold Rolled Strip Steel
Drill Rods   Drawn Bars
Swedish Iron   Sisco Welding Wire
High Grade Specialties

Catalogues and information on request

BRANCH OFFICES AND WAREHOUSES

BROOKLYN   CLEVELAND NEW ORLEANS
BOSTON   CHICAGO   DENVER
PHILADELPHIA DETROIT   MONTREAL, Can.
STOCKHOLM, Sweden

Telephone { 1700 / 1701 } Broad

Cables { "Scandinavian American Trading Newyork" }

Scandinavian-American Trading Company

PRODUCE EXCHANGE BUILDING

NEW YORK

—o—

Importers and Exporters of

WOOD PULP

and all kinds of

Chemicals and Machinery

RUSSIA'S EXTERNAL LOANS

It is estimated that at least $4,000,000,000 of Russia's external loans is in the hands of foreign investors. This is significant in view of the Bolsheviki Government's announcement that it would repudiate loans made previous to coming into power. Now that the British Government announces that it will no longer meet maturing coupons on the external Russian loans, still further interest attaches to the amounts held abroad and which are as follows: France, nearly three-fourths; England something under $500,000,000; Holland, $400,000,000; Germany, $375,000,000. Considerable amounts are also to be credited to the Scandinavian countries.

NORWEGIAN AMERICA LINE

Modern Twin-Screw
Steamers
SS.
Stavangerfjord
18,000 Tons
Displacement

SS.
Bergensfjord
16,000 Tons
Displacement

NORWEGIAN
AMERICA
LINE
PASSENGER
AGENCY, Inc.

8-10 Bridge St.
New York

General Passenger
Agents for the United
States and Canada

HOBE & CO.	BIRGER OSLAND & CO.	REIDAR GJÖLME
General Northwestern Passenger Agents	General Western Passenger Agents	General Pacific Coast Agent
123 South Third Street	115 South Dearborn Street	Arctic Bldg., Third & Cherry Streets
Minneapolis, Minn.	Chicago, Ill.	Seattle, Wash.

NORWAY MEXICO GULF LINE AND SWEDISH AMERICA MEXICO LINE

Regular service between GÖTEBORG, CHRISTIANIA and STAVAN-
GER and NEWPORT NEWS, VA., HAVANA, CUBA,
GALVESTON, TEX., and NEW ORLEANS, LA.

Passengers Carried   Wireless Apparatus

AGENTS

FEARNLEY & EGER, Christiania   SANDSTRÖM STRANNE & CO., Ltd., Göteborg

FURNESS WITHY & CO., Ltd., Furness House, Whitehall St., New York, N. Y., and Newport News, Va.

JAS. P. ROBERTSON	FOWLER & McVITIE	LYKES BROS.	GEO. PLANT
111 West Jackson Boulevard	Galveston, Tex.	Havana, Cuba	1119 Whitney Central Bldg.
Chicago, Ill.			New Orleans, La.

*The Only High-Class Scandinavian
Restaurant in New York*

NEAR HERALD SQUARE
Phone: Greeley 4782

Rendezvous for Scandinavians from all over the
world when visiting New York

Dinner with famous "Smörgåsbord." American and Scandinavian Dishes.

HENRY MALGREN, Prop.

GENERAL OFFICES: Passenger Department

117 N. Dearborn Street, Chicago, Ill.
236 Nicollet Ave., Minneapolis, Minn.
248 Washington St., Boston, Mass.

1 BROADWAY, NEW YORK

544 Market St., San Francisco, Cal.
702 Second Ave., Seattle, Wash.

SWEDISH AMERICAN LINE

(SVENSKA AMERIKA LINIEN)

Direct Passenger Service between New York and Gothenburg, Sweden

Short Route to Sweden, Norway, Denmark, Finland, Russia and other parts of the European Continent

Twin-Screw S.S. "Stockholm"

Length 565 Feet. 22,070 Tons Displacement

Largest Steamer in Service between America and Scandinavia, is provided with all modern safety appliances, and every care is taken to give the passengers a safe and comfortable journey.

Unsurpassed passenger appointments in First, Second and Third Classes.

NIELSEN & LUNDBECK, General Passenger Agents, 24 State Street, New York.

MARTIN MAURD, General Western Agent, 183 N. Dearborn Street, Chicago.

NILS NILSON, General Northwestern Agent, 127 S. Third St., Minneapolis, Minn.

BRATTSTROM & CO., General No. Pacific Agents, 117 Cherry St., Seattle, Wash.

A. HALLONQUIST, General Agent, 396 Logan Ave., Winnipeg, Man., Can.

CUNARD LINE

AQUITANIA   MAURETANIA

Fastest Passenger Service in the World
To and from the Scandinavian Countries

Record trip, New York to Gothenburg, 7 days, 7 hours, 45 minutes

Quickest Route to Europe

SERVICES AS FOLLOWS·

NEW YORK—LIVERPOOL	NEW YORK—FALMOUTH—LONDON
NEW YORK—BRISTOL	NEW YORK—MEDITERRANEAN
BOSTON—LIVERPOOL	BOSTON—LONDON
MONTREAL—QUEBEC—BRISTOL	MONTREAL—QUEBEC—LONDON

Special through rates to Egypt, India, China, Japan, Philippines,
Australia, New Zealand, South Africa and South America

TRIPS AROUND THE WORLD: $474.85 First Class, $880 Second Class

DRAFTS, MONEY ORDERS, MAIL OR CABLE

GREAT BRITAIN	SCANDINAVIA	HOLLAND	ITALY
SPAIN	PORTUGAL	FRANCE	SWITZERLAND

THE CUNARD STEAM SHIP COMPANY LIMITED

21-24 STATE STREET   NEW YORK

Offices or Agents Everywhere

The American-Scandinavian Review

VOLUME VI   NOVEMBER-DECEMBER, 1918   NUMBER 6

Published Bi-Monthly by THE AMERICAN-SCANDINAVIAN FOUNDATION, 25 West 45th Street, New York

Yearly Subscription, $1.50.   (One dollar to Associates of the Foundation.)   Single Copies, 25 cents

Entered as second-class matter, January 4, 1913, at the post-office at New York, N. Y., under the act of March 3, 1879
Copyright, 1916, The American-Scandinavian Foundation

HENRY GODDARD LEACH, *Editor*   HANNA ASTRUP LARSEN, *Literary Editor*

Advisors

New York, HAMILTON HOLT   Copenhagen, POVL DRACHMAN
Stockholm, CARL LAURIN   Christiania, CHRISTIAN COLLIN
Reykjavik, GUDMUNDUR MAGNUSSON

CONTENTS

FOUNDED BY NIELS POULSON, IN 1911

FINANCIAL

*Notes About Issues in the Financial World
Most Interesting to Readers of the Review*

FRENCH CITY ISSUES' RISE

New high records for the City of Paris 6s were made at the close of the market September 28. The previous high mark touched was 96⅛, last year. The low for 1917 was 73½. On June 13, the low price for 1918 was made at 81⅝. The new quotation is 97⅛ bid, 97¾ asked. New high records are also seen in the City of Bordeaux 6s, the City of Lyons 6s, and the City of Marseilles 6s.

SCANDINAVIAN INSURANCE COMPANIES

One of the interesting financial happenings during recent years is the increase in the representation of Scandinavian insurance companies in the United States. The first Danish insurance company to establish offices here was Skandinavia, which opened in 1916. Reinsurance is a feature in the business of this concern, and it is a gratifying sign of the times that where Germany has been entirely replaced in this respect, and the Allied countries are not quite in a position to extend operations to this side of the Atlantic, Scandinavian financial interests see their way to branch out.

NORWEGIAN AMERICAN SECURITIES CORPORATION

Owing to remarkable growth in the business of the Norwegian American Securities Corporation, the company has been compelled to enlarge greatly its quarters in the building at 74 Broadway where it has been located since its start. The entire seventeenth floor is now given over to this company, which is daily proving a strong financial link between the United States and the Scandinavian countries.

LIBERTY LOAN SUBSCRIPTIONS

While the Fourth Liberty Loan campaign exceeds anything of the kind that went before, it is pertinent to make comparisons with preceding loan subscriptions, which stood as follows: First loan, 4,000,000 separate subscriptions; second loan, 9,400,000, and third loan, 18,308,325 subscriptions. It is scarcely necessary to add that Scandinavian Americans aided materially in rolling up the grand totals.

NORWAY'S NEUTRALITY LOAN

The budget committee of the Norwegian Storting has requested the Government to grant a loan for 250,000,000 kroner to defray expenses in connection with the country's maintenance of its neutrality. The national treasury deposits on June 30 stood at only 35,320,000 kroner, while the amount in January of this year was more than 120,000,000 kroner. The provision budget has required extraordinary sums to meet expenditures.

BANK TELLS OF GERMAN MACHINATIONS

The eleventh paper in the series issued by the Guaranty Trust Company of New York treats of Germany's scheme to establish her economic leadership in the world. This paper is a most interesting exposition of what a country's ruthless masters may undertake to promote their special interests at the expense of those unable to withstand such imposition until aroused finally.   J. M.

The National City Bank of New York

has correspondence relationships with the strongest banks in Scandinavia and maintains a representative in Copenhagen to facilitate their business in the United States. It is able to offer unusual facilities for the transaction of commerce everywhere. Its Travelers' Letters of Credit and Commercial Credits command funds in all accessible countries.

Condensed Statement as of May 10, 1918

ASSETS

CASH on hand, in Federal Reserve Bank and due from Banks and Bankers and United States Treasurer	$151,779,713.92	
Acceptances of Other Banks	35,397,183.63	
UNITED STATES TREASURY CERTIFICATES Maturing in less than 90 days	140,512,500.00	$327,689,397.55
UNITED STATES BONDS	25,449,526.20	
Loans and Discounts	310,702,357.99	
Other Bonds	39,291,806.09	
Stock in Federal Reserve Bank	1,500,000.00	376,943,690.28
Due from Branches		14,058,790.31
Banking House		5,000,000.00
Customers' Liability Account of Acceptances		20,637,939.26
Other Assets		2,911,280.35
Total		$747,241,097.75

LIABILITIES

CAPITAL, Surplus and Undivided Profits	$ 74,994,970.02
DEPOSITS	628,196,322.63
Reserve for Expenses, Taxes, and Unearned Interest	4,605,767.41
Circulation	1,756,300.00
Rediscounts and Foreign Bills of Exchange Sold	9,963,889.69
Acceptances, Cash Letters of Credit and Travelers' Checks	22,181,039.01
Other Liabilities	5,542,808.99
Total	$747,241,097.75

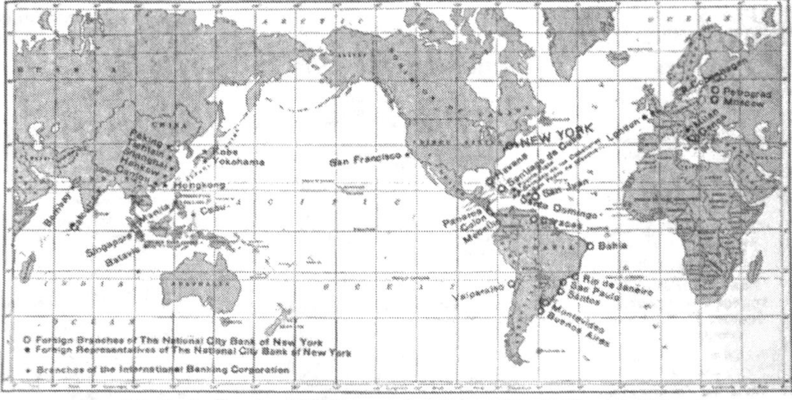

Map of the Foreign Branches of THE NATIONAL CITY BANK OF NEW YORK and its affiliate, the INTERNATIONAL BANKING CORPORATION

HANNEVIG AND COMPANY

Bankers

139 Broadway, New York

SPECIALIZING IN

SHIPPING and FOREIGN EXCHANGE

HANNEVIG AND COMPANY

139 Broadway, New York

Empire Trust Company

120 Broadway   **New York**   **580 Fifth Avenue**

London Office, 41 Threadneedle Street

Resources Over $50,000,000

The Fifth Avenue Office of this Company, corner 47th Street, is accessibly situated for anyone desiring the services of an Uptown Banking Institution. Careful and courteous attention given to any business entrusted to it.

Interest may be arranged upon accounts subject to check.

Certificates of Deposit, maturing at a date to suit the needs of the depositor, issued at favorable rates of interest.

Empire Safe Deposit Company

Safe Deposit Vaults

Norwegian American Securities Corporation

74 BROADWAY, NEW YORK CITY

Capital, $1,000,000

TRYGVE BARTH, President

LEIF H. STROM, Vice-President   GEORGE REITH, Vice-President
B. KROEPELIEN, Sec'y and Treas.   LEROY JONES, Assistant Secretary

DIRECTORS

T. BARTH, President
T. LANGLAND THOMPSON, Attorney
W. K. FRIMANN, Shipowner
B. KROEPELIEN, Treasurer
WILHELM ALME, Man. Dir. Bergen Agent a/s
TH. JULLUM, Gen. Agt. Norw'g'n Marine Ins. Co's
P. HARSEM, Merchant

L. H. STROM, Vice-Pres. New York Oversea Co.
GUNNAR HARTMANN, Pres. Hart Trading Co.
GEORGE REITH, Vice-President
C. STEENDAL, Pres. Jefferson Insurance Co.
WM. SCHENSTROM, Pres. Electric Welding Co. of America
KARL KROGSTAD, President S. O. Stray & Co.

The Norwegian American Securities Corporation was formed for the purpose of facilitating business transactions between Norway and the other Scandinavian Countries and the United States of America.

K. N. & K.

LETTERS OF CREDIT *and* TRAVELERS' CHECKS

K. N. & K. Letters of Credit and Travelers' Checks are among the oldest and best known in the banking field. Banks and Bankers will be interested in our advertising matter, especially prepared for popular distribution.

Copies of Leaflets and Booklets will be sent on request.

Knauth · Nachod & Kuhne

Members New York Stock Exchange

Equitable Building, NEW YORK CITY

BUSINESS men who are interested in Scandinavian trade will find the foreign trade service of the Irving peculiarly suited to their needs. This Bank operating direct or through its Scandinavian banking correspondents provides the information and assistance required in establishing closer relations between business men of Scandinavia and America.

IRVING

NATIONAL BANK

WOOLWORTH BUILDING   **NEW YORK**

Strictly a Commercial Bank

CONTRIBUTORS TO THE NOVEMBER-DECEMBER NUMBER

ALBERT EDELFELT is the foremost artist among the Swedish Finns. His illustrations of *Fänrik Stals Sägner* are classic interpretations of Runeberg's heroes, simple, homely types exalted by a spiritual passion of patriotism. The picture on the cover was inspired by the song "The March of the Men of Björneborg," printed in this issue in Dr. Donner's translation.

LAURENCE MARCELLUS LARSON, professor of history in the University of Illinois, is translator and author of the preface of *The King's Mirror*, published as the third in the SCANDINAVIAN MONOGRAPHS, and author of numerous historical books, including *Canute the Great* and *Short History of England*. He was born in Bergen, Norway.

JOHN BERGH is one of the younger authors in Finland who write in Swedish. "Sakari's Story" is taken from his novel *Efter Ofreden* and deals with the worst of the terrible famines that have ravaged Finland from time to time. One hundred thousand people, one-fourth of the population, are said to have perished from starvation in the reign of Charles XI.

Idylls and Epigrams are charming examples of JOHAN LUDVIG RUNEBERG's lighter vein. His fame, however, rests chiefly on his patriotic songs. The martial notes of "The March of the Men of Björneborg" have inspired audiences in all the Scandinavian countries. It was written in honor of a Finnish regiment known from the time of Gustaf Adolf and especially distinguished in the War of 1808 and 1809, when the Finns made their desperate, heroic stand against the Russian conquerors. As a companion to Runeberg's masterpiece Dr. Donner has chosen a poem by an unknown author, "March of the Finnish Cavalry in the Thirty Years' War" reminding us of the equally glorious deeds of the Finns under Gustaf Adolf.

FREDERIC SCHENCK will be remembered as the joint translator with Dr. Campbell of the first SCANDINAVIAN CLASSIC and as contributor to the REVIEW of the article "Holberg: Feminist." He represented the American Fencing Team at the Olympic Games in Stockholm in 1912. Dr. Schenck is instructor at Harvard.

CARL G. O. HANSEN is associate editor and musical critic of the Norwegian daily, *Minneapolis Tidende*, and a frequent contributor to various Norwegian publications. He is the author of the articles dealing with the Norwegians and Danes in the series on Scandinavian Music in America published by the REVIEW.

BOUNDARIES OF FINLAND PROPOSED BY L. M. LARSON

THE AMERICAN-SCANDINAVIAN REVIEW, NOVEMBER-DECEMBER, 1918

THE AMERICAN-SCANDINAVIAN REVIEW

VOLUME VI   NOVEMBER-DECEMBER · 1918   NUMBER 6

The Boundaries of Finland

By Laurence Marcellus Larson

*I believe in Finland being given its complete and absolute independence
so that it shall not be merely in name but in fact as completely independent
of Germany as of Russia; just as independent as Norway and Sweden
are. I wish that America could send its own representative at once to
the Finnish capital to counteract German propaganda and to show the
Finlanders that if they honestly and in good faith stand for their own
complete independence, we will stand by them, and give them food, and
do anything else in our power for them.*

September, 1918.   *THEODORE ROOSEVELT.*

AMONG the many Asiatic peoples that have found their way
across the Siberian steppes into eastern and southeastern
Europe are a group of Turanian tribes known historically as
the Finns. The greater part of the Finnish horde did not advance
far beyond the Ural barrier; but an important fragment, the so-called
West Finns, continued the journey up the valley of the Volga and
finally settled on the banks of the Oka, a river that drains the country
south of Moscow and joins the Volga some three hundred miles east
of that city.

It is not known when the West Finns came into central Russia,
but archæologists are disposed to believe that they had entered the
valley of the Oka three thousand years ago. After a long stay in
this region they resumed their wanderings northwestward toward
the Baltic Sea, the shores of which they reached apparently some
time in the first two centuries of the Christian era.

The migrating tribes gradually took possession of a considerable
stretch of territory north of the Düna River. Here they came to
be known as Livs and their country as Livonia. From the Düna
the migration traveled southwestward along the coast of Kurland

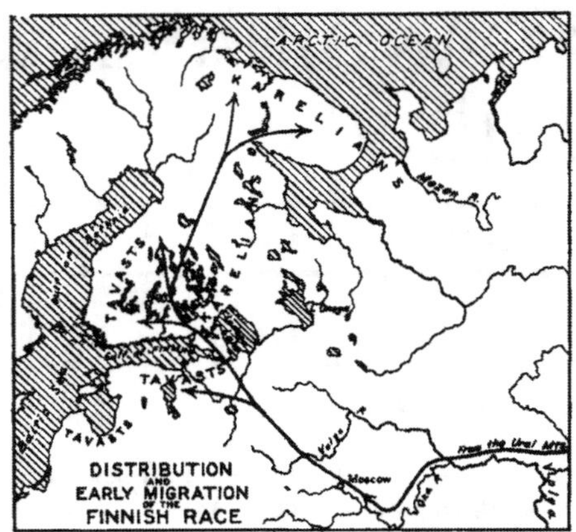

and northward into Esthonia, which, it is believed, the Finns occupied at least as early as the fifth century. The same movement carried them around or across the Gulf of Finland into what has since been called Finland, and they had come into almost complete possession of the southern parts of this land by the year 800.

The Finns who settled the shores of the great Gulf belonged to two distinct tribes, the Tavasts and the Karelians. The former remained in large part on the south shore, where they inherited the name of the people they had dispossessed and came to be known as Esths. The Tavasts who crossed over to Finland settled the southwestern part of that country from the Kymmene River to the Gulf of Bothnia. The Karelians, who seem to have migrated earlier and in greater numbers than the Tavasts, found their homes farther to the east between the Kymmene River and Lake Ladoga. Both tribes gradually extended their territories northward, but the Karelians traveled farther than the Tavasts. In their wanderings the former ultimately reached the Arctic coast, where at one time their scattered settlements might be traced from northern Norway to the Mezen River, nearly two hundred miles beyond Archangel. Some historians believe that the inhabitants of the southwestern part of Finland belong to a third tribe which they call the Finns "proper," but others maintain that these are in all likelihood merely a branch of the Tavast people.

In the earlier middle ages the limits of the territories occupied by the West Finns extended somewhat farther south than is the case to-day. In Kurland they held the larger part of the great promontory and perhaps a narrow strip of the coast along the Gulf of Riga. They controlled the northern half of Livonia and had a few settlements farther south along the Baltic shore. Esthonia was wholly Finnish, as were also the Ingrian lands south and southwest of the future site of Petrograd. The shores of the great lakes, Ladoga and Onega, were settled by Karelians in comparatively early times; and with the spread of this tribe the boundaries of Finland, in the larger sense, were gradually drawn northeastward past Shenkursk to the valley of the Mezen and probably beyond.

In more recent times, through the pressure of alien peoples, the areas of West Finnish occupation have suffered important losses. The Livs of Kurland and southwestern Livonia have practically disappeared, the stronger and more numerous Lettish population having absorbed them. The upper part of Livonia almost as far south as the Salis River, Esthonia, and the northwestern part of Ingria have, however, remained predominantly Finnish (Esthonian) to the present day. In the government of Petrograd the Finns have been forced to yield before the overwhelming advance of the Slavs, except in certain limited areas east of Ladoga and near the Esthonian boundary, as noted above. Between the two great lakes the Karelian element is still strong; but east of Onega the Russian has largely superseded the West Finn, and at present the eastern limits of Greater Finland follow a line drawn along the western shore of Lake Onega northward to the White Sea.

A state in the modern sense of the term the Finns have never created, though it is likely that their tribal groups or units might have developed into national organizations if outside forces had not interfered. Modern Finland is the result of Swedish colonization and conquest; its boundaries are the outcome of nearly eight centuries of hostility between Swedes and Slavs. Long before the Karelians and the Tavasts began to find their way into Finland, a Scandinavian people, presumably Swedes, had planted colonies in the southern part of that country. Stretching almost across the entrance to the Gulf of Bothnia lies the Åland archipelago, a group of islands that may be regarded as fragments of the Finnish land mass but has been inhabited by Swedes as long as history knows. The Ålands approach to within twenty miles of the Swedish coast and form a natural series of stepping-stones to the mainland beyond. Some writers have held that the Swedes had abandoned the settlements in the "Eastlands" before the invasion of the Tavasts; but the evidence available appears to indicate that Scandinavian culture east of Bothnia has been continuous from prehistoric times to the present, and that, at least as early as the eleventh century, there was an appreciable movement of Swedish emigrants into "the New Land" (Nyland) on the Finnish Gulf.

The history of Finland as a political unit begins with Saint Erik's expedition to the east in 1157. This venture served a double purpose: it was a crusade directed against the heathen worship of the Finns and their Swedish neighbors; and it established the authority of the Swedish Crown over the Scandinavian colonies in Nyland. King Erik no doubt also hoped to bring the native Finns into subjection; but in pursuit of this plan neither he nor his immediate successors had any marked success. For almost a century the authority of the foreigner was limited to a small area in the neighborhood of the new city of Åbo. It was not until the days of Earl Birger that a serious effort was made to conquer the Finns. In 1249 the great Earl led an expedition against the Tavasts and forced them to surrender their ancient freedom. This campaign carried Swedish civilization and the Christian faith as far as the Kymmene River; but beyond this line the heathen Karelians continued hostile and defiant.

In their opposition to Swedish expansion the Karelians received powerful support and assistance from the Christian rulers of Novgorod, a neighboring Russian republic which in the twelfth and thirteenth centuries was the greatest political and commercial center of northwestern Slavdom. The citizens of Novgorod looked with growing disfavor on the eastward progress of Swedish colonization in Nyland, and in less than a decade the two powers came into armed collision. From that year (1164) to the treaty of 1809 there was little security and peace along the Finnish frontier.

The Swedish conquest of Karelia began in 1293, when Torgils Knutsson, marshal and regent of Sweden, led a strong force into southeastern Finland, where he founded the stronghold of Viborg. The following year the Swedes penetrated as far as Lake Ladoga and seized the fortress of Kexholm, one of the outposts of Novgorod. Viborg and Kexholm in Swedish hands were regarded as direct menaces at Novgorod and immediate efforts were made to seize them. The attempt on Viborg failed, but Kexholm was retaken, and a few years later the Swedes were compelled to withdraw from eastern Karelia.

After a century and a half of intermittent warfare, the rival powers finally decided to treat for permanent peace. In 1323 their plenipotentiaries met at Nöteborg (later renamed Schlüsselburg), where the Neva River flows out of Lake Ladoga. The treaty of Nöteborg was the earliest formal agreement negotiated by Swedes and Russians of which we have any record. It drew the boundary between Finland and Novgorod from the mouth of the Sestra, a small stream emptying into the Gulf of Finland about twenty miles northwest of Petrograd, in a northerly direction to the waters of Kajana. What Kajana meant in 1323 cannot be determined; it may have been a name for the Arctic Ocean, though some historians believe that it meant the Gulf of Bothnia. Only in the south, however, where the boundary can be clearly traced, was the arrangement of any importance. Perhaps less than a third of what is now Finland had actually been colonized at the time; the remainder was a vast wilderness with no permanent population except a few groups of wandering Lapps. In the southeast the line was drawn through the disputed territory in such a way as to leave to Novgorod a strip of territory from twenty to forty miles wide west of Lake Ladoga. This lake with its

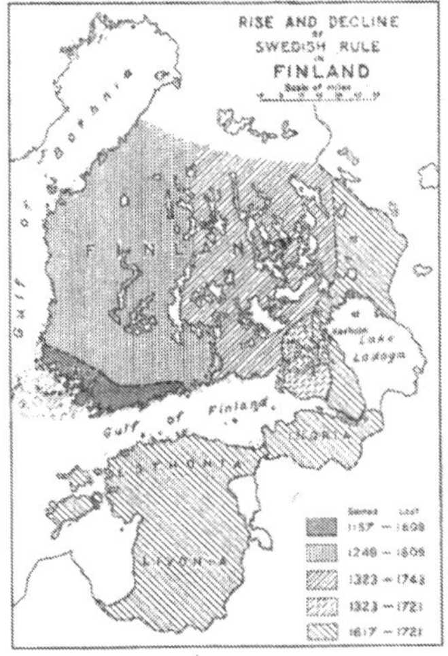

outlet, the Neva, were thus left wholly within the Russian limits, and Novgorod was able to continue the development of her commercial interests in the north and the northeast.

The Karelian tribe was divided at Nöteborg, and the division in certain respects became permanent. The western part of Karelia came under the influence of Swedish civilization and of the Roman Catholic Church; later the Lutheran reformation was preached throughout all Finland and still remains the dominant religion among the Finns. The eastern Karelians, on the other hand, accepted the civilization of Russia and the Greek Orthodox faith. A large part of their country was later added to Finland, but the old intellectual and religious divisions have not been wholly bridged.

The eastern and northern boundaries of Finland were determined in large measure by the activities of Russian monks and missionaries. Beginning early in the thirteenth century, these soldiers of the Orthodox faith had been wandering northward through eastern Karelia toward the Arctic. Two generations later the Russian Church had a series of stations from the Dwina valley almost as far as the Norwegian frontier. About 1450 the great monastery of Solovetz was founded on a group of islands near the western edge of the White Sea; it has remained an important center of Russian influence in those regions ever since. Early in the following century a Russian priest who had taken up missionary work among the northern Lapps carried the message of the Orthodox gospel along the Murman coast and built a church within a few miles of the present Norwegian boundary.

The kings of Norway had long regarded the Murman coast and the Kola peninsula as a Norwegian dependency; but this claim was soon to be disputed by Karelian adventurers who began to appear in considerable numbers on the coast of Lapland in the thirteenth century. These were subjects of Novgorod and faithful adherents of the Russian Church. In the same period Norwegian settlements were creeping forward past North Cape, and by 1300 had probably reached the present limits of Norwegian territory toward the east. The Murman coast thus came into the possession of Norway and Russia. For a long time the two countries exercised a sort of joint

The Diet House at Helsingfors, Where the First One-Chamber Diet, Elected by Universal Suffrage, Assembled in 1907, with Judge Svinhufvud as Speaker. In 1917 the Diet Met There and Declared Itself the Supreme Power in Independent Finland

A Common Type of Dwelling in Finland. Men from Such Cottages Formed the Backbone of Mannerheim's Army, Which Was Recruited Largely from the Peasantry.

Demonstration in the Cathedral Square at Helsingfors During the National Strike, in 1905, by Which the Finns Forced the Czar to Restore Their Constitutional Government

The Citizens' Guard in Åbo, Formed in 1905 to Safeguard the Country Against the "Reds"

From a Painting by Hjalmar Munsterhjelm

A CHARACTERISTIC LANDSCAPE IN TAVASTLAND, WHERE THE FIGHT BETWEEN REDS AND WHITES LATELY RAGED

jurisdiction in these regions, and the boundary was not definitely determined before 1826.

The important consideration for present purposes is that a broad belt of Russianized Karelian territory was being drawn along the east frontier of Finland and in the far north, which made the expansion in these two directions difficult and almost impossible. The kings of the Vasa dynasty saw clearly that their Finnish policy ought to include the purpose to get control of the regions about the White Sea. In 1590 a Swedish force attacked the Russian outpost at Kola, and the following year an expedition crossed from northern Finland to the White Sea; but neither venture proved successful. In 1611 the Swedish king returned to the project of northward expansion: a second effort was made to seize Kola, but again the plan failed. Finland has never had a port on the Arctic.

Though neither the Swedes nor the Russians held very faithfully to the agreement of 1323, the Nöteborg line remained the official boundary in the southeast until it was superseded by a new line drawn at Stolbova in 1617. In the war that was terminated by the treaty of that year, the Swedes had again seized Kexholm, and this time they refused to return it. The new agreement established a boundary which, beginning at the lower end of Lake Ladoga, ran for a distance of about two hundred miles northward through points located from fifty to one hundred miles east of the Nöteborg line. The limits of Swedish territory were also brought down to the Neva River.

The greater part of eastern Karelia was thus added to the possessions of the Swedish Crown. The new province of Kexholm was not, however, officially joined to the grand duchy of Finland; the same war had brought Ingria to the Swedish kingdom, and for a time this province with Kexholm formed a distinct administrative unit. The transfer called forth much dissatisfaction among the new subjects. The government at Stockholm was anxious that the Lutheran faith should be the exclusive religion of the kingdom and began a religious propaganda among the Karelians which they found extremely irritating.

For almost exactly a century the vast majority of the West Finnish population were united under a single government. Livonia, Esthonia, Ingria, Karelia, and Tavastland were all subject to the Swedish king. A few Finnish communities in Kurland and a scattered Karelian element in northern Russia were not included; otherwise the union was complete. The relationship of these various parts to the Crown was not the same in every case: Finland was counted a part of the Swedish kingdom, while Kexholm and the Baltic provinces were regarded as dependencies. It may therefore be said that, technically, the treaty of Stolbova did not change the boundaries of the grand duchy.

During the eighteenth century the territories of Finland suffered material reductions. Gustavus Adolphus had excluded Russia absolutely from the Baltic Sea, and it was not to be expected that the Muscovites would submit indefinitely to the disadvantages of such a frontier. With the accession of Peter the Great, war was resumed, and this time the Swedes were finally defeated. By the peace of Nystad (1721) much of what the Vasas had won beyond the "Eastern Sea" was lost: the Czar took the Baltic lands, the greater part of Kexholm, and a strip of the grand duchy east of and including Viborg. He was thus enabled to push the Swedish frontier nearly one hundred miles away from his new capital city. Ladoga was once more a Russian lake and the Neva a Russian river. Twenty-two years later the Swedish king was again called upon to surrender Finnish territory. By the treaty of Åbo (1743) the boundary was moved west to the Kymmene River and drawn northward and northeastward in such a way as to add nearly all of Lake Saima to the

Russian dominions.   These acquisitions, except a narrow strip north of the Neva, the Czar organized into a province of Viborg.   Nearly all of ancient Karelia was now lost to the Swedish Crown.

There were no further territorial changes along the Russian frontier before 1808, when Czar Alexander I invaded Finland and by the close of the year had conquered the entire country.   The following year (September 17, 1809), at Fredrikshamn, the Swedish envoys signed the most humiliating treaty in the history of their country, and the long connection between Sweden and Finland was terminated.

In the negotiations at Fredrikshamn Sweden was forced to surrender certain territories that could not strictly be counted as part of Finland.   These were the Åland Islands and a part of Swedish Lapland.   In vain the Swedish commissioners argued that Åland had never been Finnish in population, but the Russians were inexorable and forced the transfer.

In the dismal stretches of Lapland the frontiers had been determined only in part.   The first effort to draw a definite boundary in this region was in 1596, when Sweden and Russia agreed to accept a line drawn from the inner angle of the Varanger Fjord southward through the middle of Lake Enare.   Later, through colonization by Swedish subjects, this line was pushed somewhat farther east a few miles beyond Lake Enare.   In 1751 a definite boundary was drawn between Norway and Sweden, a line which, since 1809, has served as a boundary between Norway and Finland.   Through the greater part of its length this was traced along the ridge of the watershed, so that all the streams that empty into the Gulf of Bothnia were given to Sweden and Finland.   But these treaties left many territorial problems still unsolved.   For one thing, the Russians continued to levy tribute in the great Kemi Lappmark, though it lay west of the line of 1596 and consequently was regarded as belonging to Sweden.

The boundary between Finland and Swedish Norrland was also a matter of some doubt.   It is usually stated that Finland extended to the Kemi River, but the older maps seem to indicate that the boundary ran along the watershed between the basins of the Kemi and the Tornea.   In the negotiations at Fredrikshamn the Russians insisted on the Kalix River as the northwestern boundary of Finland, while the Swedes urged that the Kemi River was the proper line. A compromise was finally agreed upon and the rivers Tornea and Muonio were accepted as the boundary between the two countries. Two years later the Czar added the Karelian province of Viborg to the grand duchy and the boundaries of Finland in their present form were completed.

In 1917 the Finnish diet severed all connections with Petrograd and declared Finland an independent state. This action was promptly followed by a strong agitation for the rectification of the eastern frontier. So long as there remains a Russian Karelia the Finns will regard their nation as incomplete. Consequently they wish to push their boundary eastward to Lake Onega and northward to the White Sea. Such a rectification would also give their country an outlet on the Arctic coast, which seems to be necessary to their national prosperity.

It is estimated that there are approximately 350,000 Karelians who live outside the limits of the new Finnish state, nearly all of whom are to be found in the country between the Finnish frontier and the Murman Railway. This region has been under Russian control for nearly seven hundred years, and in religion, civilization, and literary culture the inhabitants have in large measure become Russianized. In the past their sympathies have been with Russia, though it is, of course, possible that in the present state of Russian affairs they would be glad to transfer their loyalty to the government at Helsingfors.

The chief obstacle in the way of establishing a Greater Finland is the Murman Railway. The building of this road was forced by the serious military situation of 1915; but in the future it is sure to have great commercial importance. Through the greater part of its course the Murman road runs close to the frontier between the Slavic and the Karelian territories. It would be possible to draw a boundary from Lake Ladoga to Kandalashka on the White Sea which would leave the railway in Russian possession and still give to Finland nearly the whole Karelian population. Russia might also be willing to surrender what she still holds of Lapland west of the railway; but it is inconceivable that she should agree to the cession of Catherine Harbor, the terminal port, without which the Murman road would be of slight value.

If the coming peace conference should approve the creation of a Greater Finland, there seems to be no good reason why the Esthonian lands should not be included in such a state. The Baltic Provinces are inhabited chiefly by two races, Letts and Finns. If the nationalistic principle is to be carried out, it would seem the logical decision to allow the Letts to follow the fortunes of their Lithuanian kinsmen and to reunite the Esthonians with the Tavasts and the Karelians. This would give Finland a total population of at least 5,000,000, nearly ninety per cent. of which would be of Turanian stock. It would also give the new state strength sufficient to maintain its sovereignty and its independence. And unless such an arrangement can be worked out, the immediate future will see the Baltic lands distributed among four weak and almost helpless states, which in the course of time can scarcely escape being forced into some form of vassal relationship either to the Slavs or to the Prussians.

From "Idylls and Epigrams"

By JOHAN RUNEBERG

[*From "Anthology of Swedish Lyrics" translated by* CHARLES WHARTON STORK,
SCANDINAVIAN CLASSICS, Volume IX]

I

From a lover's trysting came the maiden,
With red hands she came.   Her mother asked her:
"Wherefore are your hands so red, my daughter?"
And the girl said: "I've been plucking roses,
And the thorns have pricked me as I plucked them."
From her love-tryst came once more the maiden,
With red lips she came.   Her mother asked her:
"Wherefore are your lips so red, my daughter?"
And the girl said, "Raspberries I've eaten,
And they stained my lips as I was eating."
From her love-tryst once again the maiden
Came, with pallid cheek.   Her mother asked her:
"Wherefore is your cheek so pale, my daughter?"
But the girl said: "Make my grave, O mother,
Hide me there and set a cross above me,
Carve upon the cross what I shall tell you:
'Red her hands were at the first returning,
'Twas within a lover's hands they reddened.
Red her lips were at the next returning,
'Twas beneath a lover's lips they reddened.
Pale her lips were at the last returning,
They were pale because her love was faithless.'"

XVI

Counsels three the mother gave her daughter:
Not to sigh, not to be discontented,
Not to give a kiss to any lover.
Mother, if your daughter disobey not
In the last of these three things you counsel,
She will disobey in both the others.

Sakari's Story

By JOHN BERGH

Translated from the Swedish by HANNA ASTRUP LARSEN

IT ALL happened in the time when we ate bark bread, in the reign of King Karl the Eleventh—God rest his soul. Famine lay heavy over all the realm and especially over our poor frosty Finland. You might have thought the Lord was angry at the untiring care our thrifty king gave to the good things of this world and did not like his taking so much thought for the morrow. Perhaps Heaven meant to show us that it availed nothing to plan everything, arrange everything, to plough and to sow the fields, without praying for God's blessing. Though the country was perhaps in a better condition, take it altogether, than ever before, want and misery came—worse than we had known them in the days of the old spend-thrift, fighting kings. All nature was out of joint. All the plagues of Egypt went over our poor land, and we could not understand the reason; we had no Moses to show us the wound from which our life-blood was oozing away. We were like children, who only feel the sting of the rod, but don't know why it is lifted, and when I think of it all now, so long afterwards, it seems not impossible that this was the very reason why it brought us nearer to Him who was punishing us.

Our poor Juuriniemi had never been among the richer farms, and in these hard times it yielded scarcely anything. One winter we ate bread made of bark, and when the harvest again failed the next year our servants left us and went to Sweden to beg. We— my father and mother and I—lived mostly on game and fish, but with daily hunting and fishing the supply soon gave out, and the game especially was almost destroyed by men and wild beasts. When everything else was gone, mother gathered a kind of moss and boiled it.

Yet another year passed, and we went about, silent, pale, and hollow-eyed. We thought God had abandoned us and our land, and to me, young as I was, it seemed that life would never have anything to offer except misery and hunger. On all the neighboring farms, things were about the same as with us, and I began to feel that the highest imaginable bliss would be to eat my fill. My dreams, such as young people dream, dealt only with an earthly paradise where I could have a big dish of porridge and a loaf of clean bread every day. Even the stories that mother told to pass time in winter evenings were all about food and untold riches, and we gorged in fancy, since we never had anything to eat in reality.

I often roamed about for whole days in the forest, looking for game, but seeking even more the treasure of my dreams. Everywhere I seemed just about to reach something mysterious and wonderful that should help us out of our troubles, but the reality was always commonplace or baffling. I caught glimpses of the forest sprites under the dewy bushes, vanishing in the soughing reeds, and heard them laughing in the mountain clefts, but I could never get near enough to demand their hidden treasures of them. It was starvation, for I am not naturally one of those who only go about and wait for the help of others. It is hard to fight against the Lord when he is angry with a people, and that was the reason why I thought only of supernatural help out of the terrible, year-long suffering.

On Sundays, and in the morning and evening, we read the Bible and the book of sermons, but when I was alone in the forest I saw the wood-nymph with her hair down her back, beckoning and luring, and sometimes the Neck sat among the reeds playing as though to call me to him. Robin Goodfellow crept about; I could see his red cap flitting over the grayness, and the elves danced in the glade, caring nothing for the small griefs of men. But as for me I always came too late. They always had time to hide, as they do from our race.

Fall came. The rye grew sparse on the field with straight, thin straws and white, empty ears. The Black Death lurked about the villages, but we had not yet been visited by the Angel with the Sword. The fog hung thick and heavy over the fields and seemed to smell of sickness and death. In the woods there was not a breath of wind, and nothing stirred but the water that gathered and fell from the limp-hanging leaves. The oats had not had a chance to freeze and stood rotting without getting ripe. All signs pointed to another winter of starvation, but by that time I was so used to it that I hardly looked for anything else. No, the help must come from another quarter.

Again I went out into the woods among the dripping trees and searched with eager eyes for the witching shapes that I had seen flitting about. I walked and walked, until my feet could hardly carry me, and once in a while it came to me that I ought rather to be doing something useful, but I was so tired and hungry that I had not strength left to resolve on anything.

At last I came to the top of a little knoll and went over it to the opposite edge, where I knew there was a view of a small meadow. Many a time had I lain there waiting to see the elves begin their dance down below, and sometimes I had imagined I caught glimpses of them, though they always vanished before I could get down the hill.

When I reached the edge of the knoll, I saw a figure standing down below. It was a woman, a young girl, and she carried something on her arm; yet she could not be a human being, for I had never seen anything like the bodice that shone so bright and red through the mist, and no woman walked with so light and elastic a step in those days.

I lay down on the wet moss and waited for her to come nearer, for she was on her way toward the hill. It was surely the wood-nymph; I could see her golden hair falling in waves over her back; she sang in a wonderfully clear voice, and her eyes shone. But what convinced me more than anything else that she was no human being was the fact that her basket was filled to the rim with something which I took to be little bread rolls, such as I could remember from my earliest childhood when my father used to bring them home from market. It seemed to me I could still taste the delicious flavor of them in my mouth, and I felt that I must get the rolls in her basket, no matter by what means, and take them home to my mother, who was getting weaker every day.

If I could only prevent her from vanishing like all the others. I would creep toward her stealthily, but before I could get down from the knoll she might be gone. Still there was nothing for it but to try.

My heart beat, and my knees gave way under me, as I skirted round the cliff and came down upon the meadow. Softly I bent the bushes to one side and looked out. Yes, she was there yet. She stood with her back toward me, and I was surprised to see that she looked so strangely like a human being.

First I crept a little nearer, but then I suddenly became aware that she heard my step, and I rushed forward to catch her. She started and would have run away, but I was too quick and threw my arms about her. There I stood not knowing what to do, simply shaking all over. My arm held a young girl's soft, yielding body, and she, who had first gone pale, was now rosy red, and the eyes that met mine were deep like the lake on a fair summer evening. She smiled on me, and I felt the fragrance of her loosened hair, which had blown against my cheek when she turned so impetuously.

We looked at each other, and a stream of fire ran through my whole body. I forgot why I had caught her, and she did nothing but look at me with her laughing eyes. At last she bent her head back, and I kissed her.

"Boy, boy," she said softly as in a dream, "where did you come from, and why have you caught me?"

Why? I no longer knew. I only knew that all of life seemed changed, and that I had almost become a man in these short seconds. I felt that life meant more than food or hunger, and my blood, which a moment ago had been weak as sluggish water in a ditch, surged in me like spring torrents. The forest was no longer full of elves and trolls, but seemed like a mighty church, a holy place where only one being ruled, strong and powerful. The swell of organ-music was in the air, and everything in the forest sang the praise of life and love.

I understood that she too had gone about as in a dream, waiting for the miracle which the forest hid in its bosom, but to her this miracle was not food and money, as with me, but love and the fairy prince. That was the meaning of the strange, dreamy smile she had turned on me. That was why she had not torn herself from my grasp, but only kissed me and whispered, "Boy, boy!"

I was still holding her in my arms, when I saw the misty blue light die or rather sink down into the depths of her soul. Her eyes became calm, and she repeated her question in a more distinct voice.

Then I had to tell her that I thought she was the wood-nymph, and she smiled again, till her white teeth gleamed.

"A fine wood-nymph," she said, "who is Juryman Peltonen's Lisa from Isokyla."

Isokyla was a village about a mile from our own, and as I had seldom had anything to do there, I scarcely knew the people.

"But what kind of bread is that you have in your basket?" I asked.

Then she no longer smiled but laughed aloud.

"I'll show you," she said, holding out her basket to let me see that it was full of large and small mushrooms, which might easily at a distance be mistaken for bread rolls.

"What in the world are you going to do with those?" I asked her.

Then she told me that a Muscovite boyar with his servants and serfs had once visited her father's house, and these strangers had gathered mushrooms and eaten them greedily. They had taught her mother how to prepare them. Her people had been ashamed to eat such stuff before, but now in a time of famine what else could you do? In the fall they gathered enough to last for the winter, and she had come to our parts because the leafy forest, which contained the best mushrooms, grew more plentiful here than around her home.

She looked at me again and noticed my sunken eyes. Without my asking she began to show me from her basket which mushrooms were good to eat, and told me how to cook them, while I listened spellbound by the thought of all the food I had passed indifferently or trodden underfoot.

While she spoke, I looked at her and at the woods and the meadow, and it seemed to me that all was changed. The dreamy haze had vanished as if a fresh breeze had blown away the unhealthy mists, and the sun had begun to shine again. It seemed to me that reality was more beautiful than the dream and promised a thousand times greater treasures.

We sat down on a mound. I put my arm around her waist again, and she did not draw away. "Lisa," I said in a firm voice, "better days must be in store for us, and then I will come for you. I don't want any mistress of my house but you."

The misty light came into her eyes again. She leaned her head against my shoulder, nestling close to me, and I heard her crying, and held her tighter against my breast. Again it seemed to me that I understood her thoughts without the need of her uttering them. I knew that she had been longing and sighing for a little sunshine in her life, something that might warm and gladden her heart and help her to bear the terror of the evil years.

"Don't cry," I whispered stroking her fair hair, "now you are my sweetheart, and now I will work for you so hard that the corn must grow on the fields, and you shall smile till the sun can't help shining. Look at me, dearest, look at me. Happiness is coming. I hear the rushing of its wings in the forest."

She lifted her head to listen, and there was in truth a rushing in the pine-tops. First it shook down over us a glittering rain of drops, but in the next moment the sun burst forth through the clouds; the sun, which we had not seen for months, shone on her golden hair, and a quiver went through all nature as if that, too, were drawing a breath of relief. The sunbeams waxed warmer and warmer, and suddenly the wind carried the sound of church-bells from the village.

"The sun, the sun!" she cried. "May it always shine on us, dearest!"

We both rose solemnly as if we were standing before the altar in church, and we saw the clouds like vanquished hostile armies fleeing in all directions, while the sun pursued them with its flaming sword, touching the gray brow of the mountain, the bright green of the meadow, and the solemn circle of the forest standing round about.

We said never a word but stood there in wonder, until at last I pulled off my cap and threw it toward the blue sky.

"Sun! Sun!" I cried with all my strength. "The future is ours!"

But Lisa's eyes were full of tears, though her mouth smiled.

We walked together a little ways, and when we came to the lake, it glittered and shone as I had not seen it for months. Yet a while we sat there, until I remembered that I must bring my mother something to eat.

I looked at the girl, standing there by the shining waves, with the music of church-bells hovering about her, and again I kissed her. We had no need of promises; we only looked into each other's eyes and went hurriedly each our way.

As I walked, I gathered a supply of mushrooms in a basket of birch bark, but when I came home I took good care not to let my parents know what I was doing. I cleaned the mushrooms secretly and cooked them as I had been told, cutting them in such small pieces that the old folks should not know what they were eating. I told them that the sheriff had given me food which the Crown distributed among the people. They were so weakened by hunger that they did not doubt nor try to inquire farther, but simply ate, and I could see that they liked it.

When they had been eating this food for a few days and relished it, I told them what it was, and after that my mother helped me to find the mushrooms so that I might have time for other work.

I took hold of the farm in earnest, for my father had let everything drift. The weather had completely changed, and the soil dried quickly. I harnessed our one remaining horse to the plough and began preparing the ground, and when the horse was tired, I dug ditches. For a few days my father simply looked at me and sighed, but pretty soon he began to help me a little. Then I took a sack with me and went to the sheriff, who, I had been told, distributed seed. It was not yet too late to plant. The sheriff did really give me a few measures of rye, and before winter came it was sprouting and just strong enough not to be harmed by the frost.

But while it was growing, the Black Death came to our parts. The Angel of Death crept into our home too and took my mother from us. Father sat broken and silent, waiting for his turn, but it did not come. It seemed that the pestilence had lost its power with the coming of clear weather and could only take the weak and the starving. On the farms where people had been for a long time without strengthening food it took all, but I believe it was our new food that saved father and me.

We had gathered mushrooms for the entire winter and a quantity of whortleberries, which we boiled with moss. My mother, however, had felt weak for a long time, and I believe that the misery round about us sank so deep into her mind that she had no power of resistance against the sickness.

In the midst of my work and sorrow, an iron hand seemed suddenly to clutch my heart. What if death should take my sweetheart as it had taken my mother! At the thought the spade fell out of my hand, and I had no peace until I had found out the truth. Till then I had not felt the need of seeing Lisa again, but now I could not wait another day. Although it seemed impossible that the Lord could be so cruel as to take her from me, I looked about me and remembered that on almost every farm death had parted parents and children, wives and husbands, and young lovers, and I understood that it would be presumptuous in me to count on any special grace of God.

That very day I started for Isokyla. It was not a large town, though known far and wide, and the way leading to it was but a narrow forest path.

I did not, of course, know in which house Juryman Peltonen lived, and I went into the first cottage I saw to inquire. An old woman sat in a corner rocking herself and whimpering in a hopeless, tearless fashion, as women did in those days. When she caught sight of me, she stared at me as if I had been a ghost and could hardly get her thoughts together enough to answer my questions.

Yes, Peltonen's house was the second from there. It was the only one that hadn't been emptied of people by the pestilence, and she thought they must be in league with the evil one.

"They go about as if nothing had happened and tell us to eat the toadstools—as if we were cows. There's something wrong in that house. The sons are with the soldiers in Sweden, they say, but the girl's at home, and anybody can see they're friendly with the powers of darkness, for she's got that look about her like a witch."

The old woman shook her head sadly and again began her whimpering over the dead. As for me, I stood broken and weak as a child. The sudden release from anxiety made my nerves relax like bowstrings that had been too tightly strung, and for the first time I realized what it would have meant to me if she had really been gone. It was only for her sake that I had labored and striven. Yet I felt that I had not the courage to present myself before her proud father, but that I needed to work much longer before my home was fit to offer his daughter.

Silently I crept out of the cottage and started for home, but as I walked, my strength seemed to come back, and at last I ran as if I could not get home fast enough to make up for the time lost from my work.

All winter I made furniture finer than had ever been seen in our parts, and I got the farm implements ready. My father still sat broken and silent, sighing and looking on. "What's the use of all this fuss, when the Lord has left our land and nothing can grow in the fields?" he said. But somehow I felt a wonderful assurance that the bad years were over. I worked for Lisa's sake and whistled while I worked.

Spring came. Never before had I seen the blessed loveliness of everything in the spring. Nature was teeming with life, and all creatures seemed to be possessed with the same longing as I. They were all building houses for their beloved and gathering supplies; all were filled with new joy in life, and the birds whistled and sang just as I did. I understood nature as never before, from the silent fishes playing and splashing among the rushes to the circling eagles sailing over the mountains. And the rye—my rye—stood green and dainty on my little patch, and the earth was fragrant in the barley field, which I was preparing for seed. During the winter, I had shot wolves and lynx and even a bear. I had sold the skins in the city, and with the money I had bought a whole barrel of barley and two barrels of oats from the stores of the Crown. When the cranes stretched their wings over the roofs and shrieked with joy at being home again, I scattered my seed in the warm earth, and that night a soft, blessed spring rain fell.

Good God, but it was fine to see how things grew that year! I had sown but sparsely, for the soil was rich, and I had so little seed-corn, but from almost every grain there rose a whole bunch of stalks. Sunshine and rain seemed always to come when I needed them most, and at last I could see my father take a new hold on life. When he thought I didn't see him, he would steal down to the fields and stand looking at them for hours at a time, while the tears came into his eyes. Little by little, he began to help me with the fallow fields and the hay-making. I cut much hay that year, for the cow had a calf, which I meant to raise, and, moreover, I was sure Lisa would bring at least one cow as her dower.

As the harvest drew near, heavy golden ears were swaying in the breeze. I could hardly sleep for fear something would happen to the crop, and I saw that my father too lay tossing wide awake and sometimes got up in the middle of the night to go down to the fields and see that everything was safe.

But nothing happened, and when the time had come we both rose with the sun; our eyes shone, and we hardly spoke a word, while we cut and tied the grain and built up the most beautiful shocks. Not a straw was left on the ground for the birds, and the sheaves were tied as carefully as if they were meant for nosegays in the parlor. The sun shone on them and turned them into pure gold.

The next day was Sunday, and that very evening I told my father that I meant to marry Juryman Peltonen's Lisa. At that a smile spread over his old face, for he began to understand whence came my strength and enthusiasm for working, and he promised that he would go with me and be my spokesman.

I did not sleep much that night, and the rising sun found me busily polishing the cart, which had not been used for a long time, but which I had painted in bright colors one sunny day in spring. The horse had been resting for a few days, and I curried him until he shone. When my father came out, everything was ready for the journey, and again the old man smiled with a roguish light under his gray eyebrows.

In order to reach Isokyla with a cart it was necessary to take a roundabout way, which doubled the distance. But what did that

matter? The sun shone again that day, and whenever we passed
an inlet of the lake the sound of church-bells came floating to us
across the water, and the air was clear as it is only in the fall, so that
we could see far away to the opposite coast. Many houses along
the road were still empty, but the few people we saw smiled at us as
if they understood our errand, and hope shone in every eye. They
seemed to wait for the new time coming with new harvests and new
seed-time.

At last our cart rattled into Isokyla, and wherever there was
any one at home we saw pale but smiling faces looking out through
the open doors. The cows moo'd, the cocks crowed, and here too
the church-bells were ringing.

A young girl stood on the steps outside of Peltonen's house,
shading her eyes with her hand and looking out as though she were
waiting for some one. I saw at once that it was Lisa, but the strong
light prevented her from recognizing me before we were quite near
the steps. Then her cheeks became suddenly deep red, and she ran
into the house.

In her place appeared a sturdily built man who carried himself
with an air not common in those days. When I saw him, my courage
sank, but I thought: "Lisa and I love each other so much, nothing
can part us, not even if the old man disinherits her on the spot."

When we were seated in the large parlor, the two old men were
silent and solemn, until at last they began to talk about the good
crops. I could do nothing but steal glances at Lisa, who went about
helping her mother with the housework. It seemed strange, almost
impossible, that I should aspire to this proud maiden, and I did
not yet venture to speak to her. The conversation of the old men
sounded in my ears like an indistinct murmur, and I almost forgot
the purpose of our journey while I gazed at her as if she were a
beautiful picture in church, until at last she nodded to me, and our
eyes met unseen by the others. Then I knew the witching glance
of the wood-nymph in the forest glade, and my heart leaped as
when the sun shone out after months of fog.

Once I saw her wink at me with so much meaning, as she took
the bucket to go for water, that I suddenly remembered the horse
needed my attention. We met at the well, and while the horse
eagerly lapped the fresh water, we could speak undisturbed for a
few moments.

"Boy, boy," she said softly and reproachfully, "how long you
have waited. If I hadn't been so sure of you, I don't know how I
should have borne it."

Then I told her all I had done since our first and only meeting,
how I had worked the whole year only for her, and how God had
blessed my labor. At that she stole up to me behind the horse and

kissed me, and I drank her kisses as the horse drank the clear water.

When we came in again, the two old men were standing hand in hand, and smiled with equal kindness on us both.

"Come and shake hands with your future father-in-law," said my father merrily. "I had quite a hard fight for your sake, until I told him how you worked and toiled all winter, and when the mistress of the house said a good word for you, we won our case at last."

"Well, my boy," said the proud old farmer, "my people have always been stiff-necked, and I want no milksop for a son-in-law who gets down in the mouth at a little trouble. He must be a fellow who can take a Muscovite by the scruff of the neck if need be, one who can break up new ground in the wilderness, and pull in his belly-strap another hole if food is scarce. I like you, son, and when the enemy comes I'll give you my old broadsword. It's cracked a skull or two before now."

I shook hands with the two old people, and the matter was settled. The following year, when my fields were again in full growth as in the old times, the church-bells rang for me and Lisa, and I took her home to the house which stood on this very spot.

Two Patriotic Songs of Finland

Translated from the Swedish by HERMAN MONTAGU DONNER

MARCH OF THE MEN OF BJÖRNEBORG

By JOHAN LUDVIG RUNEBERG

I

Sons of heroes who have bled
On Narva's heath and Poland's sands, on Leipzig's plains, in Lützen's
   trenches,
   Finland's might is not yet dead,
Still can with foemen's blood our battlefields run red!
   Far from us be peace and rest!
The storm is loose! at cannon's flash and roar no Finnish aspect
   blenches!
   Forward, freemen, breast to breast!
On our brave warriors gaze their fathers' spirits blest.
   The noblest zeal
Shall fire us onward speeding;
   Sharp is our steel,
Our breasts inured to bleeding.
Fearless let us onward go,
And in our pulses feel our centuries' freedom glow!

Aloft, proud badge to victory leading,
From hoary ages glorified with rents and stains;
On, on, for thee we'll drain our throbbing veins
While still of Finland's storm-bleached flag one tattered strip remains!

II

Never shall this coign of earth
To foreign conqueror yield with falchions sheathed or fields with blood
        unsodden.
Never shall the cry go forth
That Finland's sons betrayed their free home in the North.
        Brave men can but fighting fall,
Nor shrink at threats, or danger fear, ne'er cower, bend, nor be down-
        trodden;
        Death to shame prefer we all,
And victory wrest from loss at honor's trumpet-call!
            Weapon in hand
        Against the foe we dash on!
            Death for one's land
        Is life's supremest passion!
        Dauntless seek we then the strife;
The Reaper's sickle waits our hour with triumph rife:
        Thinned ranks give proof in awesome fashion
Of heroes' mood and deed, of foemen's shattered chains.
Unsullied banner, on! to glory's strains—
Round thee unflinching aye thy Finnish guard remains!

MARCH OF THE FINNISH CAVALRY IN THE THIRTY YEARS' WAR

In the snows of the North is our forefathers' land;
The glow of our hearths lights a storm-beaten strand;
There hardened our arms to the swing of the brand;
There learned we for truth and for honor to stand.

The Neva has watered our foam-flecked horse;
They swam o'er the Vistula, heartening the host;
O'er the Rhine sped our falchions' retributive course,
And drank in the Danube Gustavus's toast.

And as, when o'er ashes and ruins we ride,
Sparks leap from the hoof-strokes, scattering bright,
So flashes the sun from our sabre-sweep wide,
And the gleam of our lances is liberty's light!

A Nation Without a Flag

By FREDERIC SCHENCK

WRITTEN BY DR. SCHENCK IN 1912, BEFORE THE GREAT WAR, AND PUBLISHED AT THAT TIME IN AN UNDERGRADUATE JOURNAL AT OXFORD UNIVERSITY, THESE NOTES FROM THE DIARY OF AN AMERICAN AT THE OLYMPIC GAMES IN STOCKHOLM ARE OF INCREASED SIGNIFICANCE AT THIS TIME.

MEDAL PRESENTED TO ALL PARTICIPANTS IN THE OLYMPIC GAMES IN 1912

THE "Solemn Opening" of the games, with its processions of nations, turned out, quite unexpectedly, to be a political event of considerable dramatic and emotional appeal. There was a touch of irony in the chance that gave to Norway a position exactly in the centre, so that the new Norwegian flag lined up for review under the very nose of the King of Sweden. Newer than the Norwegian flag, and more precarious, was the green and red standard of the Portuguese Republic. The newest of all, the five stripes of regenerated China, was not in evidence, but one looked for it, and found oneself wondering what new flags will unfurl at the next Olympic meeting and what old ones will have disappeared forever.

The real event, however, was the entry of the people without a flag—the Finns. Most of the spectators had hardly heard of Finland before they arrived in Stockholm, but rumors were spreading of the prowess of Kohlemainen and some of his team-mates. We were beginning to comprehend the attitude of the Scandinavians towards the slowly expanding might of Russia and the general sentiment of nationalism that pervaded the atmosphere of the games. The Russian flag came in, followed by an unimpressive band of athletes. There was desultory clapping, but more hissing. Then, at a short interval, came a little white banner, blazoned with an undecipherable coat of arms and beside it a placard, trimmed with streamers of the Russian colors—white, blue and red—bearing the name "Finland." Behind them came a squad of women gymnasts, dressed in grey, marching in perfect time with a firm, elastic, easy step; then line after line of big, broad, muscular men with solid-looking, square faces and close-cropped, blonde hair. The audience rose and yelled. It was the biggest ovation of the day; the Swedes were greeting their blood brothers in bondage—fellow Scandinavians subjected to the tyranny of the Slav. Every one understood, and men of all nations, whether they had ever seen a Finn before or not, stood up and

———

cheered with the Swedes. The procession filed round the Stadium, turned across to face the royal box, and halted. In the front rank among the standards of the nations was the Russian flag. Next to it was a gap; behind the gap stood the mighty Finns, better men physically than almost any team in the whole concourse, with their placard draped in the Russian colors and their tiny, unrecognizable banner. Hungary, Bohemia, Chile, Luxemburg, every other country, big or little, independent or subordinate, had its flag lined up with the rest. The Finns alone had none.

In the next week, the Finns proved themselves the best team from Continental Europe with the single exception of Sweden, and Kohlemainen won recognition as the greatest long-distance runner living. The Finnish arms—a golden lion surrounded by little gold billets on a red shield—became familiar to those who watched the tape, but no matter how often the Finns won, their flag never was allowed to break out from the big poles at the end of the Stadium. Instead a Russian flag went up, and after a streamer labeled "Finland." Whenever the Russian flag broke out, the crowd hissed, then, when the streamer appeared, they cheered. The Russian flag without a pennant never went up at all.

Interesting People: General Bjornstad

By Carl G. O. Hansen

THE Norwegians in the United States have always taken great pride in the achievements of those of their race who have held positions of public trust and responsibility. Especially do they glory in the deeds of those of their common stock who prove their

General Bjornstad

patriotic devotion in the military or naval service of the greatest of republics. Their record is a brilliant one, containing such names as Peter C. Assersen, the emigrant from Ekersund who worked his way up from a humble position to rear admiral in the United States Navy, who was for thirty years the head of the construction department of the Navy, and twelve of whose descendants are doing active military service in the present war; Hans C. Hegg, Porter Olsen, and Ole C. Johnson Skipsnes, all three serving as colonels in the Union Army during the Civil War; Ole Hansen Balling, lieutenant-colonel of a New York regiment in the Civil War, and others.

Hitherto, however, there has been no general of Norwegian origin in the service of Uncle Sam, and the appointment of Alfred W. Bjornstad as brigadier-general in the National Army, announced on June 28, marks the highest rank ever attained by an American of Norwegian stock. While yet in his early prime, General Bjornstad has already to his credit one of the greatest tasks entrusted to a single man in the present war; the entire plan of the officers' training camps, where thousands of young men have been made efficient officers in a comparatively short space of time, was his work.

The general's father, Julius Bjornstad, emigrated, in 1866, from Röken near Drammen in Norway, and came to St. Paul, where Alfred Bjornstad was born, forty-four years ago. He studied at Luther and St. Olaf colleges and afterwards at the University of Minnesota, where he was known as a devotee of sports and especially as a crack oarsman. In 1894, while still a student in the University, he joined the National Guard. He was with the Thirteenth Minnesota Regiment in the Spanish-American War, was commissioned a first lieutenant on May 7, 1898, and nine days later was promoted to a captaincy. He took part in all the engagements of his regiment and was wounded twice on the day Manila was captured; at one time he was shot through the lungs and taken up as dead.

In 1901, Bjornstad received his commission in the regular establishment, where he rose to be a captain, serving in the Philippines and afterwards in Cuba. He also spent some months traveling in Europe and in the Orient, and was one of the American military emissaries to the Russian-Japanese War. Meanwhile his interest in military science was growing, and he applied himself closely to study. He was an honor graduate of the Army School of the Line in 1909 and a graduate of the Army Staff College in 1910. While at the former institution, he was awarded the gold medal for a treatise on "The Military Requirements of the United States and the Best Method of Meeting Them," by many military experts considered the best work written for years on that subject.

Captain Bjornstad was a member of the General Staff of the Army for more than a year, in 1911 and 1912. From that he was appointed military attaché to the American Embassy in Berlin, and in the fall of 1912 attended the German field maneuvers. He was at that time already considered one of the most efficient tacticians of the Army. Upon his return to the United States he was appointed instructor at the Army Service School, and in 1916 he was assigned as professor of military science at Harvard University. He has made a special study of infantry organization and is the author of several text-books used in military schools.

When the war broke out, Bjornstad's large and varied experience at home and abroad made him a very valuable man to the War Department. His promotions to major, lieutenant-colonel, colonel, and brigadier-general have all come within the past two years. When the Department was confronted with the problem of organizing the officers' training camps in the shortest possible time, the task was entrusted to him, and the whole country now knows how successfully it has been carried out. In September of last year Bjornstad went to France, and this spring was made Chief of Staff of the Third Army Corps. One of his principal duties abroad is as director of the Army Staff College back of the lines, superintending the training of officers.

Slesvig Forum

I have read the Slesvig Number of the AMERICAN-SCANDINAVIAN REVIEW with great interest. So far as I know, this is the first real effort to present the problem of South Jutland to the reading public of America, and I hope that the effort will lead to something more than mere academic interest and discussion. I find that my American friends, while they appreciate the fact that a great wrong was done to Denmark in 1864, believe quite generally that the Prussians have not only tried to Germanize Slesvig, but have actually succeeded in doing so. This opinion must be eradicated before the cause of South Jutland can receive a hearing, and I believe the current issue of the REVIEW will render efficient service in this direction.

University of Illinois.   LAURENCE M. LARSON.

Pastor Bodholdt, in your Slesvig Number, tells of the old Rune stones found in South Jutland—silent, historic monuments bearing witness to Danish kings and warriors.   Allow me to add another instance in which the stones speak. In the Cathedral of the City of Slesvig, near the thousand-year-old fortification Dannevirke, there was found on the portico an old inscription which proved difficult to decipher.   The authorities called in one of their learned men, Professor Haupt of Halle, who gave the following translation:

"Drive thou away for me the German, the tyrant of the world,
and lead back the people which worshipped God in truth."

The inscription was supposed to have been made about 1530.   The late Mr. M. Andreson, President of the Danish Language League in Slesvig, who visited New York seven years ago, furnished me with the exact words of the translation which the German scientist gave in 1903.   For reasons easily understood, the German authorities have not given the contents any further publication.

New York.   FRODE C. W. RAMBUSCH.

The latest recruit to the ranks of plaintiff nationalities is little Schleswig, which occupies almost the entire current number of the AMERICAN-SCANDINAVIAN REVIEW.   The unthinking world has considered for the most part only the wrongs of the greater aggregations, Alsace-Lorraine, Bohemia, Poland, Jugo-Slavonia, Armenia.   Yet probably none of these races holds so indisputably and completely the territory it lays claim to as the Schleswigers. . . . Even if the Danes in bondage number less than half a million, and their little country covers an infinitesimal part of the earth's surface, their cause is just and undeniable, and their rights as sacred as those of any oppressed people.   They should have justice.

The New York Evening Post.

The AMERICAN-SCANDINAVIAN REVIEW has just published a South Jutland Number, and every Dane must appreciate not only the good intention, but also the brilliant and successful manner in which it has been carried out.

New York.   *Nordlyset.*

This Slesvig Number is extremely vital.

Chicago.   *Revyen.*

We hope this weighty plea will result in having the Slesvig problem taken up for consideration.

San Francisco.   *Bien.*

Editorial

Our Pact With Scandinavia With intense pleasure the Review registers the fact that our Government has now concluded agreements with all the three Scandinavian nations. First to be signed was the contract with Norway, on May 10; then followed that with Sweden, on August 22, and, shortly after, that with Denmark, on September 18. Before the first of the Scandinavian Commissions arrived in Washington, the Review published, in July, 1917, the article "Not Feeding Germany," following our press bulletins sent out through the Associated Press to clear away the wild rumors that were rampant in the newspapers. We have persistently kept the truth about Scandinavia before the American public, at the same time as we have explained to the Scandinavians the position of our Government and the necessity for safeguarding our exports against the enemy. Throughout we have advocated that policy of open diplomacy and mutual conciliation which is now happily made the basis of American relations with the Scandinavians, and we rejoice in seeing the natural friendliness between our country and theirs formally stabilized in the agreements just concluded.

Sweden Looking Westward The signing of the agreement with our Government, following that with our allies, means that Sweden has definitely turned her face westward. Though politically neutral, she will be economically closely bound to the Western Powers, with whom the mass of her people are at heart in sympathy. A powerful economic ally has been added to the circle of those who are with us, and the resources of Germany have been correspondingly narrowed. Long months of patient negotiation have gone to the framing of an agreement which should be so perfectly adjusted that it should be not only a war measure but a basis for coöperation after the war. As it finally stands, it is founded on the principle of mutual give and take which alone insures permanence.

Some idea of the contribution Sweden can make to our resources may be gleaned from the fact that in June our Government appropriated $6,000,000 as our share of the purchase price of 2,000,000 tons of Swedish iron ore bought by the authorities in Great Britain under the terms of the agreement concluded in the foregoing month, and this is only the beginning of an import that will be of the utmost importance to us. Among the chief products to be licensed for export from Sweden will be iron, steel, paper, and wood pulp, and the Swedish Government has promised to facilitate the purchase of Swedish goods by granting credits during the continuance of the present unfavorable rate of exchange.   Sweden is furthermore placing at the disposal of the Allies 400,000 tons of her shipping.

In return we are happily able to relieve the privation under which the people of Sweden have suffered.   England will release sufficient coal and coke to save them from another heatless and lightless winter. The embargo is lifted to permit them to import bread, cereals, fodder, coffee, and other goods from Australia and South America.   From this country will be sent cotton and lubricating oils, both urgently needed in Swedish factories, copper and other metals, chemicals, and various articles of food such as edible oils, dried and canned vegetables and fruit, and certain cereal products.   Altogether a fair provision is made for Sweden's needs, and Mr. Axel Robert Nordvall, Commissioner of the Royal Swedish Government, has expressed the most cordial appreciation of our Government's will to lighten the burdens of the neutrals.

WORK FOR DENMARK'S The great significance of the agreements
SKILLED LABOR between the War Trade Board and the
Danish Merchants' and Shipping Guilds, aside from their moral value as a permanent expression of mutual good-will, lies in the provision for raw materials to enable the closed factories in Denmark to open.   One-third of the population of the country is dependent on manufacturing, and, as the REVIEW pointed out last January, the world can ill afford, in these days of depleted man power, to let the skilled Danish workmen be idle.   Guaranties are, of course, given that no goods manufactured from American materials shall be sold to our enemies, and we already know from the excellent work of the Merchants' Guild in the past that it is possible to control the situation perfectly; the amount of manufactured goods that has strayed into Germany is so infinitesimal that it is not worth mentioning.

The War Trade Board guarantees that licenses will be granted for export to Denmark of commodities, including food, metals, machinery, textiles, and chemicals, amounting to more than 352,000 tons.   On the list of metals we note 150,000 tons of steel and iron products, including shipbuilding materials, while another important item is copper needed for electric wires.   The want of lubricating oil has been one of the most serious drawbacks in manufacturing and has stimulated the substitute-makers all over Scandinavia, while the dearth of kerosene and gasoline has been felt by all classes.   The allotment of 80,000 tons of non-edible oils and grease, not more than 7,000 of which may be lubricating oil, will therefore be most welcome. According to a cabled editorial in *Social-Demokraten*, the painters and carpenters are overjoyed at the prospect of linseed oil and shellac, while the tanners are delighted with the promise of chemicals required in their trade. Other trades that will be at least partially relieved are the textile workers and tobacco workers; the former are to receive about one-half the amount of raw materials used in their normal output, the latter about eighty per cent.

We note the absence of fodder from the list. This means that Denmark will not be able to maintain the output of her industrialized agriculture, although every effort is being made by the farmers to utilize their domestic resources to the last straw of hay. The list of foods is slender, since after all Denmark is better able to provide herself with the staples than are most countries in the world at present, but it is pleasant to see some luxuries included, the largest item being 16,000 tons of coffee. Coffee is emphatically the cup that cheers in the North, and the scarcity of it has been a genuine hardship.

In return for American commodities Denmark pledges herself to limit still farther her export to the Central Powers, while the export of food to Norway and Sweden is facilitated. The press comment in Denmark is uniformly very favorable.

THREE DAYS' On September 17, the cable announced that King
NEWS Christian had conferred on Dr. Maurice Francis Egan, until recently our minister in Denmark, the Grand Cross of the Order of the Dannebrog, the highest order that can be bestowed on a commoner. On September 18, the agreement between the War Trade Board and the Danish Merchants' and Shipping Guilds was signed. On September 19, Prince Axel, the sailor-prince of Denmark, now visiting this country, was entertained by the President before leaving with his suite of naval officers for Annapolis.

SELF-DETERMINATION Iceland will soon be a sovereign state, by her
FOR ICELAND own volition, and through the modern, liberal spirit of Denmark, who prefers to keep her late colony as a friend and an equal rather than as an unwilling vassal. By the agreement, signed in Reykjavik by the two delegations on behalf of their respective Governments, and now laid before the parliaments, Denmark and Iceland will be two independent states united by a common king. Iceland declares herself to be perpetually neutral, and thus will have no naval flag, but will use her own merchant flag. Denmark will continue to handle the foreign affairs of both—an arrangement reminiscent of that between Norway and Sweden, which was productive of so much friction. Fortunately, the proposed agreement seems to have more flexibility; the interests of Iceland are to be taken care of by an official in the foreign department and by attachés familiar with Icelandic affairs in the legations and consulates. There is also provision for an advisory committee to be

appointed by the two parliaments to deal with legislation affecting both and for a court of arbitration to pass on differences that may arise. In case of a failure to agree, the matter is to be submitted to an arbiter chosen alternately by the Norwegian and Swedish Governments. With regard to domestic affairs, the spirit of the agreement allows Iceland to use Danish administrative machinery for the present with the idea of ultimately taking over all the functions of government herself; among the matters specified are the inspection of fisheries, coinage, customs, postal service, telegraphs, as well as the supreme judiciary.

Iceland, in her turn, makes a concession in the paragraph which gives citizens of either country full rights of citizenship in the other. This is one of the most important points in the agreement; for it means that Danish capital will have access to utilize the magnificent natural resources of Iceland according to plans that are already under way, and we may look for a rapid economic development in the near future. Another interesting paragraph is that stipulating that Denmark is to establish two funds of one million kroner each, one at the University of Copenhagen and one at the University of Reykjavik, for the furtherance of intellectual intercourse between the two countries.

It should be remembered that Iceland was originally colonized from Norway and looks to that country rather than to Denmark as her mother land. At the treaty which separated Norway from Denmark, Iceland remained bound to Denmark by a mere oversight of the negotiators. This makes the desire of the Icelanders for a separate national life all the more reasonable, and Denmark is wise in granting it so freely. We hope she will be rewarded with the return of the Danish Slesvigers, who are her own children racially and culturally.

PRO   The Finland Constitutional League of America has come
FINLANDIA   into existence with the object of saving Finland for the
            free nations of the world and ridding her of all German dominion, moral or material. The founders of the League are convinced that the Finns never have been and are not now pro-German except in the sense of clutching at any hand that promised to save them from Russia and the Red Terror. Indeed, sympathy for the Western Powers was so strong at the beginning of the war that young Finns who took service against Russia—chiefly to learn the art of war in order to use it later to liberate their own country—made the Germans sign a pledge that they would under no circumstances be sent against the French and English; and when the power of the Czar was overthrown, they refused to fight any longer. The same spirit, it is argued, will make them revolt against the Germans when these "saviors" are revealed in their true colors.

In urging that the United States should recognize Finland as a sovereign State, the League points to the example of France, which generously recognized the new Finnish Republic simultaneously with the Scandinavian countries. England accepted the de facto government, but America's only action in regard to Finland was to withhold the 40,000 tons of grain bought here by the Finnish Government before the embargo on food went into effect. The Finns feel that they are the victims of American desire to conciliate Russia, and they are afraid that after the war they may be handed back to their old tyrant—a fear which the Germans are, naturally, doing their best to foster. To counteract this German propaganda, the League is trying to influence the Svinhufvud Government by explaining our unselfish purpose in entering the war and our determination that justice shall be done to all. At the same time, it pleads with our Government to recognize Finland and to allow the shipment of food to the starving Finns.

The president of the League is the American poet and scholar, Herman Montagu Donner, who comes of a distinguished Finnish family. Its moving spirit is P. J. Valkeapää, a Finn who has had business relations in this country for twenty years, and was entrusted by his Government with the task of buying food. Honorary vice-presidents of the League are William C. Edgar, editor of the *Bellman* in Minneapolis; John Bates Clarke, of Columbia University, and Charles H. Levermore, secretary of the New York Peace Society. Its headquarters are at 70 Fifth Avenue, New York.

LET SCANDINAVIA The REVIEW realizes the complications that
HELP! beset the path of our Administration; nevertheless we hope some way may be found of assuring the people of Finland that we are alive to their just claims. There can be no clearer case for self-determination than that of the liberty-loving, highly cultured Finns. They are emphatically a nation and were taken by Russia against their will, in 1809, just as surely as Slesvig was taken by Germany, in 1864. They have never been Russians and are not even of Slavic race. Whatever may be thought of the national aspirations of other parts of the former Russian Empire, that of Finland is no artificial flame; it has been smouldering for over a century under the crust imposed by dread of Siberian prisons.

The shipment of food to the ravaged districts of Finland, advised months ago by our consul at Helsingfors, Mr. Thornwell Haynes, would better than anything else demonstrate to the Finns our friendly spirit. Precautions must naturally be taken against having it diverted to the maw of the German army, and this can now be done by accepting the offer made by the Scandinavian countries. On

August 8, the three Scandinavian ministers called at our State Department and presented in writing identical communications from their Governments, offering their services in distributing any food sent from the United States to Finland, and pledging their honor that it would actually be used to feed the children, women, and men who are now threatened with death by starvation. The Governments of Sweden, Norway, and Denmark, have already secured the consent of the Finns to the establishment of an administrative machinery something like that of the Belgian Relief Commission. The argument against such action—that it would relieve the Germans of responsibility—was brought forward when Mr. Hoover first broached his plans for helping Belgium, but the American and British people generously brushed it aside. We hope they will do so again. The Scandinavians, having felt the pinch of hunger, are anxious to relieve their neighbors who have suffered infinitely more, and would gladly share what little they have, but by the terms of the treaties just concluded with us they are barred from re-exporting food. This makes it the more incumbent on us to give their offer consideration. It should be accepted if possible.

THE AMERICAN FINNS   According to the census of 1910, there were in the United States 129,680 persons born in Finland. The number of native and foreign born is about 300,000. They are most numerous in our mining and lumbering districts in the Far and Middle West, while in the East they have taken over numbers of farms abandoned by their former owners and have achieved wonders with them. The school and the bath-house follow the Finns to remotest corners of the wilderness. Numerous periodicals both in Finnish and Swedish are published by Finns. Coming from an oppressed country, they have naturally tended to affiliate with the most radical elements of our population; nevertheless the war has brought out splendid examples of loyalty on the part of the American Finns. They are among the most valuable workers in our shipyards; they have enlisted in great numbers, and have given freely to the Liberty Loan. They are active in the National Lutheran Commission for Soldiers' and Sailors' Welfare, and were excellently represented in the Fourth of July parade of nations in New York.

THE JOHN ERICSSON HEARING   The Joint Commission created by Congress to erect a memorial to John Ericsson in Washington, consisting of Senator John Sharp Williams, chairman; Secretary of the Navy Josephus Daniels, and Congressman James L. Slayden, held a hearing in the Committee Room of the Library, United States Senate, September 17, 1918, to

which a representation from the John Ericsson Memorial Commission
of Fifty was invited to be present.   Plans were laid for turning over
to the Government $25,000 contributed by Americans of Scandinavian descent to add to the fund of $35,000 appropriated by Congress
for the memorial.   The names of each of nearly two thousand donors
will be inscribed in the Congressional minutes.   In voicing the thanks
of the Government, Senator Williams said: "I want to express the
sentiment that I think not only this Commission but the Congress
of the United States and the people of the United States feel toward
that Committee of Fifty and toward the contributors to this fund
for the public spirit they have manifested, which will have an excellent effect in making Americans of Swedish descent and Americans
of other descent feel their identity."

The choice of location, treatment, architect, sculptor, and design
is now in the hands of the Fine Arts Commission, whom the Commission of Fifty, representing Swedish-Americans, will continue to
advise in a voluntary capacity.   The Fine Arts Commission and the
Commission of Fifty are agreed as to a site near the Lincoln Memorial, the treatment of which as well as the design are to have
the approval of Henry Bacon, the architect of the Lincoln Memorial.
Mr. Bacon has already submitted a tentative sketch of a John Ericsson
fountain.   Any sculptor in this country has the privilege of sending
in a design directly to the Fine Arts Commission, Washington, D. C.,
or to H. G. Leach, Corresponding Secretary of the John Ericsson
Memorial Commission, 25 West 45th Street, New York City, who
will forward it promptly to the Fine Arts Commission.   Other things
being equal, a sculptor of Swedish blood should have first choice, but
the prior consideration must be fidelity to the conception of John
Ericsson and the watchword "Washington Beautiful.". . . In going to
press we add the painful tidings of the death, October 9, of Chairman S. Adolph Eckberg.

THE FRIENDLY   We urge upon all Associates to send in, before Novem
AID   ber 15, names of friends whom they propose as readers
             of the REVIEW.   We ask this through the editorial
column in order to save paper and postage.   At that date it is proposed to increase regular Associate dues to $1.50 a year.   We count
on your continued loyal support of the REVIEW, which achieved this
year a maximum circulation of 10,240 copies.   During the year the
magazine has demonstrated to the country at large the loyalty and
service of her sons of Scandinavian descent.   The Boston *Herald*
voiced the general feeling when it greeted our National Service
Number with an editorial entitled "Skoal to the Northland."

Current Events
Norway

¶ The Christiania steamer *Sommerstad*, sunk by a German submarine outside the American coast, on August 12, was chartered by the Norwegian state to bring home a cargo of corn. It was in ballast between Halifax and New York when torpedoed and outside of the supposed danger zone. The case is the greater outrage because the Germans had promised safe conduct to ships carrying provisions for the state, pending negotiations between the German Government and Norwegian shipowners. ¶ Among other recent victims of the U-boats is the steamer *Hauk*, sunk on July 10, within Norwegian territorial waters, without warning or provocation, by a German boat without a national flag. The Norwegian Government sent a protest to Berlin on the basis of its injunction of January 30, 1917, barring submarines from Norwegian waters. ¶ Premier Gunnar Knudsen announced at an agricultural meeting in Christiania in August that the Government plan of a million measures (*maal*, one-fourth acre) new-tilled land in 1918 had been very nearly realized. The total amount of cultivated land before that time was about eight million measures. The state had subsidized the agriculture of the country with 27,000,000 kroner during the year and expected to increase the amount next year, applying the money to seed, artificial fertilizers, and machinery, as well as to direct subsidies. Owing to the difficulty of getting farmhands, it was possible that farm workers would have to be drafted. Much is being done through private initiative. The Norwegian Farmers' and Foresters' Credit and Loan Society have started a drive for a million kroner to stimulate cultivation of new soil and are backed by the influence of many prominent men, among them Dr. Nansen, who strongly urges his countrymen to become self-supporting, as their ancestors were in olden times. ¶ The first food ship to arrive under the American agreement was the *Bratsberg*, which docked in Christiania on one of the last days of June with a cargo of 6,000 tons, chiefly flour. The twenty thousand sacks of wheat flour, which were Christiania's share, were a welcome sight in the capital city. Since then, ship has followed ship bringing provisions, but the Norwegian stores were so depleted that it has not been possible even now to increase the bread ration. The rations of coffee and sugar have been slightly increased. ¶ The cost of living in Norway has increased 137 per cent. since the beginning of the war, as against 103 per cent. in Sweden and 82 per cent. in Denmark. ¶ The Spanish influenza reached its heigth in July, when 6,122 cases occurred in one week in Christiania alone. So many of the telephone operators were ill that the telephones had to be shut down for certain hours each day.

Denmark

¶ A conference of the prime ministers and the foreign ministers of the three Scandinavian countries was held in Copenhagen and lasted from June 26 to June 29. This is the sixth in the series which began with the meeting of the three Kings at Malmö in December, 1914. The official *communiqué* expresses gratification at the good results attained by the economic coöperation recently inaugurated, and declares that it will be continued after the war. A new feature is added in the announcement that a plan is being considered for coöperation in social legislation also. The *communiqué*, like those of the previous conferences, is framed in very general terms and repeats the expressions of continued neutrality and inter-Scandinavian friendliness. ¶ A Danish newspaper has asked Svinhufvud whether Finland would be willing to send representatives to these conferences of the Scandinavian Governments. The regent replied that Finland could not, of course, offer to take part without being invited, but if an invitation were extended the answer was a foregone conclusion. ¶ The members of the delegation sent to frame an agreement with Iceland returned to Copenhagen well satisfied with their trip. They had been received with the greatest cordiality in Reykjavik and had been taken about to see the sights of the island. ¶ Two suicides among men doing military service have caused a great stir and may possibly lead to a revision of the methods of dealing with offenders in the army. Minister of Defenses Munch announced in the Rigsdag that a thorough investigation would be made; he said that the Government was considering the abolition of military courts altogether and the handling of military offenders by the civil courts. One of the men, Marinus Richter, hanged himself in arrest because of severe disciplinary punishments. The other, a cook named Valdemar Kreutzfeldt, jumped overboard because he was accused of theft. Kreutzfeldt's funeral on Holmen churchyard occasioned the greatest demonstration seen in Copenhagen in the memory of people now living. *Politiken* estimates the crowd at 100,000 people. Anti-militarists and Syndicalists harangued the workingmen and incited them to rise against their tyrants. No serious violence was done at the time, but a few weeks later there were Syndicalist riots in the streets, in which armed men fought the police, and some damage was done to buildings. Certain members of the police force have been pointed out as enemies of the workingmen who ought to be put out of the way some dark evening. Some of the Syndicalist ringleaders were arrested, including Chr. Christensen, the editor of *Solidaritet*. ¶ The Spanish influenza has been very virulent in Copenhagen. Among the best known victims was the young Norwegian poet, Einar Solstad, who was there on his honeymoon.

Sweden

❡ A remarkable series of articles recently appeared in the pro-German organ *Stockholms Dagblad*, warning the Swedes against future German aggression in the Baltic, reminding them that the political friends of to-day would often become the enemies of to-morrow, and pointing out that the present situation with one great Power in possession of the Baltic was much more dangerous than the former division of dominion between Germany and Russia. One of the articles openly said that Germany might very conceivably wish to complete the circle by absorbing Sweden and Denmark, the only two Baltic countries yet independent of her, and force her way across Norway, in order to threaten England from the sea. ❡ Two of the most famous aviators in Sweden, Baron Cederström and Captain Krokstedt, were killed recently while flying to Helsingfors with a hydroplane bought by the Finnish Government. When they did not arrive on schedule time, search was made for them, and some splinters of their machine were found in the Åland Islands. Later Cederström's body drifted ashore. Their deaths have caused profound sorrow. ❡ A few cases of cholera have been brought from Petrograd, but the energetic measures of the health authorities in Stockholm have prevented the spread of the disease. So far as is known, no deaths have occurred. ❡ The Spanish influenza, on the other hand, has claimed many victims. Among those who have died is one of the royal princes, Prince Eric, Duke of Västmanland. The prince was born in 1889 and was King Gustaf's third and youngest son. Owing to ill health, he had taken less part in public affairs than the other members of the royal family. ❡ A national fair, or *mässe*, the first of its kind in Sweden, was held in Göteborg in the second week of August and was visited by 42,000 people. Many Norwegian and Danish as well as Swedish firms sent exhibits, and it is estimated that business to the value of 40,000,000 kronor was transacted. The war has prevented the Scandinavians from taking part as usual in the great international fairs at Leipsic and Novgorod and has stimulated them to organize their own. The Danes have for some time had similar markets known as *Köbestevner*. The success of the Göteborg *Mässe* was so great that that city and Malmö are already competing for the privilege of having the one next year. ❡ A commission which has recently completed an investigation of southern Lapland reports that region to be as rich in minerals as the northern section of the province. A copper vein found near Unna-Greisa is said to be the richest copper deposit in the world. It has been taken over by the state. ❡ The Swedish merchant marine, for the first time since the beginning of the war, shows an increase, due partly to the lessening of U-boat destruction, but chiefly to increased building.

Brief Notes

The new magazine *Atlantis*, started in Christiania under the editorship of Professor Christen Collin and Dr. Chr. Kaarböe, promises to be an important cultural link between Norway and the Western liberal nations. Among the articles we note one in French by Maurice Barrès on General Serret, one by John A. Gade on his impressions of Belgium, and a letter from the front by H. A. Angell, the distinguished Norwegian colonel, who is now serving as a lieutenant in the French Foreign Legion.

The Conrad Mohr fellowships for newspaper men have been given to Arthur Ratche of Christiania and Harald Wigum of Bergen. The former will study in the United States, the latter in France. The fellowships are to the amount of 4,500 kroner each.

Bonnier Publishing House in Stockholm will commemorate the hundredth anniversary of the birth of Zacharias Topelius by issuing a new illustrated edition of his famous cycle of historical novels *Fältskärns berättelser*. The work is of especial interest now as showing the glorious part the Finns took in the wars of Sweden under Gustaf Adolf and succeeding kings.

Erland Nordenskiöld, the Swedish explorer, writes in the magazine *Ymer* that the Indians were the first to use poisonous gases in battle. Writers of the sixteenth century relate that the Indians in Brazil and in Canada put their enemies to flight and even killed them with the smoke made by burning Cayenne pepper or the wood of certain trees impregnated with a poison, which affected the skin and membranes.

Maurice Francis Egan writes in the September *Bookman* an article on "Kultur as Patron of Danish Letters." Dr. Egan, while giving the Danes credit for an independence of mind that resists the German influence, nevertheless points out how German patronage has been the road not only to success but also to the monetary rewards of success, and describes how agents for German scientific and literary publication firms have constantly been visiting Scandinavia to make connections with scholars and men of letters. He lays stress on the necessity for offsetting this by similar American propaganda.

The same number of the *Bookman* prints an article by Henry Van Dyke on "The Tradition of Letters in American Diplomacy." To the list for Denmark, which includes so distinguished a man of letters as Dr. Egan, might have been added also that of Rasmus B. Anderson, whose *Norse Mythology*—to mention only one of his numerous works—is still the standard book on the subject. Professor Anderson was American minister to Denmark in the years 1885-89.

Madeline Z. Doty's article, "Women of the Future. In Sweden the Genius," in the February number of *Good Housekeeping*, reveals a fine understanding of the manner in which Swedish women have achieved success as women, not as imitation men. Her description of her visit to Ellen Key is most interesting. On the other hand, it shows lack of knowledge to write of the Swedes as not being "alive" because they are less garrulous than the Bolsheviki; and it is unfair to single out the present democratic royal family for blame on account of the difference between classes, which is assuredly no worse in Sweden than in the rest of the modern world.

The September number of the new magazine, *Scandinavian Trade Outlook*, edited by Julius Moritzen, is extremely attractive in appearance and full of interesting articles bearing on the increased trade relations of the United States and the Scandinavian countries.

The death of Peter Nansen at the age of fifty-seven removes another of that brilliant group of Danish writers, among whom Bang and Esman were prominent. In his youth he was known as the author of stories dealing chiefly with erotic subjects, and later he showed great versatility as a journalist, contributing regularly to *Politiken*. In 1906 he entered the great publishing firm, Gyldendal, where his tact and ready appreciation won him many friends among authors.

An instance of how the REVIEW penetrates to unexpected corners of the world was found in a letter received from the Convento S. Brigida, 1 Via Corsica, Roma. In the nuns of this convent dedicated to the Swedish woman reformer, our Woman's Number with its account of St. Birgitta found interested readers.

Australia and the Scandinavians out yonder are watching with brotherly pride the progress of America in the war. This we learn from our Australian correspondent, Mr. Henry Norman, who sends the REVIEW recent numbers of *The Age*, *The Argus*, *The Winner*, *The Mirror*, and *Health and Strength*. Australians are keeping up their sports and Swedish exercises and, judging from the prints of athletes, are generally in the pink of condition. Melba has arrived at Sidney, having crossed the equator for another winter season, and is praising America and our ice-water regime. Australians are discussing their proposed "Monroe Doctrine" and the prospect of an aeroplane route to San Francisco. The REVIEW has only a few subscribers in Australia. Who will add to their number? It costs $1.50 a year to send the REVIEW to a friend out there.

The War Service Bureau of the American Library Association began its work by asking for contributions of books, but the demand for more and better books, especially for the latest technical works of all kinds, has been so great and insistent that the Bureau now is making a drive for $3,500,000 to build up adequate camp libraries. Fiction is still supplied by gifts of books, but the men want reading that will help them to pass their military examinations or to fit themselves for the professions to which they expect to return when the war is over, and these must be purchased. Send contributions to 124 East 28th Street, New York.

Selma Lagerlöf

EVERY lover of Scandinavian literature should read and own the works of Selma Lagerlöf.

Bound in beautiful green leather and attractively stamped in gold, they would make an excellent Christmas gift for the most discriminating of your friends. This year, when so much care must be exercised in the choice of gifts, few things can be found which will be more appreciated than a book;—a beautiful book, and a *good* book.

Here are the titles included in this distinctive limp-leather edition of Selma Lagerlöf's works:

THE EMPEROR OF PORTUGALLIA	THE HOLY CITY: JERUSALEM II
JERUSALEM	INVISIBLE LINKS
FROM A SWEDISH HOMESTEAD	MIRACLES OF ANTICHRIST
THE FURTHER ADVENTURES OF NILS	THE STORY OF GÖSTA BERLING
THE GIRL FROM THE MARSH CROFT	THE WONDERFUL ADVENTURES OF NILS

Ten volumes, net, $20.00; each, $2.00

At Your Bookseller's

DOUBLEDAY PAGE & Co., GARDEN CITY, N. Y.

The Foundation will publish in November, as Volumes X and XI of the Classics, Selma Lagerlöf's first great romance which won her world recognition

GÖSTA BERLING'S SAGA

By SELMA LAGERLÖF

IN TWO PARTS

This translation is based upon the excellent British translation by Lillie Tudeer, now out of print. It has been carefully edited by Hanna Astrup Larsen, the translator of Jacobsen's *Marie Grubbe*, and the eight chapters omitted from Miss Tudeer's version have been added in masterly translation by Velma Swanston Howard. These two volumes are printed with special care from a new large type, hand set, by D. B. Updike at the Merrymount Press. The publication is rendered possible through the generous donation of Charles S. Peterson of Chicago.

The edition, as a measure of war economy, is limited to one thousand copies, after printing which the type will be distributed. Kindly order in advance. The price of each volume is $1.50; complete $3.00.

THE SCANDINAVIAN CLASSICS:

Comedies by Holberg—Poems by Tegnér—Poems and Songs by Björnstjerne Björnson—Master Olof—The Prose Edda of Snorri Sturluson—Modern Icelandic Plays—Marie Grubbe—Arnljot Gelline—Anthology of Swedish Lyrics—Gösta Berling's Saga I—Gösta Berling's Saga II.

Price $1.50 each

THE AMERICAN-SCANDINAVIAN FOUNDATION, 25 West 45th St., N. Y.

Telephone: Broad 2549   Cable Address: "Chartering," New York

V. JOHNSEN CO., Inc.

SHIP and STEAMSHIP BROKERS

23-25 BEAVER STREET, NEW YORK

AGENTS FOR

DELAWARE SHIPBUILDING COMPANY

SEAFORD, DELAWARE

Builders of Wooden Vessels and Barges

SWEDEN   U. S. A.   ARGENTINA

BRANDER, BERGSTROM & CO., Inc.

141 BROADWAY

NEW YORK

EXPORT—IMPORT

SCANDINAVIAN   AMERICAN   SOUTH AMERICAN

PRODUCTS

TRADE NOTES

*News and Comment on Exports and Trade Conditions
Between America and the Scandinavian Countries*

SWEDEN'S NEW WINDOW TO THE WEST

Up to the outbreak of the war and for a long time afterwards Sweden received its foreign news exclusively through the Swedish Telegram Bureau. No sooner had the war started than charges of one-sided pro-German orientation were made against that institution. The charges originated both with the Swedish press and with the foreign governments principally concerned. As the war went on proof accumulated that the charges were correct. Finally conditions became so serious that a number of public-spirited Swedish citizens decided to attempt a remedy. As a result of their action a new telegram bureau was started last July under the name of the "Nordiska Presscentralen." This organization is backed by a capital of 1,500,000 kronor. Among those interested in it may be noted Eliel Löfgren, Minister of Justice in the present cabinet. Its active head is Captain Olof Gylden, former Swedish minister to one of the South American republics. Hans Leander is in charge of the domestic department of the new bureau, while the foreign department is under the direction of Baltzar Roosval. Branch offices have been established at Gothenburg, Malmö and Sundsvall. Special correspondents will be sent to the principal foreign capitals. The new bureau has the backing of the principal Western news agencies, and several months ago the Reuter Bureau of London and the Agence Havas of Paris severed their connections with the Swedish Telegram Bureau in order to give their service exclusively to the new bureau.

RELEASING EMBARGOED GOODS

Negotiations pending for months have at last been successfully concluded by the United States with the Swedish Government providing for the sale of embargoed goods originally intended for Russia, but held up at Swedish ports. The total amount of goods is valued at 100,000,000 kronor, half of which is held in Sweden and half in Finland. It is believed that this transaction will have much to do with ultimately lowering Swedish exchange.

CITY COLLEGE AND FOREIGN TRADE

In accordance with plans that are being developed by the Bureau of Foreign and Domestic Commerce, the Federal Bureau for Vocational Training, and the United States Bureau of Education, the College of the City of New York, has prepared a course of training in the essential branches of foreign trade. The courses will be under the supervision of Professor Guy E. Snyder, and experts are to preside over the various branches included in the plan.

SCANDINAVIAN-U. S. TRADE AGREEMENTS

With Denmark and the United States signing a trade agreement, the situation with regard to raw materials will be relieved to some extent. Although Scandinavian economists warn against any undue optimism, at the same time the situation for the coming winter is no longer so threatening as before, and most industrial enterprises are expected to resume operations. The newspapers have nothing but kind words for the American Government in lifting the embargo partially so as to bring relief to suffering neutrals.

BUY
WAR SAVINGS
STAMPS

BACHE TRADING CO., Inc.,
Importers and Exporters,
5 Beekman Street, New York

JOHNSEN & KILDAL, Inc.,
Exporters and Importers,
26 Cortlandt Street, New York

CHR. CHRISTENSEN, Jr., Inc.,
Ship-owners and Brokers,
32 Broadway, New York

Out of the Mouth of Hell

our boys come, nerve-racked, tense, exhausted by their sleepless vigil and harassed with tragic memories.

Rest they will have, but rest is not re-creation. Mind must relax as well as body. They must forget awhile, must turn their thoughts into their normal course before facing anew the horrors of the first-line trenches.

Courage they have always, but we can put fresh heart into them; we can restore the high spirits of youth and send them singing into the fray.

They Are Fighting for You—Show Your Appreciation

When you give them arms, you give them only the instruments of your own defense; when you give for the wounded, you give only in common humanity; but when you give to the Y. M. C. A., you are extending to the boys the warm hand of gratitude, the last token of your appreciation of what they are doing for you. You are doing this by showing your interest in their welfare.

The Y. M. C. A. furnishes to the boys not only in its own "huts"—which are often close to the firing line—but in the trenches, the material and intangible comforts which mean much to morale. It furnishes free entertainment back of the lines. It supplies free writing paper and reading matter. It conducts all post exchanges, selling general merchandise without profit. It has charge of and encourages athletics, and conducts a "khaki college" for liberal education. Its religious work is non-sectarian and non-propagandist. It keeps alive in the boys "over there" the life and the spirit of "over here."

Give Now—Before Their Sacrifice Is Made

Seven allied activities, all endorsed by the Government, are combined in the United War Campaign, with the budgets distributed as follows: Y. M. C. A., $100,000,000; Y. W. C. A., $15,000,000; National Catholic War Council (including the work of the Knights of Columbus and special war activities for women), $30,000,000; Jewish Welfare Board, $3,500,000; American Library Association, $3,500,000; War Camp Community Service, $15,000,000; Salvation Army, $3,500,000.

Contributed through Division of Advertising

United States Gov't. Comm. on Public Information

This Space contributed for the Winning of the War by

K. A. KLEPPE, President KLEPPE, OSTERVOLD & CO., Inc., 11 Broadway, N. Y.

Members of
New York Produce
Exchange

Cable Address:
"Norameric" New York
A.B.C. Code Fifth Edition,
Watkins Scotts and Private

Norwegian American Trading Co.

INCORPORATED

25 Broad Street, New York, U. S. A.

and Kristiania, Norway

EXPORT:

Food Products, Metals and Machinery, Drugs, and Chemicals, Manila Rope, and Cotton Yarns

Flour, Lard, Oleo, Oil, Hams, Bacon, Beef, Pork, Sugar, Syrup, Molasses, Apples, Coffees, Peas and Beans. Steel Wire, Coke, Tin Plate, Galvanized Steel Plates, Plumbers' Supplies, Motors, and all kinds of Machinery. *Write for Catalogue*

IMPORT:

Canned, Salt, and Dry Fish, Fertilizer, Fish Oils, Wood Pulp, and Sulphites

GENERAL REPRESENTATIVE IN NORWAY:

BIRGER GRAN, Kristiania   JENS GRAN & SÖN, Bergen

References: National City Bank of New York; New York Produce Exchange Bank, N. Y.; Kristiania Bank og Kredit-kasse, Kristiania; Centralbanken for Norge, Kristiania; Bradstreet's Commercial Agency

---

S T O R M & B U L L

(INCORPORATED)

2 RECTOR STREET, NEW YORK CITY

IMPORT		EXPORT
Specialties		*Specialties*
South American and Scandinavian Products		Iron and Steel Products, Paper, Chemicals, Machinery

Own Houses:

CHRISTIANIA · STOCKHOLM · BUENOS AIRES · MONTEVIDEO
VALPARAISO—LA PAZ

Active Representation:

Principal Cities:

AUSTRALIA—BRAZIL—SOUTH AFRICA—FAR EAST

CORRESPONDENCE INVITED

Ocean Commercial Corporation

170 BROADWAY, NEW YORK

EXPORTERS = IMPORTERS

OFFICES

ENGLAND: London

SWEDEN: Stockholm

"   Gothenburg

RUSSIA: Odessa

BRAZIL: Rio de Janeiro

"   Santos

ARGENTINA: Buenos Aires

CHILE: Santiago

"   Valparaiso

PERU: Lima

JAPAN: Tokio

FORWARDING
U. S.

SCANDINAVIAN COUNTRIES

INTERSPED INC., 66 New Street, NEW YORK

MAIN OFFICE:

Internationalt Speditionsselskap

INTERSPED a/s

Sjöfartsbygningen, Christiania

INSURANCE   **WAREHOUSING**

New York Forwarding Co., Inc.

Agents   OSCAR A. OLSEN   *Branch Offices*
GOTHENBURG   General Manager   CHRISTIANIA, Kirkegaten 6 B.
STOCKHOLM   COPENHAGEN, Peder Skramsgade 28

LICENSES: Applying for American and British Licenses.

WAREHOUSE: Storing all kinds of goods.

INSURANCE: Marine, War, Fire, and all risks.

FINANCING: Value of merchandise, freight and charges payable against surrender of documents upon arrival at destination.

ANDREW GULICK & CO., Inc.

Exporters and Merchant Brokers

S. HENDRICHSEN, Agent   A. G. GULICK   256 and 257 BROADWAY
Fougstadgt .25, Kristiania   President   NEW YORK, U. S. A.

.. EXPORTING ..

Motor Attachment for Cycles	*Adding Machines*	*Hosiery*	*Tractors*
Truck Attachment to "Ford"	*Boots and Shoes*	*Raincoats*	*"Carbola"—White-washing*
Electric Lamps and Batteries	*Hide and Sole Leather*	*Folding Saw*	*Dyes*
Row Boat Motors	*Cotton Goods*	*Typewriters*	*Snap Fasteners*

CLARX 100% PURE
Whole Wheat Flour

Whole Wheat Graham Flour

Whole Rye Flour

Corn Flour and Oat Flour

CLARX MILLING COMPANY
Minneapolis

Phone Greeley 4354

M. WAIN—Tailor

Some of the best dressed men are amongst my customers. High-grade clothes made at moderate prices.

366 FIFTH AVENUE

Above 34th Street   10th Floor

NORWEGIANS STUDY TRADE HERE

A new commercial school is to be erected at Bergen which is to take as its model similar institutions in the United States. For this purpose a visiting Commission has arrived in America to inspect business colleges and general educational conditions. The members of this group are Mr. Kristofer Lehmkuhl, a former cabinet official; Mr. Sigurd Höst, dean of the Cathedral School in Christiania, and Mr. Egill Reimers, architect.

COMPLIMENTING SWEDISH CHAMBER OF COMMERCE

Secretary Oscar Marell, of the Swedish-American Chamber of Commerce, continues to receive many complimentary letters about the annual *Sweden-America*, which reflects great credit on those responsible for this valuable publication. Many Government officials, including Secretary Redfield and Secretary Daniels, express their admiration for the good work done by the Chamber of Commerce in coöperation with the Journal of Swedish-American Trade

DANISH PEAT PRODUCTION

As a substitution for other fuels, peat is proving its great value in Denmark. The fuel commission reports that the output for this year amounts so far to 4,000,-000,000 blocks, valued at 40,000,000 kroner.

DANISH SAILINGS RESUMED

For the first time in more than a year, Danish vessels in American ports resumed sailing, following the signing of the trade agreement. The Scandinavian-American Line had three big liners in American ports, *Hellig Olav, Oscar II*, and the *United States*. The largest ship, the *Frederik VIII* was laid up in Copenhagen until the embargo was lifted.

NORWEGIAN FIRMS IN NEW YORK

Nordisk Tidende recently published an illuminating account of Norwegian firms in New York City. The list is an imposing one, including as it does bankers, exporters, importers, shipping firms, and other business concerns working for the development of trade between this country and other nations.

DRAMMEN'S MEN OF WEALTH

Of the most important taxpayers in Drammen, Norway, the following are noted: Golskogen Cellulose Factory, income 1,061,800 kroner; Noested Shipping Company, 1,027,700 kroner, and Borch's Shipping Company, 814,000 kroner.   J. M.

NORWEGIAN AMERICA LINE

Modern Twin-Screw
Steamers
**SS.
Stavangerfjord**
18,000 Tons
Displacement

**SS.
Bergensfjord**
16,000 Tons
Displacement

**NORWEGIAN
AMERICA
LINE
PASSENGER
AGENCY, Inc.**

8-10 Bridge St.
New York

General Passenger
Agents for the United
States and Canada

HOBE & CO.	BIRGER OSLAND & CO.	REIDAR GJÖLME
General Northwestern Passenger Agents 123 South Third Street Minneapolis, Minn.	General Western Passenger Agents 115 South Dearborn Street Chicago, Ill.	General Pacific Coast Agent Arctic Bldg., Third & Cherry Streets Seattle, Wash.

NORWAY MEXICO GULF LINE AND SWEDISH AMERICA MEXICO LINE

Regular service between GOTEBORG, CHRISTIANIA and STAVAN-
GER and NEWPORT NEWS, VA., HAVANA, CUBA,
GALVESTON, TEX., and NEW ORLEANS, LA.

Passengers Carried   Wireless Apparatus

AGENTS

FEARNLEY & EGER, Christiania   SANDSTRÖM STRANNE & CO., Ltd., Göteborg

FURNESS WITHY & CO., Ltd., Furness House, Whitehall St., New York, N. Y., and Newport News, Va.

JAS. P. ROBERTSON 111 West Jackson Boulevard Chicago, Ill.	FOWLER & McVITIE Galveston, Tex.	LYKES BROS. Havana, Cuba	GEO. PLANT 1119 Whitney Central Bldg. New Orleans, La.

NEAR HERALD SQUARE
Phone: Greeley 4782

The Only High-Class Scandinavian Restaurant in New York

Rendezvous for Scandinavians from all over the
world when visiting New York

Dinner with famous "Smörgåsbord." American and Scandinavian Dishes.

HENRY MALGREN, Prop.

Scandinavian-American Line

Service to

NORWAY, SWEDEN and DENMARK

The Direct Passenger Line Between

NEW YORK

Christiansand, Christiania, Copenhagen

STOCKHOLM

(via Rail from Christiania)

The Largest Steamship Line in Scandinavian Passenger
Service

Four Fast, Modern Twin-Screw Passenger Steamers

FREDERIK VIII	OSCAR II	HELLIG OLAV
18,000 tons	16,000 tons	16,000 tons
	UNITED STATES	
	16,000 tons	

*Excellent Passenger Accommodations.   Modern Comfort
Unexcelled Cuisine*

For rates, sailings and other information, address

SCANDINAVIAN-AMERICAN LINE

GENERAL OFFICES: Passenger Department

117 N. Dearborn St., Chicago, Ill.
236 Nicollet Ave., Minneapolis, Minn.
248 Washington St., Boston, Mass.

ONE BROADWAY
NEW YORK

544 Market St., San Francisco, Cal.
702 Second Ave., Seattle, Wash.

SWEDISH AMERICAN LINE

(SVENSKA AMERIKA LINIEN)

Direct Passenger Service between New
York and Gothenburg, Sweden

Short Route to Sweden, Norway, Denmark, Finland, Russia and other
parts of the European Continent

Twin-Screw S.S. "Stockholm"

Length 565 Feet.   22,070 Tons Displacement
Has now resumed regular sailings

Largest Steamer in Service Between America and Scandinavia

*Unsurpassed passenger appointments in First,
Second and Third Classes,* and every care is
taken to give the passengers a safe and
comfortable journey.

NIELSEN & LUNDBECK, General Passenger
Agents, 24 State Street, New York.

MARTIN MAURD, General Western Agent,
183 N. Dearborn Street. Chicago,

NILS NILSON, General Northwestern Agent,
127 S. Third St., Minneapolis, Minn.

BRATTSTROM & CO., General No. Pacific
Agents, 115 Cherry St., Seattle, Wash.

A. HALLONQUIST, General Agent,
396 Logan Ave., Winnipeg, Man., Can.

CUNARD LINE

AQUITANIA   MAURETANIA

Fastest Passenger Service in the World
To and from the Scandinavian Countries

Record trip, New York to Gothenburg, 7 days, 7 hours, 45 minutes

Quickest Route to Europe

SERVICES AS FOLLOWS:

NEW YORK—LIVERPOOL	NEW YORK—FALMOUTH—LONDON
NEW YORK—BRISTOL	NEW YORK—MEDITERRANEAN
BOSTON—LIVERPOOL	BOSTON—LONDON
MONTREAL—QUEBEC—BRISTOL	MONTREAL—QUEBEC—LONDON

Special through rates to Egypt, India, China, Japan, Philippines,
Australia, New Zealand, South Africa and South America

TRIPS AROUND THE WORLD: $474.85 First Class, $380 Second Class

DRAFTS, MONEY ORDERS, MAIL OR CABLE

GREAT BRITAIN	SCANDINAVIA	HOLLAND	ITALY
SPAIN	PORTUGAL	FRANCE	SWITZERLAND

THE CUNARD STEAM SHIP COMPANY LIMITED

21-24 STATE STREET   NEW YORK

Offices or Agents Everywhere

·THE · AMERICAN ·
SCANDINAVIAN
REVIEW

YULE NUMBER

MARCH-APRIL · 1918

· THE · AMERICAN ·
SCANDINAVIAN REVIEW

TRAVEL NUMBER

·THE· ·AMERICAN·
SCANDINAVIAN REVIEW

SPRING NUMBER

JULY–AUGUST · 1918

·THE· AMERICAN·
SCANDINAVIAN
REVIEW

NATIONAL SERVICE NUMBER

SEPTEMBER–OCTOBER · 1918

· THE · AMERICAN ·
SCANDINAVIAN REVIEW

SLESVIG NUMBER

SCANDINAVIAN TRUST COMPANY
56 Broadway, New York
MEMBER FEDERAL RESERVE BANK OF NEW YORK

Condensed Statement of Condition at the Close of Business, June Twentieth, Nineteen Eighteen.

ASSETS		LIABILITIES	
Loans and Discounts	$20,972,846.00	Capital	$1,000,000.00
Bonds and Securities	4,457,053.71	Surplus	1,500,000.00
Cash on Hand and in Banks	3,897,700.44	Undivided Profits	206,767.84
Accrued Interest and Accounts Receivable	78,576.09	Reserve for Unearned Interest, Taxes, etc.	217,004.57
Customers' Liabilities Under Letters of Credit and Acceptances, etc.	403,410.32	Accrued Interest Payable	58,631.26
		Deposits	26,423,772.57
		Letters of Credit and Acceptances	403,410.32
	$29,809,586.56		$29,809,586.56

OFFICERS
ALEXANDER V. OSTROM, President

B. E. SMYTHE	Vice-President	DANFORTH CARDOZO	Secretary
MAURICE F. BAYARD	Treasurer	C. C. KELLEY	Asst. Secretary

BOARD OF DIRECTORS

JOHS. ANDERSEN . . . . J. Andersen & Company
KNUT BACHKE . . . . Andresens Bank, Christiania
PHILIP G. BARTLETT . . . . Simpson, Thacher & Bartlett
CHARLES E. BEDFORD . . . . Vice-President, Vacuum Oil Company
JAMES F. BELL . . . . Vice-President, Washburn-Crosby Company
JOHN E. BERWIND . . . . Vice-President, Berwind-White Coal Co.
R. R. BROWN . . . . First Vice-President, American Surety Company
WILLIAM R. COE . . . . Chairman, Johnson & Higgins
GERHARD M. DAHL . . . . Vice-President, Chase National Bank
S. E. DAHL . . . . Centralbanken for Norge, Christiania
W. EDWARD FOSTER . . . . Treasurer, American Sugar Refining Company
SAMUEL L. FULLER . . . . Kissel, Kinnicutt & Company
EDWARD F. GEER . . . . Shipowner
CHARLES S. HAIGHT . . . . Haight, Sanford & Smith
G. KAMSTRUP HEGGE . . . . Den Norske Creditbank, Christiania
EDWIN O. HOLTER . . . . Attorney
FREDERICK W. HVOSLEF . . . . Bennett, Hvoslef & Company
N. BRUCE MacKELVIE . . . . Hayden, Stone & Company
C. M. MacNEILL . . . . President, Utah Copper Company
ALEXANDER R. NICOL . . . Treasurer, Atlantic Gulf & West Indies Steamship Lines
ALEXANDER V. OSTROM . . . . President
BIRGER OSLAND . . . . General Western Agent, Norwegian-America Line
EDWIN A. POTTER, Jr. . . . . President, Finance and Trading Corporation
E. A. CAPPELEN SMITH . . . . Guggenheim Brothers
NIEL A. WEATHERS . . . . Simpson, Thacher and Bartlett

NORWEGIAN ADVISORY BOARD

KNUT BACHKE . . . . Andresens Bank, Christiania
CHR. BONGE . . . . Bergens Kreditbank, Bergen
F. BRUENECH . . . . . . Christiania Bank og Kreditkasse, Christiania
S. E. DAHL . . . . Centralbanken for Norge, Christiania
G. K. HEGGE . . . . Den Norske Kreditbank, Christiania
KR. JEBSEN . . . . Bergens Privatbank, Bergen
CHR. THAULOW . . . . . Den Nordenfjeldske Kreditbank, Trondhjem

· THE · AMERICAN ·
SCANDINAVIAN
REVIEW

THE BOUNDARIES OF FINLAND